TRANSFORMATIVE POLITICS OF NATURE

Overcoming Barriers to Conservation in Canada

Edited by Andrea Olive, Chance Finegan, and Karen F. Beazley

Transformative Politics of Nature highlights the most significant barriers to conservation in Canada and discusses strategies to confront and overcome them. Featuring contributions from academics as well as practitioners, the volume brings together the perspectives of both Indigenous and non-Indigenous experts on land and wildlife conservation, in a way that honours and respects all peoples and nature.

Contributors provide insights that enhance understanding of key barriers, important actors, and strategies for shaping policy at multiple levels of government across Canada. The chapters engage academics, environmental conservation organizations, and Indigenous communities in dialogues and explorations of the politics of wildlife conservation. They address broad and interrelated themes, organized into three parts: barriers to conservation, transformation through reconciliation, and transformation through policy and governance.

Taken together, the essays demonstrate the need for increased social-political awareness of biodiversity and conservation in Canada, enhanced wildlife conservation collaborative networks, and increased scholarly attention to the principles, policies, and practices of maintaining and restoring nature for the benefit of all peoples, species, and ecologies. *Transformative Politics of Nature* presents a vision of profound change in the way humans relate to each other and with the natural world.

ANDREA OLIVE is a professor in the Department of Geography, Geomatics, and Environment and the Department of Political Science at the University of Toronto Mississauga.

CHANCE FINEGAN was most recently a postdoctoral research fellow in the Department of Political Science at the University of Toronto Mississauga.

KAREN F. BEAZLEY is a professor emeritus in the School for Resource and Environmental Studies at Dalhousie University.

Transformative Politics of Nature

Overcoming Barriers to Conservation in Canada

EDITED BY ANDREA OLIVE, CHANCE FINEGAN,
AND KAREN F. BEAZLEY

UNIVERSITY OF TORONTO PRESS
Toronto Buffalo London

© University of Toronto Press 2023
Toronto Buffalo L ondon
utorontopress.com

ISBN 978-1-4875-4949-7 (cloth)   ISBN 978-1-4875-5305-0 (EPUB)
ISBN 978-1-4875-5051-6 (paper)   ISBN 978-1-4875-5155-1 (PDF)

Library and Archives Canada Cataloguing in Publication

Title: Transformative politics of nature : overcoming barriers to conservation in Canada /
    edited by Andrea Olive, Chance Finegan, and Karen F. Beazley.
Names: Olive, Andrea, 1980– editor. | Finegan, Chance, editor. | Beazley, Karen, editor.
Description: Includes bibliographical references and index.
Identifiers: Canadiana (print) 20230478891 | Canadiana (ebook) 20230478921 |
    ISBN 9781487549497 (cloth) | ISBN 9781487550516 (paper) |
    ISBN 9781487553050 (EPUB) | ISBN 9781487551551 (PDF)
Subjects: LCSH: Wildlife conservation – Canada. | LCSH: Landscape protection – Canada.
Classification: LCC QL84.24.T73 2023 | DDC 333.95/160971–dc23

Cover design: Will Brown
Cover image: Unsplash.com/Sergei A

We wish to acknowledge the land on which the University of Toronto Press
operates. This land is the traditional territory of the Wendat, the Anishnaabeg, the
Haudenosaunee, the Métis, and the Mississaugas of the Credit First Nation.

University of Toronto Press acknowledges the financial support of the Government of
Canada, the Canada Council for the Arts, and the Ontario Arts Council, an agency of
the Government of Ontario, for its publishing activities.

Canada Council   Conseil des Arts
for the Arts   du Canada

ONTARIO ARTS COUNCIL
CONSEIL DES ARTS DE L'ONTARIO
an Ontario government agency
un organisme du gouvernement de l'Ontario

Funded by the   Financé par le
Government   gouvernement
of Canada   du Canada

Canadä

Contents

Figures and Tables

Figures

Tables

Opening Ceremony

BEGINNING

let me
quiet
myself
the bustling breeze of my mind
whirls up branches, rattles, quivers,
then passes
not the kind of quiet that is without sound
but one full of others
it is the kind of quiet that is compassionate
observation
i trace the pulse of my heart
down into the soil
and remember
all who have come before me
what resilience
i would not be here without you
i trace the shape of me
to the pliant, tangled ground
as woven textures
of roots and trails of those who move
what fluidity
i would not be here without you
i trace the sound of my voice
to the vibrations of wind and wave
the valleys and peaks
that compose the very geography
of place:
cradling all matter
into community
let me take this in
breath like prayer
humbling
i am here
listening

shalan joudry

L'nu (Mi'kmaw) woman, mother, scholar, ecologist and artist living in southwest Nova Scotia, Canada.

   In the Mi'kmaw language, there is no stronger intonation to first person versus
collective. Consistent with this teaching, shalan chooses to not capitalize her name.

PART A

Introduction

1 From Politics to Transformative Politics of Nature in Canada

KAREN F. BEAZLEY, ANDREA OLIVE, AND CHANCE FINEGAN

It takes a monarch butterfly less than a month to metamorphosize from a larva to a butterfly. Complete transformation. There are few other living things that exemplify transformative change like a butterfly. Given its beauty and its extensive geographic range, the monarch is the symbol of collaborative conservation between Canada, the US, and Mexico. Unfortunately, the migratory *Danaus plexippus* is classified as critically imperilled (Nature Serve nd) and listed as a species at risk in Canada. Between 1995 and 2015, their population declined by over 80 per cent and the Committee on the Status of Endangered Wildlife in Canada suggests that the probability of extinction in the wildlife is at least 20 per cent in the next 20 years (Government of Canada n.d.). This iconic species, and one of the most recognizable insects in North America, is going extinct in our lifetime.

As we write this amid a global health pandemic (World Health Organization 2020, 2021), we are also experiencing existential biodiversity, climate, and humanitarian crises (Steffen et al. 2015; Intergovernmental Science-Policy Platform on Biodiversity and Ecosystem Services [IPBES] 2019; Springer et al. 2021). All are consequences of human actions rooted in dominant ideals and political systems grounded in global economic growth models, often with long histories and persistent characteristics of colonialism (United Nations [UN] 2012; Moulton and Machado 2019; Pictou 2019). Initiatives to address these interrelated crises are gaining support internationally (e.g., Kennedy et al. 2019; Convention on Biological Diversity [UN CBD] 2010, 2021, 2022) and nationally in Canada (e.g., Truth and Reconciliation Commission [TRCC] 2015a,b,c; Pathway to Canada Target 1 2018; Indigenous Circle of Experts [ICE] 2018), and yet conditions continue to worsen as damaging activities remain unabated, and in many cases accelerate, as human populations, consumption, and technology increase (IPBES 2019; Secretariat of the CBD [SCBD] 2020). As a promising landmark development, however, on December 19, 2022 in Montreal,

Canada, the 15th Conference of Parties (COP-15) to the UN CBD adopted the "Kunming-Montreal Global Biodiversity Framework." It outlines four goals and 23 targets for achievement by 2030, including "Effective conservation and management of at least 30% of the world's lands, inland waters, coastal areas and oceans, with emphasis on areas of particular importance for biodiversity and ecosystem functioning and services" (UN CBD 2022).

According to both Western science and Indigenous[1] ways of knowing, humanity is at a turning point. Either we recognize and embrace our interrelationship and interdependence with the rest of life – and the soils, water, and air – on earth and act in accordance with this reality, or much of life on earth will perish, with devastating consequences for humanity (IPBES 2019; M'sit No'kmaq et al. 2021). To effectively address the crises will require transformative shifts in the way we view ourselves in the world – our ideals, values, and responsibilities to life on earth and each other – and in governance, economic, social and knowledge systems, institutions, policies, and practices (Patterson et al. 2017; Kennedy et al. 2019; IPBES 2019). We need a new way forward that is ecologically and socially just.

Confronted with these truths, we endeavoured to initiate dialogues and conversations towards a transformative politics of nature. As co-editors of this collection emerging from those conversations, we wanted to share the insights and imaginings as to what that transformation might entail, and why it is crucial – *Where are we coming from, where are we now, and where are we going?* – as we know business as usual will not suffice. We editors are three white settler-scholars aware that transformative change will require all of us – Indigenous and non-Indigenous – working together. Andrea Olive is a settler-scholar from Treaty 4 lands in Saskatchewan and currently resides on the traditional lands of the Huron-Wendat, the Seneca, and the Mississaugas of the Credit. Chance Finegan is an American-Canadian settler-scholar on Treaty 6 territory near Saskatoon. Karen Beazley is from Mi'kma'ki, the ancestral and unceded territory of the Mi'kmaq, the people indigenous to the region. Her ancestors came to Mi'kma'ki in 1760 as pre-Loyalist planters, taking up lands from which French Acadian settlers had been expelled by the British. She is a peace and friendship ally. We are all treaty people.

Where are we coming from? Canada has a long history of wildlife protection, dating back to the 1880s when an ordinance was passed by the federal government to protect the plains bison from over-hunting (Waiser 2016). As the country grew into a federation and provinces gained power over their lands and wildlife, a patchwork of policies, programs, and laws developed to protect wildlife, nature, and, in some cases, species at risk of extinction (Beazley and Boardman 2001; Olive 2014). In 1992, Canada signed the UN CBD (1992) and made a global commitment to safeguard the country's biodiversity.

Not long after, in the mid-1990s, the government of Canada created the Canadian Biodiversity Strategy (Environment Canada 1995) as a way to follow through on its global commitments. The five goals in the strategy include sustainable use, enhanced understanding of ecosystems, increased (public) awareness of biodiversity, incentives and legislation, and international diplomacy. As part of this plan, the federal government introduced a national Species at Risk Act (SARA), which eventually passed Parliament in 2002.[2] Unfortunately, the law is limited by constitutional jurisdiction, particularly in regard to habitat protections, since wildlife, provincial crown lands, natural resources, and private property are managed at the provincial level and thus not automatically subject to SARA's provisions (Elgie 2009; Olive 2014; Westwood et al. 2019). Endangered species legislation has been adopted in some provinces and territories in Canada but not in all.

In 2010, Canada agreed to the UN Strategic Plan for Biodiversity 2011–2020 at the tenth meeting of the Conference of the Parties in Nagoya, Aichi Prefecture, Japan. The Strategic Plan included Aichi Biodiversity Targets (UN CBD 2010). In total, there were five strategic goals and 20 specific targets with a goal year of 2020. Target 11 generated the most governmental initiatives and scholarly energy (see Lemieux et al. 2019; MacKinnon et al. 2015; Zurba et al. 2019): "By 2020, at least 17 per cent of terrestrial and inland water and 10 per cent of coastal and marine areas, especially areas of particular importance for biodiversity and ecosystem services, are conserved through effectively and equitably managed, ecologically representative and well-connected systems of protected areas and other effective area-based conservation measures, and integrated into the wider landscapes and seascapes" (UN CBD 2010).

Nationally, as of the end of 2020, Canada had conserved 12.5 per cent of its land and freshwater area (11.7 per cent protected area; 0.8 per cent other effective area-based conservation measure [OECM]), and 13.8 per cent of its marine territory (8.9 per cent protected area; 4.9 per cent OECM) (Environment and Climate Change Canada [ECCC], 2021), though Canada's OECMs are highly contested as emphasizing quantity over quality, with questionable effectiveness (Lemieux et al. 2019, 2022; Lemieux and Gray 2020). Moving beyond the Aichi Biodiversity Targets, Canada is now looking into the future of conservation area goals and governance. Financial investments for nature were tabled in Canada's 2021 budget, totalling nearly $4.9 billion CA for land, freshwater and marine protected areas, Indigenous Protected and Conserved Areas, Indigenous Guardians programs; species at risk; natural/green infrastructure; and disaster mitigation and adaptation, including small-scale climate adaptation and mitigation projects for natural infrastructure (Government of Canada 2021). Recent area-based commitments aim to conserve 25 per cent of Canada's land and 25 per cent of Canada's oceans by 2025, working towards 30 per cent of each by 2030 (Trudeau 2019; ECCC 2020; Canada (Governor General)

2020; Government of Canada 2021). If achieved, conservation areas would represent the largest and most rapid allocation of land- and marine-use in the history of the country. As such it warrants careful consideration of justice and equity along with ecological imperatives.

There is scientific data and growing political consensus that Canada is no exception in the context of global emergencies. Indeed, in Canada biodiversity is in precipitous decline, exacerbated by climate change, with inequitable distribution of costs across society, disproportionately affecting nature and people, especially Indigenous communities, people of colour, women, and non-heteronormative individuals (Pictou 2019, 2020; Kennedy et al. 2019; National Inquiry into Missing and Murdered Indigenous Women and Girls [MMIWG] 2019). Despite Canada's commitments to conservation and reconciliation with Indigenous Peoples, biodiversity loss is increasing along with human rights violations (World Wildlife Fund Canada [WWF] 2017, 2020; Mother Earth and Resource Extraction [MERE] 2021). There has been a rise in the reported numbers of human rights and land and water defenders, especially Indigenous and Black women, being criminalized, harassed, and physically targeted by law enforcement and private security personnel and actors linked to natural resource extraction sectors (MMIWG 2019; MERE 2021; NDN Collective nd). Highly intensive and extensive resource extraction on the one hand and "fortress" conservation on the other have dispossessed Indigenous Peoples of their traditional territories (ICE 2018; Pictou 2019, 2020; Conservation through Reconciliation Partnership [CRP] 2021). Gains are being made in some arenas, such as with respect to the government of Canada's efforts in ethical space of engagement with Indigenous Peoples through Pathway to Canada Target 1 (2018; ICE 2018) and university-Indigenous-government partnerships for conservation through reconciliation (e.g., Zurba et al. 2019; Artelle et al. 2019; CRP 2020). Yet, for the most part, the status quo continues in resource extraction sectors, including oil and gas, renewal energy, mining, and forestry, and through the ongoing tendency to privilege private property and corporate rights over more equitable and reciprocal relations among people, lands, and waters (MMIWG 2019; Kruse and Robinson 2019; MERE 2021).

The United Nation's IPBES (2019) reported that up to a million species are at risk of extinction on the planet. The 2019–20 annual report by the Committee on the Status of Endangered Wildlife in Canada (COSEWIC) listed 810 wildlife species in various risk categories. World Wildlife Fund Canada's 2020 *Living Planet Report Canada* estimated that populations of Canadian species assessed as at risk by COSEWIC have declined by 59 per cent on average from 1970–2016, an era in which almost every existing species-at-risk policy was created. The United Nations' flagship report, *Global Biodiversity Outlook*, revealed that at the global level none of the 20 Aichi Biodiversity Targets had been fully achieved by 2020 (SCBD 2020).

Building on past strategies, the UN CBD's (2022) Kunming-Montreal Global Biodiversity Framework, adopted by the 188 Parties to the CBD at COP-15, will heavily influence international conservation efforts over the next 10 years and beyond. The first draft, released in July 2021, suggested that parties to the CBD, including Canada, will be called on to implement transformational changes, including unprecedented area expansion of well-connected networks of protected areas and OECMs, and the integration of equitable approaches that respect and uphold Indigenous rights, governance, and knowledge systems (UN CBD/WG2020/3/3 2021). Canada joined other countries in a High Ambition Coalition for Nature and People, committing to these increases nationally and globally (ECCC 2020), setting itself upon an unprecedented pathway in conservation (Dietz et al. 2021). In Canada, Prime Minister Justin Trudeau's 2019 Minister of Environment and Climate Change Mandate Letter urged the minister to "Work with the Minister of Fisheries and Oceans and the Canadian Coast Guard to introduce a new ambitious plan to conserve 25 per cent of Canada's land and 25 per cent of Canada's oceans by 2025, working towards 30 per cent of each by 2030. This plan should be grounded in science, Indigenous knowledge, and local perspectives" (Trudeau 2019). As a party to COP-15, Canada has now formally committed to achieving these and other conservation goals and targets nationally and on the international stage by 2030.

Canada has made some recent progress, especially around protected areas, but governments must immediately implement politically feasible and effective conservation policy. The next 30 years will be critical for the country's wildlife as climate change exacerbates the existing challenges to the physical conditions of the planet and as efforts to achieve current commitments and post-2020 targets are pursued. Achieving the aspirations outlined in global and Canadian national arenas will not be easy, entailing a transformative shift away from the status quo. Current social, political, and economic structures represent drivers of biodiversity loss. Transformative changes are required in "the production and consumption of energy, food, feed, fibre and water, sustainable use, equitable sharing of the benefits arising from use and nature-friendly climate adaptation and mitigation" (IPBES 2019, 15). Urgent and concerted efforts include "rapid and improved deployment of existing policy instruments and new initiatives that more effectively enlist individual and collective action for transformative change" (IPBES 2019, 16).

Unless transformative changes are made, biodiversity goals will not be achieved, and yet fundamental change will be opposed by those with vested interests in the status quo. According to the IPBES, if obstacles are overcome, multiple sectors may be transformed through a commitment to mutual goals and targets, supportive actions by Indigenous peoples and local communities, new frameworks for investment and innovation, inclusive and adaptive governance approaches and arrangements, cross-sectoral planning, and strategic policy mixes (IPBES 2019). To tackle the underlying drivers, crucial interventions entail incentives and capacity-building; multi-sectoral cooperation; pre-emptive action; decision-making in the context of resilience and uncertainty; and environmental law and implementation (IPBES 2019). Key areas where there are leverage points to initiate transformative change include societal visions of a good life; values and action; equality, justice, and inclusion; and education and knowledge systems (IPBES 2019). Transformational conservation responses will necessitate a "system-wide reorganization of our sense of reality and associated paradigms, goals, and values across economic, social, political, and technological sectors" (Lemieux et al. 2021, 202, citing IPBES 2019).

Is Change Possible?

Transformative actions are those that cause or are able to cause important and lasting changes (from Latin *transformare*: "change in shape, metamorphose"). In their deliberations, the IPBES brought significant attention to the kinds of actions required and to the most effective "leverage" for transformation. They drew heavily upon Donella Meadows's (1999) *Leverage Points: Places to Intervene in a System*. Leverage points are "places within a complex system ... where a small shift in one thing can produce big changes in everything ... Leverage points are points of power" (Meadows 1999, 1). Meadows listed 12 leverage points that remain relevant today. Those at one end of the spectrum focus on a system's material-institution-technology components (e.g., subsidies, standards, taxes) and are easier to achieve but less effective; those at the other end are most effective and are focused on ideation components, such as world views (paradigms; mindsets) and the power to transcend them. Such work supports the case for multiple leverage points, and especially for highly effective ones such as transcending paradigms or transforming worldviews.

Often the case is made that the most effective levers, such as transcending paradigms or transforming worldviews, are the most difficult to exploit and require longer time frames to achieve, and thus are considered less feasible. Others make a convincing case that worldviews can shift quickly, as Thomas Homer-Dixon argued in his book *Commanding Hope*: "In a single individual, it can happen in a millisecond" (2020). And social change can also happen quickly, especially in the face of overwhelming evidence and a growing base of support, particularly in today's context of global uniformity and connectivity (social media; information systems), which can lead to "swift, nonlinear jumps." Homer-Dixon cites examples related to apartheid, same-sex marriage, and the demise of Soviet communism. New mindsets open up the view of what is possible and what is feasible as a vision of a good life and goals and routes to a future based in "sufficiency" (enough), so as to address otherwise overwhelmingly complex crises in biodiversity, climate, and human rights.

From this perspective of hope, efforts to achieve normative shifts in our views of each other and the earth need not necessarily be assumed to be too slow and thus less feasible. At this time, there is tremendous resonance among Indigenous worldviews and alternative worldviews within Western discourse that holds up deep and relational values based in kinship and reciprocal relationships of responsibility with all of life and ecologies, often referred to as "all my relations" or ecocentrism. "Both ecocentrism and [I]ndigenous kinship ethics see life as kin and worthy of respect and a duty of care (Neidjie et al. 1985), as they accept their intrinsic value. Anthropocentrism does not do this, seeing all of nature as just a resource for human use (Crist 2012)" (Washington et al. 2018, 368). Alignment among Indigenous and non-Indigenous worldviews may provide opportunities to transcend the dominant worldview of anthropocentrism, which currently underlies the status quo, for the good of people and nature (M'sit No'kmaq et al. 2021). An "Indigenous-non-Indigenous-all-of-creation relationality" holds conciliatory possibilities towards transformative reconciliation, healing, and new possible futures that centre the rights of people and nature (Finegan 2018, as cited by Pictou, this volume).

Layout of This Collection

The chapters in this volume examine political barriers to conservation as well as possible pathways forward. Many of the authors gathered for workshops in Toronto and Halifax in 2020 before the COVID-19 pandemic. All authors in this collection wrote their chapters during various stages of lockdown and through ebbs and flows of crisis. It is more than a perfect metaphor; it is the actual lived experience of human-wildlife coexistence. Although unconfirmed at the time, COVID-19 is now known to be the third zoonotic virus, after SARS-CoV and MERS-CoV, and potential cross-species events are likely to occur in the future (Centers for Disease Control and Prevention [CDC] 2021; Mackenzie and Smith 2020). Enabling the protection of "landscape immunity – the ecological conditions that reduce the risk of pathogen spillover from reservoir hosts" – has recently been identified as an urgent "conservation and biosecurity priority" (Plowright et al. 2021, 1). Implementing both transformative change and investment for biodiversity in the midst of the COVID-19 pandemic will require extreme political will. But in some regards, the pandemic may have brought some additional imperative to biodiversity conservation (Editorial 2021). Scientific and expert guidance are being accorded more respect in some political and policy decision-making circles. Perhaps all nations, including Canada, will recognize the role of biological conservation and protected areas in safeguarding humanity and nature (Editorial 2021; Plowright et al. 2021).

The overall goal of this edited collection is to highlight the most significant barriers to conservation in Canada and then discuss strategies to confront and overcome barriers. The proximate reasons for biodiversity loss and wildlife decline are known: habitat degradation, loss and fragmentation, climate change, invasive species, pollution, and over-harvesting. Underlying causes are also well recognized: dominant economic systems and world views, colonialism, over-consumption, over-population, destructive use of technologies, war, and poverty. Many ways of addressing these problems have been proposed by Indigenous peoples, natural and social scientists, and biodiversity and social-equity advocates. However, policies at local, provincial, national, and international levels have failed to address these issues and reverse the decline for virtually all species and ecosystems. While the science is clear, the politics is not. The political barriers to effective conservation of nature in Canada need to be highlighted, debated, and confronted.

The politics and governance of biodiversity is complicated by a host of factors, such as multi-level governments, multi-agency overlap, data availability, and a rapidly changing climate (Armitage et al. 2012; Bennet 2011; Challies and Newig 2019). As pointed out by Ray et al. (2021), the fact that Canada's wildlife is declining alongside increased global conservation commitments and domestic policy responses suggests that Canada's governance systems are ill-equipped to deal with biodiversity loss. Here we take governance to mean "social political interactions" that comprise "the totality of interactions in which public as well as private actors participate" to overcome collective problems (Challies and Newig 2019; see Kooiman 2003). Governance includes everything from law and policy to environmental groups' projects to lawsuits to Indigenous law and policy.

A main focus of this collection is Indigenous rights, participation, and leadership in conservation policy and politics. In this context, we interpret politics as the total complex of relations between people living in society. Traditional constructions of "wilderness" have often engaged in colonial dispossession of Indigenous Peoples, land, and lifeways (Olive and Rabe 2016; Youdelis et al. 2020; Zurba et al. 2019). Current models of conservation need to engage in reconciliation; as Zurba et al. (2019, 10) write, "a profound shift in how the Canadian state, its conservation organizations, and its public think about conservation is required." We are called to practise conservation in ways that acknowledge and respect Indigenous rights and governance and knowledge systems (Borrows and Coyle 2017; Coulthard 2014; ICE 2018; Poezler and Coates 2015). We see a transformative vision of a good life that initiates lasting changes in complex human relations with each other and with nature or more-than-human relations to reshape/restore the natural environment in ways that are also socially just.

The following 11 chapters uncover and strategize ways around the political barriers to effective conservation governance in Canada. They provide insights that enhance understanding of key barriers, important actors, and strategies for working within and shaping policy at multiple levels of government across

Canada. They engage academics, environmental conservation organizations, and Indigenous communities in dialogues and explorations of the politics of nature conservation. Together, they demonstrate and highlight the need for increased social-political awareness about biodiversity and conservation in Canada, enhanced wildlife conservation collaborative networks (in Canada more broadly), and increased scholarly and other evidence-based attention to the principles, policies, and practices of caring for nature. They address broad themes, organized into three parts: barriers to conservation, transformation through reconciliation, and transformation through policy and governance.

Each part is followed by a "disruption." In a multi-section chapter called "We Can Do Better: Disrupting Current Approaches to Biodiversity Conservation," Finegan et al. identify and describe "conservation disruptions," or innovative perspectives that aim to push the boundaries of conservation practice. They assert that there is value in thinking about how to challenge existing approaches with the hope that new ideas will shore up weaknesses in biodiversity conservation. In keeping with the theme of disruptions, they present their chapter in multiple parts, as literal disruptions to this book, at the ends of each part.

The collection opens and closes with ceremony, in the form of two poems. In the beginning, shalan joudry[3] (Bear River First Nation, Mi'kmaq) opens us up, preparing the ground for listening. She remembers those who have come before, and those here now, with gratitude; we would not be here without them. And in acknowledging their resilience, she gives us hope, and humility, for listening, learning, and moving forward.

Following the introduction (part A), barriers to conservation in Canada are presented in part B, with four chapters addressing major challenges to transformative changes. Chapter authors identify barriers ranging from status-quo attitudes towards governance, to organizational dysfunction, to implementation and enforcement gaps, and unfulfilled and improperly implemented treaties and race-based thinking. First, in "A Pathological Examination of Conservation Failure in Canada," Lemieux et al. tackle the underlying issues as to why the organizations society entrusts to conserve biodiversity continuously fail to do so. They use pathologies as a metaphor to examine the ways in which organizational dysfunctions emerge, persist, and have become a precondition to failure in effectively conserving biodiversity in Canada. Treating these pathologies will be slow because dysfunctional organizations avoid risk and crave certainty, are not forward thinking, have closed cultures, and are not accountable because there is no legal basis. They conclude that effective achievement of conservation goals in Canada will require an integrated mix of incremental and transformative adaptations in law and policy, action plans aligned with reporting and monitoring, and alignment with other initiatives related to climate change, human health and well-being, and sustainable development, some of which are discussed in latter parts of this book.

In "Who Should Govern Wildlife? Examining Attitudes across the Country," Williamson et al. found that, despite the stark evidence to the contrary, many Canadians believe the current arrangements between federal, provincial, local, and Indigenous governments are effective for managing wildlife. This general acceptance of and preference for the status quo may pose a barrier to transformative politics for wildlife governance in Canada, with devastating consequences extending to the global level, because the status quo of shared responsibility between the federal and provincial governments is not working. The fact that Canadians by and large support this ineffective system is troubling and could be a real barrier to transformative change. Canadians might not be prepared for a change that will disrupt the federal and provincial co-management of wildlife issues. Going forward, Williamson et al. write, Canada will need to explore different and more innovative governance schema. While it is not clear whether a change in governance will help or if it will be enough, it is clear that Canada's current arrangement is failing.

Boan and Plotkin's chapter, "In a Rut: Barriers to Caribou Conservation," considers the conservation of boreal caribou as an illustration of the barriers that wildlife faces across Canada. The key driver of caribou decline is habitat fragmentation, which negatively affects many species. Despite growing agreement about how management should be undertaken to recover caribou, the authors identify significant existing barriers to implementation, including ideologies of development and growth without limits; government inaction; lack of local support; and inadequate implementation of strategies to address cumulative effects. The required approaches to maintain and restore adequate habitat for recovery of caribou and other species are hampered by these barriers. Diverging perspectives on wildlife management have led to decades of conflict and deflection that have perpetuated declines. The authors observe that legislation dealing with species at risk and wildlife is weak or non-existent, and the political will to implement legislation is weak. As a consequence, industry and development interests are typically not legally required to protect or restore habitat. Where requirements do exist, they are usually not enforced. The authors conclude that although wildlife management must be based on science, it alone cannot shape management decisions. Social and cultural dimensions, Indigenous practices and ethics, creative framing of new approaches, and a commitment to transparency also play primary roles.

Larry McDermott (Algonquin from Shabot Obaadjiwan First Nation) and Robin Roth, in "Enacting a Reciprocal Ethic of Care: (Finally) Fulfilling Treaty Obligations" (chapter 5), stress that "mere tinkering with the tools and approaches that have come to dominate wildlife management is insufficient." They identify the fundamental barrier to successful wildlife management to be "the unfulfilled and improperly implemented treaties between settler states and

Indigenous Nations," which are a symptom of "supercilious race-based thinking" that fails to recognize the value of Indigenous knowledge and governance
systems. They go on to contend that, as a consequence, mainstream Canadian
society has not inherited the knowledge of how to fulfill collective responsibilities towards each other and the natural world. While mainstream approaches
to wildlife conservation tend to disconnect humans from scarce wildlife in the
name of protection, "Indigenous approaches seek to reconnect humans to wildlife in the spirit of reciprocity and respect, leading to abundance." They make
the strong case that "reconnection" is what humanity needs right now, and "it is
what is necessary for the continuation of life."

In the disruption to part B, Sheila R. Colla and Chance Finegan discuss the
roles of narratives in conservation. Colla offers bee conservation as a cautionary
example of a time when the conservation narrative went awry with unintended
consequences. Meanwhile, Finegan draws our attention to the role of national
park managers in challenging dominant, settler narratives about Turtle Island's
natural and cultural heritage.

In part C, "Transformation through Values," four contributions directly
confront race-based thinking and other Western constructs and colonial institutional systems through resurgent Indigenous governance and knowledge
systems. Importantly, they point out that true reconciliation requires healing,
relationality, and Indigenous ways of knowing that embody the lived experience of the people and the land. First, in "Reconciliation or *Apiksitaultimik*?
Indigenous Relationality for Conservation," Sherry Pictou (Bear River First
Nation, Mi'kmaq) denotes a call for decolonizing conservation practices by
exploring how Indigenous knowledges grounded in land- and water-based lifeways are embodiments of the wild or wild species as our relatives. Indigenous
relationality encompasses the human and non-human or more-than-human
world including our ancestors and all of Creation. Pictou argues that the concept of reconciliation therefore must be mobilized as a relational practice beyond political economies and political ecologies in conservation efforts. As a
decolonizing approach, she explores how reconciliation is a form of healing
in Mi'kmaw/Indigenous relationality that holds transformative possibilities for
reframing reconciliation in conservation. She shows how a lens of Indigenous
feminism is imperative to an authentic reconciliation process. To disrupt the
dichotomies between "reconciliation efforts to transform colonial approaches
to conservation" on one hand, while "exploiting natural resources for economic development" on the other, Pictou proposes a way forward. Indigenous/
Mi'kmaw concepts of relationality, with an ethical responsibility for healing
between Indigenous-non-Indigenous-all-of-Creation, offer ways to mobilize
reconciliation beyond current political economies and political ecologies in
conservation practice. They acknowledge the inseparability of the human, natural, and spiritual worlds.

In the next chapter, three Indigenous scholars, two non-Indigenous part-ners and Elder Albert Marshall engage in dialogue on "*Etuaptmumk*/Two-Eyed Seeing and Reconciliation with Earth" (McGregor et al.). They stress that transformative change is required between humanity and the Earth, that it is a crucial form of reconciliation, and key to it is "to reconcile different ways of understanding and relating to the Earth." In their own words, Deborah McGregor (Anishinabek), Jesse Popp (Anishinabek), Andrea Reid (Nisga'a), and Mi'kmaw Elder Albert Marshall discuss different ways of understanding the world – *Two-Eyed Seeing, Two Row Wampum*, and *Dish with One Spoon*. Rooted in Indigenous cultures and embodied within the lived experience of the people and the land, these concepts offer "unique ways of knowing that can and must balance humanity's relationships with place." They provide "ethical space to ensure a coming together of peoples in the spirit of respect and collab-oration to ensure reconciliation with each other and the Earth." Their insights into the application of the concepts illustrate how we may "collectively better understand our interrelationships and inter-responsibilities, in support of rec-onciliation between societies, nations and the Earth."

In "Beacons of Teachings," Lisa Young (Eskasoni First Nation, Mi'kmaq) weaves together Indigenous stories with her lived experiences in Western and Indigenous natural resource management and protected and conserved ar-eas (IPCAs). She describes how at times it seems she is "living in two realities in which our lands and waters are in separate realms lorded over by a ruling body that wears two faces." In forestry and protected areas management, the Mi'kmaq are making headway towards arrangements that create space for In-digenous-led conservation in the spirit of reconciliation. On the water, how-ever, the Canadian government continues to ignore Mi'kmaq Treaty rights, acknowledges Indigenous knowledge only when it does not threaten their mo-nopoly over the fishery, and refuses to recognize Mi'kmaw laws and governance systems. Many of the core values of Mi'kmaw systems are held in the legends of Kluskap. They speak of the need for mutual respect for the land and "all our relations," to ensure continued interdependence and existence. They form the founding principles from which Mi'kmaw IPCAs will be created. Such teach-ings serve as beacons to light the path to reconciliation that will heal not only Mi'kmaq relationships with Canada but with the lands and waters, supporting a more sustainable future for all Canadians.

In the disruption to part C, Indigenous voices continue to be centred. Nata-sha Myhal (Sault Ste. Marie Tribe of Chippewa Indians) considers how Indige-nous sovereignty and relationships to Creation challenge Western technocratic approaches to conservation. Meanwhile, Chief Heidi Cook (Misipawistik Cree Nation) shows us how the Indigenous Guardians Program can contribute to In-digenous resurgence and biodiversity conservation, offering her community's experience in building a guardian program as a living example.

In part D, diverse approaches for "Transformation through Actions" are put forward. These range from collaborative partnerships for decolonizing education and the academy that can lead to the transformation of attitudes and practices; to shifting the conservation paradigm to ecological networks; and locating key areas of action, from whole-of-government approaches to federal leadership and law reform. In "Transforming University Curriculum and Student Experiences through Collaboration and Land-Based Learning," Zurba et al. explore an important vehicle for decolonizing education systems and building relationships between the academy and communities, which often have long histories of colonialism. Acknowledging the wrongdoing of educational institutions and improving relationships between communities and universities can be important first steps towards the process of reconciliation. They describe their collaboration, between a Mi'kmaw organization and a professor, to develop a relationship and deliver land-based learning in the context of a university course. They distill, first-hand, the aspects of collaboration that promoted relationship building and authentic student learning opportunities. Many of the outcomes, such as an appreciation for Indigenous knowledge and respect for one another, were similar for the collaborating partners and for students. These included relationality; engagement with the land and each other; and self-reflection on position and the spaces occupied in relation to the land and Indigenous peoples. The authors conclude that these are essential aspects of learning that can lead to the transformation of attitudes and practices, deepening of understanding of Indigenous knowledge and worldviews, and enhanced relationships with Indigenous peoples and the land.

In "Ecological Networks and Corridors in the Context of Global Initiatives," Hilty and Woodley stress the importance of conservation at larger spatial scales than the current system of protected and conserved areas. To stem biodiversity loss, well-designed protected and conserved areas need to be ecologically connected to create functional ecological networks. The authors present the evidence supporting large-scale conservation, ecological corridors, and ecological networks, establishing the need for ecological connectivity. They situate it within the context of the global conservation agenda, including guidance from the International Union for the Conservation of Nature (IUCN) (Hilty et al. 2020). Basic requirements for planning and implementing ecological corridors are laid out. In closing, Hilty and Woodley note that the need to define and conserve ecological corridors has never been greater. With IUCN connectivity guidelines now available, the focus shifts to questions of how to advance policy and practice from local to regional to national and global scales. Setting targets for connectivity represents an opportunity to move biodiversity conservation to also consider ecological connectivity and shift the paradigm to ecological networks for conservation.

Justina C. Ray's capstone chapter lays out "The Imperative for Transformative Change to Address Biodiversity Loss in Canada." Crucially, it entails an urgent and "fundamental re-design" that would require "wholesale changes in mindset" as an alternative to incremental change that has maintained the status quo for so many years. Ray argues that transformative change should come through mainstreaming biodiversity considerations in decision-making, which itself can only come about through a shift in values away from an unsustainable and exploitive growth ideology. Transformation will necessitate "a whole-of-government approach to budgeting and policy making, a shift in mindset to how we value nature, an embrace of Indigenous-led conservation, strong federal leadership, and accompanying law reform." Ray acknowledges that such changes will continue to be opposed by those with economic interests vested in the status quo. And yet she reminds us that we can take heart: societal transformations have occurred multiple times before in history; and an increasingly diverse set of voices (including business) is calling for such a shift, given the convergent global challenges of the loss of nature, the climate emergency, and growing inequality.

In the disruption to part D, Barbara Frei urges conservation practitioners to seek out and learn from "bright spots," or locales in which conservation is succeeding, and to share these success stories to build hope and mobilize action. Vivian Nguyen continues with this theme of knowledge production and mobilization, emphasizing the need to bring knowledge users and holders into the knowledge-generation process. She presents Living Laboratories as a step towards this. Finegan et al. conclude their disruption with a brief discussion of its implications for transforming biodiversity conservation in Canada.

In Part E, Olive and Beazley provide concluding remarks for "Achieving Transformative Change: Conservation in Canada in 2023 and Beyond." They reflect upon how we can make lasting change in complex human relations to reshape/restore the natural environment in socially just ways. Pulling together the actions and values discussed in parts C and D, the conclusion illustrates the path towards transformative change. In her closing poem, shalan joudry brings us back to gratitude and hope with ceremony, honouring the process of our coming together in storied relationships.

Together, the authors' contributions encompass an interdisciplinary variety of vexing issues, such as frustrations with federalism and bureaucracy, the exclusion of Indigenous voices, and dominant worldviews and global systems that fail to centre the rights of all peoples and nature. At the same time, they suggest transformative ways forward that overcome barriers and shine a light onto new approaches and possible futures grounded in social and ecological justice. They represent a rich diversity of shared knowledge, stories, and experiences with nature, wildlife, and species-at-risk conservation and opportunities to transform politics, policies, and practices in Canada, often with relevance well beyond its borders, in the international arena.

NOTES

1 In this book, "Indigenous" refers to First Nation, Inuit, and Métis peoples generally. The term "Aboriginal" is used when referring to specific Aboriginal Treaty rights, as this is the custom in Canadian legal scholarship and refers specifically to section 35 of the Constitution Act 1982 and section 25 of the Canadian Charter of Rights and Freedoms.

2 SARA is a federal law that applies only to federal lands, migratory birds, and some aquatic species (as the latter are federal jurisdiction). Six provinces and two territories in Canada have stand-alone legislation for species at risk. However, the provinces of British Columbia, Alberta, Saskatchewan, and Prince Edward Island, and Yukon territory only protect wildlife through various pieces of legislation like a Forestry Act or Wildlife Act. (See Olive 2019, 2021; Turcotte et al. 2021; Westwood et al. 2019.)

3 In the Mi'kmaw language there is no stronger intonation to first person versus collective. Consistent with this teaching, shalan chooses to not capitalize her name.

WORKS CITED

Armitage, D., R. de Loe, and R. Plummer. 2012. "Environmental Governance and Its Implications for Conservation Practice." *Conservation Letters* 5: 245–55. https://doi .org/10.1111/j.1755-263X.2012.00238.x

Artelle, K., M. Zurba, J. Bhattacharyya, D. Chan, K. Brown, J. Housty, and F. Moola. 2019. "Supporting Resurgent Indigenous-Led Governance: A Nascent Mechanism for Just and Effective Conservation." *Biological Conservation* 240. https://doi .org/10.1016/j.biocon.2019.108284

Beazley, K., and R. Boardman. 2001. *Politics of the Wild: Canada and Endangered Species*. Toronto, Ontario: Oxford University Press.

Bennet, E.L. 2011. "Another Inconvenient Truth: The Failure of Enforcement Systems to Save Charismatic Species." *Fauna & Flora International: Oryx* 45 (4): 476–9. https://doi.org/10.1017/S003060531000178X

Borrows, J., and M. Coyle. 2017. *The Right Relationships*. Toronto: University of Toronto Press.

Canada (Governor General). 2020. "A Stronger and More Resilient Canada: Speech from the Throne to Open the Second Session of the Forty-Third Parliament of Canada, September 23, 2020." Ottawa. Accessed April 22, 2021. www.canada.ca /throne-speech.

CDC (Centers for Disease Control and Prevention). 2021. "Importance of One Health for COVID-19 and Future Pandemics." Accessed May 28, 2022. https://www.cdc .gov/media/releases/2021/s1103-one-health.html.

Challies, E., and J. Newig. 2019. "What Is Environmental Governance? A Working Definition." *Sustainability Governance: A Blog by the Research Group Governance, Participation & Sustainability at Leuphana University.* https://sustainabilitygovernance.net/2019/06/14/what-is-environmental-governance-a-working-definition/

Conservation through Reconciliation Partnership (CRP). 2020. *Birthing Our Partnership: Year One of Our Seven-Year Journey.* https://static1.squarespace.com/static/5d3f1e8262d8ed00013cdff1/t/5ef4a43155919834bc5378ae/1593091243817/CRP+Year+1+Annual+Report+PDF.pdf

Conservation through Reconciliation Partnership (CRP). 2021. "Land Back: Governance for a Just World." CRP webinar co-hosted with David Suzuki Foundation, Ontario Nature and Decolonizing Water. April 21, 2021. https://conservation-reconciliation.ca/virtual-campfire

Coulthard, G.S. 2014. *Red Skin, White Masks: Rejecting the Colonial Politics of Recognition.* Minnesota: University of Minnesota Press.

Crist, E. 2012. "Abundant Earth and the Population Question," In *Life on the Brink: Environmentalists Confront Overpopulation*, edited by P. Cafaro and E. Crist, 141–51. Georgia: University of Georgia Press.

Dietz, S., Beazley, K.F., Lemieux, C.J., St Clair, C., Coristine, L., Higgs, E., Smith, R., Pellatt, M., et al. (21 others). 2021. "Emerging Issues for Protected and Conserved Areas in Canada." *FACETS* 6: 1892–921. https://doi.org/10.1139/facets-2021-0072

Editorial. 2021. "High Time to Invest in Biodiversity." *Nature Ecology & Evolution* 5, 263. https://doi.org/10.1038/s41559-021-01416-0

Elgie, S. 2009. "The Politics of Extinction: The Birth of Canada's Species at Risk Act." In *Canadian Environmental Policy and Politics: Prospects for Leadership and Innovation*, edited by Debora L. VanNijnatten and Robert Boardman, 197–215. Don Mills: Oxford University Press.

Environment and Climate Change Canada (ECCC). 2020. "Canada Joins the High Ambition Coalition for Nature and People," news release, September 28, 2020, Ottawa, Ontario. https://www.canada.ca/en/environment-climate-change/news/2020/09/canada-joins-the-high-ambition-coalition-for-nature-and-people.html

Environment and Climate Change Canada (ECCC). 2021. Canadian Protected and Conserved Areas Database. Accessed April 22, 2021 https://www.canada.ca/en/environment-climate-change/services/national-wildlife-areas/protected-conserved-areas-database.html.

Environment Canada (EC). 1995. *Canadian Biodiversity Strategy: Canada's Response to the Convention on Biological Diversity, 1995.* Biodiversity Convention Office, EC: Minister of Supply and Services Canada. https://www.cbd.int/doc/world/ca/ca-nbsap-01-en.pdf

Finegan, C. 2018. "Reflection, Acknowledgement, and Justice: A Framework for Indigenous-Protected Area Reconciliation." *The International Indigenous Policy Journal*, 9(3). https://doi.org/10.18584/iipj.2018.9.3.3

Government of Canada. (n.d.). "Monarch (Danaus plexippus): COSEWIC Assessment and Status Report 2016." Accessed April 26, 2021. https://www.canada.ca/en /environment-climate-change/services/species-risk-public-registry/cosewic -assessments-status-reports/monarch-2016.html

Government of Canada. 2020. *COSEWIC Annual Report presented to the Minister of Environment and Climate Change and the Canadian Endangered Species Conservation Council (CESCC) from the Committee on the Status of Endangered Wildlife in Canada (COSEWIC) 2019–2020.* https://www.canada.ca/en /environment-climate-change/services/species-risk-public-registry/cosewic-annual -reports/2019-2020.html

Government of Canada. 2021. "Budget 2021: A Recovery Plan for Jobs, Growth and Resilience." Department of Finance: Service Canada. https://www.canada.ca/en /department-finance.html. Accessed April 22, 2021.

Hilty, Jodi, Graeme L. Worboys, Annika Keeley, Stephen Woodley, Barbara Lausche, Harvey Locke, Mark Carr, et al. 2020. "Guidelines for Conserving Connectivity through Ecological Networks and Corridors." *IUCN, International Union for Conservation of Nature.* https://doi.org/10.2305/IUCN.CH.2020. PAG.30.en

Homer-Dixon, T. 2020. *Commanding Hope: The Power We Have to Renew a World in Peril.* Toronto: Alfred A. Knopf Canada.

Indigenous Circle of Experts (ICE). 2018. "Pathway to Canada Target 1: Indigenous Circle of Experts (ICE) Regional Gatherings Report." http://www.conservation2020canada .ca/ice-resources

Intergovernmental Science-Policy Platform on Biodiversity and Ecosystem Services (IPBES). 2019. "Summary for Policymakers of the Global Assessment Report on Biodiversity and Ecosystem Services of the Intergovernmental Science-Policy Platform on Biodiversity and Ecosystem Services." Edited by S. Díaz, J. Settele, E.S. Brondízio, H.T. Ngo, M. Guèze, J. Agard, A. Arneth, P. Balvanera, K.A. Brauman, S.H.M. Butchart, K.M.A. Chan, L.A. Garibaldi, K. Ichii, J. Liu, S.M. Subramanian, G.F. Midgley, P. Miloslavich, Z. Molnár, D. Obura, A. Pfaff, S. Polasky, A. Purvis, J. Razzaque, B. Reyers, R. Roy Chowdhury, Y.J. Shin, I.J. Visseren-Hamakers, K.J. Willis, and C.N. Zayas. Bonn, Germany: IPBES Secretariat. https://doi.org/10.5281 /zenodo.3553579

Kennedy, E., J. Patterson, K. Taylor, L. Steichen, M. Mulhoiiand, M. Franklin, S. Saseedhar. 2019. *Our Communities, Our Power: Advancing Resistance and Resilience in Climate Change Adaptation. Environmental and Climate Justice Program.* National Association for the Advancement of Colored People. Baltimore, MD. Accessed January 16, 2023. https://d3h55oe312fhj3.cloudfront .net/wp-content/uploads/2019/06/Our-Communities-Our-Power-TOOLKIT.pdf

Kooiman, J. 2003. *Governing as Governance.* London: Sage.

Kruse, M., and C. Robinson. 2019. "Injunctions by First Nations: Results of a National Study." Treaty Rights and Title. Yellowhead Institute. Retrieved

March 27, 2021, from https://yellowheadinstitute.org/2019/11/14/injunctions
-by-first-nations-results-of-a-national-study/

Lemieux, C., D. MacKinnon, D. Kraus, K. Beazley, A. Jacob, P. Gray. 2021. "(Re)
Connecting Canada: Setting the Table for Transformation." In *Implementing
Connectivity Conservation in Canada*, edited by C.J. Lemieux, A.L. Jacob, and P.A.
Gray, 201–7. Canadian Council on Ecological Areas (CCEA) Occasional Paper No. 22.
Waterloo, Canada: Canadian Council on Ecological Areas, Wilfrid Laurier University.

Lemieux, C.J., D.T. Kraus, and K.F. Beazley. 2022. "Running to Stand Still: The
Application of Substandard OECMs in National and Provincial Policy
in Canada." *Biological Conservation* 275. https://doi.org/10.1016/j
.biocon.2022.109780

Lemieux, C.J., and P.A. Gray. 2020. "How Canada 'Hamburger Manufactured' Its Way
to Marine Protected Area Success and a More Effective and Equitable Way Forward
for the Post-2020 Conservation Agenda." *Journal of Environmental Studies and
Sciences* 10 (4): 483–91. https://doi.org/10.1007/s13412-020-00627-4

Lemieux, C.J., P.A. Gray, R. Devillers, P.A. Wright, P. Dearden, E.A. Halpenny,
G. Groulx, T.J. Beechey, K. Beazley. 2019. "How the Race to Achieve Aichi
Target 11 Could Jeopardize the Effective Conservation of Biodiversity in
Canada and Beyond." *Marine Policy* 99: 312–23. https://doi.org/10.1016/j
.marpol.2018.10.029

M'sit No'kmaq, Marshall, A., K.F. Beazley, J. Hum, S. Joudry, A. Papadopoulos,
S. Pictou, J. Rabesca, L. Young, and M. Zurba. 2021. "'Awakening the
Sleeping Giant': Re-Indigenization Principles for Transforming Biodiversity
Conservation in Canada and Beyond." *FACETS* 6: 839–69. https://doi.org/10.1139
/facets-2020-0083

Mackenzie, J.S., and D.W. Smith. 2020. "COVID-19: A Novel Zoonotic Disease Caused
by a Coronavirus from China: What We Know and What We Don't." *Microbiology
Australia*, March 17. https://doi.org/10.1071/MA20013

MacKinnon, D., C.J. Lemieux, K. Beazley, S. Woodley, R. Helie, J. Perron, J. Elliott, C.
Haas, J. Langlois, H. Lazaruk, et al. 2015. "Canada and Aichi Biodiversity Target 11:
Understanding 'Other Effective Area-Based Conservation Measures' in the Context
of the Broader Target." *Biodiversity Conservation* 24: 3559–81. https://doi.org
/10.1007/s10531-015-1018-1

Meadows, D.H. 1999. "Leverage Points: Places to Intervene in a System." The
Sustainability Institute. https://donellameadows.org/wp-content/userfiles
/Leverage_Points.pdf

Mother Earth and Resource Extraction (MERE). 2021. "Women Defending Land and
Water." Kairos Canada. Accessed March 22, 2021. https://scalar.usc.edu/works
/mere-hub/about-mere;

Moulton, A.A., and M.R. Machado. 2019. "Bouncing Forward after Irma and
Maria: Acknowledging Colonialism, Problematizing Resilience and Thinking

Climate Justice." *Journal of Extreme Events* 6 (1). https://doi.org/10.1142 /S2345737619400037

National Inquiry into Missing and Murdered Indigenous Women and Girls (MMIWG). 2019. "Reclaiming Power and Place. Executive Summary of the Final Report." *National Inquiry into Missing and Murdered Indigenous Women and Girls.* https://www.mmiwg-ffada.ca/wp-content/uploads/2019/06/Executive _Summary.pdf

Nature Serve. (n.d.). "*Danaus plexippus* pop. 2: Monarch – Mexican Overwintering Population." Nature Serve Explorer. Accessed April 26, 2021. https://explorer.natureserve.org/Taxon/ELEMENT_GLOBAL.2.860030 /Danaus_plexippus_pop_2

NDN Collective. (n.d.). Landback Manifesto. https://landback.org/manifesto/

Neidjie, B., S. Davis, and A. Fox. 1985. *Kakadu Man: Bill Neidjie.* Queanbeyan, NSW /Australia: Mybrood P/L Incorporated.

Olive, A. 2014. *Land, Stewardship, and Legitimacy: Endangered Species Policy in Canada and the United States.* Toronto: University of Toronto Press.

Olive, A. 2019. *The Canadian Environment in Political Context.* Toronto: University of Toronto Press.

Olive, A. 2021. "Endangered Species Legislation in Canada: Convergence that Matters." In *Provincial Policy Laboratories: Policy Transfer and Diffusion in Canada's Federal System,* edited by Brendan Boyd and Andrea Olive. Toronto: University of Toronto Press.

Olive, A., and A. Rabe. 2016. "Indigenous Environmental Justice: Comparing the United States and Canada's Legal Frameworks for Endangered Species Conservation." *American Review of Canadian Studies,* 46 (4): 496–512. https://doi.org/10.1080 /02722011.2016.1255654

Pathway to Canada Target 1. 2018. "One with Nature: A Renewed Approach to Land and Freshwater Conservation in Canada. A Report of Canada's Federal, Provincial and Territorial Departments Responsible for Parks, Protected Areas, Conservation, Wildlife and Biodiversity." Ottawa. https://static1.squarespace.com /static/57e007452e69cf9a7af0a033/t/5c9cd18671c10bc304619547/1553781159734 /Pathway-Report-Final-EN.pdf

Patterson J., K. Schulz, J. Vervoot, S. van der Hel, O. Widerberg, C. Adler, et al. 2017. "Exploring the Governance and Politics of Transformations towards Sustainability." *Environmental Innovation and Societal Transitions* 24: 1–16. https://doi.org /10.1016/j.eist.2016.09.001

Pictou S. 2019. "What Is Decolonization? Mi'kmaw Ancestral Relational Understandings and Anthropological Perspectives on Treaty Relations." In *Transcontinental Dialogues. Activist Research and Alliances from and with Indigenous Peoples of Canada, Mexico and Australia,* edited by Rosalva Aída Hernández Castillo, Suzie Hutchings, and Brian Noble, 37–64. Tucson, AZ: University of Arizona Press.

Pictou, S. 2020. "Decolonizing Decolonization: An Indigenous Feminist Perspective on the Recognition and Rights Framework." *South Atlantic Quarterly* 119 (2): 371–91. https://doi.org/10.1215/00382876-8177809

Plowright, R.K., J.K. Reaser, H. Locke, S.J. Woodley, J.A. Patz, D.J. Becker, G. Oppler, P.J. Hudson, and G.M. Tabor. 2021. "Land Use-Induced Spillover: A Call to Action to Safeguard Environmental, Animal, and Human Health." *The Lancet Planetary Health.* 5 (4): e237–e245. https://doi.org/10.1016/S2542-5196(21)00031-0

Poezler, G. and K.S. Coates. 2015. *From Treaty Peoples to Treaty Nation.* Vancouver, BC, Canada: UBC Press. 272–3.

Ray, Justina, Jaime Grimm, and Andrea Olive. 2021. "The Biodiversity Crisis in Canada: Failures and Challenges of Federal and Sub-National Legal Frameworks." *FACETS* 6 (January): 1044–68. https://doi.org/10.1139/facets-2020-0075

Secretariat of the Convention on Biological Diversity (SCBD). 2020. "Global Biodiversity Outlook 5." Montreal. https://www.cbd.int/gbo5 https://www.cbd.int/gbo/gbo5/publication/gbo-5-en.pdf

Species at Risk Act (SARA). 2002. "Species at Risk Act (S.C. 2002, c. 29)." Minister of Justice, Canada. https://laws-lois.justice.gc.ca/eng/acts/s-15.3/

Springer J., J. Campese, and B. Nakangu. 2021. "The Natural Resource Governance Framework – Improving Governance for Equitable and Effective Conservation." Gland, Switzerland. *IUCN.* https://portals.iucn.org/library/sites/library/files/documents/2021-031-En.pdf

Steffen W., K. Richardson, J. Rockstrom, S.E. Cornell, I. Fetzer, E.M. Bennett, et al. 2015. "Planetary Boundaries: Guiding Human Development on a Changing Planet." *Science* 347(6223). https://doi.org/10.1126/science.1259855

Trudeau, J. 2019. "Minister of Environment and Climate Change Mandate Letter." https://pm.gc.ca/en/mandate-letters/2019/12/13/minister-environment-and-climate-change-mandate-letter

Truth and Reconciliation Commission of Canada (TRCC). 2015a. *Honouring the Truth, Reconciling for the Future: Summary of the Final Report of the Truth and Reconciliation Commission of Canada.* Winnipeg, Manitoba: Truth and Reconciliation Commission of Canada. http://www.trc.ca/assets/pdf/Honouring_the_Truth_Reconciling_for_the_Future_July_23_2015.pdf

Truth and Reconciliation Commission of Canada (TRCC). 2015b. *What We Have Learned: Principles of Truth and Reconciliation.* Winnipeg, Manitoba: Truth and Reconciliation Commission of Canada. http://www.trc.ca/assets/pdf/Principles%20of%20Truth%20and%20Reconciliation.pdf

Truth and Reconciliation Commission of Canada (TRCC). 2015c. "Calls to Action." Winnipeg, Manitoba: Truth and Reconciliation Commission of Canada. http://trc.ca/assets/pdf/Calls_to_Action_English2.pdf

Turcotte, Audrey, Natalie Kermany, Sharla Foster, Caitlyn A. Proctor, Sydney M. Gilmour, Maria Doria, James Sebes, Jeannette Whitton, Steven J. Cooke, and Joseph R. Bennett. 2021. "Fixing the Canadian *Species at Risk Act*: Identifying Major Issues and Recommendations for Increasing Accountability and Efficiency. *FACETS* 6: 1474–94. https://doi.org/10.1139/facets-2020-0064

United Nations (UN). 2012. "Renewable Resources and Conflict: Toolkit and Guidance for Preventing and Managing Land and Natural Resources Conflict." United Nations Interagency Framework Team for Preventive Action, UN Environment Programme. https://www.un.org/en/land-natural-resources -conflict/pdfs/GN_Renew.pdf

United Nations Convention on Biological Diversity (UN CBD). 1992. "Convention on Biological Diversity." https://www.cbd.int/convention/text/

United Nations Convention on Biological Diversity (UN CBD). 2010. "The Strategic Plan for Biodiversity 2011-2020 and the Aichi Targets." UNEP/CBD /COP/DEC/X/2. October 29, 2010. https://www.cbd.int/doc/decisions/cop-10 /cop-10-dec-02-en.doc

United Nations Convention on Biological Diversity (UN CBD). 2021. "First Draft of the Post-2020 Global Biodiversity Framework." CBD/WG2020/3/3. July 5, 2021. https://www.cbd.int/doc/c/abb5/591f/2e46096d3f0330b08ce87a45/wg2020-03 -03-en.pdf

United Nations Convention on Biological Diversity (UN CBD). 2022. "Nations Adopt Four Goals, 23 Targets for 2030 in Landmark UN Biodiversity Agreement," official CBD press release. December 19, 2022. Montreal. https://www.cbd.int/article /cop15-cbd-press-release-final-19dec2022

Waiser, B. 2016. *A World We Have Lost: Saskatchewan before 1905*. Toronto: Fifth House Publishers.

Washington, H., G. Chapron, H. Kopina, P. Curry, J. Gray, and J.J. Piccolo. 2018. "Foregrounding Ecojustice in Conservation." *Biological Conservation* 228: 367–74. https://doi.org/10.1016/j.biocon.2018.09.011

Westwood, A.R, S.P. Otto, A. Mooers, C. Darimont, K.E. Hodges, et al. 2019. "Protecting Biodiversity in British Columbia: Recommendations for Developing Species at Risk Legislation." *FACETS* 4: 136–60. https://doi.org/10.1016/j .biocon.2018.09.011

World Health Organization. 2021. "WHO Strategic Action and Resource Requirements to End the Acute Phase of the COVID-19 Pandemic 2021." February 16, 2021. https://www.who.int/emergencies/diseases/novel-coronavirus-2019 /strategies-and-plans

World Health Organization. 2020. "2019 Novel Coronavirus (2019-nCoV): Strategic Preparedness and Response Plan." February 4, 2020. https://www.who.int /emergencies/diseases/novel-coronavirus-2019/technical-guidance-publications ?publicationtypes=01bc799c-b461-4a52-8c7d-294c84cd7b2d

World Wildlife Fund Canada (WWF). 2017. "Living Planet Report: A National Look at Wildlife Loss." WWF Canada, Toronto, Ontario. https://wwf.ca/wp-content /uploads/2020/02/WEB_WWF_REPORT_v3.pdf

World Wildlife Fund Canada (WWF). 2020. "Living Planet Report Canada: Wildlife at Risk." WWF Canada, Toronto, Ontario. https://wwf.ca/living-planet-report-canada -2020/

Youdelis, M., R. Nakoochee, C. O'Neil, E. Lunstrum, and R. Roth. (2020), "'Wilderness' Revisited: Is Canadian Park Management Moving beyond the 'Wilderness' Ethic?" *The Canadian Geographer / Le Géographe canadien* 64: 232–49. https://doi.org /10.1111/cag.12600

Zurba, M., K.F. Beazley, E. English, and J. Buchmann-Duck. 2019. "Indigenous Protected and Conserved Areas (IPCAs), Aichi Target 11 and Canada's Pathway to Target 1: Focusing Conservation on Reconciliation." *Land* 8(10): 1–20. https://doi .org/10.3390/land8010010

Introducing Disruptions

CHANCE FINEGAN

Many challenges confront conservation practitioners; these range from the seemingly straightforward (e.g., habitat fragmentation) to the obviously complex (e.g., climate crisis). While one may be able to address one or two such challenges at once, the speed at which new problems emerge and their sheer volume threaten to overwhelm conservation efforts. Alongside this, well-established tools like the Endangered Species Act (USA) and the Species at Risk Act (Canada) are proving to be less effective (Henson, White, and Thompson 2018; Creighton and Bennett 2019; McCune et al. 2013) than desired, despite evidence that the public values wildlife and conservation (McCune et al. 2017). Meanwhile, recent attempts to meet international commitments such as Aichi Biodiversity Target 11 were inconsistent to the point of failure (Lemieux et al. 2019; Convention on Biological Diversity 2020). Inconsistency has also been observed in the ability of protected areas to achieve conservation goals (Geldmann et al. 2019; McCune, Van Natto, and MacDougall 2017). Alongside this, concern is growing about "misplaced conservation ... where a failed appreciation for cooperation, evidence, or both have eroded efforts to conserve biodiversity" (Ford et al. 2021, 252). And, finally, the role of Indigenous Peoples, rights, and relationships with Creation are increasingly (if belatedly) recognized by non-Indigenous policy elites as key to effective conservation in the future (Reed et al. 2020; Tran et al. 2020; Rist et al. 2019).

In this collection, we identify and describe "conservation disruptions," or innovative perspectives that aim to push the boundaries of conservation practice. It is not our contention that current approaches should be wholly condemned. Rather, we assert there is value in thinking about how to challenge those approaches with the hope that new ideas will shore up weaknesses in biodiversity conservation.

WORKS CITED

Convention on Biological Diversity. 2020. *Global Biodiversity Outlook 5*. Montreal. Accessed March 11, 2021. https://www.cbd.int/gbo/gbo5/publication/gbo-5-en.pdf

Creighton, Maria J.A., and Joseph R. Bennett. 2019. "Taxonomic Biases Persist from Listing to Management for Canadian Species at Risk." *Écoscience* 26 (4): 315–21. https://doi.org/10.1080/11956860.2019.1613752.

Ford, Adam T., Abdullahi H. Ali, Sheila R. Colla, Steven J. Cooke, Clayton T. Lamb, Jeremy Pittman, David S. Shiffman, and Navinder J. Singh. 2021. "Understanding and Avoiding Misplaced Efforts in Conservation." *FACETS* 6 (1): 252–71. https://doi.org/10.1139/facets-2020-0058.

Geldmann, Jonas, Andrea Manica, Neil D. Burgess, Lauren Coad, and Andrew Balmford. 2019. "A Global-Level Assessment of the Effectiveness of Protected Areas at Resisting Anthropogenic Pressures." *Proceedings of the National Academy of Sciences* 116 (46): 23209LP–23215. https://doi.org/10.1073/pnas.1908221116.

Henson, Paul, Rollie White, and Steven P. Thompson. 2018. "Improving Implementation of the Endangered Species Act: Finding Common Ground through Common Sense." *BioScience* 68 (11): 861–72. https://doi.org/10.1093/biosci/biy093.

Lemieux, Christopher J., Paul A. Gray, Rodolphe Devillers, Pamela A. Wright, Philip Dearden, Elizabeth A. Halpenny, Mark Groulx, Thomas J. Beechey, and Karen Beazley. 2019. "How the Race to Achieve Aichi Target 11 Could Jeopardize the Effective Conservation of Biodiversity in Canada and Beyond." *Marine Policy* 99: 312–23. https://doi.org/https://doi.org/10.1016/j.marpol.2018.10.029.

McCune, Jenny L., William L. Harrower, Stephanie Avery-Gomm, Jason M. Brogan, Anna-Mária Csergő, Lindsay N.K. Davidson, Alice Garani, et al. 2013. "Threats to Canadian Species at Risk: An Analysis of Finalized Recovery Strategies." *Biological Conservation* 166: 254–65. https://doi.org/10.1016/j.biocon.2013.07.006.

McCune, Jenny L., Alyson Van Natto, and Andrew S. MacDougall. 2017. "The Efficacy of Protected Areas and Private Land for Plant Conservation in a Fragmented Landscape." *Landscape Ecology* 32 (4): 871–82.

Reed, Graeme, Nicolas D. Brunet, Sheri Longboat, and David C. Natcher. 2020. "Indigenous Guardians as an Emerging Approach to Indigenous Environmental Governance." *Conservation Biology*. https://doi.org/10.1111/cobi.13532.

Rist, Phil, Whitney Rassip, Djalinda Yunupingu, Jonathan Wearne, Jackie Gould, Melanie Dulfer-Hyams, Ellie Bock, and Dermot Smyth. 2019. "Indigenous Protected Areas in Sea Country: Indigenous-Driven Collaborative Marine Protected Areas in Australia." *Aquatic Conservation: Marine and Freshwater Ecosystems* 29 (S2): 138–51. https://doi.org/10.1002/aqc.3052.

Tran, Tanya C., Douglas Neasloss, Jonaki Bhattacharyya, and Natalie C. Ban. 2020. "'Borders Don't Protect Areas, People Do': Insights from the Development of an Indigenous Protected and Conserved Area in Kitasoo/Xai'xais Nation Territory." *FACETS* 5 (1): 922–41. https://doi.org/10.1139/facets-2020-0041.

PART B

Barriers to Conservation in Canada

2 A Pathological Examination of Conservation Failure in Canada

CHRISTOPHER J. LEMIEUX, MARK W. GROULX, TREVOR SWERDFAGER, AND SHANNON HAGERMAN

We are faculty members in resources and sustainability-oriented programs in four universities, two in British Columbia and two in Ontario. Between us we have over 100 years of combined experience in dealing with a wide span of conservation issues from the perspective of conservation partners, researchers, and educators and, in the case of one of us, as a government-based conservation practitioner. Our work has brought us into constant and regular contact with members of a wide range of equity-deserving community members, and our interactions with them have tremendously deepened our awareness of the many of the conservation-related challenges they face, even though these challenges are not a part of our lived experiences. We have become impatient for change on this front and are committed to finding ways to move the conservation community forward in an inclusive way. Our ties to nature are diverse and deep, our passion for conservation strong, which we can use to unite us and drive change in the regions in which we live and work. These backgrounds and commitments no doubt shape our values and views, and we highlight them explicitly here in order that the reader is aware of them as they travel through these pages with us.

Second, throughout our discussion we refer regularly to the "conservation community" and to "conservation organizations." We chose the word "community" with care, with the intent of being inclusive and embracing of a wide range of players with interests in the protection and conservation of nature. Our goal is to avoid the all too common polarization of "industry groups and environmentalists," or "government and civil society" and the like. We consider this community to include elected and non-elected members of Indigenous, federal, provincial, territorial, and municipal agencies, the leaders and members of resource harvesting enterprises, academics, and a wide range of conservation organizations. By this latter term, we refer primarily to non-governmental, non-industry organizations whose primary mission is oriented around the protection and conservation of nature and the environment more generally. These organizations range in size and scope from small community naturalist groups to much larger nationally focused and internationally linked organizations like the World Wildlife Fund or Oceana Canada. And finally, while several of the examples we touch on to highlight the various points we make are taken from the provinces in which we live, our chapter's analysis is fundamentally national in scope and intent, and our views, we would suggest, are broadly applicable across Canada and, perhaps, globally.

1. Introduction

Whatever happens, will be for the worse, and therefore it is in our interest that as little should happen.
— Robert Gascoyne-Cecil, Third Marquess of Salisbury and three-time British prime minister

To address widespread biodiversity declines and concurrent ecological degradation, parties to the United Nations (UN) Convention on Biological Diversity (CBD) agreed in 2010 to a *Strategic Plan for Biodiversity 2011–2020*, including the 20 Aichi Biodiversity Targets. While final reporting has yet to occur by parties, the current literature suggests that most trends continue to decline (Díaz et al. 2019; Rounsevell et al. 2020; Green et al. 2019; Secretariat of the Convention on Biological Diversity 2020). Preliminary reporting on progress on the targets in Canada has been inconsistent and potentially misleading. For example, Canada's sixth national report to the CBD, published in 2019, painted an optimistic picture, claiming that 12 targets were on track to be met. However, Hagerman and Pelai (2016) found that most of Canada's responses to the Aichi Biodiversity Targets were aspirational, with only a few being implemented (Hagerman and Pelai 2016). Furthermore, the World Wildlife Fund (WWF) report *2020 Living Planet Report for Canada* revealed that populations of Canadian species assessed as "at risk" have declined by an average of 59 per cent, and species assessed as globally at risk have seen their Canadian populations fall by an average of 42 per cent (World Wildlife Fund Canada 2020).

Concerns about shortcomings in implementing the *Strategic Plan for Biodiversity 2011–2020* and achievement of the Aichi Biodiversity Targets has led to calls for enhanced planning, reporting, and review under the CBD (Guarás, Weissenberg, and Rivera-mendoza 2021). Building on the *Strategic Plan for Biodiversity 2011–2020*, parties to the CBD, including Canada, are now focused implementing the "Kunming-Montreal Global Biodiversity Framework" (Convention on Biological Diversity (CBD) 2022), which will guide global conservation efforts to 2030. As these and other related conversations about the future of conservation are active, evolving, and consequential, it is timely to identify the deep underlying issues as to why the organizations society entrusts to conserve biodiversity continuously fail to do so.

In this chapter, we use **"pathologies" as a metaphor** to examine the ways in which organizational dysfunction emerges and persists, and how it becomes a precondition to failure in the context of effectively conserving biodiversity in Canada. By "failure" we broadly mean an inability to achieve the goals and objectives that Canada's diverse and growing conservation community sets out to achieve. Specifically, we examine **six pathologies** that are chronically affecting conservation in Canada today and use a series of examples to illustrate their impacts on conservation. We strive to present more of a diagnosis of the pathologies, based on symptoms we have observed in conservation, and leave it to our colleagues in other chapters to take on the more difficult task of identifying the various prescriptions and treatments needed to achieve improved conservation outcomes that can support both biodiversity and people.

2. The Pathology Approach to Understanding Conservation Failures

The evidence is clear: despite some successes (e.g., Bolam et al. 2020), the conservation of biodiversity has failed more often than not. In a quantitative sense, there is no comprehensive set of indicators of ecosystem or biodiversity health at any regional scale that are trending in a positive direction. Even commonly celebrated aspects of conservation, such as the expansion of protected areas networks, have not necessarily led to gains in outcomes for biodiversity (Geldmann et al. 2019; Carrasco et al. 2021). Although temporal lags in species' responses to conservation action could be masking our ability to observe progress towards conservation success (Watts et al. 2020), in the Canadian context, as elsewhere, the weight of evidence indicates that conservation failures persist, no matter how one defines success.

It is generally accepted that much of the failure to effectively conserve biodiversity can be attributed to a number of issues, including, for examples, a lack of mainstreaming of biodiversity in public policy (Whitehorn et al. 2019); ineffective integration of different forms of knowledge into conservation planning (Lemieux et al. 2021); inadequate human and financial resources (Waldron et al. 2013; Barbier, Burgess, and Dean 2018); failure to value nature adequately (Dasgupta 2021); and limitations in raising the profile of biodiversity loss for politicians and the public (Legagneux et al. 2018) (several of these challenges are discussed in more detail in chapter 11 by Justina Ray). That said, we argue that it is the unrecognized yet persistent symptoms of "pathological management" that coalesce to produce a gateway through which all other threats to biodiversity emerge and transform ecosystems and, ultimately, prevent Canada from achieving its conservation goals.

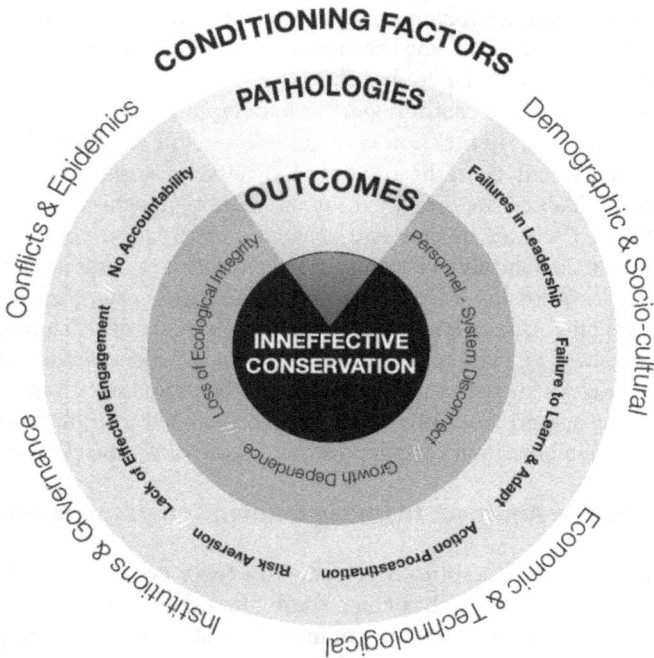

Figure 2.1. Conceptual model of the biodiversity conservation pathology in Canada. Ineffective conservation outcomes are shaped by several pathologies and conditioning factors (values and behaviours).

Originating in healthcare, pathology is the branch of medicine that investigates the nature of disease – its structural and functional effects on the body that produces deviations from a healthy (i.e., optimal or ideal) condition. As detailed in figure 2.1, several pathologies lead to ineffective and undesirable conservation outcomes, in reference to the deficiencies associated with traditional management approaches and institutions that focus on maximizing short-term benefits to people, a result of unsustainable environmental, social, and economic outcomes of command-and-control resource management (Holling and Meffe 1996; Allen and Gunderson 2011; Briggs 2003).

First introduced by Holling and Meffe (1996), the authors argued that institutions managed by command and control have low resilience to new challenges because the system discourages innovation and penalizes or ignores alternative perspectives by employees. Institutions faced with these problems attempt to solve them by applying more control, which further reduces natural variability. Expanding on these original insights, we identify the repeated and often unacknowledged patterns of behaviour and the systems within which their behaviours are embedded, that co-evolve, coalesce, and continue to lead to a decline in ecosystem integrity in Canada, with a focus on biodiversity conservation.

Here, we focus on six interrelated pathologies, which represent repeated sources of failure. The pathologies as identified and highlighted are matters of judgment and perspective. There are certainly other pathologies that we do not address due to space limitations (perverse incentives, for example), and readers may justifiably take the position that the pathologies presented here may be less significant than others in terms of affecting Canada's ability to achieve desired conservation outcomes. Given that our goal is to stimulate dialogue and to contribute to the identification of the transformative changes required to address these debilitating pathologies, we welcome this critique.

In addition to preventing the ability to achieve conservation goals, it is our argument that these six pathologies result in frustrated conservation professionals (who are *literally* trained to contribute to effective conservation outcomes but are unable to maximize their contributions due to these pathologies), a related inability to meaningfully consider and incorporate different forms of knowledge into conservation planning and management, an inability to assess performance with respect to key conservation policy objectives and, ultimately, a misinformed and confused public. We provide specific examples related to these pathologies to help illuminate these problems and, more generally, better understand how they continue to paralyze Canada's ability to achieve desired conservation outcomes.

Pathology 1: Chronic Failures in Leadership

Signs and Symptoms:

- inadequate direction, including inadequate/incompatible laws, plans, policies, and planning processes
- constant dismantling and reinventing
- inadequate human and financial resources
- inability to exert authority
- inadequate research and monitoring programs

While the conservation and enhancement of components or elements of biodiversity is a key objective of hundreds of laws and related policies at multiple levels of government, Canada's conservation policy landscape continues to be fragmented and lacks leadership and coordination across the political, program, and process activities of government. A major challenge in Canada has been the chronic lack of leadership and coordination provided by Canada's

National Focal Point to the CBD, Environment and Climate Change Canada (ECCC). Criticisms have ranged from "having no plan" to failures in implementation, such as falling short of exercising its authority to protect critical habitat for species at risk in a timely way (Palm et al. 2020; Bird and Hodges 2017). Independent audits and assessments by science-based non-governmental organizations (NGOs), researchers, and others have detailed the rather spectacular number of ways in which ECCC has failed to meet its legislated goals and responsibilities (Office of the Auditor General of Canada 2018b; Palm et al. 2020; CPAWS 2016).

For example, in 1998, ECCC was criticized for having no plan to implement the 1996 *Canadian Biodiversity Strategy* and – wait for it – again in 2000, 2005, 2013, and 2018 (Office of the Auditor General of Canada 2018b). The reasons for this failure in leadership are complicated. However, it is clear that there have been failures in both the *implementation stage,* where ECCC has taken on the implementation of too many policies and goals and targets so complicated and so beyond their capacity to provide meaningful results, and during the *evaluation stage,* where they have failed to properly evaluate outcomes pertaining to various policy objectives and international commitments.

These problems stretch back decades and, to some extent, have become normalized within the agency. This could be linked to an inability to exercise authority, which has resulted in, for examples, establishing or agreeing to establish overburdened or unattainable policy agendas, and in wasting resources through repeated litigation (especially related to species at risk). These failures can also be linked to ECCC's poor ability to consult and coordinate efforts across Canada's diverse conservation community, including other provinces and territories and Indigenous peoples. These issues are discussed in more detail in Pathology 5 below. The collective result has been a spiraling organizational decline with corresponding failure to achieve conservation goals, and associated declines in ecosystem health.

For our second example, we turn our attention to another federal department, Fisheries and Oceans Canada (DFO) and the issue of marine protection standards (or lack of). Canada's Oceans Act, which came into effect in 1997, was considered exemplary ocean management legislation (Bailey et al. 2016). It provided a framework through which Canada could effectively integrate ocean management, ecosystem-based management, and marine protected area (MPA) implementation. Despite this positive step in legislation, serious concerns have emerged regarding Canada's commitment to implementing the Oceans Act, essentially since its inception (Office of the Auditor General of Canada 2018a).

In addition to a failure to develop integrated management plans for ocean areas other than the Pacific, of particular concern in recent years has been the ineffectiveness of DFO in achieving its marine conservation objectives, whether related to establishing MPAs under the Oceans Act or for managing aquatic species listed under the Species at Risk Act. We are particularly concerned about the frequency in which DFO reviews and changes laws, programs, and policies and announces new ones to give the false impression that the agency is both forward looking and able to solve problems.

For example, in 2016 DFO severed itself from Canada's Pathway to Target 1 conservation initiative, effectively unlinking an integrated terrestrial, freshwater, and marine planning process that included all provinces and territories, the private conservation sector, and Indigenous organizations working to achieve Canada's area-based protection targets (as per the former Canada Target 1/Aichi Biodiversity Target 11 and recently adopted Target 3 of the Kunming-Montreal Global Biodiversity Framework). This action represented a classic example of "turf protection," which occurs when agencies protect their power preserves and perceive the sharing of power and resources as a zero-sum game (Kearney et al. 2007). The action resulted in DFO taking a unilateral approach to "shoe-horn" nearly 60 fisheries closures into a new type of "other effective area-based conservation measure" (OECM) to achieve Canada's 10 per cent marine protection target as per the Aichi Biodiversity Target 11, literally overnight (Lemieux and Gray 2020).

In the process of establishing what DFO misleadingly refers to as "marine refuge" OECMs, national and international conservation standards and guidelines were ignored (Lemieux et al. 2019; Lemieux et al., 2022), setting the agency on a seemingly endless loop of "dismantling and reinvention" of laws and associated policies, such as those related to conservation standards. Public concerns as well as concerns by the scientific conservation community over the efficacy of converting fisheries closures to marine refuges, which continue to permit both non-renewable and renewable resource extraction (including oil and gas exploration), and a focus on single-species management (as opposed to protecting biodiversity as a whole), prompted expert reviews of both its marine protected area standards in 2018 and marine refuge standards in 2020 (figure 2.2).

Through these reviews, it became clear that regulatory conflict within DFO, an organization responsible for both exploiting *and* conserving biodiversity, was compromising the integrity of science and decision-making with respect to conservation, as well as public perception of that integrity. Consequently, recommendations by the expert panel were released in 2019 (National Advisory Panel on Marine Protected Area Standards 2019), which was followed by changes to the Ocean's Act to expel bottom trawling, mining, dumping, and oil and gas extraction, effectively reconciling activities that should have never been permitted in MPAs in the first place.

There are many other interrelated issues that lead to chronic conservation policy failure in Canada, including failures to (1) integrate measurable endpoints and timelines into law (e.g., completion of protected areas networks); (2) include

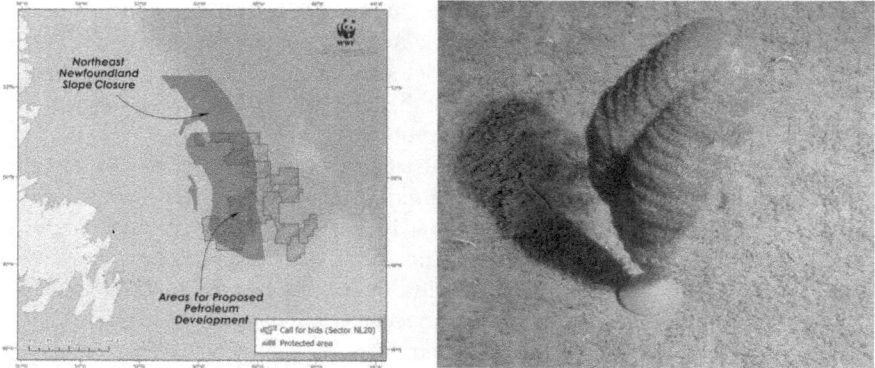

Figure 2.2. The Northeast Newfoundland Slope Closure, roughly the size of Denmark, was designated as a "marine refuge" by DFO in 2017 to protect slow-growing, fragile, cold-water corals and sponges that provide essential habitat for fish and other species. However, exploratory oil and gas leases have been granted to British Petroleum (BP), which will cover roughly one-quarter of the so-called refuge that currently contributes nearly 1 per cent to Canada's declared conserved area. (Map Source: WWF; Sea Pen Phonot Source: DFO)

mitigation in the first stage of planning processes (e.g., integrate biodiversity protection in EA/IA processes and F/P/T infrastructure projects); (3) include mandatory research and monitoring upon which to adequately measure policy success; and (4) address policy conflicts: for example, those that either neglect biodiversity conservation or provide incentives to exploit it. Perhaps most significantly, there remains no requirements in law to report on the state of any aspect of biodiversity. This is cause for concern, as lack of baseline and trends data can result in "shifting baseline syndrome," where a persistent downgrading of perceived normal ecological conditions over time lead to under-estimation of the true magnitude of long-term ecosystem degradation (Jones et al. 2020). Other challenges associated with leadership and policy are detailed by Justina Ray in chapter 11.

Pathology 2: Failure to Learn

Signs and Symptoms:

- learning from only limited types of knowledge, or not learning at all
- lack of institutional incentives and processes that support consideration and incorporation of diverse forms of knowledge
- tendencies to suppress new information, and/or resist new ideas or information from outside of organizations

It is a common refrain among conservation scientists and in the literature that a key barrier to effective conservation is failure to incorporate science into policy (Lemieux et al. 2021) – or, put differently, failure to learn from new information (Allen and Gunderson 2011). While it is certainly the case that science – or more accurately knowledge – ought to be a central consideration for public policy, including for conservation, it is also true that most examinations of this pathology simplify two crucial points.

First, by virtue of how the pathology is constructed, there is a tendency to characterize science and policy as separate spheres and activities and the relationship between them as being unidirectional and linear (Beck 2011). This is known as the "linear model of science and policy." By this pervasive yet empirically unsupported view, science may become politicized through this process, but science itself is seen as inherently objective and independent of social and historical context (figure 2.3). Second, this pathology tends to be defined too narrowly, most often, with a focus on information produced within Western scientific traditions and worldviews. While it is true that we do often fail to learn in the context of conservation policy development, we are failing to learn from a limited stock of knowledge.

These two issues are related. In contrast to the assumptions inherent to the linear model of science and policy, the realms of science and policy are more accurately understood as mutually constitutive of each other – a relationship described by the knowledge co-production model (Jasanoff and Simmet 2017). By this perspective, science is inextricably embedded within, produced by, and reproducing of social practices, identities, norms, and structures of power (Jasanoff and Simmet 2017). Overcoming this pathology requires recognizing these complexities to develop a more fulsome diagnosis of why challenges of knowledge, decision-making and learning are (even) greater than typically recognized.

This is particularly problematic when it comes to considering the process of knowledge co-production referenced above. We wish to be clear that knowledge should be a central input to decision-making. But attention to the co-produced nature of knowledge invites awareness and reflection on the institutional processes, learning processes, social order, and the values that underpin and produce knowledge to begin with. These processes matter for how they shape the types of knowledge that are deemed credible for decision-making, and they help explain how dominant regimes of knowledge, once in place, reinforce and reproduce existing institutional commitments and norms (Jasanoff 2004). We offer two examples below.

While we have argued in other sections for the importance of institutions that ensure accountability, monitoring, and target setting, there is simultaneously the need to be reflective about how such regimes of measurement – including targets – can have unintentional consequences, specifically when

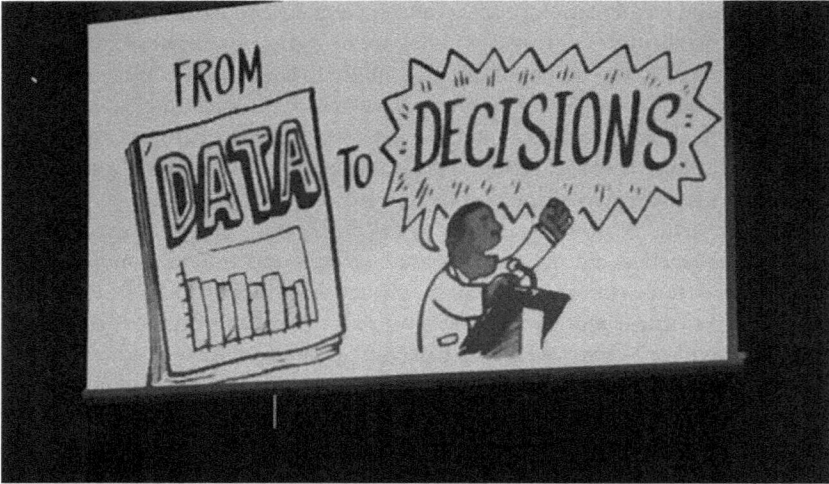

Figure 2.3. Slide presented by one of the large conservation NGOs to parties to the Convention on Biological Diversity at SBSTTA 21 (November 2017) during a presentation about how to better link "data" to "conservation decision-making." The presentation and this slide are illustrative of the linear model of the relationship between science and policy at work in practice. (Photo Source: Shannon Hagerman)

it comes to the types of knowledge that enter the realms of decision-making (Turnhout, Neves, and De Lijster 2014). The Aichi Biodiversity Targets of the former 2011–2020 Strategic Plan for Biodiversity and the newly adopted 23 targets of the Kunming-Mongreal Global Biodiversity Framework provide illustrative examples of this. Despite clearly being co-produced products of science and politics (Campbell, Hagerman, and Gray 2014), once negotiated, targets tend to operate in scientific and policy spheres as a set of neutral objects. Furthermore, by focusing attention on aspects of the challenge targets can serve to reinforce particular visions of what conservation is and what information and knowledge that are deemed important and actionable to support it (Hagerman et al. 2021). Simply put, it is one thing to say that diverse knowledge is valued throughout the conservation community but quite another to be deliberate in thinking about the institutional rules and processes that serve to winnow out ways of knowing in practice.

We see stark evidence of this winnowing in the context of forest conservation and management in BC's publicly managed forests. This winnowing arises from the politics of knowledge (Forsyth and Walker 2008; Vadrot 2014) that we have described above and speaks directly to the second simplification of this pathology – that of the tendency to focus on only one type of knowledge (Western scientific) as "information." For example, BC's forest sector is trialing the use of genomics technologies to identify resilient populations of tree species for reforestation programs that are anticipated to be more robust to expected changes wrought by climate – an approach known as assisted migration.

BC Ministry of Forests, Lands, and Natural Resource Operations (MFL-NRO), the agency responsible for conserving and managing forests in BC, has a mandate to "strengthen public trust in natural resource management practices by promoting values-based decision-making principles and engaging with stakeholders and communities" (Ministry of Forests Lands and Natural Resource Operations 2017). Yet despite proclamations to engage and consider diverse forms of expertise in the development and implementation of assisted migration policies, and not to mention the myriad uncertainties and values embedded in these policies (St-Laurent, Hagerman, and Kozak 2018), in-depth interviews with agency scientists and managers reveal the subtle and consequential knowledge politics that have led to the consideration and incorporation of a limited stock of knowledge and, concerningly, the systematic exclusion of knowledge produced within other worldviews, namely Indigenous knowledge (Pelai, Hagerman, and Kozak 2021). This matters because contributions from different forms of knowledge are essential to better understand and ultimately address conservation challenges at multiple scales.

All this being said, a slightly different diagnosis and associated set of concerns are illuminated by an "organizational learning" perspective. From this latter perspective, at least three pre-conditions are notable. First, there must be an organizational willingness to learn that is predicated on a culture that sees learning as a valued activity and a primary tool for boosting program performance (Collins 2001). In a more government-centered focus, Barber (2015) draws particular attention to the need for public service learning as a key to improved service delivery. Second, it requires a reliable stream of data or information from which the organization can learn. This stream can, for example, take the form of raw data about a particular resource or a series of external audits (e.g., Oceana 2020). Third (and consistent with a knowledge co-production perspective), it requires an openness to differing knowledge systems and ways of understanding nature and its various elements, including how different groups know, interact with, and value nature. Organizations with this more open-minded approach would likely feature decision-making that explicitly includes local knowledge, Indigenous systems of learning, or inputs from different communities of practice from outside the agency. It is difficult to conclude that these conditions are commonly met in today's conservation organizations or that the Canadian conservation community could be accurately characterized as predisposed to learning or to integrating different knowledge systems into its functioning.

Addressing the already thorny pathology of information and learning thus invites engagement with the even stickier aspects of power, values, and institutions within which that information is produced and considered. But this complexity comes with a potential upside. If meaningful progress can be made in this area, including through the creation of organizations, institutions, and processes that can foster consideration of previously overlooked or actively ignored knowledge, this holds great promise for addressing some of the failures of the past and unlocking solutions for the future.

Pathology 3: Irrational Action Procrastination

Signs and Symptoms:

- delay dealing with known problems
- focus on problems and not causes
- rely on quick fixes usually with a big stick (crisis management)
- miss opportunities
- focus on planning and not action (stuck in planning loop)
- be unwilling to experiment and consider the future

Allen and Gunderson (2011) discuss a temporal gap between identifying political obstructions, halting of action with calls for "more science," and the pursuit of perfection in plan development as contributors to action procrastination in natural resources management. In their review of Great Lakes restoration efforts, McLaughlin and Krantzberg (2012) provide additional context to the behavioural patterns that can affect regulatory organizations and policy regimes they belong to, where they identify a pattern of long delay and the subsequent need to pursue rapid, large-scale, and often unilateral action (i.e., action procrastination) as a troublesome organizational dysfunction. Procrastination in conservation is so common yet so precarious and completely irrational: not only are we aware that we are not addressing a problem, but we also know that it is probably a bad idea to keep delaying action.

The smokescreen of information deficit can be a common ingredient in stalled implementation processes across the conservation fields. A recent study by Lemieux et al. (2021) clearly illustrates that there is adequate information to support decisions related to many conservation problems, but that a host of systemic institutional barriers prevent its effective utilization. Conservation of Canada's woodland caribou (*Rangifer tarandus caribou*) populations (also known as Boreal caribou), listed as threatened under the federal Species at Risk Act since 2003, illustrates the difference between not having sufficient information to move forward, and – to the point made under Pathology 1 above – not

Figure 2.4. Despite woodland caribou being listed as threatened on Canada's Species at Risk Act (SARA) since 2003, it took over a decade to develop a draft recovery plan. As of early 2021, critical habitat is yet to be protected in most provinces and territories. (Photo: rob56vt, iNaturalist)

being able to link legislative mandates to effective leadership and timely action (figure 2.4). With contributions from a blue-ribbon panel comprised of a national pool of leading scientists over a five-year period, along with a wealth of additional academic scholarship, Taylor and Walker (2017) argue that the delay in effective protection since woodland caribou were listed "is not due to the lack of information" but an inability to prioritize critical habitat for protection after it is identified.

In 2013, the auditor general of British Columbia reported on the status of biodiversity conservation in BC, concluding among other things that the "[g]overnment does not know whether its actions are resulting in the conservation of biodiversity" (Office of the Auditor General of British Columbia 2013). Having audited the authority responsible for adoption and implementation of the province's conservation framework, the report concluded that an inability to move from identification of priority actions to implementation was perpetuated because priorities had been abandoned in the annual business planning of responsible ministries.

Like the BC auditor general's report, Palm et al. (2020) identify the lack of provincial species-at-risk legislation and inadequate protection under the current policy regime as a driver of on ongoing decline of BC's southern mountain woodland caribou population. They also note, however, that protection of necessary critical habitat to ensure long-term recovery represents an estimated loss of $94 million in annual forest revenue. These economic costs are no doubt a key motivator of the (often local) political opposition underpinning the staggering lack of political will that continues to delay the landscape level protection measures that are required to ensure the longevity of the population. In Alberta, Hebblewhite (2017) argues even more forcefully that while short-term emergency measures like wolf control were able to stabilize the Little Smoky caribou population, the time bought through such measures was merely taken by the Alberta government as license to pursue political benefit by permitting more oil and gas drilling, ensuring a renewed cycle of decline and planning, and ultimately allowing even more delays in implementing long-term measures to protect critical habitat. For a more detailed discussion on caribou management including recovery in Canada, see chapter 4 by Boan and Plotkin.

In addition to the factors identified above, scholars examining the implementation gap across various conservation fields have pointed to a range of key contributing factors, including the lack of integrated implementation planning within conservation science assessment processes, limited efforts to define and measure implementation success, and the over-utilization of "one size fits all" implementation processes that ignore context-specific barriers and enablers (Adams et al. 2019; Knight et al. 2008). Yet, beneath these (and other) structural elements is a vast and dynamic network of human interactions within and beyond conservation organizations that (re)produce the attitudes, values, beliefs, and ultimately organizational cultures that form and reinforce factors that constrain action. To more fully understand how such cultures contribute to the implementation gap, Papworth (2017) calls for greater attention to the nuances of decision-making within conservation organizations through the lens of conservation psychology. Responding to this call, in the following section we explore risk aversion in individual and organizational psychologies as a pathology that is deeply intertwined with those just discussed.

Pathology 4: Decision-Makers Are Risk Averse

Signs and Symptoms:

- craving for certainty of outcomes
- discomfort with decisions that generate uncertainty or potentially negative outcomes
- fear of looking bad
- avoiding hard truths

Uncertainty in management outcomes and expected benefits complicates just about all conservation decisions (Canessa et al. 2019). And while risk analysis, a method to deal with uncertainty, is routine in the health, financial, and insurance sectors, it is a relatively new field of study within biodiversity conservation (excluding fire risk), but increasingly used in the area of invasive species (Mandrak and Cudmore 2015), species-at-risk assessments (e.g., via Committee on the Status of Endangered Wildlife in Canada (COSEWIC)) (Favaro et al. 2014) and, more recently, climate change adaptation planning (Mantyka-Pringle et al. 2015; Hagerman and Satterfield 2014). For a discussion on how uncertainty affects local support for caribou recovery, once again refer to chapter 4 by Boen and Plotkin.

Canadian conservation regimes generally exhibit a pathological and deeply embedded craving for certainty of outcomes, which is mirrored by an equally entrenched discomfort with decisions that generate uncertainty and pose risks of negative outcomes. Conservation agencies constantly face the dilemma of whether to invest in actions with high probability of success (guaranteed benefits) or to choose projects with a greater risk of failure but might provide higher benefits if they succeed. As Tulloch et al. (2015) note, "In conservation, the consequences of making a risky decision and being wrong include failing to adequately mitigate threats, wasting resources on an action that does not succeed, and damaging the reputation of the management organization." And while our experience suggests that most conservationists see themselves as change advocates committed to innovation in achieving conservation objectives, examples of significantly risk-laden innovations at the organizational level are few, exemplifying a personality mismatch between the practitioner and the rigid organization that resists learning and change (Pathology 2 above).

In our view, rather than simply repeating the "bureaucracies are risk averse" bromide, a more nuanced approach to considering risk in the conservation community context is to focus on how a regime manages the risks that various conservation challenges pose. It should be emphasized that conservation regimes don't just fear risk, they *crave certainty*. This is not mere semantics; the magnetic pull of certainty is very strong and consistently deflects bureaucratic attention towards decisions that generate highly predictable outcomes and that present virtually zero risk. This is the primary underlying factor why protected-areas organizations remain paralyzed with respect to adaptation to climate change (despite a growing information base and significant concern identified by practitioners for over two decades) (Barr et al. 2020) and tend to prefer conventional management strategies over unconventional ones (Hagerman and Satterfield 2014). In most conservation challenges, however, zero-risk options are not available, and the regimes must instead consider and balance a suite of unavoidable risks.

The way conservation regimes have responded to the widespread call for the adoption of biodiversity indicators is instructive in terms of how they do so. Despite widespread calls by the international conservation community for the need of biodiversity indicators and monitoring frameworks (Convention on Biological Diversity (CBD) 2020; Bhatt et al. 2020), indicators pose at least two major risks for bureaucracies, which have yet to be acknowledged in the extant literature. First, the establishment of indicators and the collection of data with respect to them create a substantial risk that program failures will be highlighted, or that substantial new problems will be discovered and lead to more pressures on the program. In national organizations, like federal/provincial/territorial (F/P/T) departments, a wrinkle on this risk is that consistently adopted indicators can expose differences in program performance within a department, something senior leaders could view as a negative dynamic that promotes internecine rivalries and other staff morale problems. Some indicators, while globally considered important, continue not to be reported on at all. For example, we are not aware of a single F/P/T agency that reports on traditional knowledge and customary sustainable use.

Second, the creation of a widely endorsed indicator suite poses financial risks. Indicators data collection is typically labour intensive, monotonous, politically uninteresting, and expensive. Moreover, because the power of most environmental data sets only really becomes apparent after a significant time series is built up, most investments in this area feature large upfront expenditures that only generate benefits over the medium- to long-term. Accordingly, indicator programs can be seen as high-cost, low-reward initiatives posing clear and present danger to a program's financial integrity (see Waldron et al. 2017). The absence of a climate change impacts monitoring program in Parks Canada, or in the National Wildlife Area (NWA) program of ECCC, or the demise of Environment Canada's Ecological Monitoring and Assessment Network (EMAN) offer good examples of this dynamic at play.

These twin risks are real and cannot simply be avoided, as they will not just disappear. Management of these unavoidable risks typically involves the deployment of a cascading set of risk management strategies, including (1) blocking the establishment of the indicator suite in the first place; (2) assigning indicator development to a multi-stakeholder process and insisting that only when consensus emerges can the indicators be adopted (which is another form of action procrastination, as detailed above); or (3) assigning no resources to any new data collection associated with the accepted targets. Should data collection against an indicator become unavoidable, data are often kept confidential and not placed in the public domain where they can be used to form critiques of a regime (e.g., CWS's waterfowl population data or DFO's annual fish stock survey data, which are not made easily available).

In the absence of accountability structures described in Pathology 6 below, regime leaders are left to make their own risk calculations and to determine what is acceptable or not. The net effect of these risk management calculations and strategies is generally to preserve the status quo and to put in place a set of generally invisible obstacles to innovation and change. This dynamic often exacerbates or accentuates the other pathologies detailed in this chapter, and creates cultural norms that render innovation, transparency, and creativity "abnormal" and difficult to foster and maintain. As a result, most of Canada's conservation regimes are left to deal with the challenges of today and the future with the tools and programs of the past.

Pathology 5: Lack of Effective and Meaningful Engagement

Signs and Symptoms:

- poor mechanisms and funding to support stakeholder participation
- blocked communications
- stakeholders reject results
- constrained roles of different actor groups
- managers lack training in social sciences

Holling and Meffe (1996) present the reduction of natural variation in a system and the consequent loss of system resilience as a core feature of the pathology of natural resource management. To this, they add a burgeoning disconnect between agency staff and the systems they manage and society's axiomatic belief in the need for growth, delivered through tightly managed systems of control. The topic of stakeholder and rights-holder engagement, and, more relevant here, the lack of effective engagement is extensively discussed within the conservation literature, and we believe is inextricably and intimately related to the persistence of this pathology within the conservation realm.

Emphasizing the specific, and in their words, "common failure" of adaptive management programs, Allen and Gunderson (2011) present the omission of key actors in management processes and networks as a key contributing driver to the ongoing pathology of natural resource management and its downstream environmental impacts. Scholars from the fields of conservation management, public participation, and collaborative planning broadly agree, arguing that processes that draw narrowly on perspectives, lived experiences, and knowledge systems (e.g., as in Pathology 2) contribute to the institutional, legal, and cultural barriers that condition the failure of conservation goals (Fischer 2000; Sterling et al. 2017).

For instance, engagement initiatives can be "externally driven" by individual or institutional actors like government agencies or researchers, or "self-organized" by local groups who have active influence over management issues (e.g., NGOs) (Sterling et al. 2017). In either case, there is a similar risk of poor engagement practices becoming an impediment to conservation goals when engagement (1) occurs late in planning and/or decision making processes; (2) promotes the recurrent inclusion of actors/groups at the expense of the recurrent exclusion of others; (3) follows a one-size-fits-all approach without consideration of cultural and place-based context; and (4) takes a transactional form that emphasizes narrow management objectives rather than a whole-systems approach (Shackleton et al. 2019; Charles et al. 2020).

A comprehensive discussion of the roadblocks that are perpetuated through poor engagement is beyond the scope of this chapter, but the implementation gap within conservation appears to be widened when individuals or groups are treated as passive information recipients or sources of public perception, rather than necessary partners in co-defining conservation challenges, and thereby the nature of the pathway to addressing their root causes (Jolibert and Wesselink 2012). A rapidly growing literature on citizen/community science aptly illustrates the press for greater democratization of Western science and the management processes it feeds (Charles et al. 2020). Although still taking the weakly democratized form of contributory citizen science, as opposed to a co-creation approach that includes community actors in defining research goals (Dickinson et al. 2012), the adoption of the iNaturalist mobile platform by both Ontario Parks and Parks Canada illustrates the needed shift to greater active public engagement in conservation practice. At Cape Merry, near Churchill, Manitoba, this includes the opportunity to join a "BioBlitz" documenting the biodiversity surrounding the 250-year-old Fort Prince of Wales and, at least in theory, the opportunity to collect evidence that informs conservation management decisions.

The issue of engagement in conservation practice is often expressed in terms of absent engagement processes or absent voices and representation within engagement processes. While we do not dispute these challenges, to the point made under Pathology 2 above, even when stakeholder and rights-holder mapping has carefully identified potential contributors, processes can fail when actors are unwilling to challenge the dominance of certain knowledge systems or their own limited frames of knowing. Within Canadian conservation practice, there are growing calls to recognize the complicity of conservation tools like protected areas in the dispossession of traditional territories from First Nations and the need to fully recognize Indigenous knowledge systems as a *distinct and equal* source of wisdom informing conservation efforts (Youdelis 2016; Zurba et al. 2019) (see also chapter 5 by McDermott and Roth and chapter 6 by Pictou).

As an alternative to inviting Indigenous rights-holders into engagement processes that have (often unilaterally) been defined by state actors, Barry and Porter (2012) define the need for "contact zones," where new approaches to upholding legally recognized Indigenous rights and title, self-determination, governance innovation, and environmental stewardship might be explored. Set within the context of Indigenous land rights and title in Australia, Porter (2006) explores the structure and function of the Wimmera Indigenous Resource Management Partnership (WIRMP) as a point of connection for social learning. The WIRMP was established as a deliberative space to facilitate ongoing relationship building between state agencies (the Department of Sustainability and Environment) and the Wotjobaluk people as rights and title holders (represented by the Wotjobaluk Traditional Land Council) in support of shared land and water management. As a deliberative space that included joint scheduling, agenda setting, and chairing, the WIRMP created opportunities for shared problem solving before management considerations ever entered the formal realm of consultation. In particular, Porter (2006) notes that the WIRMP sought an ongoing conversation and means for relationship building, even the in absence of specific projects or plans, highlighting the importance of engagement that moves beyond instrumental transactions.

Pathology 6: Lack of Accountability and Transparency

Signs and Symptoms:

- lack of clear, measurable goals
- lack of timelines
- inability to consider biodiversity as a whole (i.e., single species management)
- poor reporting
- lack of enforcement and repercussions for poor performance

Conceptually speaking, accountability is often used as a conceptual umbrella for a series of evaluative steps related to "active responsibility," including transparency, responsiveness, equity, efficiency, and effectiveness (Bovens 2007) and is often used interchangeably with "good governance." There are many examples of mechanisms that flow under the guise of accountability at various levels of governance in Canada. At the international level, parties to the UN CBD must submit national reports every six years (submitted by ECCC). At F/P/T levels, ministerial mandate letters and government accountability offices levels, where they exist, represent formal, administrative types of accountability, the latter of which various agencies are provided with the opportunity to respond to. For example, in a recent audit of protected area performance in Ontario, the auditor general of Ontario recently concluded that "Ontario lacks an overall plan or long-term target and the staff it takes to protect the province's parks and other protected areas." (Office of the Auditor General of Ontario 2020). Finally, private conservation organizations, such as the Nature Conservancy of Canada, are mostly held accountable to their donors through annual reports, which represent financial statements and do not include aspects of conservation outcomes.

Although these types of mechanisms exist, we must ask whether organizations or officials who exercise public authority are subject to accountability at all, as the mechanisms tend to be "soft" in the sense that there are very little or no possibilities for sanctions – that is, there are no consequences for not achieving goals and commitments. As our first Pathology indicates, *laws should matter*. Some may argue that the role of law in conservation is of diminishing importance and that future success lies primarily in the meaningful engagement of conservation actors collaborating to forge common solutions based on shared interests and a pooling of resources. While this is certainly relevant, the reality is that conservation outcomes for which no agency or actor is legally accountable are rarely achieved.

In considering the accountability issue, a nuanced consideration of the societal niche occupied by legislation suggests that laws should matter deeply and that their impact on conservation should be dramatic. Legislation confers a societal value or priority to one or more dimensions of conservation. It codifies society's conservation values and expectations, and it circumscribes acceptable behaviours with respect to nature and its resources. In many instances, it has created conservation institutions, such as the Canadian Wildlife Service (1947) and COSEWIC (1977) at the federal level and the Environmental Bill of Rights in Ontario (1993) at the provincial level.

This is of critical importance in understanding the accountability pathology infecting conservation in Canada. In our view, most conservation theorists and practitioners would likely agree that achieving conservation goals requires, *inter alia,* the establishment of biodiversity focused programming, the collection, storing, and sharing of ecosystem indicator information, the establishment of effective and equitable decision-making systems, and rigorous and regular reporting of conservation program results to Canadians.

Unfortunately, despite some of the mechanisms noted in the first paragraph of this section, no minister or her department is legally accountable to undertake *any* of these initiatives. Perhaps most importantly, no conservation goals or targets are set in law, and no F/P/T minister is required to report to Parliament or a provincial legislature regarding progress towards achieving conservation program goals. This creates problems with vertical and horizontal aspects of accountability within and between F/P/T departments responsible for biodiversity. Only the Oceans Act speaks to the need for integrated ecological planning but, as noted in our first Pathology, implementation of the act has been poor overall.

The consequence of this void is that much of the burden for accountability has fallen to NGOs, which have grown in number and power to drive improvements in performance and to identify capacity gaps, a service that governments are either unwilling, unable, or ineffectively provide (Lehman 2007; Jepson 2005). Most prominently in Canada, the Canadian Parks and Wilderness Society (CPAWS) has taken a lead role in holding the federal government accountable for its terrestrial and marine protected areas effectiveness, while WWF Canada has focused on biodiversity status and trends.

At the international level, while the Conference of the Parties (COP) to the CBD have undertaken reviews, the impacts of these reviews in terms of stepping up and broadening action to implement the CBD and the *Strategic Plan for Biodiversity 2011–2020* are not reported, monitored, or tracked. It is not known to what extent, if at all, they feed into subsequent (or ongoing) national planning, implementation, monitoring, and reporting. In addition, the CBD does not enforce any accountability on parties whatsoever, leaving countries to report on the status of biodiversity and various conservation initiatives without any form of peer review. The lack of a review process within the CBD leaves little room to assess whether actions taken are really leading to improvements in the status and trends of biodiversity (Lemieux et al. 2019).

The overall situation in Canada coalesces and accumulates to stifle innovation in conservation. Problematically, the legal accountability risk of being non-compliant with laws requiring setting biodiversity goals, advancing data sharing, or establishing transparent and inclusive decision-making systems, for example, are nil because there are no such requirements. Therefore, it comes as no surprise that conservation regimes deflect to tried and true approaches and away from program initiatives or innovations which they are not required to consider or support. These accountability deficiencies make it difficult if not impossible to determine where conservation successes to emulate and challenges to remedy lie and further impede conservation success in Canada.

3. Conclusions

Twenty-five years ago, Holling and Meffe (1996) warned that institutions that are dominated by cultures of control, resistance to new ideas, and unwillingness to change contribute to on-going degradation of ecosystems. We have detailed the many ways in which conservation in Canada is deeply affected by pathological management and chronic organizational dysfunction. Treating these pathologies will be painfully slow because, as we have detailed, dysfunctional organizations have closed cultures, avoid risk, crave certainty, are not forward thinking, and are not accountable because there is nothing to be accountable for in law.

The pathologies we detail have become so entrenched, there is little reason to believe that they will change in the short- to medium-term. To learn, appropriate lessons must be drawn about the specific type of failures involved in past, present, and future biodiversity conservation policies and policy proposals, and about all their program, process, and political sources. Effective achievement of the UN CBD Kunming-Montreal Global Biodiversity Framework , the goals of the *2030 Agenda for Sustainable Development*, and the scenarios for the *2050 Vision of Biodiversity* in Canada will require an integrated mix of incremental and transformative adaptations in law and policy, action plans aligned with reporting and monitoring, and more effective alignment with other national initiatives related to climate change, human health and well-being, and sustainable development, some of which are discussed in the second half of this book.

ACKNOWLEDGMENTS

This chapter was inspired by personal discussions on organizational pathologies and management dysfunction with Dr. Paul A. Gray, a retired civil servant who dedicated his career to conserving our Home Place. Paul, you made a difference.

WORKS CITED

Adams, Vanessa M., Morena Mills, Rebecca Weeks, Daniel B. Segan, Robert L. Pressey, Georgina G. Gurney, Craig Groves, Frank W. Davis, and Jorge G. Álvarez-Romero. 2019. "Implementation Strategies for Systematic Conservation Planning." *Ambio* 48 (2): 139–52. https://doi.org/10.1007/s13280-018-1067-2

Allen, Craig R., and Lance H. Gunderson. 2011. "Pathology and Failure in the Design and Implementation of Adaptive Management." *Journal of Environmental Management* 92 (5): 1379–84. https://doi.org/10.1016/J.JENVMAN.2010.10.063

Bailey, Megan, Brett Favaro, Sarah P. Otto, Anthony Charles, Rodolphe Devillers, Anna Metaxas, Peter Tyedmers, et al. 2016. "Canada at a Crossroad: The Imperative for Realigning Ocean Policy with Ocean Science." *Marine Policy* 63: 53–60. https://doi.org/10.1016/j.marpol.2015.10.002

Barber, Michael. 2015. *How to Run a Government So That Citizens Benefit and Taxpayers Don't Go Crazy*. London, UK: Penguin Random House.

Barbier, Edward B., Joanne C. Burgess, and Thomas J. Dean. 2018. "How to Pay for Saving Biodiversity." *Science* 360 (6388): 486–8. https://doi.org/10.1126/science.aar3454

Barr, Stephanie L., Brendon M.H. Larson, Thomas J. Beechey, and Daniel J. Scott. 2020. "Assessing Climate Change Adaptation Progress in Canada's Protected Areas." *The*

Canadian Geographer/Le Géographe Canadien, 1–14. https://doi.org/https://doi
.org/10.1111/cag.12635

Barry, Janice, and Libby Porter. 2012. "Indigenous Recognition in State-Based
Planning Systems: Understanding Textual Mediation in the Contact Zone." *Planning
Theory* 11 (2): 170–87. https://doi.org/10.1177/1473095211427285

Beck, Silke. 2011. "Moving beyond the Linear Model of Expertise? IPCC and the
Test of Adaptation." *Regional Environmental Change* 11 (2): 297–306. https://doi
.org/10.1007/s10113-010-0136-2

Bhatt, Rashi, Michael J. Gill, Healy Hamilton, Xuemei Han, Helaine M Linden, and
Bruce E. Young. 2020. "Uneven Use of Biodiversity Indicators in 5th National
Reports to the Convention on Biological Diversity." *Environmental Conservation* 47
(1): 15–21. https://doi.org/10.1017/S0376892919000365

Bird, Sarah C., and Karen E. Hodges. 2017. "Critical Habitat Designation for Canadian
Listed Species: Slow, Biased, and Incomplete." *Environmental Science & Policy* 71
(May): 1–8. https://doi.org/10.1016/j.envsci.2017.01.007

Bolam, Friederike C., Louise Mair, Marco Angelico, Thomas M. Brooks, Mark
Burgman, Claudia Hermes, Michael Hoffmann, Rob W. Martin, Philip J.K.
McGowan, and Ana S.L. Rodrigues. 2020. "How Many Bird and Mammal
Extinctions Has Recent Conservation Action Prevented?" *Conservation Letters*.
https://doi.org/10.1111/conl.12762

Bovens, Mark. 2007. "Analysing and Assessing Accountability: A Conceptual
Framework." *European Law Journal* 13 (4): 447–68.

Briggs, Sue. 2003. "Command and Control in Natural Resource Management:
Revisiting Holling and Meffe." *Ecological Management and Restoration* 4 (3): 161–2.
https://doi.org/10.1046/j.1442-8903.2003.00151.x

Campbell, Lisa M., Shannon Hagerman, and Noella J. Gray. 2014. "Producing Targets
for Conservation: Science and Politics at the Tenth Conference of the Parties to the
Convention on Biological Diversity." *Global Environmental Politics* 14 (3): 41–63.
https://doi.org/10.1162/GLEP_a_00238

Canessa, Stefano, Gemma Taylor, Rohan H. Clarke, Dean Ingwersen, James
Vandersteen, John G. Ewen, and Wildlife Health Ghent. 2019. "Risk Aversion and
Uncertainty Create a Conundrum for Planning Recovery of a Critically Endangered
Species." https://doi.org/10.1111/csp2.138

Carrasco, Luis, Monica Papeş, Kimberly S. Sheldon, and Xingli Giam. 2021. "Global
Progress in Incorporating Climate Adaptation into Land Protection for Biodiversity
since Aichi Targets." *Global Change Biology*. 27: 1788–801. https://doi.org/10.1111
/gcb.15511

Charles, Anthony, Laura Loucks, Fikret Berkes, and Derek Armitage. 2020.
"Community Science: A Typology and Its Implications for Governance of Social-
Ecological Systems." *Environmental Science & Policy* 106: 77–86. https://doi.org
/10.1016/j.envsci.2020.01.019

Collins, James Charles. 2001. *Good to Great*. HarperCollins.

Convention on Biological Diversity (CBD). 2020. "Update of the Zero Draft of the Post-2020 Global Biodiversity Framework." https://www.cbd.int/doc/c/3064/749a /0f65ac7f9def86707f4eaefa/post2020-prep-02-01-en.pdf.

CPAWS. 2016. "Protecting Canada's National Parks: A Call for Renewed Commitment To Nature Conservation." https://cpaws.org/wp-content/uploads/2019/07/CPAWS -Parks-Report-2016.pdf.

Dasgupta, P. 2021. *The Economics of Biodiversity: The Dasgupta Review*. London: HM Treasury.

Díaz, Sandra, Josef Settele, Eduardo S. Brondízio, Hien T. Ngo, John Agard, Almut Arneth, Patricia Balvanera, et al. 2019. "Pervasive Human-Driven Decline of Life on Earth Points to the Need for Transformative Change." *Science* 1327 (6471). https:// doi.org/10.1126/science.aaw3100

Dickinson, Janis L., Jennifer Shirk, David Bonter, Rick Bonney, Rhiannon L. Crain, Jason Martin, Tina Phillips, and Karen Purcell. 2012. "The Current State of Citizen Science as a Tool for Ecological Research and Public Engagement." *Frontiers in Ecology and the Environment* 10 (6): 291–7. https://doi.org/10.1890 /110236

Favaro, B., D.C. Claar, C.H. Fox, C. Freshwater, and J.J. Holden. 2014. "Trends in Extinction Risk for Imperiled Species in Canada." *PLoS ONE* 9 (11). https://doi .org/10.1371/journal.pone.0113118

Fischer, Frank. 2000. *Citizens, Experts, and the Environment: The Politics of Local Knowledge*. Durham, NC: Duke University Press.

Forsyth, Tim, and Andrew Walker. 2008. *Forest Guardians, Forest Destroyers: The Politics of Environmental Knowledge in Northern Thailand*. Seattle, Washington: University of Washington Press.

Geldmann, Jonas, Andrea Manica, Neil D. Burgess, Lauren Coad, and Andrew Balmford. 2019. "A Global-Level Assessment of the Effectiveness of Protected Areas at Resisting Anthropogenic Pressures." *Proceedings of the National Academy of Sciences of the United States of America* 116 (46): 23209–15. https://doi.org/10.1073 /pnas.1908221116

Green, Elizabeth J., Graeme M. Buchanan, H.M. Stuart, M. Butchart, Georgina M. Chandler, Neil D. Burgess, Samantha L.L. Hill, and Richard D. Gregory. 2019. "Relating Characteristics of Global Biodiversity Targets to Reported Progress." *Conservation Biology* 33 (6): 1360–9. https://doi.org/10.1111/cobi.13322

Guarás, Daniela, Marina Von Weissenberg, and Hugo René Rivera-Mendoza. 2021. "Post-2020 Expertise on #19 Transparency and Accountability for Delivering Goals." Post-2020 Biodiversity EU Support. https://4post2020bd.net/resources/expertise -on-19-building-transparency-and-accountability-for-delivering-global-biodiversity -goals/

Hagerman, Shannon M., and Ricardo Pelai. 2016. "'As Far as Possible and as Appropriate': Implementing the Aichi Biodiversity Targets." *Conservation Letters* 9 (6): 469–78. https://doi.org/10.1111/conl.12290

Hagerman, Shannon M., and Terre Satterfield. 2014. "Agreed but Not Preferred: Expert Views on Taboo Options for Biodiversity Conservation, Given Climate Change." *Ecological Applications* 24 (3): 548–59. https://doi.org/10.1890/13-0400.1

Hagerman, Shannon M., Lisa M. Campbell, Noella J. Gray, and Ricardo Pelai. 2021. "Knowledge Production for Target-Based Biodiversity Governance." https://doi .org/10.1016/j.biocon.2021.108980

Hebblewhite, Mark. 2017. "Billion Dollar Boreal Woodland Caribou and the Biodiversity Impacts of the Global Oil and Gas Industry." *Biological Conservation* 206: 102–11. https://doi.org/10.1016/j.biocon.2016.12.014

Holling, C.S., and Gary K. Meffe. 1996. "Command and Control and the Pathology of Natural Resource Management." *Conservation Biology* 10 (2): 328–37. https://doi .org/10.1046/j.1523-1739.1996.10020328.x

Intergovernmental Science-Policy Platform on Biodiversity and Ecosystem Services (IPBES). 2019. "Summary for Policymakers of the Global Assessment Report on Biodiversity and Ecosystem Services of the Intergovernmental Science-Policy Platform on Biodiversity and Ecosystem Services." Bonn, Germany. https://ipbes .net/system/tdf/ipbes_global_assessment_report_summary_for_policymakers .pdf?file=1&type=node&id=35329.

Jasanoff, Sheila. 2004. *States of Knowledge: The Co-production of Science and the Social Order*. Routledge.

Jasanoff, Sheila, and Hilton R. Simmet. 2017. "No Funeral Bells: Public Reason in a 'Post-Truth' Age." *Social Studies of Science* 47 (5): 751–70. https://doi.org/10.1177 /0306312717731936

Jepson, Paul. 2005. "Governance and Accountability of Environmental NGOs." *Environmental Science & Policy* 8 (5): 515–24. https://doi.org/https://doi.org /10.1016/j.envsci.2005.06.006

Jolibert, Catherine, and Anna Wesselink. 2012. "Research Impacts and Impact on Research in Biodiversity Conservation: The Influence of Stakeholder Engagement." *Environmental Science & Policy* 22: 100–11. https://doi.org/10.1016/j .envsci.2012.06.012

Jones, Lizzie P., Samuel T. Turvey, Dario Massimino, and Sarah K. Papworth. 2020. "Investigating the Implications of Shifting Baseline Syndrome on Conservation." *People and Nature* 2 (4): 1131–44. https://doi.org/10.1002/pan3.10140

Kearney, John, Fikret Berkes, Anthony Charles, Evelyn Pinkerton, and Melanie Wiber. 2007. "The Role of Participatory Governance and Community-Based Management in Integrated Coastal and Ocean Management in Canada." *Coastal Management*. https://doi.org/10.1080/10.1080/08920750600970511

Knight, Andrew T., Richard M. Cowling, Mathieu Rouget, Andrew Balmford, Amanda T. Lombard, and Bruce M. Campbell. 2008. "Knowing but Not Doing: Selecting Priority Conservation Areas and the Research–Implementation Gap." *Conservation Biology* 22 (3): 610–17. https://doi.org/10.1111/j.1523-1739.2008 .00914.x

Legagneux, Pierre, Nicolas Casajus, Kevin Cazelles, Clément Chevallier, Marion Chevrinais, Lorelei Guéry, Claire Jacquet, et al. 2018. "Our House Is Burning: Discrepancy in Climate Change vs. Biodiversity Coverage in the Media as Compared to Scientific Literature." *Frontiers in Ecology and Evolution.* https://doi .org/10.3389/fevo.2017.00175

Lehman, Glen. 2007. "The Accountability of NGOs in Civil Society and Its Public Spheres." *Critical Perspectives on Accounting* 18 (6): 645–69. https://doi .org/10.1016/j.cpa.2006.04.002

Lemieux, C.J., and P.A. Gray. 2020. "How Canada 'Hamburger Manufactured' Its Way to Marine Protected Areas Success and a Better Way Forward for the Post-2020 Conservation Agenda." *Journal of Environmental Studies and Sciences.* https://doi .org/10.1007/s13412-020-00627-4

Lemieux, C.J., P.A. Gray, R. Devillers, P. Wright, P. Dearden, E.A. Halpenny, M.W. Groulx, T.J. Beechey, and K. Beazley. 2019. "How the Race to Achieve Aichi Target 11 Could Jeopardize the Effective Conservation of Biodiversity in Canada and Beyond." *Marine Policy* 99 (November 2018): 312–23. https://doi.org/10.1016/j.marpol.2018.10.029

Lemieux, C.J., E.A. Halpenny, T. Swerdfager, M. He, A.J. Gould, D. Carruthers Den Hoed, J. Bueddefeld, G.T. Hvenegaard, B. Joubert, and R. Rollins. 2021. "Free Fallin': The Decline of Evidence-Based Decision-Making by Canada's Protected Area Managers." *FACETS.* https://doi.org/10.1139/facets-2020-0085

Mandrak, Nicholas E., and Becky Cudmore. 2015. "Risk Assessment: Cornerstone of an Aquatic Invasive Species Program." *Aquatic Ecosystem Health and Management* 18 (3): 312–20. https://doi.org/10.1080/14634988.2015.1046357

Mantyka-Pringle, S. Chrystal, Piero Visconti, Moreno Di Marco, Tara G. Martin, Carlo Rondinini, and Jonathan R. Rhodes. 2015. "Climate Change Modifies Risk of Global Biodiversity Loss Due to Land-Cover Change." *Biological Conservation* 187 (July): 103–11. https://doi.org/10.1016/j.biocon.2015.04.016

McLaughlin, Chris, and Gail Krantzberg. 2012. "An Appraisal of Management Pathologies in the Great Lakes." *Science of the Total Environment* 416: 40–7. https:// doi.org/10.1016/j.scitotenv.2011.12.015

Ministry of Forests Lands and Natural Resource Operations. 2017. "Ministry of Forests, Lands and Natural Resource Operations 2017/18 – 2019/20 Service Plan." Victoria, BC. https://www.bcbudget.gov.bc.ca/2017/sp/pdf/ministry/flnr.pdf.

National Advisory Panel on Marine Protected Area Standards. 2019. "Final Report of the National Advisory Panel on Marine Protected Area Standards." Ottawa, Ontario.

Oceana. 2020. "Fishery Audit 2020: Unlocking Canada's Potential for Abundant Oceans." https://doi.org/10.5281/zenodo.4266773

Office of the Auditor General of British Columbia. 2013. "An Audit of Biodiversity in BC: Assessing the Effectiveness of Key Tools." http://www.bcauditor.com/sites /default/files/publications/2013/report_10/report/OAGBC-Audit of Biodiversity in B.C assessing the effectiveness of key tools.pdf.

Office of the Auditor General of Canada. 2018a. "2018 Fall Reports of the Commissioner of the Environment and Sustainable Development to the Parliament

of Canada. Report 2 – Protecting Marine Mammals." Ottawa, Ontario. 2018. https://
www.oag-bvg.gc.ca/internet/English/parl_cesd_201810_02_e_43146.html.

– 2018b. "2018 Spring Reports of the Commissioner of the Environment and
Sustainable Development to the Parliament of Canada: Report 3 – Conserving
Biodiversity." Ottawa, Ontario. https://www.oag-bvg.gc.ca/internet/English/parl
_cesd_201804_03_e_42994.html.

Office of the Auditor General of Ontario. 2020. "Value-for-Money Audit: Conserving
the Natural Environment with Protected Areas." https://auditor.on.ca/en/content
/annualreports/arreports/en20/ENV_conservingthenaturalenvironment_en20.pdf.

Palm, Eric C., Shaun Fluker, Holly K. Nesbitt, Aerin, L. Jacob, Mark Hebblewhite, and
W.A. Franke. 2020. "The Long Road to Protecting Critical Habitat for Species at Risk:
The Case of Southern Mountain Woodland Caribou." https://doi.org/10.1111/csp2.219

Papworth, Sarah. 2017. "Decision-Making Psychology Can Bolster Conservation."
Nature Ecology & Evolution 1 (9): 1217–18. https://doi.org/10.1038/s41559-017
-0281-9

Pelai, Ricardo, Shannon M. Hagerman, and Robert Kozak. 2021. "Seeds of Change?
Seed Transfer Governance in British Columbia: Insights from History." *Canadian
Journal of Forest Research* 51 (2): 326–38. https://doi.org/10.1139/cjfr-2020-0235

Porter, Libby. 2006. "Planning in (Post) Colonial Settings: Challenges for Theory and
Practice." *Planning Theory & Practice* 7 (4): 383–96. https://doi.org/10.1080
/14649350600984709

Rounsevell, Mark D.A., Mike Harfoot, Paula A. Harrison, Tim Newbold, Richard D.
Gregory, and Georgina M. Mace. 2020. "A Biodiversity Target Based on Species
Extinctions." *Science* 368 (6496): 1193–5. https://doi.org/10.1126/science.aba6592

Secretariat of the Convention on Biological Diversity. 2020. "Global Biodiversity
Outlook 5: Summary for Policymakers." Montreal, QC. https://www.cbd.int/gbo
/gbo5/publication/gbo-5-spm-en.pdf.

Shackleton, Ross T., Tim Adriaens, Giuseppe Brundu, Katharina Dehnen-Schmutz,
Rodrigo A. Estévez, Jana Fried, Brendon M.H. Larson, Shuang Liu, Elizabete
Marchante, and Hélia Marchante. 2019. "Stakeholder Engagement in the Study and
Management of Invasive Alien Species." *Journal of Environmental Management* 229:
88–101. https://doi.org/10.1016/j.jenvman.2018.04.044

St-Laurent, Guillaume Peterson, Shannon Hagerman, and Robert Kozak. 2018. "What
Risks Matter? Public Views about Assisted Migration and Other Climate-Adaptive
Reforestation Strategies." *Climatic Change* 151 (3): 573–87. https://doi.org/10.1007
/s10584-018-2310-3

Sterling, Eleanor J., Erin Betley, Amanda Sigouin, Andres Gomez, Anne Toomey, Georgina
Cullman, Cynthia Malone, Adam Pekor, Felicity Arengo, and Mary Blair. 2017.
"Assessing the Evidence for Stakeholder Engagement in Biodiversity Conservation."
Biological Conservation 209: 159–71. https://doi.org/10.1016/j.biocon.2017.02.008

Taylor, Stephanie, and Tony R. Walker. 2017. Letter, "Canada Fails to Protect Its
Caribou. North Atlantic Right Whales in Danger. Let Experts Judge Research
Potential." *Science* 358 (6364): 730–1. https://doi.org/10.1126/science.aar2402

Tulloch, Ayesha I.T., Richard F. Maloney, Liana N. Joseph, Joseph R. Bennett, Martina M.I. Di Fonzo, William J.M. Probert, Shaun M. O'Connor, Jodie P. Densem, and Hugh P. Possingham. 2015. "Effect of Risk Aversion on Prioritizing Conservation Projects." *Conservation Biology* 29 (2): 513–24. https://doi.org/10.1111/cobi.12386

Turnhout, Esther, Katja Neves, and Elisa De Lijster. 2014. "'Measurementality' in Biodiversity Governance: Knowledge, Transparency, and the Intergovernmental Science-Policy Platform on Biodiversity and Ecosystem Services (IPBES)." *Environment and Planning A* 46 (3): 581–97. https://doi.org/10.1068/a4629

Vadrot, Alice B.M. 2014. *The Politics of Knowledge and Global Biodiversity*. Oxon and New York: Routledge.

Waldron, Anthony, Daniel C. Miller, Dave Redding, Arne Mooers, Tyler S. Kuhn, Nate Nibbelink, J. Timmons Roberts, Joseph A. Tobias, and John L. Gittleman. 2017. "Reductions in Global Biodiversity Loss Predicted from Conservation Spending." *Nature* 551 (7680): 364–7. https://doi.org/10.1038/nature24295

Waldron, Anthony, Arne O. Mooers, Daniel C. Miller, Nate Nibbelink, David Redding, Tyler S. Kuhn, J. Timmons Roberts, and John L. Gittleman. 2013. "Targeting Global Conservation Funding to Limit Immediate Biodiversity Declines." *Proceedings of the National Academy of Sciences of the United States of America* 110 (29): 12144–8. https://doi.org/10.1073/pnas.1221370110

Watts, Kevin, Robin C. Whytock, Kirsty J. Park, Elisa Fuentes-Montemayor, Nicholas A. Macgregor, Simon Duffield, and Philip J.K. McGowan. 2020. "Ecological Time Lags and the Journey towards Conservation Success." *Nature Ecology & Evolution* 4 (3): 304–11. https://doi.org/10.1038/s41559-019-1087-8

Whitehorn, Penelope R., Laetitia M. Navarro, Matthias Schröter, Miguel Fernandez, Xavier Rotllan-Puig, and Alexandra Marques. 2019. "Mainstreaming Biodiversity: A Review of National Strategies." *Biological Conservation* 235: 157–63. https://doi.org/https://doi.org/10.1016/j.biocon.2019.04.016

World Wildlife Fund Canada. 2020. *WWF Canada: Living Planet Report Canada*. Toronto, ON. https://doi.org/10.13140/RG.2.2.16556.49280

Youdelis, Megan. 2016. "'They Could Take You out for Coffee and Call It Consultation!': The Colonial Antipolitics of Indigenous Consultation in Jasper National Park." *Environment and Planning A: Economy and Space* 48 (7): 1374–92. https://doi.org/10.1177/0308518X16640530

Zurba, Melanie, Karen F. Beazley, Emilie English, and Johanna Buchmann-Duck. 2019. "Indigenous Protected and Conserved Areas (IPCAs), Aichi Target 11 and Canada's Pathway to Target 1: Focusing Conservation on Reconciliation." *Land* 8 (1): 10. https://doi.org/10.3390/land8010010

3 Who Should Govern Wildlife? Examining Attitudes across the Country

MATTHEW A. WILLIAMSON, STACY LISCHKA, ANDREA OLIVE,
JEREMY PITTMAN, AND ADAM T. FORD

Canada is the world's second largest country with roughly 10 million km^2 of terrestrial and freshwater ecosystems (NWWG 1997), and approximately 80,000 species, with at least 300 of those being endemic species (CESCC 2016, Enns et al. 2020). It also has the "most wilderness of any nation in the world (26%) and is ranked relatively low, nineteenth, in its proportion of heavily human-disturbed land (1%)" (Coristine et al. 2019, 1220). This suggests potential for large and connected protected areas that could support biodiversity. Recent data suggests, however, that Canada is struggling to protect wildlife. Of 30,000 species for which there is sufficient information, 20 per cent are imperiled to some degree (CESCC 2016). Between 1970 and 2014, 50 per cent of monitored wildlife species in Canada declined in abundance, with an average decline of 83 per cent (WWF Canada 2020). This decline is particularly alarming because it coincides with the Canadian government's creation of legislation and policy to protect wildlife and species at risk. For example, the national Species at Risk Act, created in 2002, is struggling to protect species on the list, as species populations declined an average of 28 per cent (WWF Canada 2020).

The drivers of wildlife decline are varied and complex, including habitat loss and fragmentation, climate change, pollution, and overharvesting. However, declines are often related to the "cumulative and cascading" impacts of various stressors (WWF Canada 2020). For example, habitat loss and climate change are independent threats to species like polar bears or caribou, but combined they produce a devastating threat to both the species and their habitats. As a result, successful management of wildlife populations and habitats requires confronting and managing all these other threats simultaneously.

The *2020 WWF Living Planet Report* suggests "efforts to protect and recover vulnerable wildlife at local, provincial, and national scales are not nearly enough." From a governance standpoint, Canada must do more to protect its wilderness and reverse species decline in human-dominated ecosystems like urban centres and working landscapes. This chapter presents results from a

survey of 11,500 Canadian residents across the 10 provinces and three territories about their preferences for different actors and governance approaches.
The analysis focuses on responses to three main questions:

- Is the government making good decisions about how wildlife and habitats
  are managed?
- What level of government is most appropriate to manage wildlife and
  habitat?
- Who should be most influential in making decisions related to wildlife and
  habitat management/regulations?

This is a first step in understanding what Canadians feel about the appropriate
role of government and actors outside government, such as non-governmental
organizations, private industry, and scientists, in managing wildlife and the habitats on which they depend.

All authors are settler-scholars living and working in the traditional territories of Indigenous Peoples in the United States and Canada. Matthew Williamson is originally from the traditional territory of the Očhéthi Šakówiŋ in South
Dakota and currently lives and works in the territory of the Shoshone and
Bannock Tribes in Idaho. Stacy Lischka currently lives and works in the traditional territory of the Očhéthi Šakówiŋ, Núu-agha-tuvu-pu (Ute), Cheyenne,
and Arapaho Tribes in Colorado. Andrea Olive is from Treaty 4 lands in Saskatchewan and currently resides on the traditional lands of the Huron-Wendat,
the Seneca, and the Mississaugas of the Credit. Jeremy Pittman grew up in the
Treaty 6 Territory, the traditional lands of the nêhiyawak, and the homeland of
the Métis. He currently resides on the traditional territory of the Neutral, Anishinaabeg, and Haudenosaunee peoples. He works and lives on the Haldimand
Tract, which is the land granted to the Six Nations. Adam Ford currently lives
and works in unceded Sylix territory in British Columbia. We acknowledge that
the themes presented in this chapter primarily reflect settlers across Canada
and urge those who read this to reflect upon the ways in which surveys such as
ours may obscure truths that cannot be revealed by numbers alone.

The chapter begins with a brief literature review of prior studies that have
examined attitudes towards wildlife in Canada. We then explain our method-
ology and present our results. Overall, we find that, despite the stark evidence
to the contrary, many Canadians believe the current arrangement between
federal, provincial, local, and Indigenous governments is effective for managing wildlife. Most respondents prefer that the federal government make decisions about species at risk and conservation incentive programs, but favour
provinces for decisions about protected areas and hunting regulations. As the
introduction to this volume suggests, and other chapters in this book demonstrate, Canada needs widescale transformative change if wildlife indicators are

to improve. However, our data suggest that acceptance of – and preference for – the status quo may be a barrier to transformative politics for wildlife governance in Canada.

Understanding Wildlife Governance in Canada

In Canada, wildlife is managed and protected through a "bewildering array of policy instruments administered by different levels (federal, provincial, and territorial) or scales of government" (Ray et al. 2021). This is largely due to the constitutional division of powers, and it is worth briefly outlining here the governance structure for wildlife and habitat regulation in Canada. Figure 3.1 below illustrates the array of actors that influence wildlife policy but does not mean to suggest that all actors have equal influence. This section highlights the concentration of power in the federal and provincial governments with respect to policy creation and implementation.

Provinces have jurisdiction and constitutional authority over most natural resources, as well as provincial Crown lands and private property. The land jurisdiction aspect is the critical issue because wildlife require habitat for persistence. In some respects, this places provinces at the centre of wildlife governance and at the very heart of species-at-risk conservation (where habitat loss and human activities are the main drivers of decline). In an extensive review of all biodiversity statutes in Canada, Ray et al. (2021) found 201 "laws across all jurisdictions in Canada that directly consider biodiversity in some fashion" with 21 of those statutes being at the federal level and the remaining 180 spread across the sub-national jurisdictions.

Indeed, all provinces and territories have wildlife acts and policy guidelines for hunting and fishing as well as access to recreational spaces like parks. Only six provinces and two territories have stand-alone legislation for at-risk wildlife. British Columbia, Alberta, Saskatchewan, Prince Edward Island, and Yukon rely on various forestry or wildlife acts to protect imperiled wildlife rather than a single policy (Olive 2014). In most parts of Canada, the federal government does not have strong jurisdiction over wildlife and instead tends to share responsibility with provinces and territories. One clear area of federal jurisdiction is the ability to enter into international treaties, such as the UN Convention on Biological Diversity and the UN Declaration of the Rights of Indigenous Peoples. The federal government also shares jurisdiction when it comes to international issues like migratory birds and ocean life.

There are federal lands, including National Parks and Marine Conservation Areas, from coast to coast to coast. South of the 60th parallel there is very little federal land (less than 10%) but across the three territories the vast majority of land is federal or co-managed through land claim agreements with Indigenous Peoples. On federal lands, federal laws apply. One important example is the

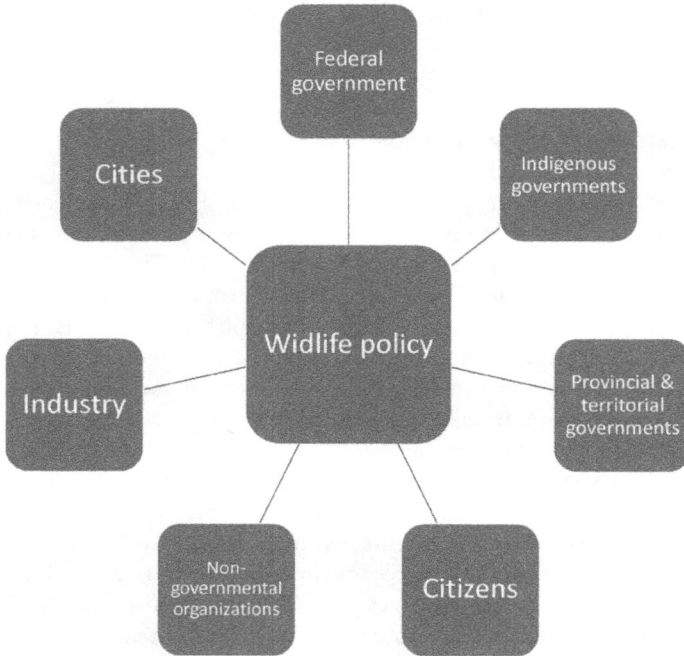

Figure 3.1. Actors that influence wildlife policy in Canada.

national Species at Risk Act (SARA), which is the most important federal law for protecting wildlife. SARA is fairly limited in scope, especially as compared to the national Endangered Species Act in the US (see Olive 2014) but does extend protection to all listed species on federal lands.

Wildlife species are assessed by an independent scientific body, the Committee on the Status of Endangered Wildlife in Canada (COSEWIC) and added to SARA at the discretion of the Minister of Environment. Once a species is added to SARA, Environment and Climate Change Canada and Fisheries and Oceans Canada are responsible for both designating and then protecting critical habitat. If critical habitat occurs on non-federal lands and there is imminent risk of the species going extinct, the federal government does have the power to invoke an emergency order to protect the species on provincial or private land (sometimes with compensation). In the past 20 years, the emergency clause has been used for two species but only to regulate on provincial crown land. The first was the case of the Greater Sage Grouse in Saskatchewan and Alberta in 2013, and the second was for the Western Chorus Frog in Quebec. By and large, the federal government leaves it to the provinces to protect wildlife on non-federal lands.

Cities and urban municipalities are known as "creatures of the province" because their authority is granted to them by the provincial government (see Tindal and Tindal 2017). Toronto or Winnipeg, for example, are only as powerful as Ontario and Manitoba allow them to be. There is nothing in the Canadian Constitution that specifies their jurisdiction or grants them authority to make and enforce laws. Not surprisingly, the role that municipalities play in wildlife governance varies across the provinces and territories. Some cities, like Vancouver and Montreal, are G40 cities and considered leaders in climate and environmental issues. Other cities, like Regina or Edmonton, have comparatively very little environmental policy in place. Of course, all cities own land and as such are subject to provincial and federal wildlife laws that pertain to property. It would be impossible to present a comprehensive overview of what municipalities are doing in terms of wildlife regulation. The important thing to note is that cities do not have any formal or defined powers when it comes to biodiversity and habitat protection.

Beyond the federal-provincial shared responsibility for wildlife, there is an older, often unseen, and unacknowledged system of governance and stewardship that overlays the country. As outlined in chapter 1 and made clear in later chapters, Indigenous-led conservation remains essential to wildlife (see Artelle et al. 2019). There are layers of case law and policy to support Indigenous rights to wildlife and land title, which are formally recognized in historic and modern treaties as well as the Constitution. Through the Truth and Reconciliation Commission of Canada, the federal government and provinces are committed to implementing the 96 Calls to Action. Related to that, Canada has also, with much consternation, endorsed the United Nations Declaration of the Rights of Indigenous Peoples[1] (UNDRIP).

Non-governmental organizations (NGOs) like World Wildlife Fund Canada or Canadian Parks and Wilderness Society as well as hunter and angler groups, agriculture producer groups, and land-use groups can also play an important role in Canadian wildlife and habitat management. Traditionally, NGOs play the role of lobbying government for policy, communicating issues to the public, and serving as watchdogs of government implementation (or lack thereof) of policy (Olive 2019). Private industry and the business community are also actors with influence and impact in wildlife management. These actors may pose threats to biodiversity through their normal operations, such as forestry operations or a cement production facility, or they may lobby the government for laxer legislation or donate significant sums of money for wildlife research and protection. The last actor with an important role in wildlife management is the individual citizen. Average people are landowners – some owning or leasing huge tracts of land or significant habitat for at-risk species – and voters. These roles cannot be overlooked or downplayed in the larger governance structure.

We know that Canada's wildlife is experiencing significant declines and that ecosystems are in trouble across the country. This means that the current governance structure is inadequate. It is failing to protect wildlife and ensure a sustainable balance between biodiversity and the economic and social or spatial needs of Canadians. The WWF 2020 *Living Planet Report* concludes that "a different approach to conservation is needed: one that can more effectively address multiple threats to biodiversity and Canada's ecosystems" (WWF Canada 2020). This chapter explores existing attitudes towards governance arrangements in Canada and looks for possible openings to transformation.

Examining Attitudes towards Wildlife in Canada

Very little is known about Canadian attitudes towards wildlife and wildlife management. There is only one prior national study in the academic literature. McCune et al. (2017) polled public opinion using a phone survey to determine Canadian's support for measures designed to prevent the listing of endangered species. Of the 1000 respondents, there was significant support for conservation and preventing extinction of wildlife. Indeed, "eighty-nine percent of respondents somewhat or strongly agreed that it is important to prevent the extinction of wild plants and animals in Canada" (184). When it came to the governance issue, 60 per cent agreed that the federal government should have primary responsibility for preventing the extinction of plants and animals in Canada. This was followed by environmental NGOs (13%), provincial government (10%), individuals or landowners (7%), municipal government (3%), and private business (less than 1%). Thus, while Canadians want species at risk protected, they want it to be the federal government's responsibility.

Outside of this national study, there is public opinion from regional or issue-specific surveys regarding public preference for governance or preferences related to species and habitat management (Jung et al. 2018; Harshaw 2008; McFarlane et al. 2007; Olive 2014; Thorton and Quinn 2009). These studies generally find low levels of public awareness but strong support for federal responsibility in wildlife and habitat management. Support for the role of the federal government in regulating hunting, access to public lands, and private industry vary by species and issue.

Decisions about environmental management are not made in a political vacuum. Indeed, controversies over endangered species management may be as much about trust in a particular government agency as they are arguments about determining the appropriate approach for avoiding extinction. As political discourse becomes increasingly polarized, we might imagine that wildlife conservation preferences may become proxies for deeper beliefs about who should govern public life, in general. As these divides deepen, the difficulty of true transformation increases.

Our survey is intended to fill an empirical gap in the literature. Ours is the first large-scale national survey that examines public attitudes towards wildlife governance. The focus is not on species at risk nor any specific species, park, or issue. Instead, our goal is to get a snapshot of how Canadians feel about wildlife management. This will help policy-makers understand current levels of support, potential areas of conflict, and avenues for changes in the future.

Methodology

The analysis draws on a survey of 11,556 respondents, conducted with Canadian residents in July–August 2020 under UBC Behavioural Research Ethics Board protocol H19–02427 and Boise State Institutional Review Board protocol 090-SB20–141.[2] The sample was random, drawn from a non-probability panel provided by Dynata, a large international survey firm that recruits through both online and offline partners and targeted advertising. The non-probability panel accounts for variation in response rates by adjusting sampling rates based on response rate throughout the period that the survey is open. Quotas and recruitment balancing were used to develop a sample that is reflective of national census data with respect to gender and age while also attempting to balance urban and rural responses. In addition, recruitment efforts and quotas emphasized rural residents in order to obtain a more geographically uniform distribution of samples. Dynata incentivizes participation using a variety of rewards to reflect the diversity of motivations for participating; however, the cash value of the incentive is the same for all participants. The survey was open to all residents of Canada over the age of 18 and delivered online in French, Spanish, and English, according to the respondent's preference.

We present high-level descriptions of the results of this survey as a means of setting the broader context for the discussions taken up in this book. We avoid statistical analysis of these survey results because comprehensive statistical treatment of the hypotheses tested within the survey would far exceed the scope of this chapter. More importantly, the range of philosophical, ethical, and legal issues this book engages represent a level of complexity that does not align well with reductionist statistical approaches (e.g., multivariate regression, analysis of variance, etc.). Finally, our sample was intentionally designed to reach more rural residents. Although one might argue that the opinions of those in population centres are more politically important in democratic systems of governance, the role of primarily rural locales (e.g., northern Alberta or southern Saskatchewan) in driving national energy and agricultural policy suggests that rural voters may play an outsized role in determining national and provincial responses ot wildlife conservation challenges. We leave it to the other authors in this volume and the reader to consider the role that power plays in environmental governance and where those who have power derive it.

Sample versus Population Data

Our sample includes 53 per cent female respondents and 46 per cent male, with 1 per cent preferring not to answer. The average age of respondents was 53, with a median age of 55. In total, 42 per cent of respondents have at least an undergraduate university education while 17 per cent have high school only. This means our sample of respondents is older and more educated than the national population. Census data shows that of the 38 million people in Canada, 51 per cent are female and the average age of Canadians is 41. As of the 2016 census, 23 per cent of Canadians (18 and older) have at least an undergraduate university education while 26 per cent have high school only (Statistics Canada, n.d.). Data indicates that older and more educated Canadians are more likely to vote (Statistics Canada n.d.). Thus, our sample is likely more representative of the average Canadian voter as opposed to the average Canadian.

In thinking about generalizability and the cultural and socio-demographics of our respondents, it is worth noting that 21 per cent of respondents reported living in an urban area, 48 per cent in a suburban area and 31 per cent in a rural area. Overall, 10 per cent of respondents claimed to be agricultural producers. Eight percent of respondents indicated having grown up on a farm, while an additional 13 per cent grew up in a rural area. In comparison, 44 per cent of respondents reported having grown up in a small town, subdivision, or rural subdivision. Thirty-five per cent reported having grown up in an urban or metropolitan area. Overall, this means our sample is less urban than national statistics suggest – as of 2019, 82 per cent of Canadians live in an urban or suburban area with only 19 per cent living in a rural area (Stats Canada n.d.).

In terms of political beliefs, we asked respondents to place themselves on a scale from 1 (very liberal) to 7 (very conservative). Here, 26 per cent chose 4 (slightly more conservative) while 36 per cent lean liberal and 30 per cent lean conservative. In terms of who the respondent voted for in federal elections, 41 per cent reported voting for Liberal party candidates, 34 per cent voted for Conservative Party candidates, 12 per cent voted for NDP candidates, 8 per cent voted for Green candidates, and 2 per cent voted for Bloc Quebecois candidates. For perspective, in the most recent federal election (2021), 33 per cent of Canadians voted for the Liberal Party, 34 per cent for the Conservative Party, 18 per cent for the NDP, 2 per cent for the Green Party, and 8 per cent for the Bloc. Thus, our sample has more centre-left respondents than may exist nationally.

As seen in table 3.1, the proportion of respondents varied across the country but aligns with population estimates from the last national census for most regions. We group responses by province for three largest provinces: BC, Ontario, and Quebec. We then grouped responses by region in the case of the less populated provinces in the East (Nova Scotia, Prince Edward Island, New Brunswick, and Newfoundland) and in the West (Alberta, Saskatchewan, and Manitoba).

Table 3.1. Total number and percentage of survey respondents and their proportion to the regional population in Canada

	Total number of respondents	Per cent of sample	Proportion of population in Canada (2016 census)
British Columbia	1642	14%	13%
Eastern Provinces	1308	11%	7%
Northern Territories	17	0.1%	0.3%
Ontario	4671	40%	38%
Quebec	1317	11%	23%
West	1966	17%	18%
No answer	586	5%	NA
Total	11, 556		

The sample in Quebec is much lower than its proportion of the Canadian population. Those respondents comprise only 11 per cent of our sample but are 23 per cent of Canada's population. Otherwise, the sample is representative of the provinces or regions. In the North (Nunavut, Northwest Territories, and Yukon), we had only 17 total respondents, which represents 0.1 per cent of our sample. This is because the northern territories' population is 0.3 per cent of Canada's population. While these 17 respondents remain in the data set when looking at all Canadian respondents, we have removed them from regional analysis in this chapter. We did not feel that it was appropriate to represent the views of people living across 60 per cent of the country's landmass from 17 survey responses.

Results

The results are presented in three sections that map onto the focus questions of the chapter: quality of governance, appropriate level of government, and influential actors for wildlife and habitat decision-making. In each section we present national data (that includes all respondents in the 10 provinces and three territories) and data by region (excluding the three territories due to insufficient samples).

Quality of Governance

We asked respondents how much they agree with a series of statements related to the ability of the government to make good decisions about how wildlife and their habitats are managed. There were 11 statements, and respondents could strongly agree, agree, neither agree/disagree, disagree, and strongly disagree with each of them. A full list of statements is available in

Table 3.2. Attitudes towards the quality of governance for wildlife, by all respondents (Canada) and by region

	n	Mean	Standard Deviation	Mode
Canada	10,932	2.57	1.00	2
British Columbia	1,566	2.59	1.03	2
Eastern Provinces	1,244	2.54	1.00	2
Ontario	4,389	2.52	0.99	2
Quebec	1,246	2.56	0.97	2
West	1,871	2.65	1.03	2

the appendix, but they ranged from government actions "are guided by clear goals and aims" to "are backed by reliable information" to "respond to the needs of local people."

Overall, we found that respondents felt that the quality of governance decisions made about wildlife-related issues was of moderate quality, with a mean score 2.57 on a scale from 1 (strongly agree) to 5 (strongly disagree).[3] This did not vary across regions, as table 3.2 illustrates. The most negative-leaning region is the West, and the least negative-leaning region is Ontario.

Appropriate Government Actors for Wildlife Regulation

We asked respondents: "How appropriate do you feel it is for the following groups to regulate wildlife populations and habitats?" We provided options for different levels of government. As table 3.3 illustrates, 79 per cent thought the federal government was very appropriate or somewhat appropriate, 84 per cent said the same about the provincial government, 64 per cent for local, and 71 per cent for Indigenous governments.

However, the only actor type where more than 50 per cent of respondents felt it was very appropriate for wildlife and habitat regulation was the provincial government. Only 31 per cent felt a local government was very appropriate. On the flip side, 15 per cent felt local governments were inappropriate or very inappropriate, and 13 per cent said Indigenous governments were inappropriate or very inappropriate. There are a considerable number of respondents who were unsure, especially when it came to the role of local governments as appropriate actors for regulating wildlife and habitat.

Looking at the data by region, (table 3.4) there is least support for the federal government in the Western provinces with less than 40 per cent thinking it is very appropriate for the federal government to regulate wildlife management. There is most support, although less than a majority (49%), for federal regulation in Quebec.

Table 3.3. Canadians' attitudes about the appropriateness of different levels of government for regulating wildlife and habitat (n = 10,932)

	Federal (%)	Provincial (%)	Local (%)	Indigenous (%)
Very appropriate	47	52	31	42
Somewhat appropriate	32	32	33	29
Neither	13	11	22	16
Somewhat inappropriate	4	3	8	5
Very inappropriate	3	3	7	8

Table 3.4. Respondents' attitudes, by region, about the appropriateness of different levels of government for regulating wildlife and habitat

	Very Appropriate (%)	Somewhat Appropriate (%)	Neither (%)	Somewhat Inappropriate (%)	Very Inappropriate (%)
Preference for federal action on wildlife management					
British Columbia	44	33	13	5	3
East	47	30	11	4	4
Ontario	47	29	12	4	3
Quebec	49	29	12	3	2
West	38	34	14	5	5
Preference for provincial action on wildlife management					
British Columbia	56	29	9	2	2
East	54	29	9	3	3
Ontario	47	31	12	3	2
Quebec	46	30	14	3	3
West	50	32	9	3	3
Preference for local action on wildlife management					
British Columbia	28	32	21	9	7
East	30	31	20	7	7
Ontario	31	32	20	6	5
Quebec	27	28	24	8	7
West	27	32	23	8	7
Preference for Indigenous action on wildlife management					
British Columbia	35	29	15	6	10
East	38	26	15	5	8
Ontario	41	27	15	5	8
Quebec	43	25	16	4	5
West	31	29	16	6	11

Over half of respondents on two coasts saw the province as very appropriate to manage wildlife. Ontario respondents were (marginally) more likely to say that it was appropriate or very appropriate for the local government to regulate wildlife and populations and habitat than respondents from other regions.

Support for Indigenous governments as appropriate actors to manage wildlife and habitat was strongest in Ontario and Quebec and weakest in the West and British Columbia. However, even in those regions, over 60 per cent of respondents chose appropriate or very appropriate. Opposition – or reporting that Indigenous Peoples are very inappropriate actors – was highest in the West and BC, with 10 per cent or more of respondents selecting that category.

Actor Influence in Decision-Making

We asked respondents: In your mind, which of the following groups do you feel *should be most influential* in making decisions about the following:

(a) establishing new parks and protected areas for the benefit of wildlife
(b) deciding how and when legal hunting can occur
(c) determining the status of specific wildlife populations (such as listing species as threatened or endangered, or allowing hunting)
(d) providing financial incentives to encourage people to take actions that benefit wildlife

See the appendix for the exact question wording and format. We provided as options the actors in column one of table 3.5. We worded this question specifically around *influence* because we did not want people to answer based on whose responsibility things actually are. For example, scientists are not responsible for any decisions about wildlife management, but it is possible to think they should be the most influential actor in making decisions about a certain management issue, like listing a species as at risk in Canada.

As seen in table 3.5, respondents felt that provincial governments should be most influential in decisions about protected areas and hunting regulations, whereas the federal government should be most influential in decisions about threatened and endangered status and providing incentives. Very few respondents thought that any other actor should have influence for decisions about these actions. One standout result is that 15 per cent of all respondents felt that scientists should be most influential for determining the status of wildlife populations. Almost no respondents thought private industry should be most influential in any area of wildlife management.

Table 3.5. Canadians' attitudes about who the most influential decision-maker should be for different wildlife management actions (n= 10,932)

	Protected Areas (%)	Wildlife Status (%)	Hunting (%)	Providing incentives (%)
Federal gov't	28	36	18	42
Provincial gov't	39	27	54	32
Local gov't	6	4	7	4
Indigenous gov't	4	3	4	2
Non-government Organization	6	6	3	4
Individuals	2	1	1	2
Private sector	0	0	0	1
Scientists	8	15	4	2
Other	1	1	1	1
Not sure	8	8	8	10

The regional results are fairly consistent across the country (table 3.6). In terms of protected areas, respondents in Quebec were more likely to say the federal government should be most influential and least likely to say the provincial government. The reverse is true in BC, where respondents were least likely to choose the federal government and most likely to choose the provincial government. On decisions about wildlife status, respondents in Ontario and Quebec were slightly more likely to say the federal government – and least likely to say the provincial government – should be most influential. In every region more respondents choose the federal government than any other actor. Six to eleven percent of respondents in each region answered "not sure" across the four issues, with the most "not sure" responses coming regarding incentives.

Examining hunting decisions, there was clear consensus that the province should be most influential in making decisions. Indeed, as many as 63 per cent of respondents in the East choose the province. In BC, the East, and the West only about 15 per cent choose the federal government. Finally, regarding incentives, there was clear consensus for the federal government. Of note, this is the only category where respondents chose private industry as an influential actor with about 1 per cent of respondents in each region.

Discussion

Overall, our survey demonstrates Canadians' support for the current governance arrangement for wildlife and habitat. Most Canadians, across all regions,

Table 3.6. Canadians' attitudes, by region, about who the most influential decision-maker should be for different wildlife management actions

	Federal (%)	Provincial (%)	Local (%)	Indigenous (%)	NGO (%)	Individual (%)	Private (%)	Scientists (%)	Not Sure (%)
Influential actor for decisions on protected areas									
British Columbia	25	46	4	4	5	2	0	8	6
East	27	42	3	3	6	2	0	8	8
Ontario	28	37	8	3	5	2	0	8	8
Quebec	36	30	7	5	5	2	0	8	7
West	26	43	5	3	6	1	0	8	7
Influential actor for decisions on status of wildlife populations									
British Columbia	34	30	3	4	5	0	0	16	7
East	34	29	2	2	6	1	0	17	8
Ontario	38	25	4	3	6	1	0	14	9
Quebec	38	23	3	5	7	1	0	14	9
West	33	30	4	2	6	1	0	16	7
Influential actor for decisions on hunting									
British Columbia	15	59	5	5	3	1	0	5	7
East	14	63	4	3	3	1	0	5	7
Ontario	20	49	9	5	3	1	0	4	9
Quebec	24	49	5	6	3	1	0	4	8
West	15	58	7	3	3	2	0	4	7
Influential actor for providing incentives to encourage people to take actions that benefit wildlife									
British Columbia	42	35	4	2	3	1	1	2	9
East	44	34	3	2	4	2	1	2	10
Ontario	43	31	5	2	4	2	1	2	10
Quebec	46	27	4	3	4	2	1	2	11
West	41	34	4	2	4	2	1	2	10

think the government is doing an adequate job of managing wildlife. There is a general acceptance and preference for federal and provincial involvement in wildlife issues, with little appetite for other actors, including Indigenous governments. Given the widely publicized failure of Canadian biodiversity conservation efforts, these preferences for the status quo may indicate that for the average Canadian voter, the fate of wildlife populations is not particularly salient. This is likely the most insidious obstacle to transformative change. Without widespread recognition of a broken system, the appetite for changing that system is unlikely to emerge.

Appropriate Actors

Almost 80 per cent of our respondents think the provincial and federal governments are appropriate actors when it comes to regulating wildlife populations and habitat. By and large, it is these levels of government that are responsible, as per the design of federalism and the jurisdiction laid out in the Constitution. Canada is one of the most decentralized government systems in the world. In a 2020 survey of over 5,000 Canadians, Environics Institute found that 50 per cent of Canadians want to see a shift in the division of power, with 31 per cent saying the provincial or territorial government should take charge of things currently handled by the federal government. However, 50 per cent of respondents supported the status quo and did not seek any change (Environics Institute for Survey Research 2020).

Looking at our regional data, we see the least support for the federal government in the West. This might be a more general attitude towards governance and not just wildlife governance. For example, in the Environics Institute survey, respondents in Alberta and Saskatchewan were most favourable (at 40% of respondents) of having the provinces take charge of current federal issues. In public opinion of the federal government and current Prime Minister Justin Trudeau, residents of the Western provinces, especially rural regions, have unfavourable opinions (for example, Augus Reid 2021). In the environmental realm, in studies examining attitudes towards the federal carbon tax, residents of Alberta and Saskatchewan are often very opposed (Mildenberger et al. 2016; Besco et al. 2021). Thus, our survey could be capturing these more anti-federal attitudes in the West.

We see the most support for federal action on wildlife management in Ontario and Quebec. Give the data limitations in Quebec (only 11% of the sample is drawn from the region, which makes up 23% of Canada's population), it is difficult to make inferences or draw conclusions. Only half of respondents in Quebec thought the federal government was an appropriate actor, but it is surprising given that the province refused to participate in the 1995 National Accord for Species at Risk because it already had provincial regulations in place for wildlife and species at risk (Olive 2014). The relationship between Quebec and the federal government is likely to be tested in the years to come as SARA measures could be used to protect caribou inside the province (Jonas 2022). More data is required to understand how voters and/or the general public in Quebec feel about wildlife governance and federalism.

It is worth noting that of all the regions, Ontario had the strongest support for local governments. This could be because the province has stronger local governments in general, or it could point to the history and experience of conservation authorities. Finally, it might be because there are programs like the Conservation Land Tax Incentive Program and other tax incentives in Ontario that are administered at the municipal level. In other surveys, such as the Environics Institute survey, Ontario respondents were not more favourable to municipal governments having more power or responsibility. Thus, this could be a finding related more to wildlife specifically.

Support for Indigenous governments was weakest in the provinces that have the most Indigenous peoples (by percent of population). Residents of the western part of the country, including BC, were least likely to choose Indigenous governments as appropriate actors – although the majority still choose very appropriate or appropriate. Opposition was also the greatest in those regions – 10 per cent of respondents in BC and 11 per cent in the West said Indigenous governments are very inappropriate. Given our research design, it is difficult to interpret these results. The survey was not designed to examine the Indigenous governance or support for Indigenous Protected Conservation Areas or Indigenous-led conservation. Moreover, through its sampling strategy, Dynata targets the majority view. While we did oversample rural areas, we did not target areas that have successful Indigenous-led wildlife management.

Influential Actors

Designating protected areas to achieve conservation goals is an increasingly hot-button issue across the globe. Through the UN CBD and the Aichi Biodiversity Targets, the Canadian federal government committed to protecting, by 2020, at least 17 per cent of the terrestrial area of the country and 10 per cent of the coastal and marine area. Failing to reach that goal, the prime minister has recommitted Canada to 25 per cent by 2025 and set a goal of 30 per cent by 2030. Of course, this is a difficult target for the federal government because they do not control or own 30 per cent of the land in Canada. They will require help from the provinces and potentially private individuals. Looking at our survey results, we see that Canadians think provinces should be influential when it comes to making decisions about protected areas, followed closely by the federal government. We see this result play out across all regions, except in Quebec where more respondents choose the federal government as most influential over provinces. In order to successfully reach the modified land protection goals set forth by the prime minister, it will likely be most effective to have provincial leadership on land protection to build public support, even if the federal government is playing a strong role behind the scenes.

Given a variety of possible actors, our respondents felt the federal government should be most influential on decisions about wildlife populations, with 36 per cent of respondents choosing that actor. Twenty-seven percent thought the provincial government should be most influential. In reality, it is an independent federal body of scientists, COSEWIC, that assesses all flora and fauna in Canada and then recommends a status to the Minister of Environment and Climate Change Canada to consider in decisions about listing under the SARA. However, only 15 per cent of our respondents felt that scientists should be most influential in making decisions about wildlife. It is difficult to interpret this result. On the surface, it would suggest that 85 per cent think that decisions about designation of threatened or endangered species should be a political decision. It could also suggest that respondents think the provincial and federal government scientists already working on these issues could be supported by academics or researchers outside of government. The relatively high rate of support for scientists (15%) stands out compared to other non-federal and provincial actors, and support for the role of scientists in other contexts.

The split between a preference for provinces making decisions about protected areas and a preference for the federal government making decisions about the status of wildlife populations is interesting. First, it shows support for the status quo – since this is largely what happens on the ground in Canada. Second, it demonstrates support for a division of powers and federalism. Third, it suggests that Canadians want both levels of government to be involved in the protection of species at risk in Canada. In their nation-wide survey on species at risk in Canada, McCune et al. (2017) found that most respondents (60%) agreed that the federal government should have *primary* responsibility for preventing the extinction of plants and animals in Canada. This was followed by environmental non-government organizations (13%), provincial government (10%), individuals or landowners (7%), municipal government (3%), and private business (less than 1%). While we did not ask the same question, it is difficult to argue that our respondents would agree that the federal government should hold a primary responsibility, especially given that almost 40 per cent think the province should be most influential in protected areas and almost a quarter think the province should be most influential in wildlife population status decisions. Our data indicate that shared responsibility for these actions would likely build public support.

Most Canadians prefer provincial leadership on hunting regulations, with a majority of respondents choosing the provincial government as the most appropriate actor and fewer than 1 in 5 choosing the federal government.

In the East, just over 60 per cent of respondents selected the provincial government. In reality, the federal government regulates hunting in parks and other federally protected areas and is also responsible for regulating hunting in regard to any protected animals and species at risk. The provinces and territories set their own regulations for hunting all other animals (game and fish). This might include selling hunting licences, setting hunting seasons, issuing firearm regulations, and setting harvest quotas. Our respondents suggest there is support for this form of provincial regulation of hunting.

Last, in terms of providing incentives to encourage people to take action to benefit wildlife, there was a split between the federal and provincial government as the most influential actor, with 40 per cent choosing the former and 30 per cent choosing the latter. In 2018, the federal government announced that it would invest $1.3 billion in wildlife and nature programs (Government of Canada 2018). The money is earmarked for a variety of critical issues like species-at-risk, protected areas, and Indigenous conservation. In addition, the federal government has numerous environmental funding programs that include wildlife (Government of Canada, n.d.). The provinces, however, also administer numerous programs that fund wildlife protection. Thus, a split between those two levels of governments, with over 70 per cent choosing one of those two governments, in our survey results is not surprising.

Conclusion

Biodiversity loss is occurring globally and across Canada. The current wildlife management governance system in Canada is failing to protect wildlife and reverse declines. Many ecosystems are vulnerable, especially in the south, and species at risk are declining across the country (WWF Canada 2020). Natural resource extraction is occurring in over half of the areas that provide key ecosystem services (Mitchell et al. 2021) and demands for agricultural and forestry are only growing. Canada is struggling to protect habitat and is failing to connect existing protected areas in most of the country (Lemieux et al. 2021). This is particularly alarming because "Canada's land-protection policies are of particularly high global relevance" (Coristine et al. 2019, 1220, see also Lamb et al. 2018) given that Canada has the most wilderness of any nation. If Canada cannot adequately protect wildlife and habitat, the consequences will be devastating at the global level.

The status quo – shared responsibility between the federal and provincial governments – is not working. The fact that Canadians by and large support this system is troubling and could be a real barrier to transformative change. As noted in the introduction to this volume, the IPBES 2019 report makes clear that global declines in biodiversity can only be addressed through transformative change. This will necessitate a "system-wide reorganization of our sense of reality and associated paradigms, goals, and values across economic, social, political, and technological sectors" (Lemieux et al. 2021, 2021b). Our chapter suggests that Canadians might not be ready or prepared for a change that will disrupt the federal and provincial co-management of wildlife issues. Going forward, Canada will need to explore different and more innovative governance schema. Of course, we don't know if changing governance will help or if it will be enough. However, we do know that our current arrangement is failing.

APPENDIX

Survey Questions

Please share how much you agree with the following statements related to the ability of government to make good decisions about how wildlife and their habitats are managed. For each item, please check one box.

Actions taken by government to ensure that wildlife populations are healthy ...	Strongly agree	Somewhat agree	Neither agree, nor disagree	Somewhat disagree	Strongly disagree	Not sure
are guided by clear goals and aims.						
are coordinated with other responsible organizations.						
are backed by the necessary funding to be successful.						
are backed by reliable information.						
consider input from residents and affected people.						
are made by individuals who can be held responsible for the outcomes.						

(Continued)

Actions taken by government to ensure that wildlife populations are healthy …	Strongly agree	Somewhat agree	Neither agree, nor disagree	Somewhat disagree	Strongly disagree	Not sure
use resources efficiently to maximize benefits for wildlife.						
are evaluated to determine if goals were achieved.						
are based on long term planning and foresight.						
are adapted when necessary.						
use new approaches to solve problems when appropriate.						
respond to the needs of local people.						

How appropriate do you feel it is for the following groups to regulate wildlife populations and habitats?

	Very appropriate	Somewhat appropriate	Neither appropriate, nor inappropriate	Somewhat inappropriate	Very inappropriate	Not sure
Federal government						
provincial government						
Local/ Municipal government						
Indigenous government						

In your mind, which of the following groups do you feel *should be most influential* in making decisions about

- establishing new parks and protected areas for the benefit of wildlife?
- how and when legal hunting can occur?
- the status of specific wildlife populations (such as listing species as threatened or endangered, or allowing hunting)?
- providing financial incentives to encourage people to take actions that benefit wildlife?

(Please check one.)

Federal government
State/provincial government
Local/municipal government
Tribal governments
NGO
Individuals
Private businesses
Scientists
Other (Please indicate. _____)
I am not sure

NOTES

1 UNDRIP Article 24, Section 1: "Indigenous Peoples have the right to their traditional medicines and to maintain their healthy practices, including the conservation of their vital medicinal plants, animals, and minerals. Indigenous individuals also have the right to access, without any discrimination, to all social and health services."
   UNDRIP Article 32, Section 1: "Indigenous Peoples have the right to determine and develop priorities and strategies for the development or use of their lands or territories and other resources." UNDRIP Article 18, Section 1: "Indigenous Peoples have the right to participate in decision-making in matters which would affect their rights, through representatives chosen by themselves in accordance with their procedures, as well as to maintain and develop their own Indigenous decision-making institutions."
2 Supported by the Liber Ero Foundation; Environment Climate Change Canada (Project # GCXE20S018); Wildlife Conservation Society; Wilburforce Foundation.
3 These scores are the means and modes taken across the items in the survey question for each respondent; the grand mean/mode is across all respondents. See the appendix for a list of the nine survey questions used to compile the means and modes.

Factor analysis revealed that all components of governance quality loaded onto a single factor – that is, the pattern in responses was consistent across all factors in predicting overall perceptions of quality. This justifies using an overall mean as a representation of these responses at the individual level.

WORKS CITED

Angus Reid. 2021. "Time for a Change in Canadian Politics?" https://angusreid.org/federal-politics-conservative-leadership

Artelle, Kyle A., Melanie Zurba, Jonaki Bhattacharyya, Diana E Chan, Kelly Brown, Jess Housty, and Faisal Moola. 2019. "Supporting Resurgent Indigenous-Led Governance: A Nascent Mechanism for Just and Effective Conservation." *Biological Conservation* 240. https://doi.org/10.1016/j.biocon.2019.108284

Besco, Randy, Andrea Olive, and Emily Eaton. 2021. "Public Opinion and Energy Politics in the Saskatchewan and North Dakota." *The Extractive Industries and Society* 8, no. 2: 100890.

CBD. "Strategic Plan for Biodiversity 2011–2020 and the Aichi Targets." In *Report of the Tenth Meeting of the Conference of the Parties to the Convention on Biological Diversity*. 2010.

CESCC (Canadian Endangered Species Conservation Council). 2016. "Wild Species 2015: The General Status of Species in Canada." National General Status Working Group. https://www.registrelep-sararegistry.gc.ca/virtual_sara/files/reports/Wild%20Species%202015.pdf

Coristine, Laura E., Sheila Colla, Nathan Bennett, Anja M. Carlsson, Christina Davy, Kimberley T.A. Davies, Brett Favaro et al. 2019. "National Contributions to Global Ecosystem Values." *Conservation Biology* 33, no. 5 (2019): 1219–23.

ECCC (Environment and Climate Change Canada). 2020. "Canada Joins the High Ambition Coalition for Nature and People." https://www.newswire.ca/news-releases/canada-joins-the-high-ambition-coalition-for-nature-and-people-847311784.html

Ecojustice. 2012. "Failure to Protect: Grading Canada's Species at Risk Laws." https://www.ecojustice.ca/wp-content/uploads/2014/08/Failure-to-protect_Grading-Canadas-Species-at-Risk-Laws.pdf

Environics Institute for Survey Research. 2020. "Survey of Canada, Report 2: The Division of Power and Resourses." PDF available at https://www.environicsinstitute.org/docs/default-source/default-document-library/confederation-survey-2020-2-final-aug-14.pdf?sfvrsn=c7674fd1_0

Enns, A., D. Kraus, and A. Hebb. 2020. *Ours to Save: The Distribution, Status and Conservation Needs of Canada's Endemic Species.* NatureServe Canada & Nature Conservancy of Canada.

Federal, Provincial, and Territorial Governments of Canada. 2014. *2012 Canadian Nature Survey: Awareness, Participation, and Expenditures in Nature-Based Recreation, Conservation, and Subsistence Activities.* Ottawa, ON: Canadian Councils of Resource Ministers.

Government of Canada. 2018. "Government of Canada Puts $175 Million into Projects That Protect Nature. https://www.canada.ca/en/environment-climate-change/news/2018/12/government-of-canada-puts-175-million-toward-projects-that-protect-nature.html

Government of Canada. (n.d.) "Environmental Funding Programs." https://www.canada.ca/en/environment-climate-change/services/environmental-funding/programs.html

Harshaw, H.W. 2008. *British Columbia Species at Risk Public Opinion Survey 2008: Final Technical Report*. Vancouver, BC: University of British Columbia Collaborative for Advanced Landscape Planning.

Indigenous Circle of Experts. 2018. "We Rise Together: Achieving Pathway to Target 1 through the Creation of Indigenous Protected and Conserved Areas in the Spirit and Practice of Reconciliation." https://static1.squarespace.com/static/57e007452e69cf9a7af0a033/t/5ab94aca6d2a7338ecb1d05e/1522092766605/PA234-ICE_Report_2018_Mar_22_web.pdf

IPBES. 2019. *Global Assessment Report of the Intergovernmental Science-Policy Platform on Biodiversity and Ecosystem Services*, edited by S. Díaz, J. Settele, E. Brondízio and H.T. Ngo. Bonn, Germany: IPBES Secretariat. https://doi.org/10.5281/zenodo.3553579

Ipsos Reid. 2012. "Three In Five Canadians (62%) Say the Federal Government Is Doing Too Little to Protect Species at Risk." December 12, 2012 (updated: September 3, 2020). https://ecojustice.ca/pressrelease/3-in-5-canadians-say-federal-government-doing-too-little-to-protect-endangered-species/

Jonas, Sabrina. 2022. "Ottawa Threatens to Use Species at Risk Act to Protect Quebec Caribou." CBC. Accessed May 28, 2022. https://www.cbc.ca/news/canada/montreal/ottawa-intervene-caribou-protection-1.6416835

Jung, Thomas S., Julie P. Thomas, Frank Thomas, Ron Chambers, Douglas A. Clark, Saleem Dar, Darcy Doran-Myers, et al. 2018. "Results of a Public Survey about Grizzly Bears (*Ursus arctos*) and Their Management in Yukon, Canada." *Yukon Fish and Wildlife Branch Report MR-18-01. Whitehorse, Yukon, Canada* (2018).

Lamb, Clayton T., Marco Festa-Bianchet, and Mark S. Boyce. 2018. "Invest Long Term in Canada's Wilderness." *Science* 359.6379: 1002.

Lemieux, Christopher J., Aerin L. Jacob, and Paul A. Gray. 2021a. 'Implementing Connectivity Conservation in Canada." Canadian Council on Ecological Areas (CCEA) Occasional Paper No. 22. Canadian Council on Ecological Areas. Waterloo, Ontario: Wilfrid Laurier University.

Lemieux, C., D. MacKinnon, D. Kraus, K. Beazley, A. Jacob, P. Gray. 2021b. "(Re) Connecting Canada: Setting the Table for Transformation." In *Implementing Connectivity Conservation in Canada*, edited by C.J. Lemieux, A.L. Jacob, and P.A. Gray: 201–7. Canadian Council on Ecological Areas (CCEA) Occasional Paper No. 22. Canadian Council on Ecological Areas. Waterloo, Ontario: Wilfrid Laurier University.

McCune, Jenny L., Sheila R. Colla, Laura E. Coristine, Christina M. Davy, D.T. Tyler Flockhart, Richard Schuster, and Diane M. Orihel. 2019. "Are We Accurately Estimating the Potential Role of Pollution in the Decline of Species at Risk in Canada?" *FACETS* 4, no. 1 (2019): 598–614. https://doi.org/10.1139/facets-2019-0025

McFarlane, Bonita Lynn, David Oliver T. Watson, and R.C.G. Stumpf-Allen. 2007. *Public Perceptions of Conservation of Grizzly Bears in the Foothills Model Forest: A Survey of Local and Edmonton Residents*. Vol. 413. Canadian Forest Service, Northern Forestry Centre.

Mildenberger, Matto, Peter Howe, Erick Lachapelle, Leah Stokes, Jennifer Marlon, and Timothy Gravelle. 2016. "The Distribution of Climate Change Public Opinion in Canada." *PloS one* 11, no. 8 (2016): e0159774.

Mitchell, Matthew G.E., Richard Schuster, Aerin L. Jacob, Dalal E.L. Hanna, Camille Ouellet Dallaire, Ciara Raudsepp-Hearne, Elena M. Bennett, Bernhard Lehner, and Kai M.A. Chan. 2021. "Identifying Key Ecosystem Service Providing Areas to Inform National-Scale Conservation Planning." *Environmental Research Letters* 16, no. 1 (2021): 014038.

NWWG (National Wetlands Working Group). 1997. *The Canadian Wetland Classification System*, 2nd ed., edited by B.G. Warner and C.D.A. Rubec. Wetlands Research Centre, Waterloo, ON: University of Waterloo. https://www.gret-perg .ulaval.ca/fileadmin/fichiers/fichiersGRET/pdf/Doc_generale/Wetlands.pdf

Ray, Justina C., Jaime Grimm, and Andrea Olive. 2021. "The Biodiversity Crisis in Canada: Failures and Challenges of Federal and Sub-National Strategic and Legal Frameworks." *FACETS* 6 (1) : 1044–68.

Statistics Canada. "Factors Associated with Voting." https://www150.statcan.gc.ca/n1 /pub/75-001-x/2012001/article/11629-eng.htm#a2

Thornton, Clarisse, and Michael S. Quinn. 2009. "Coexisting with Cougars: Public Perceptions, Attitudes, and Awareness of Cougars on the Urban-Rural Fringe of Calgary, Alberta, Canada." *Human-Wildlife Conflicts* 3, no. 2: 282–95.

Tindal, C. Richard, and Susan Nobes Tindal. 2017. *Local Government in Canada*, 5th ed. Toronto: Nelson Thomson Learning.

WWF Canada. 2020. *Living Planet Report Canada: Wildlife at Risk*, edited by J. Currie, J. Snider, and E. Giles. WWF Canada. Toronto, Canada.

4 In a Rut: Barriers to Caribou Recovery

JULEE BOAN AND RACHEL PLOTKIN

The global biodiversity crisis will severely affect ecosystem services that are key to human survival. It also threatens the inherent value of living beings, particularly those in spaces not dominated by human industries and modern-day infrastructure, regardless of their benefits to humans. From 1970 to 2014, about half of 903 monitored wildlife species in Canada declined (World Wildlife Fund Canada 2017). The Government of Canada has responded nationally with commitments under the Species at Risk Act (2002), and internationally as a party to the UN Convention on Biological Diversity. Provinces and territories have made conservation commitments under the Accord for the Protection of Species at Risk. As outlined below, it has been easier for federal, provincial, and territorial governments to make promises than to uphold them.

Twenty percent of the approximately 30,000 species in Canada (for which there is sufficient information) are imperiled to some degree (Canadian Endangered Species Conservation Council 2016). Of the almost 800 wildlife species that are at risk of extirpation (local extinction) and extinction in Canada (Committee on the Status of Endangered Wildlife in Canada 2020), one of the most iconic is the boreal caribou (*Rangifer tarandus caribou*). Although only one species of caribou exists globally, differences in habitat use, behaviour, and migration patterns have resulted in the identification of Designatable Units (Festa-Bianchet et al. 2011; Committee on the Status of Endangered Wildlife in Canada 2011). Canada has 12 Designatable Units (DU), including boreal caribou in the boreal forest from British Columbia and the Northwest Territories and across northern forests to Labrador (known as DU6). Boreal caribou throughout Canada is one of the ecotypes experiencing range loss and, in some cases, precipitous declines (Schaefer 2003; Venier et al. 2014). Of the 51 existing populations, only 15 are considered self-sustaining – that is, likely to persist without human intervention (Environment and Climate Change Canada 2020).

In 2011, the government of Canada completed a meta-analysis to examine the relative contribution of various pressures on boreal caribou populations. The results showed a significant relationship between levels of cumulative disturbance in a caribou range – the combination of roads, clearcuts, seismic lines, forest fires, and other developments – and calf survival (Environment Canada 2011). Multiple regional studies have also linked caribou declines to the cumulative disturbance that results from increases in linear features and fragments habitat (e.g., Mumma et al. 2018; Rudolph et al. 2017; Stewart et al. 2020; Winder et al. 2020; Fryxell et al. 2020). Recently, Johnson et al. (2020) stated that their "nation-wide analysis, representing the full spectrum of regional variation in environmental conditions across the distribution of boreal caribou in Canada, re-affirms that anthropogenic disturbances are *the primary agent* contributing to boreal caribou declines across Canada" (1323, emphasis added).

Many species are not well researched, as it is costly to compile the multiple years of data collection that are often required to understand habitat use and population viability. In addition, wildlife surveys to support monitoring of population health are also expensive, and species under study can be elusive and difficult to accurately track. However, boreal caribou are one of the most well-studied species in Canada, and a sufficient level of scientific knowledge exists to guide management decisions using a risk-based approach. In 2012, the federal recovery strategy for boreal caribou directed provinces to maintain or restore each caribou range such that a minimum of 65 per cent is undisturbed as part of critical habitat protection. This disturbance threshold is expected to result in a minimum 60 per cent probability of caribou persistence (Environment Canada 2012) and was based on an empirical relationship between disturbance and calf recruitment (Environment Canada 2011). The disturbance threshold is, however, a social determination that reflects the level of risk Environment Canada has deemed acceptable and, based on the studies of population responses to habitat disturbances completed to date, still maintains a risk of 40 per cent probability that caribou will not persist.

Across Canada, despite the science, caribou continue to decline, and several boreal caribou populations are on the brink of extirpation, such as the V'al Dor herd in Québec and the Little Smoky herd in Alberta. The Lake Superior caribou population in Ontario, which was isolated from the mainland boreal caribou population many decades ago, is now almost completely lost from the shores of Lake Superior.

In some cases, in British Columbia and Alberta, boreal caribou continue to survive only because of significant human interventions, including killing predators and alternate prey that support predators and putting fences around caribou to reduce the risk of predation (Johnson et al. 2020). Some penning operations enclose calves and then release them when their chances of survival are higher (i.e., they are considered fast enough to have a chance to escape predators), while others permanently keep female caribou enclosed. Although these measures can slow rates of caribou decline, they have not succeeded in advancing caribou recovery (Hervieux et al. 2014), which can be defined as moving populations towards becoming self-sustaining. "Self-sustaining" is defined by Environment Canada as "a stable or increasing population that was large enough to persist without human intervention" (Environment Canada 2011). Caribou recovery requires simultaneous, integrated habitat protection and restoration.

In this chapter, we consider the conservation of boreal caribou and their habitat, with a focus on Ontario, as an illustration of the barriers that caribou and other wildlife face across Canada. We are both settlers who have worked for two decades on caribou habitat conservation in Ontario for our respective environmental non-governmental organizations – the David Suzuki Foundation and Natural Resources Defense Council (and previously Ontario Nature). These experiences have included, between us, completing a PhD in forest sciences, publishing peer-reviewed papers on post-logging caribou habitat restoration, serving on advisory committees to the federal and Ontario governments, reviewing draft recovery strategies, conducting aerial surveys of caribou, working cooperatively with the forestry sector to develop plans to support economic development and caribou habitat conservation (e.g., through standard development for Forest Stewardship Council certification in Canada), engaging in dialogue with Indigenous communities on their approaches to caribou conservation, reviewing and providing input into legislation and policy affecting boreal caribou, and delivering dozens of public presentations on caribou decline and the need for critical habitat protection and restoration. Our efforts, and the efforts of others working to support caribou recovery, have had varying degrees of impact. We have had some success in working with policy-makers to develop strong habitat protection legislation but have found most governments lacking the political will required to apply any significant restrictions on development, despite overall public support for environmental protection. Our meetings with communities across northern Ontario have been valuable, but we lack the lobbying resources of our economic counterparts, who have so far been successful in dominating caribou narratives that inflate claims of job loss, dismiss scientific consensus, and/or overstate the effectiveness of their mitigation measures.

Evidence shows that boreal caribou can serve as a focal or "umbrella" species (Bichet et al. 2016; Drever et al. 2019). The key driver of caribou decline, habitat fragmentation, also negatively affects many other species at risk. Thus, if provinces and territories can manage the boreal forest (the vast majority of which is public/Indigenous homelands) for caribou survival and recovery, these management approaches should benefit other wildlife that rely on un-fragmented older, conifer forests, too.

Caribou conservation efforts can also help achieve other biodiversity and environmental goals (Drever et al. 2019). For example, setting aside large tracts of boreal forests from industrial development to achieve caribou conservation can deliver on Canada's international protected areas commitments (e.g., Convention on Biological Diversity) and potentially on its climate obligations and nature-based climate solutions (e.g., United Nations 2015; Yona et al. 2019).

Despite growing agreement among caribou experts about how forest management should be undertaken to sustain boreal caribou and their recovery (e.g., through limiting cumulative disturbance within caribou population ranges), significant barriers exist to implementing these strategies. We consider four such barriers: (1) ideologies of development and growth without limits, (2) government inaction, (3) lack of local support (exacerbated by misinformation campaigns), and (4) inadequate implementation of strategies to address cumulative effects.

Ideologies of Development and Growth without Limits

Canada uses natural resources faster than the environment can regenerate them (Earth Overshoot Day 2020). This reflects a widely held and misguided notion that the planet can support ever-expanding resource extraction in perpetuity. In North America (and elsewhere), the benefits of continual economic growth are accepted as self-evident and are for the most part unexamined in mainstream discourse.

The idea of economic growth through "sustainable development" was first widely articulated in 1987 in *Our Common Future*, also known as the "United Nations Brundtland Report" (World Commission on Environment and Development). The report defines sustainable development as "development that meets the needs of the present without compromising the ability of future generations to meet their own needs" (16). It posits that the only truly sustainable form of progress is that which simultaneously addresses the interlinked pillars of the economy, environment, and social well-being.

Yet the term "sustainable development" has become increasingly dominated by vague or biased definitions. As a result, many interests promote the term as a "vehicle to perpetuate many and varied corporate and institutional interests whilst giving the impression of adherence to, and observance of, environmentally-sound principles" (Johnston et al. 2007). While the adoption of UN sustainable development goals was a significant step in embedding environmental objectives into the collective understanding of sustainability, the notion that sustainable development can be achieved alongside the prioritization of economic growth and increasing resource use remains entrenched.

Under this predominant framework, the term "sustainable" has been co-opted to focus primarily on job creation and retention, the so-called third pillar in the sustainability stool, while environmental and social needs are often simplified, considered secondary, or essentially disregarded altogether. In resource-extraction planning, it has become accepted that negative environmental impacts will occur and need only to be mitigated and that the social pillar is represented primarily by jobs created in industrial development sectors. In the measurement of social and economic benefits, healthy ecosystems are rarely if ever understood as the foundations of vibrant societies and strong economies. Rather, the dominant societal narrative often places wildlife protection in direct conflict with economic growth and wealth accumulation. Frequently, significant public resistance arises when actions are taken to establish limits to industrial or other development expansions, usually due to fear of job loss, even when scientific evidence has shown that much of our consumption is wasteful, unnecessary, and does not meaningfully contribute to our quality of life, and studies have determined that a significant portion of recent job losses in the forestry industry can be attributed to global markets and mechanization (Capeluck and Thomas 2015). Further, the growth-focused economic model does not address the unequal distribution of resources and wealth in our society. The need for economic growth is often portrayed simplistically, and profit maximization tends to be at the foundation of land-use decisions (M'Gonigle and Takeda 2012; Bond et al. 2020).

Environmental impacts such as biodiversity loss are underestimated and rarely, if ever, accounted for. Nor do growth-focused models describe the complex layers of social impacts that occur from the boom-and-bust cycles that often accompany industrial projects, or the social values of unfragmented forests such as climate change adaptation, spiritual, recreation, and mental health support (e.g., Baker and Spracklen 2019; Watson et al. 2018; Gillespie et al. 2018; Karjalainen et al. 2010).

As an example of this approach, the Ontario Forest Sector Strategy published in 2020 (Province of Ontario 2020) emphasized a simple "growth is good" perspective; it proposes to vastly increase the amount of logging in the province without any acknowledgment of the potential impacts that increased logging will have on biodiversity.

The primacy of economic objectives is also demonstrated through protected areas management, in which protection of ecological integrity is supposed to be prioritized. Even in the renowned Jasper National Park, a mountain caribou herd recently became extirpated and two more are on the brink of extirpation. As Edward Struzik, a Fellow at Queen's Institute for Energy and Environmental Policy, notes, "science-based conservation programs in the mountain parks have long been pitted against tourism" (Struzik 2020). In 2020, conservationists expressed concerns that managers were failing to set appropriate limits to human use and access by continuing to allow recreational activities in prime caribou habitat in Jasper National Park (Alberta Wilderness Association 2020).

This sense of the limitless bounty of nature can be traced back to the frontier mindset of colonialists in Canada. The country was established on the false belief that the land was *terra nullius*, "nobody's land," and that it was wide open for exploitation. Its large size, with an abundance of water and vast tracts of forest, has given rise to the perspective that significant negative ecological impacts are unlikely and can always be mitigated.

On the rare occasions when decision-making authorities have attempted to impose limits to development or extraction activities to protect species at risk and their habitat, economic stakeholders who believe their interests may be negatively affected often challenge protection measures (Boan et al. 2018). In several instances, the challenges reflect the fact that while boundless growth of the human footprint is generally embraced without constraint, perspectives calling for the prioritization of wildlife are only seen as valid when a handful of individual animals remain.

For example, in 2016, the federal government intervened in Quebec to protect a small area of threatened habitat (totalling approximately 2 km^2) for the western chorus frog. It had disappeared from 90 per cent of its range in the province and there were concerns for its survival over the next 10 to 25 years. In response to federal habitat protection measures, the developer sued the federal government, arguing that, among other things, because the frog existed elsewhere it did not require protection at that location (The Maison Candiac Group Inc. c. Canada (Attorney General) 2020). Similarly, in 2018, after 12 right whales were killed over one summer, the Environmental Commissioner of Canada remarked that the government did not implement recovery measures for the highly imperiled species until the whales were on the verge of extinction (Office of the Auditor General of Canada 2018.)

In Alberta, recent research (Stewart et al. 2020) has revealed that to sustain boreal woodland caribou populations, forest management practices need to change. The authors recommended that "harvest rates should not exceed the historical fire regime of these Alberta populations, 0.9% annually, or a harvest rotation of roughly 110 years" (Stewart et al. 2020, 1442).

Yet this proposed shift in rotation age – in keeping with the concept of a circular economy where natural resources are extracted at rates that do not upend or disrupt pre-industrial, natural cycles (Raworth 2017) – is unlikely to ever be adopted by industrial forestry, which views older trees past their prime economic value as "decadent" (Forest Service British Columbia, 1994). Even for the Little Smoky caribou herd in Alberta, where resource extraction activities have disturbed over 96 per cent of the range, protection measures for remaining habitat have still been contested when they are proposed, and energy lease holders continue to expand fragmentation (Weber 2014).

Government Inaction

In Canada, two orders of government have legislative powers: the federal government and 13 provincial and territorial governments. Provinces and territories have constitutional rights to manage their own non-renewable resources, forestry resources, and electrical energy. Both jurisdictions have responsibilities for species at risk, such as boreal woodland caribou. In addition to the federal and provincial/territorial division of responsibilities, departments, agencies, and ministries within these jurisdictions each have unique responsibilities.

Each province and territory is responsible for managing the wildlife within it on behalf of its citizens, and provinces are also responsible for overseeing the allocation of permits and tenures for industrial resource-extraction activities. In 1996, each province made a commitment under the Accord for the Protection of Species at Risk to "establish complementary legislation and programs that provide for effective protection of species at risk throughout Canada, that will … provide protection for the habitat of threatened or endangered species" (Government of Canada 1996).

However, as provinces and territories also tax industrial activities, this can (and often does) task departments with, at best, contradictory mandates – to recover wildlife and grow industrial activity – and, at worst, conflicts of interest. Only a few provinces have fulfilled their commitment to develop species-at-risk legislation. At the time of writing, six of 13 provinces and territories have no specific laws devoted to species-at-risk conservation. Those with laws have received poor implementation grades on evaluation (Ecojustice 2012; Ray et. al, 2021).

For example, Ontario's Endangered Species Act, once celebrated as a gold standard, has been significantly weakened by a series of amendments that exempt industry from complying. In late 2020, the forestry industry was granted a permanent exemption from the act's prohibitions against habitat destruction (Bergman et al. 2020; McIntosh 2020).

The federal Species at Risk Act, brought into force in 2002, applies directly to land and waters within federal jurisdiction. It mandates the completion of recovery strategies that identify a species' critical habitat – habitat required for survival and recovery. The federal recovery strategy for boreal woodland caribou, released in 2012, directed provinces to develop range plans within five years that limit the total amount of disturbance in each caribou range and, where the limit had been surpassed, plan for restoration (Environment Canada 2012). Yet, ten years later, no range plans have been finalized and implemented anywhere in Canada.

The federal government has the power to intervene in provincial jurisdiction under the Species at Risk Act to protect endangered species if the minister of environment and climate change determines that a province is not "effectively protecting" the habitat of an at-risk species (Section 61) or if a species faces an imminent threat to its survival (section 80, referred to as an "emergency order"), but it rarely does so.

The minister has intervened only three times for terrestrial species under these provisions, and only after being petitioned to do so by non-governmental conservation organizations – for the sage grouse in Saskatchewan and Alberta and twice for the western chorus frog in Quebec. Cabinet received a ministerial recommendation for a habitat protection order for boreal caribou in Alberta in October 2020, but the minister of environment and climate change then negotiated with the province to sign a voluntary conservation agreement that framed federal intervention as unnecessary. The conservation agreement outlined processes for range plan completion but failed to provide interim habitat protection measures to anchor caribou survival during planning.

When provinces and territories report on caribou and caribou habitat protection efforts to comply with federal requirements under the SARA, pages are filled with descriptions of existing provincial laws, policies, and initiatives that could be used to protect wildlife (Environment Canada 2018), but these are not accompanied by discussions or analysis of how well, if at all, the policies are being implemented. Enforcement is not addressed.

In Ontario, a Caribou Conservation Plan was published in 2009. The plan included an "insurance policy" to recognize that new information could require adaptation. It stated that before new logging areas are accessed, certain conditioned need to be met, based on a range level assessment of caribou presence, population size, and demographic trends. It is necessary to show that both a sufficient amount and arrangement of currently suitable habitat exists, and there needs to be evidence that the local caribou population is viable (i.e., not declining. In 2011, the Ministry of Natural Resources and Forestry completed assessments of all boreal caribou populations within the managed forest and documented them in integrated range assessment reports for each range. Most populations exhibited declining trends. Despite the restrictions that should have been required on industrial logging "until it [could] be demonstrated that there is sufficient habitat, successful habitat renewal, and a persistent caribou population" (Ontario Ministry of Natural Resources 2009, 11), new areas were, and continue to be, logged.

In fact, Ontario has moved in the opposite direction: rather than implementing the insurance policy, it has doubled down on increasing the amount of wood logged. When Ontario released its 2020 *Forest Sector Strategy*, it acknowledged that due to economic factors over the past decade, the forestry sector had only been logging about half of its allowable cut. It stated that "the current volume of timber harvested is less than 60% of what it was in 2000" (Province of Ontario 2020, 5). Instead of viewing this new reality as an opportunity to address high disturbance levels in many boreal caribou ranges by conserving habitat for caribou, the province announced that it would endeavour to almost double industrial logging in Ontario over the next 10 years by striving to reach the maximum cut (30 million cubic metres per year) by 2030.

The plan was met with vocal public opposition. Environmental non-governmental organizations, scientists, and non-timber forest users, such as tourism operators, were excluded from the face-to-face consultation sessions, which were by invitation only. The Province of Ontario received more than 32,000 form letters through a mail-in campaign, and almost 500 direct comments through the Environmental Registry from the public, Indigenous communities, and municipalities. Of those, 47 per cent were against the Forest Sector Strategy, 23 per cent were neutral and only 30 per cent were in support.

Despite strong evidence that Ontarians have broader values and objectives than a single-minded focus on the potential for economic growth and that many do not view environmental safeguards as obstacles, the province proceeded with approval for its Forest Sector Strategy, a key component of which is to remove perceived barriers to accessing wood.

Deregulation initiatives are often accompanied by shifts in inspection, monitoring, and enforcement measures. In recent years, provincial governments have increasingly devolved these tasks to industry, resulting in increased levels of industry self-regulation. For example, the Ontario environmental commissioner notes that under the suite of exemptions granted to the industry from prohibitions in the Endangered Species Act, monitoring and evaluation of compliance "is largely based on self-assessment" (Environmental Commissioner of Ontario 2017).

In BC, over the past decade the "government embarked on a major law reform initiative to reduce the 'regulatory burden' on industries, reduce the size of the civil service and its role in resource management governance, and thereby increase our collective dependence upon professionals employed by industry proponents to meet the public interest in natural resource management and environmental protection" (Haddock 2015).

Moreover, this trend has changed the degree to which information about species at risk protection is publicly available. For example, in Ontario, the environmental commissioner noted:

> The MNRF [Ministry of Natural Resources and Forestry] now has no intention of publicly sharing information on registered activities under the ESA. Instead, the MNRF informed the ECO that members of the public can only obtain such

information by submitting a freedom of information request under the Freedom of Information and Protection of Privacy Act. (Environmental Commissioner of Ontario 2017, 242)

In British Columbia, an academic review of the province's trend towards industrial self-regulation stated:

> When independent professionals are delegated various roles and functions formerly undertaken by the government, important issues relating to record keeping, public disclosure and transparency inevitably arise. When the functions reside in government, these issues are governed by laws governing public records, such as the Document Disposal Act, Freedom of Information and Protection of Privacy Act, and by government's Operational Records Classification System policies. Government has legal duties regarding the retention and disposal of records, and the provision of public access to those records. However, when the relevant information is held by independent professionals outside of government, those rules do not apply unless there is a legal duty to provide the documents to the government and they become government records. (Haddock 2015, 54)

The impacts of provincial inaction and devolvement of responsibilities to industry have been clear: in 2017, the federal Report on the Progress of Recovery Strategy Implementation for the Woodland Caribou concluded, "while boreal caribou continue to occur in all 51 ranges identified in the 2012 Recovery Strategy, habitat condition in the majority of ranges has worsened since 2012. Moreover, the boreal caribou population as a whole has continued to decline" (Environment Canada 2017, vi). The divide between federal and provincial/territorial jurisdiction, the move away from direct provincial oversight and enforcement, and the ensuing pivot away from public reporting have all played a role in advancing boreal caribou decline across Canada.

Lack of Local Support

The success of wildlife habitat conservation is often assumed to be predicated on local support for conservation initiatives and, in particular, on the perspectives of local people regarding potential impacts on their livelihoods. Brockington (2004) refers to this as the "principle of local support," (411) which asserts that the long-term effectiveness of land protection requires local people – the people most likely affected by these decisions – to support decisions or at least not declare strong opposition. Consequences of lack of support for wildlife conservation initiatives can include local protests, resistance by local politicians to support conservation plans, and, in the most extreme cases, intentional killing of species and/or destruction of remaining habitat (Lueck and Michael 2003).

A lack of local support is influenced by several factors, real and perceived. In some instances, industrial interests have scripted narratives for local leaders, often based on "cherry-picking" facts to promote their own interests (Boan et al. 2018). Misinformation campaigns have proliferated over the past decade.

Throughout society, specific groups of people have lost confidence in science. In many cases, this is because the uncertainty found in science is not well understood. The fact that science "inevitably entails some degree of uncertainty" (Ascher 2004) makes science and scientists particularly vulnerable to misinformation campaigns that can fuel distrust about the role of scientists and their motivations.

When scientific uncertainty is exploited to undermine the scientific evidence on which regulations are built, it can lead to public confusion and greater polarization of views. This "manufactured uncertainty" (Michaels and Monforton 2005) is a significant barrier to implementing public policy to protect wildlife. Instead of helping various interests come to a shared understanding of the problem and pathways to solving it, it gives the impression that such uncertainty outweighs the benefits of moving forward. In this context, "all opinions are equal," and facts are subjective.

There are also examples where local stakeholders and Indigenous Peoples lack trust in the regulators' (federal and provincial) willingness or ability to look out for local interests, and where stakeholders and Indigenous Peoples have been excluded from decision-making. In some cases, representation in decision-making is through industry associations or municipal/council resolutions, instead of local individuals.

For example, in 2019, several First Nations in Ontario launched protests against Ontario's Woodland Caribou Conservation Plan. In the plan's implementation, the Ontario Ministry of Natural Resources and Forestry proposed changes to land use in northwestern Ontario. The plan proposed to connect the near-extirpated Lake Superior caribou population to the mainland herds through large, connected, undisturbed corridors. This could have resulted in forestry road closures and reduced harvesting. Some Indigenous communities along the Lake Superior north shore raised concerns that these decisions would affect their mining and energy interests. Chief Matthew Dupuis of the Red Rock Indian Band accused the province of failing to consult, stating, "we're just being force-fed this new policy" (Ross 2019).

Lastly, in any natural resource extraction sector a significant level of precariousness is associated with a reliance on global commodity markets. Job loss can be cyclical, and when large industrial facilities such as mills or mines close, the impacts can be devastating to small, resource-dependent communities. In addition to reliance on global markets and commodity prices, the forestry sector itself is also undergoing significant changes. "Wood and pulp and paper industries have traditionally been the main vehicle of economic development in Northern Ontario. Globalization, shifting demand, and automation have impacted these industries significantly. Employment in forest-based manufacturing sectors declined significantly between 1991 and 2016" (Northern Policy Institute 2019). Further,

> the substitution of routine tasks by machines has been happening steadily in the logging and forestry sector. The advent of skidders, mechanical harvesting, and remote chipping has modernized bush operations. GIS, telemetry, and satellite imagery have also optimized harvest planning and access development. Remote sensing of harvesters can grade, sort, and scale product in one operation. These technologies have led to a significant reduction in employment in the logging and forestry industry. (Northern Policy Institute 2019, 9)

Job insecurity undoubtedly puts economic and social pressure on forest-dependent communities and explains some of the resistance to implementing conservation strategies that may – whether in reality or perceived as a result of misinformation campaigns – impact local jobs.

> The ongoing process of automation in the forestry sector implies that most of the remaining jobs in these sectors can also be automated. Therefore, the prospects of increasing employment to the levels experienced in the 1980s and 1990s during the future cyclical uptrend is slim. (Northern Policy Institute 2019, 33)

Amid significant lobbying and misinformation campaigns that have convinced community members their livelihoods are at risk due to environmental regulation rather than challenges inherent to the economic development itself, including increasing mechanization, local people are less likely to support the implementation of conservation regulations.

When there is local support for conservation measures that will affect industrial development, it is too often subjected to protracted processes by the provincial government. For example, members of Grassy Narrows First Nation have expressed their opposition to clearcut logging in their territory for over two decades. Yet while the province has stated that it "take[s] the concerns of Grassy Narrows First Nation very seriously," and that the ministry "ensure[s] the views of Grassy Narrows First Nation and other Indigenous communities are considered in all decisions regarding forestry and natural resource management" (Prokopchuk 2018), the province has not formally recognized the Nation's declaration of a Sovereign and Protected Area within its traditional territory, nor has it formally, at the time of writing, amended the Forest Management Unit within which the Nation resides. With the ongoing resolution of land claims and expressions of Aboriginal title, this will hopefully change.

Inadequately Addressing the Impact of Cumulative Effects

Anthropogenic activities, directly and indirectly, impact species and ecosystems and the services they provide to people. The combination of activities results in a variety of outcomes at multiple scales that are difficult to predict because they are often nonlinear in relation to metrics such as habitat loss and fragmentation, and they are not detected due to time lags and insufficient monitoring (e.g., Raiter et al. 2014).

The effects of human activities in the dynamic boreal ecosystem provide a prime example of cumulative impacts at the landscape level. Resource development activities such as industrial logging, oil and gas extraction/distribution, hydroelectric dams, energy transmission projects, and mineral exploration and mining have increased dramatically in the boreal forest over the past 50 years (Brandt et al. 2013; Andrew et al. 2014; Venier et al. 2014). Compared to other parts of the world, Canada's boreal forests are undergoing some of the most rapid transformations due to human activities and climate change (Hansen et al. 2013).

Cumulative effects – including both human activities and natural disturbance – may be considered in impact assessment for new land uses and activities, but these processes rarely (if ever) prevent additional activities from proceeding. Most, if not all, provincial governments lack planning or policies to effectively address cumulative impacts.

If mandated, the requirement to maintain biodiversity is usually housed within a single ministry – often the Ministry of Natural Resources or the Ministry of Environment. But ministries are ill-equipped to conduct broad-scale or regional land-use planning that can consider the rate, intensity, and location of human activities and land use, as they tend to operate independently of one another. For example, if a Ministry of Forestry chooses to set aside an area from industrial logging to protect biodiversity, the area may continue to be negatively affected by mining or energy corridor development under the responsibility of the Ministry of Energy, Northern Development and Mines, or a newly paved road under the responsibility of the Transportation Ministry.

Cumulative effects frameworks and regional planning to coordinate how development is considered and approved (or not) within the habitat of at-risk species are integral to managing multiple human activities and climate change impacts. Where ecological thresholds are fairly well understood as they are for caribou, they must be explicitly considered in planning and approval processes.

Cumulative impact lenses must be accompanied by the authority to say no to projects based on such assessments.

To date, implementation of these tools is inadequate. For example, according to Ontario's Environmental Commissioner in 2016,

> The cumulative effects of multiple projects are usually not assessed. Despite international best practices, project owners are not required to consider the cumulative effects of other relevant activities such as known future projects and those that are already occurring in the project area; this can result in projects going ahead in areas that are already subject to significant environmental stresses. (Environmental Commissioner of Ontario 2016, 340)

With respect to the changes that weakened the Endangered Species Act, the environmental commissioner of Ontario notes,

> This is particularly troubling because the MNRF is not tracking the cumulative impact of harmful activities on species. In April 2017, the ECO asked ministry staff whether the MNRF considers cumulative effects in its approvals process or under permit-by-rule, and whether it has conducted a cumulative effects analysis for the ESA. The ministry stated that it does not consider cumulative effects and has not undertaken any such analysis. This potentially puts many species in a "death by a thousand cuts" situation that could cause irreparable harm, especially since the MNRF does not deny ESA authorizations." (Environmental Commissioner of Ontario 2017, 236)

In Alberta, home of Canada's most fragmented caribou ranges, a conservationist writes that "… effective management of cumulative effects requires institutional change, both in policy and law, that has been persistently rejected due to Alberta's economic priorities" (Huynh 2018). While in British Columbia,

> The BC Forest Practices Board has noted that not only is there no legal framework for managing cumulative effects in BC, but "to the extent that there is an issue, there is no one to tell – there is no decision maker when it comes to cumulative effects of multiple developments." These failings have been emphasized by BC's Auditor General, who found in 2015 that BC's "current legislation and directives do not effectively support the management of cumulative effects." (Smith et al. 2018, 3)

Lack of political will to commit to regional planning, particularly in the context of cumulative effects, makes it increasingly challenging to maintain sufficient habitat for wildlife in the face of the cumulative impacts of development and climate change. The result is habitat loss and decreased connectivity in already affected landscapes, and growth-inducing development and impacts in relatively undisturbed regions, such as road and mine development in remote regions like the Ring of Fire in Ontario (Chetkiewicz and Litner 2014). Unless landscape-level planning, including regional and strategic impact assessments, is prioritized to consider cumulative effects and their impacts on biodiversity, we will continue to see declines, extirpation, and extinctions as activities damage and destroy habitat one patch at a time. This is especially true as, in many cases, there is an unwillingness to incur the full costs required to recover or restore ecosystems once they have been significantly impacted.

Conclusion

Wildlife populations in Canada are under stress from many factors, including climate change, pollution, invasive species, and over-exploitation, among others. Yet habitat loss and degradation continue to be a primary threat for most species at risk in Canada.

For the recovery of at-risk species, including boreal caribou, successful recovery measures should be based on science and Indigenous knowledge, protection of currently (or recently) utilized habitat, and restoration of degraded habitat. Yet approaches to maintaining and restoring adequate amounts of habitat to advance wildlife recovery and survival are hampered by ideologies of growth without limits, government inaction, lack of local support (often driven by misinformation campaigns), and a lack of understanding of cumulative impacts and risk.

Diverging perspectives on wildlife management – in the case of boreal caribou, whether additional limits to industrial logging are warranted or not – have led to decades of conflict and deflection that have perpetuated caribou declines rather than recovery. In most instances in Canada, due to weak or non-existent species-at-risk and wildlife legislation and/or lack of political will to implement legislation that exists, industry and development operators are not legally required to protect the habitat that species need to survive and recover. Where requirements do exist, they are often not enforced (Nixon et al. 2012). Instead, loss and/or degradation of habitat continues.

If we are to manage wildlife in Canada to advance the recovery of at-risk species while sustaining more common species, we must recognize limits to the expansion of our human footprint beyond which wildlife will not survive, and implement policies accordingly. We must use resources conservatively with an ongoing focus on the ways their use will impact their quality and abundance in the future. A major collective effort will be required to shift natural resource use to within sustainable limits (Hawken 2007).

To reverse declining wildlife trends, governments must take responsibility for protecting and restoring habitat, employ a "cumulative effects lens" for resource extraction project approvals, and increase transparency on reporting wildlife decline. We must better engage the public to understand economic and ecological landscapes. Wildlife management must be based on science, but science alone cannot shape management decisions. Social and cultural dimensions, Indigenous practices and ethics, creative framing of new approaches, and a commitment to transparency should each play a primary role (Artelle et al. 2018). Further, our organizations are committed to supporting laws, policies, and management approaches that respect and uphold Indigenous laws. As our colleagues explain in the next chapter, Western approaches to wildlife management lack recognition of the roles that gratitude, reciprocity, and obligation play in living cooperatively with all life and supporting abundance. Across North America, many of the most dramatic examples of caribou recovery efforts are led by Indigenous nations and organizations.

WORKS CITED

Alberta Wilderness Association. 2020. "Where Is Parks Canada's Plan for Jasper's Disappearing Caribou?" Press release, Alberta Wilderness Association, October 6, 2020. https://albertawilderness.ca/where-is-parks-canadas-plan-for -jaspers-disappearing-caribou/

Andrew, Margaret E., Michael A. Wulder, and Jeffrey A. Cardille. 2014. "Protected Areas in Boreal Canada: A Baseline and Considerations for the Continued Development of a Representative and Effective Reserve Network." *Environmental Reviews* 22 (2): 135–60. https://doi.org/10.1139/er-2013-0056

Artelle, Kyle A., John D. Reynolds, Adrian Treves, Jessica C. Walsh, Paul C. Paquet, and Chris T. Darimont. 2018. "Hallmarks of Science Missing from North American Wildlife Management." *Science Advances* 4 (3). https://doi.org/10.1126 /sciadv.aao0167

Ascher, William L. 2004. "Scientific Information and Uncertainty: Challenges for the Use of Science in Policymaking." *Science and Engineering Ethics* 10 (3): 437–55. https://doi.org/10.1007/s11948-004-0002-z

Baker, Jessica C.A., and Dominick V. Spracklen. 2019. "Climate Benefits of Intact Amazon Forests and the Biophysical Consequences of Disturbance." *Frontiers in Forests and Global Change* 2: 47. https://doi.org/10.3389/ffgc.2019.00047

Bergman, Jordanna N., Allison D. Binley, Rowan E. Murphy, Caitlyn A. Proctor, Thuong Tran Nguyen, Elise S. Urness, Michelle A. Vala, Jaimie G. Vincent, Lenore Fahrig, and Joseph R. Bennett. 2020. "How to Rescue Ontario's Endangered Species Act: A Biologist's Perspective." *FACETS* 5 (1): 423–31. https://doi.org/10.1139 /facets-2019-0050

Bichet, Orphé, Angélique Dupuch, Christian Hébert, Hélène Le Borgne, and Daniel Fortin. 2016. "Maintaining Animal Assemblages through Single-Species Management: The Case of Threatened Caribou in Boreal Forest." *Ecological Applications* 26 (2): 612–23. https://doi.org/10.1890/15-0525

Boan, Julee J., Jay R. Malcolm, Mallory D. Vanier, Dave L. Euler, and Faisal M. Moola. 2018. "From Climate to Caribou: How Manufactured Uncertainty Is Affecting Wildlife Management." *Wildlife Society Bulletin* 42 (2): 366–81. https://doi .org/10.1002/wsb.891

Bond, Alan, Jenny Pope, Monica Fundingsland, Angus Morrison-Saunders, Francois Retief, and Morgan Hauptfleisch. 2020. "Explaining the Political Nature of Environmental Impact Assessment (EIA): A Neo-Gramscian Perspective." *Journal of Cleaner Production* 244. https://doi.org/10.1016/j.jclepro .2019.118694

Brandt, James P., M.D. Flannigan, D.G. Maynard, Ian D. Thompson, and Jan A. Volney. 2013. "An Introduction to Canada's Boreal Zone: Ecosystem Processes, Health, Sustainability, and Environmental Issues." *Environmental Reviews* 21 (4): 207–26. https://doi.org/10.1139/er-2013-0040.

Brockington, Dan. 2004. "Community Conservation, Inequality and Injustice: Myths of Power in Protected Area Management." *Conservation and Society*: 411–32.

Canadian Endangered Species Conservation Council. 2016. "Wild Species 2015: The General Status of Species in Canada." National General Status Working Group.

Capeluck, Evan and Jasmin Thomas, 2015. "A Detailed Analysis of Productivity Trends in the Forest Products Sector in Ontario, 2000–2013: Sunset Industry or Industry in Transition?" CSLS Research Reports 2015–06, Centre for the Study of Living Standards.

Chetkiewicz, Cheryl, and Anastasia Litner. 2014. "Getting It Right in Ontario's Far North: The Need for a Regional Strategic Environmental Assessment in the Ring of Fire [Wawangajing]." WCS Canada and EcoJustice.

Committee on the Status of Endangered Wildlife in Canada (COSEWIC). 2011. "Designatable Units for Caribou (*Rangifer tarandus*) in Canada." Committee on the Status of Endangered Wildlife in Canada. Ottawa. https://www.canada.ca /content/dam/eccc/migration/cosewic-cosepac/4e5136bf-f3ef-4b7a-9a79 -6d70ba15440f/cosewic_caribou_du_report_23dec2011.pdf

Committee on the Status of Endangered Wildlife in Canada (COSEWIC). 2020. "Canadian Wildlife Species at Risk." Committee on the Status of Endangered Wildlife in Canada. https://www.cosewic.ca/index.php/en-ca

Drever, C. Ronnie, Chantal Hutchison, Mark C. Drever, Daniel Fortin, Cheryl A. Johnson, and Yolanda F. Wiersma. 2019. "Conservation through Co-occurrence: Woodland Caribou as a Focal Species for Boreal Biodiversity." *Biological Conservation* 232: 238–52. https://doi.org/10.1016/j.biocon.2019.01.026

Earth Overshoot Day. 2020. "Country Overshoot Days." https://www.overshootday .org/newsroom/country-overshoot-days/

Ecojustice. 2012. "Failure to Protect: Grading Canada's Species at Risk Laws." https://www
    .ecojustice.ca/wp-content/uploads/2014/08/Failure-to-protect_Grading-Canadas
    -Species-at-Risk-Laws.pdf
Environment Canada. 2011. "Scientific Assessment to Inform the Identification of
    Critical Habitat for Woodland Caribou *(Rangifer tarandus caribou),* Boreal Population,
    in Canada: 2011 Update." Ottawa, Ontario, Canada. https://www.registrelep
    -sararegistry.gc.ca/virtual_sara/files/ri_boreal_caribou_science_0811_eng.pdf
Environment Canada. 2012. "Recovery Strategy for the Woodland Caribou *(Rangifer
    tarandus caribou),* Boreal Population, in Canada." Species at Risk Act Recovery
    Strategy Series. Ottawa: Environment Canada.
Environment Canada. 2017. "Report on the Progress of Recovery Strategy
    Implementation for the Woodland Caribou *(Rangifer tarandus caribou),* Boreal
    Population, in Canada for the Period 2012 to 2017." Species at Risk Act recovery
    strategy series. Ottawa: Environment Canada.
Environment Canada. 2018. "Woodland Caribou *(Rangifer tarandus caribou),* Boreal
    Population: Progress Report on Unprotected Critical Habitat." https://www.canada
    .ca/en/environment-climate-change/services/species-risk-public-registry/critical
    -habitat-reports/woodland-caribou-boreal-population-2018.html
Environment and Climate Change Canada. 2020. "Amended Recovery Strategy for
    the Woodland Caribou *(Rangifer tarandus caribou),* Boreal Population, in Canada."
    Species at Risk Act Recovery Strategy Series. Environment and Climate Change
    Canada, Ottawa. https://wildlife-species.canada.ca/species-risk-registry/virtual_sara
    /files/plans/Rs-CaribouBorealeAmdMod-v01-2020Dec-Eng.pdf
Environmental Commissioner of Ontario. 2016. "Chapter 3.06, Environmental
    Assessments." In *2016 Annual Report of the Office of the Auditor General of
    Ontario.* https://www.auditor.on.ca/en/content/annualreports/arreports/en16
    /v1_306en16.pdf
Environmental Commissioner of Ontario. 2017. "Good Choices, Bad Choices."
    https://www.auditor.on.ca/en/content/reporttopics/envreports/env17/Good
    -Choices-Bad-Choices.pdf
Festa-Bianchet, Marco, Justina C. Ray, Stan Boutin, Steeve D. Côté, and Anne Gunn.
    2011. "Conservation of Caribou (*Rangifer tarandus*) in Canada: An Uncertain Future."
    Canadian *Journal of Zoology* 89 (5): 419–34. https://doi.org/10.1139/z11-025
Forest Service British Columbia. 1994. "Forest, Range, and Recreation Resource
    Analysis." https://www.for.gov.bc.ca/hfd/library/frra/1994/index.htm
Fryxell, John M., Tal Avgar, Boyan Liu, James A. Baker, Arthur R. Rodgers, Jennifer
    Shuter, Ian D. Thompson, Douglas E.B. Reid, Andrew M. Kittle, Anna Mosser, and
    Steven G. Newmaster. 2020. "Anthropogenic Disturbance and Population Viability
    of Woodland Caribou in Ontario." *Journal of Wildlife Management* 84 (4): 636–50.
    https://doi.org/10.1002/jwmg.21829
Gillespie, Nathaniel, Jonas Epstein, Susan Alexander, Michael Bowker, Ron Medel,
    Mike Leonard, and Andrew Thoms. 2018. "Socioeconomic Benefits of Recreational,

Commercial, and Subsistence Fishing Associated with National Forests." *Fisheries* 43 (9): 432–39. https://doi.org/10.1002/fsh.10127

Government of Canada. 1996. "Protection of Species at Risk: Federal, Provincial, and Territorial Accord." https://www.canada.ca/en/environment-climate-change /services/species-risk-act-accord-funding/protection-federal-provincial-territorial -accord.html

Haddock, Mark. 2015. "Professional Reliance and Environmental Regulation in British Columbia." University of Victoria Environmental Law Centre. http://www .elc.uvic.ca/wordpress/wp-content/uploads/2015/02/Professional-Reliance-and -Environmental-Regulation-in-BC_2015Feb9.pdf

Hansen, James, Pushker Kharecha, Makiko Sato, Valerie Masson-Delmotte, Frank Ackerman, David J. Beerling, Paul J. Hearty, Ove Hoegh-Guldberg, Shi-Ling Hsu, Camille Parmesan, and Johan Rockstrom. 2013. "Assessing 'Dangerous Climate Change': Required Reduction of Carbon Emissions to Protect Young People, Future Generations and Nature." *PloS One* 8 (12): e81648.

Hawken, Paul. 2007. *Blessed Unrest: How the Largest Movement in the World Came into Being and Why No One Saw It Coming.* New York: Viking USA.

Hervieux, Dave, Mark Hebblewhite, Dave Stepnisky, Michelle Bacon, and Stan Boutin. 2014. "Managing Wolves (*Canis lupus*) to Recover Threatened Woodland Caribou (*Rangifer tarandus caribou*) in Alberta." *Canadian Journal of Zoology* 92 (12): 1029–37. https://cdnsciencepub.com/doi/full/10.1139/cjz-2014-0142

Huynh, Mai-Linh. 2019. "A Boreal Forest Divided Cannot Stand – A Cumulative Effects Story." Alberta Wilderness Association. March 1, 2019. https:// albertawilderness.ca/a-boreal-forest-divided-cannot-stand-a-cumulative -effects-story/

Johnson, Cheryl A., Glenn D. Sutherland, Erin Neave, Mathieu Leblond, Patrick Kirby, Clara Superbie, and Philip D. McLoughlin. 2020. "Science to Inform Policy: Linking Population Dynamics to Habitat for a Threatened Species in Canada." *Journal of Applied Ecology* 57 (7): 1314–27. https://doi.org/10.1111/1365-2664.13637

Johnston, Paul, Mark Everard, David Santillo, and Karl-Henrik Robèrt. 2007. "Reclaiming the Definition of Sustainability." *Environmental Science and Pollution Research International* 14 (1): 60–6. https://doi.org/10.1065/espr2007.01.375

Karjalainen, Eeva, Tytti Sarjala, and Hannu Raitio. 2010. "Promoting Human Health through Forests: Overview and Major Challenges." *Environmental Health and Preventive Medicine* 15 (1): 1–8. https://doi.org/10.1007/s12199-008-0069-2

Lueck, Dean, and Jeffrey A. Michael. 2003. "Preemptive Habitat Destruction under the Endangered Species Act." *Journal of Law & Economics* 46 (1): 27–60. https://doi .org/10.1086/344670

The Maison Candiac Group Inc. c. Canada (Attorney General). 2020. "Western Chorus Frog Judgement, 2020 CAF 88 (CanLII)." http://canlii.ca/t/j7tsw

McIntosh, Emma. 2020. "Doug Ford Moving to Permanently Exempt Logging Industry from Endangered Species Law." *The National Observer.*

November 13, 2020. https://www.nationalobserver.com/2020/11/13/news
/doug-ford-permanently-exempt-logging-endangered-species-law

M'Gonigle, Michael, and Louise Takeda. 2012. "The Liberal Limits of Environmental
Law: A Green Legal Critique." *Pace Environmental Law Review* 30 (3).
http://digitalcommons.pace.edu/pelr/vol30/iss3/4

Michaels, David, and Celeste Monforton. 2005. "Manufacturing Uncertainty:
Contested Science and the Protection of the Public's Health and Environment."
American Journal of Public Health 95 (S1): S39–S48. https://doi.org/10.2105
/AJPH.2004.043059

Mumma, Matthew A., Michael P. Gillingham, Katherine L. Parker, Chris J. Johnson,
and Megan Watters. 2018. "Predation Risk for Boreal Woodland Caribou in Human-
Modified Landscapes: Evidence of Wolf Spatial Responses Independent of Apparent
Competition." *Biological Conservation* 228: 215–23. https://doi.org/10.1016
/j.biocon.2018.09.015

Nixon, Sean, Devon Page, Susan Pinkus, Liat Podolsky, and Sasha Russell. 2012.
"Failure to Protect: Grading Canada's Species at Risk Laws." Ecojustice.

Northern Policy Institute. 2019. "Are Robots Coming for Our Jobs? The Economic
Impact of Automation on Northern Ontario's Economy." https://www.nswpb.ca
/wp-content/uploads/2020/10/FINAL_-_EN_Economic_Impact_of
_Automation-1-1-2.pdf

Office of the Auditor General of Canada. 2018. "Fall Reports of the Commissioner
of the Environment and Sustainable Development to the Parliament of Canada,
Report 2—Protecting Marine Mammals." https://www.oag-bvg.gc.ca/internet
/English/parl_cesd_201810_02_e_43146.html

Ontario Ministry of Natural Resources. 2009. "Ontario's Woodland Caribou
Conservation Plan." Toronto: Queen's Printer for Ontario, https://files.ontario.ca
/environment-and-energy/species-at-risk/277783.pdf

Prokopchuk, Matt. 2018. "Grassy Narrows Declares Logging Ban in Its Territory
ahead of Forest Management Planning." CBC News, October 11, 2018. https://www
.cbc.ca/news/canada/thunder-bay/grassy-narrows-logging-ban-1.4856870

Province of Ontario. 2020. "Ontario Forest Sector Strategy." https://files.ontario.ca
/mnrf-fid-forest-sector-strategy-en-2020-08-20.pdf

Raiter, Keren G., Hugh P. Possingham, Suzanne M. Prober, and Richard J. Hobbs. 2014.
"Under the Radar: Mitigating Enigmatic Ecological Impacts." *Trends in Ecology &
Evolution* 29 (11): 635–44. https://doi.org/10.1016/j.tree.2014.09.003

Raworth, Kate. 2017. *Doughnut Economics: Seven Ways to Think Like a 21st-Century
Economist*. White River Junction, VT: Chelsea Green Publishing. https://www
.kateraworth.com/

Ray, Justina, Jaime Grimm, and Andrea Olive. 2021. "The Biodiversity Crisis in
Canada: Failures and Challenges of Federal and Sub-National Strategic and Legal
Frameworks." *FACETS* 6 (June): 1044–66. https://doi.org/10.1139/facets-2020-0075.

Ross, Ian. "Northwest First Nations Protest Provincial Caribou Strategy." Northern Ontario Business. May 29, 2019. https://www.northernontariobusiness.com /industry-news/forestry/northwest-first-nations-protest-provincial-caribou -strategy-1479695

Rudolph, Tyler D., Pierre Drapeau, Louis Imbeau, Vincent Brodeur, Sonia Légaré, and Martin-Hugues St-Laurent. 2017. "Demographic Responses of Boreal Caribou to Cumulative Disturbances Highlight Elasticity of Range-Specific Tolerance Thresholds." *Biodiversity and Conservation* 26 (5): 1179–98. https://doi.org/10.1007 /s10531-017-1292-1

Schaefer, James A. 2003. "Long-Term Range Recession and the Persistence of Caribou in the Taiga." *Conservation Biology* 17 (5): 1435–9. https://doi.org/10.1046 /j.1523-1739.2003.02288.x

Smith, Gavin, Anna Johnston, and Hannah Askew. 2018. "Why It's Time to Reform Environmental Assessment in British Columbia." BC Assessment and Planning Reform Backgrounder. West Coast Environmental Law. https://www.wcel.org/sites /default/files/publications/2018-01-bc-eareform-backgrounder-web-final.pdf

Stewart, Frances E.C., J. Joshua Nowak, Tatiane Micheletti, Eliot J.B. McIntire, Fiona K.A. Schmiegelow, and Steven G. Cumming. 2020. "Boreal Caribou Can Coexist with Natural but Not Industrial Disturbances." *Journal of Wildlife Management* 84 (8): 1435–44. https://doi.org/10.1002/jwmg.21937

Struzik, Edward. 2020. "This May Be Our Last, Best Chance to Save Jasper's Dwindling Caribou Population." *The Narwhal.* December 28, 2020. https://thenarwhal.ca /opinion-caribou-breeding-jasper-national-park/

United Nations. 2015. "The Paris Agreement." https://unfccc.int/process-and-meetings /the-paris-agreement/the-paris-agreement

Venier, Lisa A., Ian D. Thompson, Richard Fleming, Jay R. Malcolm, Isabelle Aubin, John A. Trofymow, David Langor, Rona N. Sturrock, Cynthia Patry, R.O. Outerbridge, and Steven B. Holmes. 2014. "Effects of Natural Resource Development on the Terrestrial Biodiversity of Canadian Boreal Forests." *Environmental Reviews* 22 (4): 457–90. https://doi.org/10.1139/er-2013-0075

Watson, James E.M., Tom Evans, Oscar Venter, Brooke Williams, Ayesha Tulloch, Claire Stewart, Ian Thompson, Justina C. Ray, Kris Murray, Alvero Salazar, Clive McAlpine, Peter Potapov, Joe Walston, John G. Robinson, Michael Painter, David Wilkie, Christopher Filardi, William F. Laurance, Richard A. Houghton, Sean Maxwell, Hedley Grantham, Cristián Samper, Stephanie Wang, Lars Laestadius, Rebecca K. Runting, Gustavo A. Silva-Chávez, Jamison Ervin, and David Lindenmayer. 2018. "The Exceptional Value of Intact Forest Ecosystems." *Nature Ecology & Evolution* 2 (4): 599–610. https://doi.org/10.1038/s41559-018-0490-x

Weber, Bob. 2014. "Alberta Wolf Cull Stabilizes Caribou Numbers, but Just Buys Time: Study." City News, November 23, 2014. https://toronto.citynews.ca/2014/11/23 /alberta-wolf-cull-stabilizes-caribou-numbers-but-just-buys-time-study/

Winder, Richard, Frances E.C. Stewart, Silke Nebel, Eliot J.B. McIntire, Andrew
    Dyk, and Kangakola Omendja. 2020. "Cumulative Effects and Boreal Woodland
    Caribou: How Bow-Tie Risk Analysis Addresses a Critical Issue in Canada's Forested
    Landscapes." *Frontiers in Ecology and Evolution* 8 (1). https://doi.org/10.3389
    /fevo.2020.00001
World Commission on Environment and Development. 1987. *Report of the World
    Commission on Environment and Development: Our Common Future.*
    https://sustainabledevelopment.un.org/content/documents/5987our-common
    -future.pdf
World Wildlife Fund Canada. 2017. "The Living Planet Report Canada: A National
    Look at Wildlife Loss." https://wwf.ca/wp-content/uploads/2020/02/WEB_WWF
    _REPORT_v3.pdf.
Yona, Leehi, Benjamin Cashore, and Oswald J. Schmitz. 2019. "Integrating Policy and
    Ecology Systems to Achieve Path Dependent Climate Solutions." *Environmental
    Science & Policy* 98: 54–60. https://doi.org/10.1016/j.envsci.2019.03.013

5 Enacting a Reciprocal Ethic of Care: (Finally) Fulfilling Treaty Obligations

LARRY McDERMOTT AND ROBIN ROTH

As you will know, respect for Mother Earth and all species and forms of life is fundamental to the true Indigenous way of life. Over the course of my lifetime, I have witnessed our natural heritage damaged almost irrevocably at every level by unbridled greed, opportunism, and development, and uncoordinated federal and provincial management – evident particularly in the history of logging, hydro-electric generation, nuclear development, and mining within the Ottawa River Watershed, the ancestral territory of the Algonquin Peoples, and the land that originally gave life to the dream of Canada. The record of devastation now impacts not just Aboriginal peoples, reserves, and wildlife, but our national health and global future. Indigenous peoples have been impoverished and rendered invisible and voiceless by this ceaseless exploitation of our natural resources, while others have appeared to thrive. But now the time for reckoning is upon us.

– William Commanda, Algonquin Elder, 2006, 1–2.

Indigenous relationships with the web of life, of which we are part, is based on natural law and the active expressions of gratitude and reciprocity leading to abundance. This is significantly different than the Western approach to wildlife management where populations are managed to avoid depletion or even extirpation. Indigenous world views are most often based on the perspective that we are one species among many, and our well-being is directly connected to the well-being of other species. This is achieved through not only the physical and mental processes of observation and adaptation but through empathic and spiritual expression and connection to and with other life forms.

Until recently, most in the Western science community held supercilious views towards Indigenous approaches to wildlife, resulting in notable conflict around polar bear, American eel, Atlantic salmon, lobster, caribou, buffalo, and other species management and relationship systems. Wildlife management rooted exclusively in Western science has failed to take seriously the approaches and assessments of Indigenous Peoples.[1] For example, in 1977 the

US delegate to the International Whaling Commission used a US government survey to support a quota of zero for bowhead whales, an important species for Indigenous hunters in coastal Alaska (Mitchell and Reeves 1980). Local hunters found the assessment way too low and so formed the Alaska Eskimo Whaling Commission and conducted their own census, successfully advocating for a return to hunting. Eventually a local government hired their own scientists who found that the US government report undercounted the bowhead whale population because the conventional scientific wisdom that bowhead whales only travelled in open water was wrong. In fact, bowhead whales frequently swim under the ice, undetected by government scientists but known to Indigenous hunters (Albert 2001). These sorts of conflicts around hunting quotas have routinely happened throughout North America, with the polar bear (Clark, VanBeest, and Brook 2012) the caribou (Bechtel 2016), and salmon (Barringer, 2018), to name but a few.

Furthermore, there are divergent perceptions of hunting bans. Western wildlife management enacts them to keep humans away from the designated animal, whereas, from an Indigenous perspective, the reciprocal relationship between humans and animals needs to be maintained for the health of both. So, a ban on hunting breaks the relationship, which, when maintained with respect and integrity, leads to abundance. Such a sentiment is expressed when the Niitsitapi (Blackfoot People) say "the buffalo did not leave us, we left the buffalo" (Littlebear, pers. comm.). What drove the buffalo to near extinction was not Indigenous hunting, nor is Indigenous hunting or fishing the reason behind the decline of the caribou, polar bear, cod, salmon. or American eel. When Indigenous Nations enact bans on hunting, they do so as a last resort to fulfill their duty of care, whereas mainstream wildlife management uses hunting bans as the primary means of protection.

While these sorts of conflicts resulting from a lack of recognition or respect for the reciprocal relationship that underpins Indigenous multi-dimensional approaches to wildlife are not exclusively in the past, we are seeing some signs that the future holds hope for our collective ability to improve our relationships to wildlife through a meaningful engagement with Indigenous knowledge systems. We see the recent progress made through the Pathway to Canada's Target 1 process, where the process was opened and closed with a Ceremony, as indicative of a better future. This is a rare national example where oral Indigenous and Western written systems were upheld and both knowledge systems were engaged strategically to guide Canada in fulfilling its obligations to the Convention on Biological Diversity. Pathway to Canada's Target 1 process is a unique example where Aichi Biodiversity Target 18[2] was taken seriously and brought together with the other targets to create a national strategy. Canada now has a global responsibility to share this example of reconciliation, cooperation, and partnership in the service of conservation for wildlife, including lands and waters, recognizing a "bio-cultural" approach and practice. See chapters 6 and 7 of this volume for a more thorough discussion of the potential of reconciliation for transformative change.

The opportunity in front us now – to learn from and amplify Indigenous approaches and to respect them similarly to Western science – has been offered settlers before. To understand our collective journey to this more hopeful place, it is critical to understand Canada's origin story, early Indigenous-settler relations, Treaty-making, and the path not taken. We argue in this chapter, that the fundamental barrier to responsible wildlife management/relationships is the unfulfilled and improperly implemented Treaties between settler states and Indigenous Nations.

There are two of us telling this story. The first author, Elder Larry McDermott, is from Shabot Obaadjiwan First Nation, and he brings decades of teachings, oral history, and vast experience in Indigenous conservation in Canada and around the world to the collaboration. The second author is Dr. Robin Roth, a scholar of mixed European heritage, who brings years of learning from Indigenous Peoples in Canada and abroad and her training in finding, understanding, and synthesizing the written record to this work. We most frequently use the collective pronoun to indicate the collaborative nature of the work but, where appropriate, name ourselves individually as the source of a particular statement or observation. What follows is our exploration of what we see as the fundamental barrier to advances in wildlife management.

Indigenous Relations – Natural Law – Treaty Making

> Our relationship with the moose nation, the deer nation, and the caribou nation is a treaty relationship like any other, and all the parties involved have both rights and responsibilities in terms of maintaining the agreement. The treaty outlines a relationship that, when practised in perpetuity, maintains peaceful coexistence, respect, and mutual benefit. (Simpson 2011, 111)

In an era of reconciliation, it is common to state that "we are all Treaty people" and provide support for the idea that Canada must honour its Treaties. But what is in a Treaty? More, we think, than most Canadians realize. A Treaty spells out the responsibilities of two or more parties (whether human beings or the natural world) to one another and contain a commitment in perpetuity to hold up those responsibilities in the interest of maintaining good relations. Early treaties were not between European sovereigns and Indigenous Nations but between Indigenous Peoples and the rest of nature, or between Indigenous nations *about* the rest of nature (Borrows 2021). Treaties between Indigenous Nations existed before European settlement and had always been used to recognize relations with the Sky, Earth, Creator, and all beings while ensuring peaceful co-existence of sovereign nations. The Dish with One Spoon Treaty is a good example of a pre-European settlement Treaty that was used to commit the Anishinaabeg and Haudenosaunee Peoples of the Great Lakes region to sharing the land and its resources in peaceful co-existence: never taking more than you need, keeping the bowl clean, and making sure there is some food in the bowl for future needs. As Elder Rick Hill states, the Dish with One Spoon "has got to do with hunting, fishing, and gathering. But it has also got to do with a healthy frame of mind" (Glover 2020). Anishinaabe legal scholar Aimée Craft locates Treaty principles in the legal obligations and relationships that "exist among humans, animals, fish, plants, rocks, and *adisookan* (spirits), among and between themselves individually and collectively" (Craft 2013, 70). Treaties were and are ultimately about upholding *bimaadiziwin*, an Anishinaabe conception of well-being that emphasizes balanced and healthy relationships with all relations (Simpson 2008, 32). Treaties are thus rooted in Natural Law; they are a legal expression of our responsibilities.

Onondaga Faith Keeper Oren Lyon, in an oral statement before the Royal Commission on Aboriginal Peoples on 3 May 1993, at Akwesasne, explained Natural Law thus:

> Indians are spiritual, religious people, always have been and, hopefully, always will be because that is the fundamental law. That's the main law of survival. That is the law of regeneration. Any law that you make you must bind to that spiritual law. If you don't, you're not going to make it, because the spiritual law, the law of reality that is outside here, that you must drink water to live, that you must eat to survive, that you must build shelter for your children, that you must plant, that you must harvest, you must work with the seasons – that law does not change. That's the major law that governs all life on this earth. If nations don't make their law accordingly, they will fail eventually because no human being is capable of changing that law. (Erasmus and Dussault 1996, 668)

While Natural Law and the obligations of humanity towards the rest of the natural world are expressed in Treaties, so too are Indigenous teachings frequent reminders of our collective responsibilities. The Seven Grandmother/Grandfather Teachings and other similar teachings, such as the Haudenosaunee "words before all else" otherwise known as the Thanksgiving Address, or the Nuu-chah-nulth principle of *tsawalk,* remind us of our responsibilities and relationships to the web of life. These teachings, though varied according to specific cultures and traditions, contain common themes of being one species among many, the interconnectedness of life, the importance of reciprocal relationships, the expression of gratitude and our collective responsibility to maintain balance, well-being, and the continuation of Life.

These philosophies and cultural practices contain principles and values that provided guidance that informed early Treaty making with European settlers and through which we need to understand the early Peace and Friendship Treaties, the Royal Proclamation of 1763 and the diplomatic proceedings at Fort Niagara in 1764.

On 7 October 1763, King George III officially claimed British territory in North America after Britain had defeated the French in the Seven Years War. The military victories by the Anishinaabeg and Haudenosaunee warriors precipitated the declaration of the Royal Proclamation of 1763. The Royal Proclamation is sometimes referred to as the "Indian Magna Carta" because of its importance in recognizing Indigenous rights and title. The proclamation clearly states that only the British Crown had the right to negotiate with Indigenous Peoples for territory. It thus "explicitly states that Aboriginal title has existed and continues to exist, and that all land would be considered Aboriginal land until ceded by treaty" (Indigenous Foundations.arts.ubc.ca). The Royal Proclamation set a foundation for inclusion of both British and Indigenous People's ways of knowing, cultural protocols and legal systems (Borrows 1997).

The Royal Proclamation set in motion the subsequent process for the Treaty of Niagara or Treaty of 1764, where two thousand or more Indigenous representatives from across Turtle Island (North America) travelled, in some cases for months, to Niagara to be joined by British representatives of the Crown. "First Nations were not passive objects, but active participants in the formulation and ratification of the Royal Proclamation." (Borrows 1997, 20).

John Borrows (1994, 20), an Anishinaabe legal scholar, explains the importance of the Treaty of Niagara: "At this gathering a nation-to-nation relationship between settler and First Nation peoples was renewed and extended, and the Covenant Chain of Friendship, a multinational multination alliance in which no member gave up their sovereignty, was affirmed."

The Royal Proclamation led to the Treaty process in the summer of 1764. Both the British and Indigenous representatives had the cross-cultural capacity to communicate in both the written word and through oral knowledge transfer. Both parties had the capacity to produce wampum belts and exchanged them as a means of recording what was agreed to at the Treaty of Niagara. The recording through wampum and in oral representations was surrounded and consummated in Ceremony. The wampum belts serve as a mnemonic device that connected to the oral tradition and the spiritual commitment expressed by both parties as part of the Treaty process. Wampum also contributed to the recorded written process.

In Delgamuukw v. British Columbia (1997), the Supreme Court of Canada recognized the importance of oral history and recognized it as sometimes providing a more in-depth contextual understanding and accuracy than the written record. Extending that principle to the Treaty of Niagara allows us to build on the oral teachings that Elder Larry McDermott has received, confirming that the 2000 or so Indigenous peoples present at the Treaty of Niagara communicated the collective responsibility to care for the Earth and all its inhabitants to the Crown, who accepted that responsibility in Ceremony. These kinds of commitments were also at the core of earlier agreements enshrined in, for instance, the Welcoming and Sharing Three Figure Sacred Wampum Belt negotiated in the early eighteenth century. McDermott and Wilson 2010 refer to it as one of the first Access and Benefit Sharing (ABS) agreements produced in Canada. The belt depicts three figures representing the French and the English flanking the Algonquin. Esteemed Elder William Commanda was responsible for sharing the legal history of the agreement and informs us "that the commitment expressed through the Wampum Belt was to accept the sacred responsibilities to care for the life-givers, to respect each other, and to share the 'grand resources of the land'" (McDermott and Wilson 2010, 7).

In *Treaty Elders of Saskatchewan*, Cardinal and Hildebrandt write that the purpose of the Treaties was to secure "the Crown's guarantee that the Crown would respect the integrity of the First Nations relationship with the Creator" (2000, 31). They further argue that the Treaties were intended to protect First Nations connections to land. We would go a step further and argue that the Crown, through Treaty, was agreeing to share that responsibility with First Nations to ensure both of our Nation's collective connection to land, which includes all its inhabitants (human and other than human) and ensure that we are able to fulfill our inherent responsibilities that come with that connection.

Non-Indigenous Canadians frequently understand Nation-to-Nation Treaties as agreements to give and protect the rights of Indigenous peoples. More inclusive or progressive understandings suggest the Treaties were not about giving anything that didn't already exist but were about sharing the land. But really those early Treaties contained instructions on how to share the *responsibility* for the land and, utilizing the principles and practices of the Dish with One Spoon Wampum Treaty before them, were understood by the Indigenous nations who affirmed them to protect their relationship to the land and to all their relations. The Sharing and Friendship Wampum Belt carried by William Commanda and the voices of Indigenous representatives at the Treaty of 1764 are just a few examples of where Indigenous Peoples attempted to lead and affirm the shared relationship to the land in harmony with Natural Law. The failure to accept this instruction is the root cause of environmental destruction, race-based violence, and other injustices, that can be healed by pursing true reconciliation – meaning reconciliation with each other and the land. The reciprocal relationship with nature and the agreement to abide by Natural Law were legal principles that colonial sovereigns and their settlers have (thus far) failed to recognize or uphold.

Indigenous Relations – "Wildlife"

We have established that Indigenous traditions recognize that Natural Law governs human relationships to the rest of the web of life. The reciprocal ethic of care can be seen very tangibly in the ways Indigenous peoples approach their relationship to "All of Our Relations," what is commonly referred to as "wildlife." We put the term in quote marks to indicate how the concept, as expressed in English, inherently divides life into that which is "wild" (outside human influence) and that which is "domesticated" (that which is under human control). In an Indigenous worldview, this is a false dichotomy that privileges the human as a superior species and denies our equal responsibility to maintain good relations with all aspects of the web of life (Eichler and Baumeister, 2018). This section will look specifically at examples of how relations are maintained with species of great importance. Indigenous care for wildlife is not presumed a neutral, objective task to ensure enough resources to consume, but rather an active spiritual ethic of care meant to maintain and enhance good relations resulting in mutual benefit between humans and animals. Key to this ethic is a pervasive understanding in many Indigenous Nations and communities that humans are a new animal, not superior to others, who have the opportunity and responsibility to learn from their animal relatives. Below we tell the stories of the buffalo, the American eel, and the goose as ways of illustrating this ethic. All three animals are iconic and critically important for different Indigenous cultures. Together they cover a wide geography and diversity of management/relationship strategies and represent the land, water, and sky worlds.

Tales of Resurgence, Recovery, and Abundance: Buffalo

Consistent with the Treaty-making traditions described above, in early fall of 2014 representatives from tribes on either side of the US-Canada border gathered in Ceremony to confirm their commitment to the buffalo (the American Bison) through a historic signing of the Buffalo Treaty, the first inter-tribal treaty in 150 years (Johns, 2020). The Plains Buffalo (*Bison bison*) is a cultural keystone species for many Indigenous Peoples throughout North and Central America. Cultural keystone species, like an ecological keystone species, denotes a species of such central importance that its absence leads to a significant collapse and then reorganization of the system in which it is embedded (Garibaldi and Turner, 2004).

The buffalo once roamed in the millions across much of North America and predominately on the central plains and provided Indigenous Peoples with food, shelter, tools, and spiritual guidance. The buffalo provided a healthy source of protein but also, through its hoof prints, wallowing behaviour, and dung, was integral to the diversity of prairie grasslands. The American commercial buffalo hunter's devastation of the Plains Bison, symbolized by the mountains of buffalo skulls at the turn of the century, resulted from a combination of factors, including market hunting to feed industries in the East but was significantly helped along by the military's push eastward and an explicit effort to separate plains Indigenous Peoples, such as the Blackfoot, from their main source of food, shelter, and spiritual well-being. Frank Mayer (Smits 1994, 314) quotes a high-ranking US military officer as saying, "If we kill the buffalo, we conquer the Indian." And Sir John A. Macdonald, in 1883, said in response to the near disappearance of the bison, "I am not at all sorry that this happened. So long as there was a hope that buffalo would come into the country, there was no means of inducing the Indians to settle down on their reserves" (Commons Debates 1883, 1102). The winters of 1882–4 are referred to as the "starvation winters," due to the amount of starvation experienced by the Blackfoot and numerous Indigenous Nations of the plains. The slaughter of the buffalo was also the demise of the Indigenous Peoples of the plains and their unique and distinct ways of Life. It also precipitated a massive decline in prairie grassland diversity, with insect diversity and bird abundance declining along with much prairie wildlife that co-evolved with the buffalo for millennia (Olsen 2021). It is thus both an ecological and cultural keystone species.

> Dr Littlebear, professor emeritus at Lethbridge University and member of Kainai First Nation, had this to say about the signing of the Buffalo Treaty. Through the renewal and application of North American Indian paradigms, one discovers that sustainability, leaving the land as pristine as possible, and having humans fit themselves into the ecological balance are fundamental to the life-ways of Indian peoples. But the buffalo is a major player in this ecological scenario. The near extinction of the buffalo left a major gap. The treaty on buffalo restoration aims to begin to fill that gap and once again partner with the buffalo to bring about cultural and ecological balance. (WCS, 2014) Excerpts from that Treaty speak directly to the reciprocal ethic of care indicative of Indigenous relations to wildlife. As expressed in the preamble to the Buffalo Treaty, Since time immemorial … BUFFALO has been our relative. BUFFALO is part of us and WE are part of BUFFALO culturally, materially, and spiritually.

And the first article of the Treaty, on conservation, says this:

> Recognizing BUFFALO as a practitioner of conservation, WE, collectively, agree to perpetuate conservation by respecting the interrelationship between us and "all our relations" including animals, plants, and Mother Earth; to perpetuate and continue our spiritual ceremonies, sacred societies, sacred languages, and sacred bundles to perpetuate and practise as a means to embody the thoughts and beliefs of ecological balance.

The Buffalo Treaty illustrates the reciprocal ethic of care inherent in Indigenous relationships to wildlife and recognizes that conservation of the buffalo requires the protection and practice of Indigenous biocultural relations. To conserve Indigenous language and ceremony serves the buffalo and ensures its return to the people and the land, where it can once again take up its important place as a central figure in Indigenous ways of life, governance, and spiritual relations that serve to privilege ecological integrity and function. This is the central goal of the Iinnii Initiative, a Blackfoot-led effort to return buffalo to their people and the land. The effort is unique in that a conservation organization based in Western science is involved (Wildlife Conservation Society) but takes its direction from Blackfoot Elders and Knowledge Keepers (Keyser, 2018). Oral tradition, Ceremony and Blackfoot knowledge is central to the effort to return free-roaming buffalo to northern Montana and Southern Alberta (Fox 2018).

Tales of Resurgence, Recovery, and Abundance: American Eel

Similarly, the American eel is an ancient species that has served Indigenous peoples in parts of South, Central, North America, Greenland, and Iceland for thousands of years. The American eel is a Clan animal among some Indigenous Peoples, and provides food, medicine, durable and waterproof material, along with spiritual relationship.

The American eel spawns in the Sargasso Sea and drifts with ocean currents. Consequently, all habitat is crucial to the well-being of the species because of its reproductive and recruitment (distribution) characteristics. Indigenous Peoples have long understood the interconnectedness of this habitat matrix and how cumulative effects on its functioning may impact the health of the American eel everywhere within its habitat.

The Committee on the Status of Endangered Wildlife in Canada (COSEWIC) wrote in its 2006 report: "Indices of abundance in the Upper St. Lawrence River and Lake Ontario have declined by approximately 99% since the 1970's ... Possible causes of the observed decline, including habitat alteration, dams, fishery harvest, oscillations in ocean conditions, acid rain, and contaminants, may continue to impede recovery" (2006, iii).

The cumulative effects study for the American Fishery Society determined the chance of an eel surviving the dams on its way to spawn in the Sargasso Sea are low: "The probability of survival could be as low as 2.8%. It is evident from our analysis that the effects of turbine mortality are cumulative along the Mississippi and Ottawa Rivers causing significant reduction in overall probability of survival" (MacGregor et al. 2015, 156).

Larry McDermott was a member of both the Ontario and Canadian American Eel Recovery teams and concludes that the main problem in Canada and US was a lack of political will to deal with the requirement for upstream and downstream passage along with the impact of improper sewage treatment and other toxic migrations. William Commanda, Algonquin Elder and Officer of Canada, had this to say about the American eel:

> Where at the 1987 Constitutional Discussions, I raised concerns about the pollution transforming our lands and wildlife to federal and provincial leaders; today, the American Eel, a unique and irreplaceable fish, and source of nutrition and sustenance to my ancestors, is now on the Endangered Species List ... We are living in times of prophecy. The balance of the cycle of life and nature has been seriously disturbed, and we are all seeing the impacts in our daily lives at every turn ...
>
> Today, the plight of the American Eel must awaken us to the crucial need to transform our relationship with Mother Earth and All Our Relations, and to awaken us to the pivotal role of Indigenous Peoples in the process.
>
> (Manoshkadosh the American Eel, email to the Canadian Department of Fisheries and Oceans, March 31, 2007, 1)

This connection to the eel was so critical that Donald Marshall Jr., who is known for establishing Aboriginal fishing and Treaty rights by taking the Crown to court over being charged for netting eels in 1993, started a petition to save the species. The petition stated he would surrender his rights as a result of a Supreme Court of Canada victory to harvest eels if it meant more of them could make it to the Ottawa and St. Lawrence watersheds. Just before his death in 2009, Marshall was committed to re-establishing relationships with the eel and Indigenous youth as a key step in the recovery of the species.

This commitment to care for the species and the reciprocal relationship with the Eel that it suggests, is mostly lost on the state-led management of the fish. Two exceptions, however, can be found in John Cassleman, a world-recognized Canadian fish scientist, and team lead Rob MacGregor, who understood this concept and supported the full inclusion of Indigenous Peoples in the governance of the Ontario Recovery Strategy process. The recovery strategy team opened every meeting in Ceremony and closed them that way too. This level of mutual respect and accommodation was rare then but produced a much more powerful and comprehensive report than would have been achieved by Western science alone.

Tales of Resurgence, Recovery, and Abundance: Goose

The previous two stories are stories of destruction and attempted recovery. This one is about abundance and imbalance. While geese populations were low a few decades ago, they are now abundant, and even the Snow and Ross's geese and Canada geese are now considered overabundant by Environment Canada in some locations (Canada 2021). While all species of goose have long been an important source of food for many Indigenous Peoples, the relationship between the Canada goose and the Cree is particularly important. The return of the geese in the spring was the first source of fresh meat after winter, and its importance to the cultural traditions of the Cree cannot be underestimated. The Cree relationship to the Canada goose suffered during the height of the assimilationist policies and industrial activities of the 1960s and '70s, which impacted the traditional lands and waters.

Instead of living off the land in the bush, Cree people reluctantly began living in permanent villages and relying on other sources of food. Now the annual spring goose hunt is a time of cultural renewal, ceremony, and inter-generational knowledge transfer. Schools and businesses close for goose week so that everyone may participate in the hunt camps. John Turner, of Moose Cree First Nation, speaks of the importance of the hunt camps: "People have an interest in protecting and conserving bird habitat as the spring hunt is such an important part of life in the community. The spring goose hunt also has a spiritual aspect in terms of the return of the birds and the renewal of life and the warming weather" (Boutsalis 2020).

The Wemindji Cree in northern Quebec build dikes and cut corridors in preparation for the geese, and some are experimenting with prescribed burns to create new grass for the geese to eat (Sayles 2015). These practices, new and old, demonstrate both respect and reciprocity, where the geese are provided safe passage and suitable habitat and some geese give themselves to the hunters for sustenance after a long winter. And while geese are more abundant than ever, climate change and changing development landscapes means that their migration patterns are shifting. The Cree continue to modify the landscapes to match goose behaviour and provide safe passage to ensure continued abundance and the maintenance of the reciprocal relationship. These are the activities that allow for the hunt, the culture, and geese to continue.

Colonial Wildlife Management

> ... ethos of care; engaging in reciprocal relationships; and celebrating intercon-nectedness. Each of these ideas serves to deeply unsettle the assumption of the separation and superiority of humans in environmental management. (Muller et al. 2019, 403)

While the objective of Indigenous approaches to wildlife conservation is to cultivate and maintain good relations and connections between all species, as discussed with the buffalo, eel and goose, the objective of mainstream conservation and wildlife management is to protect (usually a dwindling number of) a particular species from humans, who are understood in the Western paradigm as separate from nature. This very fundamental distinction can be traced back to European colonization of what is now referred to as North America.

Whereas Indigenous relations with other animals was (and remains) rooted in natural law, with the related understanding that we are one animal among many, settlers brought with them deeply held beliefs about the "dominion of man" over all species (Eichler and Beaumister, 2018). Also part of a hierarchical worldview was the belief that some humans were more human than others due to their perceived separation from nature (Castree and Nash 2006). To put it bluntly, Enlightenment thinking promoted a divide between humans and nature, and positioned women, children, and nature, including wildlife, as a resource to be owned and thus exploited. It also provided a racist rationale for the belief in who was "human" enough to deserve recognition as a self-governing people. Settlers relied on the Papal Bull of (1493) "Doctrine of Discovery" to judge Indigenous people as less human because they were not Christian and had governance traditions that emphasized their connection to nature rather than their superiority to it (Borrows 2020). It is on these twin foundations that both colonialism and North American wildlife management continues to rest.

After a period of early settlement driven in large part by a desire to extract and profit from the continent's natural resources, including wildlife as food products, pelts, fish, and timber, came a period of concern for dwindling resources. In the case of wildlife, the earliest conservation efforts were in reaction to the actions of commercial hunters who decimated wildlife populations, such as the Plains bison[3] and aligned with the interests of sport hunters, who wished to conserve wildlife in order to pursue them for recreation (Loo 2006; Eichler and Beaumister 2018). Early interventions were thus created to keep market hunting in check and conserve game for the personal enjoyment of a (non-Indigenous) settler public, who wished to hunt for sport and who desired interactions with wildlife as a form of respite from the difficulties of modern urban life (Loo 2006). This had dire consequences for Indigenous Peoples and others who hunted for sustenance.

In Canada, the turn of the century marked the creation of more centralized bureaucracies enacted to rationalize and regulate the use of some wildlife (game) and control other wildlife (vermin) for the good of a (bourgoisie) "public." Early in the twentieth century, both the provincial and the federal levels of government imposed a licencing system that, in addition to providing revenue, allowed game departments to track and regulate kill (Loo 2006). With the exception of having to register their traplines,[4] Indigenous Peoples were exempt from the licencing provisions (only if it did not impede upon white traplines). The federal Department of Indian Affairs (DIA) argued that Indigenous people were "not bound by any provincial game act by virtue of the treaties they had signed, which guaranteed their hunting and fishing rights" (Loo 2006, 23). Not surprisingly, the provinces, which had gained authority over wildlife with the British North America Act, did not share this perspective and frequently enforced their rules on Indigenous residents as well, thus creating significant conflict in the early part of the century that continues to exist today.

Tina Loo, in her book *States of Nature: Conserving Canada's Wildlife in the Twentieth Century*, argues that game laws were "instruments of colonization," serving to impose not only limits on harvesting animals and fish but also a particular moral code about appropriate relationships to wildlife being those restricted to recreation and pleasure, thus serving to marginalize Indigenous people's cultural, social, and ceremonial practices, and their own relationship to animals. These early management interventions in the form of hunting quotas effectively turned Indigenous people's right to harvest into poaching and sought to sever their relationship with the animals they harvested.

The common set of regulatory tools employed by the state to manage wildlife in Canada have come to be known as the North American Model of Wildlife Conservation (NAM), the underlying principles of which promote particular versions of equity and morality that do not recognize Treaties with Indigenous Nations, or the inherent rights and responsibilities of Indigenous Peoples. (Eichler and Beaumeister 2018, 76) identify the core principles as follows:

> (1) Wildlife resources are a public trust. (2) Markets for game are eliminated. (3) Allocation of wildlife is by (state) law. (4) Wildlife can be killed only for a legitimate purpose. (5) Wildlife is considered an international resource. (6) Science is the proper tool to discharge wildlife policy. (7) Democracy of hunting is standard.

These principles, once interrogated, reveal a bias towards an economy of sport hunters, who are overwhelmingly of European descent and male, and the state, which in Canada is a colonial state. Tina Loo (2006, 26) writes how early wildlife law was as much about creating and enforcing a particular morality, a particular version of environmental citizenship that effectively "pushed subsistence and commercial hunters to the moral margin" as it was about managing wildlife numbers (Loo 2006, 26). The sportsman creed asserted that wildlife was too important to be eaten. The only legitimate reason for killing wildlife was as part of "a larger purpose, namely, elevating the human condition by providing sport and diversion for modern men" (Loo 2006, 27). The principles elevate the state as the appropriate management body and source of law which can manage for the public good and assert that Western science is not only the best but the *only* relevant knowledge system. Consistent with conservation ideals that informed early protected area establishment (Nash 2001), wildlife, and nature more generally, are the source of recreation and aesthetic enjoyment, not a source of livelihood and certainly not as older relatives who have lessons to teach us from the Indigenous perspective. NAM also repeatedly refers to wildlife as a resource, both words, especially in relation to one another, are both disrespectful and make little sense from an Indigenous worldview. NAM asserts that animals are objects to be owned and managed as a commodity while not providing space for animals to be kin who offer their bodies in a relationship of respect, relationality, reciprocity, and gratitude. In short, NAM ignores the values, needs, and interests of Indigenous peoples (Eichler and Beaumeister 2018).

Critical scholarship has routinely documented ways that state-based wildlife management programs alienate and criminalize Indigenous relationships to wildlife. Nadasdy (2007) describes how Yukon officials listen politely to First Nation accounts of animals as having agency equal to that of humans but, despite their public affirmation of traditional ecological knowledge, "conceptions of animals as persons who engage in reciprocal social relations with humans never seem to form the basis for wildlife management decisions, nor do they find their way into the provisions of First Nation land claim agreements" (Nadasdy 2007, 25). And Snook et al. (2020) observe that despite the importance of species such as caribou to Indigenous Peoples, the dominant management framework provides Indigenous People with little to no authority, voice, or meaningful recognition.

The North American model of wildlife management not only marginalizes Indigenous Peoples knowledge and governance of wildlife but, through its very ontological assumptions, serves to sever Indigenous Peoples' relationship to species in their territories, thus severely undermining their ability to practise a reciprocal ethic of care, as a lesson of practice for all peoples. Mainstream wildlife management in this country has travelled far from the intent in those original agreements and Treaties between settler states and Indigenous Peoples, at the expense and degradation of wildlife species. NAM does not deliver on the promise to share responsibility for the health and well-being of wildlife species. Rather it asserts singular authority over wildlife and, as a growing list of species at risk will tell you, has failed to protect wildlife and the biodiversity and ecological integrity that we all depend upon. Mikma'q Elder Albert Marshall would call this "one-eyed seeing," where we only look through one eye, with one knowledge system, and one governance system. He advocates for *Etuaptmumk*, or "Two-Eyed Seeing," where practitioners "see from one eye with the strengths of Indigenous ways of knowing, and see from the other eye with the strengths of Western ways of knowing, and to use both of these eyes together" (Bartlett, Marshall, and Marshall 2012, 335). This concept is expanded upon in chapter 7 of this volume. It is with this approach that we return to our hope that wildlife management can turn a corner and begin to honour Indigenous Treaties, recognize Natural Law, and listen again to those instructions, and reconnect Indigenous principles of respect, reciprocity, and interconnectedness into our collective relationship to wildlife for the benefit of All Life.

The Opportunity

Canada's continued willingness to ignore the intent behind the early and current Treaties with Indigenous Nations and the instructions held within them has led to a nature deficit as an impoverishment of Canadian society. The ongoing undermining of these Treaties leads to a lack of trust and dishonourable relationships between the Crown, conservation agencies and organizations, and Indigenous Nations and communities. It also represents a lost opportunity to learn governance processes, knowledge systems and worldviews that centres on a reciprocal ethic of care, reciprocity, and respect resulting in a wildlife management/relationships practice that is rather designed in accordance with colonial logics of division, hierarchy, and control with devastating results.

We are faced again, then, with an opportunity. Our current approaches are dominated by an attempt to maximize commercial and industrial development opportunities, and conservationists are left to try and save whatever scarce habitat they can at the continued expense of wildlife, lands, and waters. The current paradigm allocates a narrow role to wildlife conservation – one of attempting to protect dwindling wildlife all the while the world has been unable to achieve a single Aichi Biodiversity Target by the end of 2020. There is a global awakening of how damaging this economically driven paradigm is (see Nenquimo 2020). It is time and the opportunity to fully recognize that we must live within Natural Law. The possibility in front of us is to finally take up the responsibilities in the Treaties affirmed by our Ancestors and once again learn from Indigenous worldviews that can teach a reciprocal ethic of care and responsibility to future generations of All Life that is currently lacking, not only in wildlife management but in the governance of our relationship to the rest of nature.

In a 2015 American Fisheries Society Symposium, cross-cultural application was cited as important to the work of species decline analysis and recovery: As steps are hopefully taken to mitigate cumulative effects on American Eel across whole watersheds, the long-held but often ignored Indigenous principle of *Ginawaydaganuk* is gaining attention because it resonates with statements about interconnectedness and cooperative aspects in watershed management planning … *Ginawaydaganuk*, the Algonquin law of "interconnectedness" which is documented in the Welcoming and Sharing Wampum Belt carried by Algonquin First Nations, outlines responsibilities to each other and to the Earth. It requires cumulative effects of actions on the entire web of life, a consideration which reflects the Algonquin definition of sustainability, notions of reconciliation and respect jointly of human rights and environmental protection. (MacGregor 2015, 172–3; see also McDermott and Wilson 2010)

We see the beginning of this shift happening and cross-cultural applications becoming more widespread in the work done by the Pathway to Canada Target 1. In March 2018, after 18 months of deliberation by a panel of Indigenous and non-Indigenous conservationists, foresters, agriculturalists, and representatives from industry, the National Advisory Panel's report, titled *Canada's Conservation Vision*, states in Recommendation 1 that "all governments in Canada adopt a shared conservation vision that embraces Indigenous worldviews that acknowledge that we are one species among many that share the earth with the rest of life; achieves our collective conservation goals within a framework of reconciliation and the creation of Ethical Space" (NAP 2018, 2).

In short, the mainstream wildlife management toolbox, which is dominated by ways of restricting or limiting the use of wildlife, needs to be rebalanced to include Indigenous knowledge and practices that seek to maintain and enhance relations with all species to ensure their abundance and ecological integrity. The trust and understanding built through the Pathway process are now being acted upon through changes to how conservation agencies approach and partner with Indigenous Peoples, their willingness to develop greater cultural competency among their staff, the generosity of Indigenous thought leaders and Traditional Knowledge Holders in sharing their experiences, teachings and knowledge and most importantly, the support – Canada-wide – for recognizing Indigenous leadership in conservation.

We return now to the words of the late esteemed Algonquin Elder William Commanda, Keeper of the Seven Fires Prophecy Wampum Belt, as cited in Thumbadoo, 2005 (capitalization in original):

These Difficult Times We Live In Were Foreseen By Spiritual Visionaries Across the World. My Ancestors Warned Us About This Time And The Choices We Would Have To Make, In The Seven Fires Prophecy, Which Was Inscribed in Sacred Wampum Shell In The Late 1400s. The Prophecy Holds A Vision For The Future Where We
- Honour Our Relationship To Mother Earth And All Creation
- Celebrate Our Individual Gifts and Diversity, And Still
- Recognize and Respect Our Place Within A *Circle Of All Nations*

We contend that the decisions we make today, to practise Two-Eyed Seeing, to honour the original Treaties with Indigenous Nations, and to live up to our mutual and collective responsibilities towards the whole web of life, will result in the future of which Elder William Commanda spoke, and our Ancestors envisioned!

NOTES

1 We choose to capitalize Indigenous when referring to Peoples or Nations to indicate
   a respectful recognition that Indigenous is not an adjective but rather references
   an identity, much like Canadian or Spanish. We recognize significant variation
   amongst different groups of Indigenous Peoples. Throughout the chapter we also
   capitalize words such as Natural Law, Sky, Treaty, Creator when using these words
   to refer to nouns of elevated status. In these instances, we are referencing concepts
   articulated through a framework that comes with Creation and cannot be changed
   or manipulated and thus are distinct from the more common use of these terms.
2 Aichi Target 18: "By 2020, the traditional knowledge, innovations and practices of
   indigenous and local communities relevant for the conservation and sustainable use
   of biodiversity, and their customary use of biological resources, are respected, subject
   to national legislation and relevant international obligations, and fully integrated and
   reflected in the implementation of the Convention with the full and effective participation of indigenous and local communities, at all relevant levels" (CBD, 2010).
3 The demise of the plains bison resulted from a combination of factors, including
   market hunting to feed industries in the East but was significantly helped along
   by the military's push eastward and an explicit effort to separate plains Indigenous
   Peoples, such as the Blackfoot, from their main source of food, shelter, and spiritual
   wellbeing.
4 The DIA allowed for the trapline exemption because they felt it was in the best interest of the Aboriginal Peoples given the increased conflict caused by an influx of
   white trappers drawn to the trade.

WORKS CITED

Albert, T.F. 2001. "The Influence of Harry Brower, Sr., an Iñupiaq Eskimo Hunter, on
   the Bowhead Whale Research Program Conducted at the UIC-NARL Facility by the
   North Slope Borough." In *Fifty More Years Below Zero: Tributes and Meditations for
   the Naval Arctic Research Laboratory's First Half Century at Barrow, Alaska*, edited
   by D.W. Norton, 265–78. Fairbanks, AK and Calgary, Alberta: University of Alaska
   Press, and Arctic Institute of North America.
Barringer, F. 2018. "In the Pacific Northwest, Native Fishing Rights Take on a Role as
   Environmental Protector ... & the West." Stanford University. https://west.stanford
   .edu/news/blogs/and-the-west-blog/2016/pacific-northwest-native-fishing-rights
   -take-role-environmental-protector. Accessed May 14, 2021.
Bartlett, C., M. Marshall, and A Marshall. 2012. "Two-Eyed Seeing and Other Lessons
   Learned within a Co-learning Journey of Bringing Together Indigenous and
   Mainstream Knowledges and Ways of Knowing." *Journal of Environmental Studies
   and Sciences*. 2 (4): 871–86. https://doi.org/10.1007/s13412-012-0086-8

Bechtel, R. 2016. "Oral Narratives: Reconceptualising the Turbulence between Indigenous Perspectives and Eurocentric Scientific Views." *Cultural Studies of Scientific Education* 11: 447–69. https://doi.org/10.1007/s11422-014-9659-z

Borrows, J. 1994. "Constitutional Law from a First Nation Perspective: Self-Government and the Royal Proclamation." *UBC Law Review* 28: 1.

– 1997. "Wampum at Niagara: The Royal Proclamation, Canadian Legal History, and Self-Government." In *Aboriginal and Treaty Rights in Canada: Essays on Law, Equality and Respect for Difference*, edited by Michael Asch, 155–72. Vancouver: University of British Columbia Press.

– 2020. "Webinar – Demystifying the Doctrine of Discovery." Conservation through Reconciliation Partnership. Oct 14, 2020. https://conservation-reconciliation.ca/virtual-campfire

– 2021. "Treating: The Terms of Indigenous Permissions." J.V. Clyne Lectures at Green College, BUC: Indigenous Resurgence and Colonial Fingerprints in the 21st Century. March 2, 2021. https://www.youtube.com/watch?v=nehcpc7YHuo

Boutsalis, K. 2020. "For These Cree First Nations, Canada Geese Are Central to Cultural Revival." *Audobon Magazine*. https://www.audubon.org/news/for-these-cree-first-nations-canada-geese-are-central-cultural-revival

Canada 2021. "Overabundant Species Special Conservation Measures." Accessed April 25, 2021. https://www.canada.ca/en/environment-climate-change/services/migratory-game-bird-hunting/overabundant-species-special-conservation-measures.html.

Cardinal, Harold, and Walter Hildebrandt. 2000. *Treaty Elders of Saskatchewan: Our Dream Is That Our Peoples Will One Day Be Clearly Recognized as Nations.* Calgary: University of Calgary Press.

Castree, N., and C. Nash. 2006. "Posthuman Geographies." *Social and Cultural Geography* 7 (4): 501–4. https://doi.org/10.1080/14649360600825620

CBD. 2010. "Aichi Biodiversity Targets." Accessed May 14, 2021. https://www.cbd.int/sp/targets/

Clark, D., F. Van Beest, and R. Brook. 2012. "Polar Bear–Human Conflicts: State of Knowledge and Research Needs." Canadian Wildlife Biology and Management 1 (1): 21–9.

Commanda, W., 2006. "Manoshkadosh: The American Eel." Circle of All Nations: Algonquin Territory. Retrieved March 12, 2021. https://www.circleofallnations.ca/http___circleofallnations_2014NEW_Welcome.html/Circle_Blog/Entries/2014/2/28_Grandfather_inspires_protection_of_the_Eel_files/AmEelManoshkadosh2007FinalWithOrigEmailandGWClinkBiling.pdf.

Commons Debates. 1883. "Offical Report: Volume 2." May 9. E. Cloutier, Queen's Printer and Controller of Stationery. https://play.google.com/store/books/details?id=IFLnAAAAMAAJ&rdid=book-IFLnAAAAMAAJ&rdot=1

Craft, Aimée. 2013. *Breathing Life into the Stone Fort Treaty: An Anishnabe Understanding of Treaty One*. Saskatoon, SK: Purich Publishing.

Eichler, L., and D. Baumeister. 2018. "Hunting for Justice: An Indigenous Critique of the North American Model of Wildlife Conservation." *Environment and Society: Advances in Research* 9: 75–90. https://doi.org/10.3167/ares.2018.090106

Erasmus, G., and R. Dussault. 1996. *Report of the Royal Commission on Aboriginal Peoples*. Ottawa: The Commission.

Fox. P. 2018. "*Tapestry* Episode on CBC: Indigenous Scientist Argues Bison Should Return to Blackfoot Reserve." Feb 22, 2018. https://www.cbc.ca/radio/tapestry /sacred-space-2-the-power-of-the-land-1.4482906/indigenous-scientist-argues -bison-should-return-to-blackfoot-reserve-1.4482914

Garibaldi, A., and N. Turner. 2004. "Cultural Keystone Species: Implications for Ecological Conservation and Restoration." *Ecology and Society,* 9 (3). Accessed May 17, 2021. http://www.jstor.org/stable/26267680

Glover, F. 2020. "A Dish with One Spoon. Voices from Here. The Canadian Encyclopedia." *The Canadian Encyclopedia*. Accessed May 3, 2021. https:// thecanadianencyclopedia.ca/en/article/a-dish-with-one-spoon

Johns, Elizabeth Louise. 2020. "Buffalo Renaissance: The Northern Plains Tribes' Path to Self-Determination." Graduate student theses, dissertations, and professional papers. 11639. https://scholarworks.umt.edu/etd/11639

Keyser, E. 2018. Collaborative Conservation: Reconnecting People, Land and Bison through the *Iinnii Initiative*. MA thesis, University of Guelph.

Littlebear, Leroy. Personal Communication. September 29, 2016.

Loo, Tina. 2006. *States of Nature: Conserving Canada's Wildlife in the Twentieth Century*. Vancouver and Washington: University of British Columbia Press and University of Washington Press

MacGregor et al., 2015 "The Demise of American Eel in the Upper St. Lawrence River, Lake Ontario, Ottawa River, and Associated Watersheds: Implications of Regional Cumulative Effects in Ontario" http://www.ontarioriversalliance.ca/wp-content /uploads/2015/06/macgregor_cumulative-effects_finalfinal.pdf

McDermott, L., and P. Wilson. 2010. "'Ginawaydaganuk': Algonquin Law on Access and Benefit Sharing." *Policy Matters*. 17: 205–14

Mitchell, Edward, and Randall R. Reeves. 1980. "The Alaska Bowhead Problem: A Commentary." *Arctic* 33 (4) 4: 686–723. https://doi.org/10.14430/arctic2591

Muller, S., S. Hemming, and D. Rigney. 2019. "Indigenous Sovereignties: Relational Ontologies and Environmental Management." *Geographical Research*. 57 (4): 399–410. https://doi.org/10.1111/1745-5871.12362

Nadasdy, P. 2007. "The Gift in the Animal: The Ontology of Hunting and Human–Animal Sociality." *American Ethnologist*. 34 (1): 25–43. https://doi.org/10.1525 /ae.2007.34.1.25

NAP (National Advisory Panel). 2018. "Canada's Conservation Vision: A Report of the National Advisory Panel" Her Majesty the Queen in Right of Canada.

Nash, R. 2001. *Wilderness and the American Mind*, 4th edition. New Haven, CT: Yale University Press.

Nenquimo, N. 2020. "This Is My Message to the Western World – Your Civilization Is Killing Life on Earth." *The Guardian*. October 12, 2020. https://www.theguardian .com/commentisfree/2020/oct/12/western-worldyour-civilisation-killing-life-on -earth-indigenous-amazon-planet

Olsen, W. 2021. "The Ecological Buffalo: Following the Trail of a Keystone Species." Talk given for the Alberta Chapter of the Wildlife Society. March 24, 2021.

Sayles, J. 2015. "No Wilderness to Plunder: Process Thinking Reveals Cree Land-Use via the Goose-Scape." *The Canadian Geographer*. 59 (3): 297–303. https://doi .org/10.1111/cag.12201

Simpson, Leanne Betasamosake. 2008. "Looking after Gdoo-Naaganinaa: Precolonial Nishnaabeg Diplomatic and Treaty Relationships." *Wicazo Sa Review* 23 (2): 29–42. https://doi.org/10.1353/wic.0.0001

– 2011. *Dancing on Our Turtle's Back: Stories of Nishnaabeg Re-creation, Resurgence and a New Emergence*. Winnipeg, MB: Arbeiter Ring Publishing.

Smits, David. 1994. "The Frontier Army and the Destruction of the Buffalo: 1865–1883." *The Western Historical Quarterly*. **25** (3): 312–38. https://doi.org /10.2307/971110

Snook, J., A Cunsolo, D. Borish, C. Furgal, J. Ford, I. Shiwak, C. Flowers, and S.L. Harper. 2020. "'We're Made Criminals Just to Eat off the Land': Colonial Wildlife Management and Repercussions on Inuit Well-Being." *Sustainability* 12. https://doi.org/10.3390/su12198177

Thumbadoo, R. 2005. "Learning from a Kindergarten Dropout: William Commanda Ojigkwanong: Cultural Sharing and Reflections." Circle of All Nations.

Wildlife Conservation Society. 2014. Press release: "Historic Buffalo Treaty Signed by Tribes and First Nations along U.S. and Canada Border." Newsroom (wcs.org)

Disruptions, Part B

Disrupting Dominant Narratives for a Mainstream Conservation Issue: A Case Study on "Saving the Bees"

SHEILA R. COLLA

Pollinator decline has emerged as a conservation issue of intense public interest over the past decade in North America. It is estimated that 75 per cent of the world's flowering and crop plants rely on or benefit from animal pollination, with bees being the most important animal group (Potts et al. 2016). Despite a large, and growing, body of science, the dominant narratives of bee declines and requisite conservation actions have largely been driven by industry, media, ENGOs, and a misinformed public. Deconstructing common narratives and examining them for biases and determining whose interests they reflect is critical to effectively conserve declining pollinator species.

Using evidence of drastic bee declines, the beekeeping industry has framed policy and media narratives to benefit them, despite that European honeybees are not at risk of extinction, are not native, and cannot replace the pollination services wild pollinators provide (Colla & MacIvor 2017). Two high profile policy examples include President Obama's National Pollinator Health Strategy and Ontario Premier Wynne's Pollinator Action Plan. Both policies were developed largely due to public support around helping struggling bee populations, but in the end both policies reflected industry support instead of evidence-based conservation action (Nicholls et al. 2020). For example, the beekeeping industry is highly impacted by insecticide use because honeybees are brought into degraded agricultural landscapes. The industry has pushed for restricted use of certain pesticides designed to harm insects (i.e., neonicotinoids) (e.g., Carreck 2017). While restricting neonicotinoids use or replacing them with less harmful insecticides are likely also to benefit other declining pollinators at the local scale, it does not change the broader threats to native pollinators associated with unsustainable agriculture. As a sole priority, it serves only to address one threat and only at the scale relevant to the beekeeping.

Another example of prioritizing industry needs is the policy focus on the creation of and access to pollinator forage habitat for beekeepers to bring their hives, including on public lands and protected areas. Beekeepers require ample forage for bees when hives are not being used to pollinate crops for the hive's nutrition and to produce honey. A recent study found that a single honeybee hive removes pollen needed for 33,000 native solitary bees over three months in a landscape (Cane & Tepedino 2017). The policy focus on flowers and not nesting or overwintering habitat indicates critical habitat for wildlife is not a priority, but instead only nutritional resources for transient managed hives. Given the competition for forage and habitat (i.e., pollen and nectar resources), along with research showing the transmission of diseases from managed bees to wild bees (Alger et al. 2019; Colla et al. 2006), policies allowing managed bees to forage freely in protected areas and public lands is particularly risky for wild pollinator communities.

Like most invertebrates, the vast majority of pollinators have not been properly assessed for extinction risk. However, where good data exists, there is evidence that species have declined rapidly in recent decades. According to the IUCN Red List, about one in four North American bumblebee species are at risk of extinction, with some species, like the Rusty-Patched bumblebee, exhibiting sharp declines over a large geographical region. For this species and other at-risk bees, the threat of pathogen spillover from managed bees seems to best describe observed declines (Kent et al. 2018; Colla 2016). Thus, regulating these industries and the movement of bees within and between countries are critical steps towards conserving native bees. Distracting from these issues can lead to a confused public and to misallocated resources, which are in short supply in wildlife conservation (Ford et al. 2021). Even worse, they may increase the threats of competition and disease spillover. Indeed, van Vierssen Trip et al. (2020) found that the general public overwhelmingly incorrectly believe bee populations are in decline due to loss of flowers and pesticide use; about 50 per cent of Canadians believe all bees are endangered and that the European honeybee is a wild, native bee; and 66 per cent were unsure if the honeybee could replace wild bees. A media analysis showed a disproportionate focus on honeybees as the most important, or only, relevant pollinator insect, with less than 20 per cent of articles mentioning native bees or non-bee pollinators (Smith & Saunders 2016).

While the concern around pollinator declines has largely focussed on agricultural crop pollination, wild and diverse bee communities also ensure the pollination of wildflowers, shrubs and trees, which provide food and shelter for other organisms, making them critical components of resilient ecosystems. Additionally, wild pollinators have co-evolved mutualisms with culturally important food and medicine plants, making them important components of Indigenous cultural sovereignty (Lemelin et al. 2020). And wild pollinators provide their free ecosystem services to community gardens, often found in poor and racialized densely populated urban neighbourhoods, thus contributing to food security.

The Role of National Parks in Disrupting Heritage Interpretation on Turtle Island

CHANCE FINEGAN

National parks are key sites of biodiversity conservation. But their dual mandate – to preserve ecological integrity alongside public use – means they are also places of education. In Canada and the US, heritage interpretation is necessarily bound up in settler-colonialism. Whose heritage is interpreted? With what knowledge? By whom? By considering these questions and challenging protected area managers to interpret both settler and Indigenous heritage, we disrupt staid approaches to park management.

Heritage sites (which includes parks) are often closely intertwined with telling nationalist stories (Rosenkranz 2020; Lonetree 2012; Thomas 2001). In the US, parks have their roots in a desire to highlight that country's distinctiveness from Europe (Runte 1997). This mirrors one of the key characteristics of settler states: they separate themselves from the imperial metropole to form new states. In Canada, Sandilands (2009) argues protected areas are similarly nationalistic. Indeed, placing settlers at the centre of national stories is a primary way settler-colonialism is operationalized (Lowman and Barker 2015; Starblanket and Hunt 2020).

What can park managers do about this? I have five suggestions. First, leadership should set a clear expectation that Indigenous heritage be interpreted. In Canada, both the Truth and Reconciliation Commission (TRC) and the Missing and Murdered Indigenous Women and Girls (MMIWG) Inquiry have made it clear that a lack of knowledge about Indigenous peoples contributes to the ongoing violence against them (although, rather obviously, the solution does not rest on education alone). Turtle Island's heritage cannot be preserved and/or interpreted if practitioners focus only on settlers.

Second, interpretation is a profound exercise of power (Finegan 2019b). Interpreters speak with the authority of the uniform they wear. Additionally, like researchers, interpreters exercise their power when they decide which stories to tell and with whose knowledge. If I work at Thousand Islands National Park and choose to interpret Kanien'kehá:ka connections to the

St. Lawrence River but only rely on European knowledge and sources to inform my program, I do my site, the Kanien'kehá:ka, and visitors a grave disservice. Particularly given the close connections between European knowledge-gathering (both explorers and contemporary academics) and settler-colonialism (Smith 2009), I would be risking active harm and the reproduction of negative stereotypes.

Third, current interpretation practice emphasizes dialogic interpretation, which positions the interpreter not as the source of knowledge but as a facilitator. "In this role, the facilitator strives to provide a space where people feel comfortable talking with each other," write (Beck et al. 2019, 208–9). "... each person has something to say based upon their personal experiences...". In Indigenous contexts – when interpretation is explicitly about violently racialized people – this is dangerous. As Sensoy and DiAngelo (2014, 5) write:

> The discourse of personal experience has particularly significant consequences for dialogues in which the stated goals are to gain understanding of minoritized perspectives ... the claim of personal experience removes the political dimensions and preserves conventional arrangements.

Facilitated dialogue is inappropriate for interpreting Indigenous heritage, particularly when we consider how interpreters are trained to engage in it.

A recent interpretation textbook (Beck et al. 2019, 209) instructs that in dialogic interpretation, "facilitators should place minimal value judgment on responses ...". Taken at face value, such an approach would freely permit visitors to spout whatever racist stereotypes they may have about Indigenous peoples and lifeways. A freely available US National Park Service (2015, 2) worksheet online suggests questions like "What impact does immigration have on your daily life? What images come to your mind when you hear the word 'immigrant?' What do you value most about being a citizen of the US?" Such questions serve as prompts for a dialogic interpretation program on immigration. Again, the first and second do little to guard against creating space for stereotypes, and the third assumes all audience members are US citizens. Such flawed training must be urgently re-evaluated, particularly in Indigenous contexts. Otherwise, interpreters risk the continued marginalization of Indigenous Peoples.

Fourth, managers must ensure their staff are adequately trained to engage in this work. Interpreting Indigenous heritage is not the same as interpreting settler (particularly dominant European) heritage. Nor is it the same as interpreting natural heritage. It is inherently more complex, difficult, and loaded. Interpreters must be aware of these differences and understand how to grapple with them.

Fifth, as all of this suggests, Indigenous Peoples themselves should interpret their heritage. I am not suggesting that non-Indigenous people cannot ever do this work. Rather, it is that wherever possible, Indigenous people should do so. Barriers exist to increasing (and maintaining) Indigenous employment within agencies like Parks Canada or the US Park Service (Parks Canada 2019; Nelson 2016; Finegan 2019a). But these barriers do not negate the basic principle that those best positioned to interpret, say, Chinook heritage are the Chinook rather than settlers.

Biodiversity conservation and heritage interpretation exist alongside one another. Even those practitioners who do not work in parks (where this connection is most apparent) may find themselves educating the public about the natural and/or cultural heritage of Turtle Island. Conservation benefits when these efforts are expanded to include Indigenous heritage. As I have outlined here, there are a variety of ways in which conservation organizations and managers can begin to engage in this important work, disrupting settlers' primacy in the narratives we tell about this continent.

WORKS CITED

Alger, Samantha A., P. Alexander Burnham, Humberto F. Boncristiani, and Alison K. Brody. 2019. "RNA Virus Spillover from Managed Honeybees (*Apis mellifera*) to Wild Bumblebees (*Bombus spp.*)." *PloS one* 14, no. 6. https://doi.org/10.1371/journal.pone.0217822

Beck, Larry, Lawrence Beck, Ted Cable, and Douglas Knudson. 2019. *Interpreting Cultural and Natural Heritage: For a Better World*. Champaign, Illinois: Sagamore.

Carreck, N.L., 2017. "A Beekeeper's Perspective on the Neonicotinoid Ban." *Pest Management Science* 73 (7): 1295–8. https://doi.org/10.1002/ps.4489

Colla, Sheila R. 2016. "Status, Threats and Conservation Recommendations for Wild Bumble Bees (*Bombus spp.*) in Ontario, Canada: A Review for Policymakers and Practitioners." *Natural Areas Journal* 36, no. 4: 412–26. https://doi.org/10.3375/043.036.0408

Colla, Sheila R., Michael C. Otterstatter, Robert J. Gegear, and James D. Thomson. 2006. "Plight of the Bumble Bee: Pathogen Spillover from Commercial to Wild Populations." *Biological Conservation* 129, no. 4: 461–7. https://doi.org/10.1016/j.biocon.2005.11.013

Colla, Sheila R., and J. Scott MacIvor. 2017. "Questioning Public Perception, Conservation Policy, and Recovery Actions for Honeybees in North America." *Conservation Biology* 31, no. 5: 1202–4. https://doi.org/10.1111/cobi.12839

Convention on Biological Diversity. 2020. *Global Biodiversity Outlook 5*. Montreal. Accessed March 11, 2021. https://www.cbd.int/gbo/gbo5/publication/gbo-5-en.pdf

Creighton, Maria J.A., and Joseph R. Bennett. 2019. "Taxonomic Biases Persist from Listing to Management for Canadian Species at Risk." *Écoscience* 26 (4): 315–21. https://doi.org/10.1080/11956860.2019.1613752

Finegan, Chance. 2019a. *Protected Areas, Indigenous Peoples, and Reconciliation in the United States of America*. Toronto: York University.

– 2019b. "The Interpreter as Researcher: Ethical Heritage Interpretation in Indigenous Contexts." *Journal of Heritage Tourism*, 1–13. https://doi.org/10.1080/1743873X .2018.1474883

Ford, Adam T., Abdullahi H. Ali, Sheila R. Colla, Steven J. Cooke, Clayton T. Lamb, Jeremy Pittman, David S. Shiffman, and Navinder J. Singh. 2021. "Understanding and Avoiding Misplaced Efforts in Conservation." *FACETS* 6 (1): 252–71. https:// doi.org/10.1139/facets-2020-0058

Geldmann, Jonas, Andrea Manica, Neil D. Burgess, Lauren Coad, and Andrew Balmford. 2019. "A Global-Level Assessment of the Effectiveness of Protected Areas at Resisting Anthropogenic Pressures." *Proceedings of the National Academy of Sciences* 116 (46): 23209 LP–23215. https://doi.org/10.1073/pnas.1908221116

Henson, Paul, Rollie White, and Steven P. Thompson. 2018. "Improving Implementation of the Endangered Species Act: Finding Common Ground through Common Sense." *BioScience* 68 (11): 861–72. https://doi.org/10.1093/biosci/biy093

Kent, C.F., A. Dey, H. Patel, N. Tsvetkov, T. Tiwari, V.J. MacPhail, Y. Gobeil, B.A. Harpur, J. Gurtowski, M.C. Schatz, and S.R. Colla. 2018. "Conservation Genomics of the Declining North American Bumblebee *Bombus terricola* Reveals Inbreeding and Selection on Immune Genes." *Frontiers in Genetics* 9: 316.

Lemelin, R.H., A. Hutter, K.P. Whyte, and G. Root. 2020. "From Aamoo (Bees) to Memengwaa (Butterflies), Living Well with Manidoons (Insect Pollinators) and Ninwish (Milkweed): Indigenous Peoples and Insect Pollinators on Turtle Island (North America)." *American Entomologist*, 66 (4): 42–7. https://doi.org/10.1093/ae/tmaa064

Lemieux, Christopher J., Paul A. Gray, Rodolphe Devillers, Pamela A. Wright, Philip Dearden, Elizabeth A. Halpenny, Mark Groulx, Thomas J. Beechey, and Karen Beazley. 2019. "How the Race to Achieve Aichi Target 11 Could Jeopardize the Effective Conservation of Biodiversity in Canada and Beyond." *Marine Policy* 99: 312–23. https://doi.org/10.1016/j.marpol.2018.10.029

Lonetree, Amy, ed. 2012. *Decolonizing Museums: Representing Native America in National and Tribal Museums*. Chapel Hill: University of North Carolina Press.

Lowman, Emma Battell, and Adam Barker. 2015. *Settler: Identity and Colonialism in 21st Century Canada*. Black Point, Nova Scotia: Fernwood Publishing.

McCune, Jenny L., Anja M. Carlsson, Sheila Colla, Christina Davy, Brett Favaro, Adam T. Ford, Kevin C. Fraser, and Eduardo G. Martins. 2017. "Assessing Public Commitment to Endangered Species Protection: A Canadian Case Study." *FACETS* 2 (1): 178–94. https://doi.org/10.1139/facets-2016-0054

McCune, Jenny L., William L. Harrower, Stephanie Avery-Gomm, Jason M. Brogan, Anna-Mária Csergő, Lindsay N.K. Davidson, Alice Garani, et al. 2013. "Threats to Canadian Species at Risk: An Analysis of Finalized Recovery Strategies." *Biological Conservation* 166: 254–65. https://doi.org/10.1016/j.biocon.2013.07.006

McCune, Jenny L., Alyson Van Natto, and Andrew S. MacDougall. 2017. "The Efficacy of Protected Areas and Private Land for Plant Conservation in a Fragmented

Landscape." *Landscape Ecology* 32 (4): 871–82. https://doi.org/10.1007/s10980
-017-0491-1

Nelson, Glenn. 2016. "Why Has the National Park Service Gotten Whiter?" *High Country News*, August 2016.

Nicholls, A.A., G.B. Epstein, and S.R. Colla. 2020. "Understanding Public and Stakeholder Attitudes in Pollinator Conservation Policy Development." *Environmental Science & Policy* 111: 27–34.

Parks Canada. 2019. "Report on Gatherings on Indigenous Cultural Heritage." Gatineau, Quebec.

Potts, S.G., V. Imperatriz-Fonseca, H.T. Ngo, M.A. Aizen, J.C. Biesmeijer, T.D. Breeze, L.V. Dicks, L.A. Garibaldi, R. Hill, J. Settele, and A.J. Vanbergen, 2016. "Safeguarding Pollinators and Their Values to Human Well-Being." *Nature*, 540 (7632): 220–9.

Reed, Graeme, Nicolas D. Brunet, Sheri Longboat, and David C Natcher. 2020. "Indigenous Guardians as an Emerging Approach to Indigenous Environmental Governance." *Conservation Biology*. https://doi.org/10.1111/cobi.13532

Rist, Phil, Whitney Rassip, Djalinda Yunupingu, Jonathan Wearne, Jackie Gould, Melanie Dulfer-Hyams, Ellie Bock, and Dermot Smyth. 2019. "Indigenous Protected Areas in Sea Country: Indigenous-Driven Collaborative Marine Protected Areas in Australia." *Aquatic Conservation: Marine and Freshwater Ecosystems* 29 (S2): 138–51. https://doi.org/10.1002/aqc.3052

Rosenkranz, Leah. 2020. "History and Memory in the Intersectionality of History and Memory in the Intersectionality of Heritage Sites and Cultural Centers in the Pacific Heritage Sites and Cultural Centers in the Pacific Northwest and Hawai'i Northwest and Hawai'i." Unpublished MA thesis, Portland State University.

Runte, Alfred. 1997. *National Parks: The American Experience*. Lincoln: University of Nebraska Press.

Sandilands, Catriona. 2009. "The Cultural Politics of Ecological Integrity: Nature and Nation in Canada's National Parks, 1885–2000." *International Journal of Canadian Studies*, no. 39–40: 161. https://doi.org/10.7202/040828ar

Sensoy, Özlem, and Robin DiAngelo. 2014. "Respect Differences? Challenging the Common Guidelines in Social Justice Education." *Democracy and Education* 22 (2): 1–10.

Smith, Linda Tuhiwai. 2009. *Decolonizing Methodologies: Research and Indigenous Peoples*. 2nd ed. New York: Zed Books.

Smith, T.J., and M.E. Saunders. 2016. "Honey Bees: The Queens of Mass Media, Despite Minority Rule among Insect Pollinators." *Insect Conservation and Diversity* 9 (5): 384–90. https://doi.org/10.1111/icad.12178

Starblanket, Gina, and Dallas Hunt. 2020. *Storying Violence: Unravelling Colonial Narratives in the Stanley Trial*. Winnipeg: ARP Books.

Thomas, Nicholas. 2001. "Indigenous Presences and National Narratives in Australasian Museums." In *Culture in Australia: Policies, Publics and Programs*, edited by Geoffrey Brennan and Tony Bennett, 299–313. Cambridge: Cambridge University Press. https://doi.org/10.22459/hr.1997.01

Tran, Tanya C., Douglas Neasloss, Jonaki Bhattacharyya, and Natalie C. Ban. 2020. "'Borders Don't Protect Areas, People Do': Insights from the Development of an Indigenous Protected and Conserved Area in Kitasoo/Xai'xais Nation Territory." *FACETS* 5 (1): 922–41. https://doi.org/10.1139/facets-2020-0041

US National Park Service. 2014. "The Arc of Dialogue, NPS Interpretive Development Program – 03/2014 Professional Standards for Learning and Performance." Accessed January 13, 2022. https://mylearning.nps.gov/wp-content/uploads/2015/11/IFT-Arc-of-Dialogue-HO.pdf

van Vierssen Trip, N., V.J. MacPhail, S.R. Colla, and B. Olivastri. 2020. "Examining the Public's Awareness of Bee (*Hymenoptera: Apoidae: Anthophila*) Conservation in Canada." *Conservation Science and Practice*, 2 (12): e293.

PART C

Transformation through Values

6 Reconciliation or *Apiksitaultimik*?
Indigenous Relationality for Conservation

SHERRY PICTOU

When I return to the shores and inlets of what is known today as the Bay of Fundy and Tuitnuk (at the out-flow), known as the Digby Gut, or when I walk familiar wooded trails straddling rivers, streams, and brooks, I remember these places as learning to swim and fish, to harvest dulse, to harvest sweet grass, dig and bake clams beneath beach sand, cook trout on an open fire, or how to choose the perfect alder branch to slide trout on to carry home. I can still hear the laughter and voices of my younger brother and cousins as though it were yesterday, and voices of the old ones who guided and taught us how to live and story these places. Little did I realize then how these spaces were microscopic in scale compared to our ancestral homelands delineated by broader natural boundaries, beyond the reserve, making up our ancestral hunting and fishing district – Kespukwitk (end of the flow or the last flow of water) (Sable & Francis 2012). The inlets, coves, and bays I remember are now marked by dense enclosures of private properties (waterfront properties), and our canoe portages/carries have been replaced by logging roads, some say better than main roads. At the same time, within Kespukwitk lies Kejimkujik National Park, established in 1969 and as a Heritage Site, established in 1995 – land of the little people or fairies. I remember listening to stories told to me by my Grandmother about how Kejimkujik is comprised of sacred land and waterscapes that greatly shaped her own learning as a child (before the park). And buried in the burial grounds there are her (and my) ancestors.

I open with this story of my experience as a Mi'kmaw woman and scholar from Kespukwitk because, upon reflection, it offers a teaching about how colonialism (and capitalism) continue to impact the Mi'kmaq and many Indigenous Peoples of Turtle Island (North America) (and around the world). The ongoing dispossession of ancestral homelands by setter-state colonialism is marked by neoliberal exploitation of natural water and landscapes (private and public/ Crown property) on one end of the spectrum or what is referred to as "fortress conservation"[1] or no/low human footprint (parks or protected areas) on the other. It is important to note, though, that there have been increased efforts to engage with Indigenous Peoples, including the Mi'kmaq, in the planning and management of National Parks over the past decade (Kejimkujik n.d; Parks Canada 2019). Recent environmental literature indicates that conservation practice is now at a point in time when the past meets the present, and reconciliation is being examined as a way to open up transformative possibilities for the future (e.g., Artelle et al. 2019; Garnett et al. 2018; Schuster et al. 2019). In particular, reconciliation is being explored as a way for transforming colonial approaches to conservation coinciding with the endorsement of the Universal Declaration on the Rights of Indigenous Peoples (UNDRIP) in 2007 (M'sit No'kmaq et al. 2021; Zurba & Sinclair 2020; Zurba, Beazley, English, & Buchmann-Duck 2019; Moola and Roth 2018).

This chapter contributes to this discussion – denoting a call for decolonizing conservation practices – by exploring how Indigenous knowledges grounded in land- and water-based lifeways are embodiments of the wild or wild species as our relatives: an Indigenous relationality that encompasses the human and non-human or more-than-human world including our ancestors and "all of Creation" (McGregor 2018, 244). I argue that the concept of reconciliation therefore must be mobilized as a relational practice beyond political economies and political ecologies in conservation practice. In other words, reconciliation cannot exist politically, conceptually, or materially "outside of our relationship to Place" (Wilson & Hughes 2019, 8). I first highlight some of the tensions and politics regarding Traditional Ecological Knowledge (TEK) and Indigenous Knowledge (IK), followed by the politics of reconciliation, and I discuss how TEK/IK within political and academic discourses can intersect. As a decolonizing approach, I explore how reconciliation is a form of healing in Mi'kmaw/ Indigenous relationality that holds transformative possibilities for reframing reconciliation in conservation principles and practices. This is followed by a discussion about how reconciliation and conservation through the lens of Indigenous feminism is imperative to a truthful or authentic reconciliation process. This chapter by no means offers a definitive analysis about reconciliation and conservation. Instead, it broadens the discussion by posing critical questions to consider in efforts to mobilize reconciliation for transforming and decolonizing conservation practice.

Tensions between TEK, IK, and Conservation

The (in)validity and (mis)use of traditional ecological knowledge (TEK) or Indigenous Knowledge (IK) has been contested over several decades and continues to this day. As early as 2001, Michi Saagiig Nishnaabeg (Anishinaabe) author Leanne Betasamosake (2001, 154) noted that "I found it very difficult to identify with the perspectives on TEK found in mainstream Environmental Science journals and I was extremely concerned about the lack of Aboriginal voices and perspectives in the field.... I have now recognized that Western science is the primary tool used by government and industry to justify the destruction of Aboriginal Territories for short-term profit." Simpson is stating how Western science, government, and capitalism are interrelated, inferring an inter-institutional complicity in the dispossession and violence against Indigenous Peoples and the environmental destruction of their ancestral homelands.

Anishinaabe scholar Deborah McGregor (2004) also observes "even when non-Native definitions incorporate valid aspects of TEK, they tend to consider TEK as a 'body of knowledge,' something that can be considered as being separate from the people who hold it" (78), and "the way in which TEK is understood and implemented within a Western perspective means that the insights into the nature of the environmental crisis and approaches to its resolution that TEK offers get lost" (72; also see Starblanket & Stark 2019, 181). In other words, "seeking knowledge is not just for the sake of knowledge" (McGregor, Restoule, & Johnston 2018, 241). Even today, "views of conservation held by local communities whose languages do not directly translate the concept of conservation as it is described in the environmental sciences" (Nuna, Sable, Foxcroft & Simbine 2021, 52) are excluded.

At the same time, national and international consortia of sustainable development and conservation agencies are making additional exerted efforts to engage with TEK and IK, especially since the passing of UNDRIP (2007). For example, the Intergovernmental Science-Policy Platform on Biodiversity and Ecosystem Services (IPBES) extended the mandate of the task force on Indigenous Local Knowledge (ILK) to implement "Enhanced recognition of and work with [I]ndigenous and local knowledge systems" up to 2030 (IPBES 2019). The International Union for Conservation of Nature (IUCN) has been coordinating efforts with the Commission on Environmental, Economic and Social Policy (CEESP), and since 2011 with the Specialist Group on Indigenous Peoples, Customary Law and Human Rights (SPICEH), to work towards Indigenous Protected Areas (IPAs), or as referred to in Northern Turtle Island (Canada), Indigenous Protected and Conserved Areas (IPCAs) (Indigenous Circle of Experts (ICE) 2018; Zurba et al. 2019). IUCN will also be hosting a World Summit of Indigenous Peoples and Nature in 2021 (IUCN 2021). Yet, challenges remain regarding how to "integrate" or engage with TEK/IK, similar to those pointed out 16 to 20 years ago by Simpson and McGregor. In assessing the IPBES approach to ILK, Hill et al. (2020, 17) argue that crucial gaps remain in "shared governance with IPLC [Indigenous Peoples and Local Communities] and a commitment to equity between ILK and science; transformation, loss and innovation within ILK; protection of intellectual property rights associated with ILK; and the requirement for experts in boundary-crossing and bridging knowledge systems. Power asymmetries remain a formidable barrier to working across knowledge systems in IPBES and other environmental assessments." IUCN/CEESP Chair Kristen Walker Painemilla (2021, xi) states that "we also must recognise that nature managed by IPLCs is under increasing pressure, including from resource extraction, commodity production, mining, and transport and energy infrastructure, which has only been exacerbated with the COVID-19 global pandemic." Environmental sciences (and other disciplinary knowledges) and unsustainable resource exploitation mark both ends of a spectrum – academia and political economies – while at the same time they can intersect, as elucidated by Simpson and Paineilla, as key parts of a Western-colonial system or framework. Therefore, the task of decolonizing environmental sciences involves "simultaneous engagements with, and resistances to, those same sciences" (Dhillon 2020, 486) and the knowledge (and other) systems that underly them.

To get beyond simply applying TEK/IK/ILK within a Western science system requires embracing Indigenous knowledge systems as a whole, including restoring human relationships to the land/waters. In Northern Turtle Island, such conversations have been especially mobilized in the context of IPCAs through the work of the Indigenous Circle of Experts (ICE). ICE was formed to advise and make recommendations towards Target 1 of Canada's 2020 Biodiversity Goals and Targets, focusing on the terrestrial and inland waters of Canada (based on Target 11 of the Aichi Biodiversity Targets set out by the Convention on Biological Diversity). Through insights gained in gatherings of governments and Indigenous Peoples across Canada, ICE outlined 28 key recommendations, mostly geared towards federal, provincial, and territorial governments, in their report *We Rise Together: Achieving Pathway to Canada Target 1 through the Creation of Indigenous Protected and Conserved Areas in the Spirit and Practice of Reconciliation* (ICE 2018). While it is not within the scope of this chapter to explore the politics involved in seeking recognition of Indigenous knowledges and rights from settler governments (Coulthard 2014; Zurba & Sinclair 2020; Zurba et al. 2019; Finegan 2018), it is important to point out that a key underlying message identified in the ICE report is that reconciling tensions between conservation practice and Indigenous knowledges relies on a process of "healing" by restoring a sustainable human relationship to the land/waters (ICE 2018, 36, 48, 103; also see Zurba et al. 2019, 14; Nuna et al. 2021). For example, ICE (2018, 48) asserts that IPCAs "could be areas where the focus is on restoring not only the land, but also humans' relationship to it, with the intention of leaving the land and the relationship 'better than we found it.'" While I will later come back to the concept of healing within the context of reconciliation, what is significant about this assertion is that it opens up possibilities for transcending the barriers or silos pronounced in Western science that view humans as being separate from nature. Viewing humans as separate from nature has resulted in competing or contradictory policies that support the dualistic aims of unsustainable economic exploitation on one hand and fortress conservation on the other. The possibilities opened up by acknowledging and restoring human relationship with the land could result in new policies that offer healthier alternatives to these false dichotomies.

Bridging Tensions in the Conservation–Exploitation Divide through Reciprocal Relationship

Although ICAs, IPCAs and other similar arrangements offer promising ways forward – beyond fortress conservation and towards reconciliation for people and the land – tensions remain between conservation and exploitation. There is a cautionary lesson offered by some of the preliminary analyses of the Great Bear Rainforest Agreements, covering 6.5 million hectares and the ancestral homelands of 26 Indigenous communities. The Agreements are being hailed as a step towards reconciliation with Indigenous Peoples, but at the same time the communities continue to face challenges in implementing an ecosystem-based management approach against unsustainable industrial forestry practices (ICE 2018; Price, Roburn & MacKinnon 2009; also see Loucks 2021). These tensions between conservation and industrial exploitation impact Indigenous Peoples around the world in asserting self-determining approaches to sustainable land- and water-based lifeways. In other words, alternative visions for sustainable or biocultural conservation are usually pre-empted by a binary of two extremes – either fortress conservation or unsustainable industrial exploitation – and are often presented within the language of conservation and reconciliation as the only two choices (Corntassel 2012; Pictou 2018; Washington et al. 2018). Yet, with respect to conservation practice, as Merle Sowman, Wayne Rice, A. Minerva Arce-Ibarra, and Ivett Peña-Azcona (2021, 23) state:

> There are different meanings associated with the term conservation in different cultural contexts. The Western notion of conservation has a strong focus on restricting access to and protection and stewardship of resources, whereas in many Indigenous and local communities, cultural identity and practices are inextricably linked to relationships with the use and conservation of resources and the environment … Therefore, an awareness of the meanings and motivations that guide conservation behaviour in local contexts, and a respect for the customary and cultural institutions that inform resource access, use and governance, are critical to promoting conservation outcomes that are socially just and ecologically sustainable.

There are also similar tensions that need to be resolved between social justice and ecological justice, with respect to which aspect prevails when social and ecological rights are seen as separate or in opposition. Washington et al. (2018), for example, explore how to reconcile social justice with eco-justice through an ecocentric worldview. While they "accept that social justice is by no means universally supported in Western society and that the neoliberal focus on competition represents a key problem to advancing social justice," they also argue that a "theory of justice must rank ecojustice as at least equally important as social justice" (371). Eco-justice provides a means to speak for the trees, plants, fish, rivers, animals, etc. Therefore, Washington et al. offer an eco-justice framework for social and ecological justice that attends to the power dynamics of privilege, internalized dominance, and oppression as a way forward to ensure effective conservation by countering the dominant Western, anthropocentric worldview. In an important way, eco-justice, as framed here, has some commensurability with many Indigenous worldviews grounded in ways of knowing that regard human and non-human worlds as inseparable. "Both ecocentrism and [I]ndigenous kinship ethics see life as kin and worthy of respect and a duty of care, as they accept their intrinsic value. Anthropocentrism does not do this, seeing all of nature as just a resource for human use" (368).

Accordingly, a conservation lens grounded in ecocentrism could bring Indigenous and non-Indigenous perspectives into closer alignment, disrupting dominant Western anthropocentrism, and serving to decolonize both people and nature in ways that are socially and ecologically just. Bringing Western and Indigenous values into closer alignment opens up opportunities for conservation insights from both knowledge systems for the good of all (M'sit No'kmaq et al. 2021). Mi'kmaw Elder Dr. Albert Marshall has long introduced *Etuaptmumk* (Two-Eyed Seeing), a concept in the Mi'kmaw language for bringing the best of two worldviews – Western knowledges and Mi'kmaw/Indigenous knowledges – to learn and "use both of these eyes together for the benefit of all" (ICE 2018, 57; also see M'sit No'kmaq et al. 2021; Popp, Reid, Marshall, McGregor, Miller and Sritharan; Young; Myral in this section). When Elder Dr. Albert Marshall speaks about the "benefit of all" he is referring to the interdependence of the human and non-human worlds and therefore he also speaks to how we have "inherit responsibilities ... for ensuring that no action that we will take will ever compromise the ecological integrity of the area.... Because our overall objective is to ensure that the next seven generations will also have the same opportunities as we have, and hopefully better opportunities than we have, of not just being able to sustain themselves and harvest the gifts from the creator but also be able to enjoy and learn from her just as our ancestors have learned from her" (ICE 2018, 37).

As with many Indigenous worldviews, Elder Dr. Albert Marshall is speaking to a relational responsibility that is reciprocal, or a "reciprocal responsibility" (ICE 2018, 36), a concept that is greatly theorized and practised in Indigenous scholarship and research (McGregor, Restoule, & Johnston 2018; Wilson, Breen, & Dupié 2019). Another key element of his concept of relational responsibility is how we learn from Mother Earth. His late wife, Elder Dr. Murdena Marshall (u.d., 1), explains further:

Traditional knowledge is known through watching and listening, not in the motionless way that educational institutions now demand. It is experienced through songs and ceremonies, through the activities demonstrated through hunting, fishing, and gathering medicine. Knowledge interacts with, and is visible in, the daily life of a person, in our association with animals and trees, with plants and with the spirit world. It is present in our dreams, in our visions, in our ceremonies and with all of creation. It is felt in the spirit of the people.

So, within this broader concept of Indigenous Relationality, is it possible to transform our relationship with the land/waters (or 'conservation') in ways that invoke a reciprocity of responsible relationships "between persons ... and with important ecological species and places [that] are central features of Indigenous environmental governance" (Dhillon 2020, 487)? As a way to explore how we might answer this question I interrogate the concept of reconciliation as a transformative element in conservation or vice versa as being elucidated in recent conservation and reconciliation literature (e.g., M'sit No'kmaq et al. 2021; Zurba & Sinclair 2020; Zurba, Beazley, English, & Buchmann-Duck 2019; Moola and Roth 2018; ICE 2018).

The Politics and Intersections of Reconciliation

While state-sanctioned approaches to reconciliation have been in process for over 30 years (Coulthard 2014), efforts towards "Advancing Reconciliation with Indigenous Peoples" living in Northern Turtle Island (Canada 2019) have been galvanized by the Truth and Reconciliation Commission's Calls to Action (CTA) in 2015. The CTA was a result of an investigative response to the genocidal impacts of the Residential Schools commissioned by the federal government. Since the release of the CTA, reconciliation discourses have accelerated, especially within the political contours of state-Indigenous leadership and within academic institutions in Canada. However, governmental reconciliation policies have been greatly contested, by Indigenous scholars among others, as being rhetorically monopolized by state and industry as a way to contemporize colonialism and dispossession under the cloak of economic advancement as a basis for reconciliation (Coulthard 2014; Daigle 2019; Simpson 2017; also see McGregor 2018; Wilson, Breen & Dupre 2018). And while Indigenous knowledges have started to take their rightful place within academia, the need for post-secondary efforts at implementing the related CTA to education and research must move beyond the limitations of token land acknowledgments and the hiring of more Indigenous faculty without transforming the constructions of "epistemic violence" experienced by Indigenous scholars (Cormier & Ray 2018, 114; also see Daigle 2019).

Nicole Penak (2018, 142) explains how land acknowledgments can serve to erase Indigenous presence by positioning Indigenous existence as being in the past and removed from cities:

> These reconciliation-era acknowledgments, some kind of an effort to capture the Indigeneity of this space in a pronouncement, bound by the strict confines of the past tense. Though they are being tediously worked over by committees of expert consultants, the story they tell still seems to place Indigenous people outside of this time and outside of this space. When people talk about connecting to the land, they often point outside of the city. That Indigenous lives, culture, stories live somewhere separate from here. These *land* acknowledgments do little to correct this, as they fail to talk about land but centre ... political dealings. As Indigenous Peoples our connection to land is somewhat dialectic. The trickery that removes the land – the landless – from the city's story appears to take Indigenous Peoples and our stories with it.

Mushkegowuk (Cree) scholar Michelle Daigle (2019, 704) argues how most reconciliation efforts mandated by Canadian post-secondary institutions are merely playing lip service and placing most of the responsibility and labour on Indigenous Peoples, while at the same time implicitly reproducing dispossession and violence against Indigenous Peoples in ways such as affording privilege to extractive industries to "hold political and material space" across university campuses (714). Like Simpson and Painemilla in the discussion about TEK/IK, Daigle explicates the intersections of academia and political economy/ecologies marking reconciliation efforts as disingenuous. This being said, should we be delving into reconciliation, whether in academic or political efforts, without looking for ways to operationalize more conciliatory practices towards reconciliation, beyond administrative gestures such as land acknowledgments? Or should we instead be focusing our reconciliation efforts towards conciliatory practices for transforming knowledges in general, and in our case, conservation knowledges, principles, and practices in particular to Indigenous ways of knowing? I would argue that some of the answer lies within practices of Indigenous relationality – underscored by land- and water-based relations denoting the inseparability of humans and land/waters (rural and urban).

At the beginning of the documentary film *We Story the Land* (Stiegman & Pictou 2016), produced in my ancestral homelands, Councillor Carol Ann Potter (who also participated in the ICE Eastern Regional Gathering) states:

> When you are out in the woods or on the water, you become very in tune. You are part of it ... then you realize our people have been here. When you are standing there, you can start thinking really about what it means about actually where you

are standing. There's not a time that we don't know that we haven't been here, or our ancestors haven't been here. So, to me we are a part of this land. We are like the blood that runs through the veins of the trees and streams. We are part of that.

Councillor Potter is speaking to the inseparability of the ontological (land/water) from the epistemological (Indigenous ways of knowing) and how land/waters "occupy as an ontological framework for understanding relationships" (Coulthard 2014, 60). As Indigenous feminists Gina Starbanket and Heidi Kiiwetinepinesiik Stark (2018, 182) argue, "it is not enough to make space for Indigenous knowledge. We must allow this space to be reconfigured by Indigenous knowledge." This builds on the concept of "ethical space" in conservation as a space "that respects the integrity of all knowledge systems" (ICE 2018, 6; also see M'sit No'kmaq et al. 2021) and towards Elder/Dr. Albert Marshall's teaching about the responsibility of not compromising the ecological integrity of our environment, which is itself a source of knowledge, and in relationship, a way of knowing. McGregor (2018, 253) describes how, from an Indigenous researcher perspective, we are "living the knowledge … not just seeking knowledge, it is the way we conduct ourselves and relate to other beings in Creation. The research that is enacted to pursue these goals is informed by an 'ethic of responsibility.'" So, while ethical space is a space where knowledges can come together, it also must be driven by an ethical and relational responsibility to knowledge as living, learning, and researching in and with all of Creation.

Thus, if we can learn to understand and live this inter-relationship between the ontology and epistemology of land (and water) and human existence, what Glen Coulthard (2014) calls "grounded normativity," while enacting "ethical responsibility," then I would argue that there is an opportunity for reconciliation to be a transformative element in broader knowledge systems, and in conservation practice, as well as for transforming the anthropocentric valuing of the natural world solely as a commodity for one species and one mode of development – the human global economy.

While not speaking to reconciliation specifically, John N. Kittinger et al. (2021, 89–90) point to how training programs for conservation practitioners "must become more inclusive and incorporate diverse epistemologies, knowledge systems, and cultural norms." I further contend that reconciliation in conservation practice must also prioritize land and waterscapes as sources of food and water and local livelihoods or "local Indigenous economies" (ICE 2018, 5) and serve to confront mega-industrial development. But in order to do this, I am suggesting that Indigenous concepts of reconciliation embedded in Indigenous Knowledge or TEK have something to offer that has so often been overlooked, as also noted by McGregor (2004). Mi'kmaq and other Indigenous approaches to relationality in reconciliation include crucial processes for healing, an important instrumental concept emphasized throughout the ICE report.

Reconciliation or *Apiksitaultimik*? Indigenous Relationality and Healing

The Mi'kmaw equivalent to the concept of reconciliation is *apiksitaultimik*. Yet one "cannot demand *apiksiktuek* ('that which forgives')" without "*nijkitekek* ('that which heals')." Nijkitekek "through *ilsutekek* ('to make right') guides relations toward reintegration and healing" (McMillan 2016, 198; also see Young 2016, 95). This process is usually achieved through ceremonies and feasts referred to as *Wi'ku-paltimk*. The Mi'kmaw linguistic inference is that reconciliation consists of actions that are relational, dialectical, and ceremonial. Mi'kmaw scholar Tuma Young (2016, 95) explains that "through the prism of the L'nu [Mi'kmaw] worldview ... the centrality of balance and harmony – 'correction,' as the recovery of correct relationship – begins to emerge, together with an emphasis on the importance of story, song, ritual, and ceremony in reaching this goal." Together, apiksituek, nijkitekek, and ilsutekek for achieving reconciliation – apiksitaultimik – offer teachings that are inherently relational and critical in transforming the structures that reproduce colonialism. Relationality is the impetus for moving reconciliation beyond the risks of just paying lip service and instead towards a process for healing relationships that include our non-human relatives of the wild and all of Creation – our relationships to water and landscapes and our ancestors from which our knowledge lives. It is interesting to point out that the process for reconciliation from an L'nu perspective is not dissimilar to Elder/Dr. Murdena Marshall's description of traditional knowledge as learning "experienced through songs and ceremonies" – the intersection of the ontological and epistemological. "So, coming back and using the land, and using it properly, it puts us back into it and it is like we are healing. Not only are we healing the land, but we are healing ourselves" (Potter in Stiegman & Pictou 2016).

At the same time, we must be prepared to accept how the work of healing in "reconciliation is hard" (Young 2020), and "while captivating, reconciliation can be frustrating" (Whitlow & Oliver 2019, 206). Furthermore, we must be careful of placing a greater emphasis on forgiveness than the actual healing aspect, which has been a criticism of most state-sanctioned reconciliation policies as noted previously. In doing so, the onus is placed on Indigenous Peoples to forgive without nijkitekek, that which heals. In learning from the Truth and Reconciliation Commission process, "events had become confessional spaces of white guilt that were shaped by an ask-the-Indian dynamic whereby white people take up the majority of the space by asking Indigenous peoples what they could do to 'achieve' reconciliation and be a reconciled settler. Responsibility was oftentimes put on Indigenous peoples to do the emotional and time-consuming work of mitigating white guilt and creating a forgiving space to move forward – a key point which was repeatedly critiqued by Indigenous peoples at such events" (Daigle 2019, 705; also see Simpson 2017; and Coulthard 2014).

In this regard, I agree with statements in the ICE report that "it is up to each [Indigenous] nation to define reconciliation for itself. In this manner, reconciliation means identifying the appropriate healing process for restoring relationships" (2018, 7). Importantly, however, I also caution that it is debateable whether healing is possible "first, between Crown and Indigenous Peoples, recognizing what has not worked in the past so it is corrected moving forward in the spirit of peace and friendship; and second, between all people (Indigenous and non-Indigenous) and the lands" (7). I have described in other publications how neoliberalism, colonialism, and capitalism work in tandem as a framework for state-driven negotiations and consultations with Indigenous Peoples about land claims, treaty, and Indigenous rights that pre-empt if not further dispossess Indigenous Peoples, especially Indigenous women and two-Spirited, lesbian, gay, bi-sexual, transgender, queer, questioning, intersex, asexual (2SLGBTQQIA) persons, from their ancestral homelands (Pictou 2019, 2020). Therefore, I have argued that we must look beyond these formal processes and create spaces for what I have cast as building "small-t" treaty relationships between the broader Indigenous and Canadian public. What I mean by small-t-treaty relationships are those we build beyond formal treaty negotiation processes as a way to make space for Indigenous relationality as a way of knowing, and for working towards Indigenous-non-Indigenous-all-of-creation relationality. I contend these spaces hold conciliatory possibilities towards a transformative reconciliation described by Chance Finegan (2018, 20) as a "space for healing."

Without healing from a Mi'kmaw/Indigenous relational perspective as an operative element of reconciliation, such work risks becoming ineffective and even more difficult and frustrating. Healing in reconciliation, and in conservation in particular, implies healing with Indigenous Peoples, and just as important, includes restoring our relationship with the land and waters. "An emphasis on how history has shaped conservation practices and priorities will help future leaders avoid perpetuating historical and current inequalities" (Washington et al. 2018, 371). In the context of establishing IPCAs, Zurba et al. (2019, 4) further suggest that "acknowledging the truth is an important precursor to reconciliation, and thus examining Canada's colonial past and present is a critical component of moving forward with IPCAs." In other words, as Zurba et al. are suggesting, truth telling must be part of the healing in the reconciliation process in conservation. Thus, we must also ask ourselves, in conceptualizing reconciliation in conservation, will our thinking and actions regarding healing be only in a context of a conservation futurity, while leaving the already damaged human and natural world relations in place? As ICE asserts, "some pre-existing protected areas share a 'dark history' and will have a greater need for truth-telling and reconciliation work" (2018, 44–5; also see Finegan 2018). Accordingly, ICE further emphasizes that "IPCAs do not necessarily need to be landscapes that are ecologically intact. They could also serve as 'restoration areas' where lands and waters are aided in healing from industrial and human development that have led to serious ecosystem breakdowns" (2018, 48). Both human-to-human and human-to-nature relations need truth and healing as fundamental precursors and on-going processes of reconciliation and conservation.

As part of truth telling and healing, I suggest it is crucial that we also examine how our existing relationships with one another intersect with our relationships with nature and natural resources beyond protected areas, to include destructive relationships (such as resource extraction) that are not conducive to reconciliation, especially for Indigenous women and 2SLGBTQQIA persons. For example, the Missing and Murdered Indigenous Women and Girls Final Inquiry Report (MMIWG Final Report 2019) directly links the influx of male labourers mobilized by hyper-intensive resource extraction to the violence and death of not only ancestral homelands but also against the bodies of MMIWG and 2SLGBTQQIA persons (Final Report 2019; Pictou 2020). Yet even during a pandemic, resource extraction is considered an essential service (Désilets 2020), while the MMIWG final report recommendations are put on hold (Global News 2020). Moreover, the controversial proposed Site C dam in British Columbia, a water source for fracking, was approved (CBC News 2021), while Indigenous Peoples still do not have adequate access to healthy drinking water (Office of the Auditor General of Canada 2021). And many Indigenous food systems in the North and Indigenous communities throughout Turtle Island, including Asubpeeschoseewagong (Anishinaabeg) First Nation (formerly known as Grassy Narrows First Nation) in Ontario and my own ancestral homelands, Kespukwitk in Nova Scotia, are exposed to industrial pollutants such as mercury (UN Human Rights Council 2020). How do we heal these relations? Will the transformative possibilities in conservation, especially in Indigenous-led conservation, be limited by the settler-state dynamic of reconciliation in so far as such efforts will not be permitted to disrupt hyper-intensive industrial activities such as these on Indigenous ancestral homelands and waters? And just as importantly, will there be room for Indigenous food and lifeways from which our knowledge is lived, to inform visions of local sustainable economies or conservation economies, while at the same time addressing biodiversity loss, climatic change, and other environmental issues? These are the tough questions of truth telling and healing that ethical responsibility demands in our efforts to create ethical spaces for genuine reconciliation in conservation. To answer these and other critical questions, Indigenous feminism provides an important and promising foundation for our ethical responsibilities in creating spaces for reconciliation in conservation.

Reconciliation and Conservation through an Indigenous Feminist Lens

When talking truth about state-sanctioned concepts of reconciliation, we must remember that the state also sanctioned the Indian Residentials Schools and related atrocities that led to over 20 years of judicial and political actions on the part of Indigenous People. By "October 2002, more than 11,000 legal cases had been filed against the federal government and the churches" invoking the federal government to establish the TRC in 2008 (Jung 2009, 7). Not surprisingly, then, the sincerity of state-sanctioned policies such as reconciliation efforts in both academic and political contexts are called into question, as discussed earlier. Just as important, like residential school survivors, Indigenous women have been challenging gender discrimination in the judicial system over the past several decades, eventually leading to the total removal of gender discrimination from the Indian Act in 2019. Despite this victory, we must continue to learn about and come to terms with how settler-colonial governance structures imposed on Indigenous societies over generations are deeply steeped in patriarchal colonialities and continue to impact Indigenous women, 2SLGBTQQIA persons and children. For example, patriarchy and heteropatriarchy have become internalized in ways that predominantly privilege a masculinist mode of governance and males as the prime beneficiaries of neoliberal economic development models imposed in treaty and land claim negotiations and consultation processes (Pictou 2020), at great cost to Indigenous women, 2SLGBTQQIA persons, children, and all of nature/creation.

Indigenous women and 2SLGBTQQIA persons often find themselves excluded from these processes, while trying to protect and defend lands and waters in their ancestral homelands, at times against both their own leadership and resource exploitation projects (Pictou 2018; also see Pictou 2020). Yet as land and water defenders/protectors, they are the ones who are mostly criminalized through court injunctions, indicating a hierarchy of laws that privilege corporate rights over human rights and rights of nature in general and over Indigenous rights and Natural Law in particular – especially when compared to the low number of successful injunctions launched by Indigenous Peoples to protect their Aboriginal and Treaty rights (Kruse & Robinson 2019).

I suggest that these acts of oppression also represent a form of the internalized domination that Washington et al. (2018) allude to in their proposed framework integrating social and ecological justice. They also intersect with Carla M. Dhillon's (2020) article "Indigenous Feminisms: Disturbing Colonialism in Environmental Science Partnerships," where she explicitly references the role of Indigenous feminism in countering inequities through relational reciprocity, inclusion of all ages and genders, and Indigenous knowledge systems. Dhillon argues that inequities in "ecological sciences remain an ongoing problem, while dominant climate change discourses tend not to focus on such critical questions." She states further that "Indigenous peoples have long argued that decolonization work must focus on original values such as relational reciprocity and inclusion of all ages and genders" (Ibid. 484). She further asserts that Indigenous feminism can counter these inequities as a way to ensure an inclusive mode of Indigenous governance and for decolonizing environmental sciences. Indeed, McGregor (2018) discusses how she learned from Indigenous women participating in a research project on water governance that one of their traditional roles involves "speaking for the water" (251). She goes on to explain how, as Indigenous researchers, we have a relational responsibility to integrate our personal learning with our academic work in ways that share and mobilize the research rather than just "extract" knowledge (252; also see Pictou 2019). The importance of these interrelationships among inclusion, equity, and knowledge systems is reinforced by Elders' concerns about not having the capacity to share IK with youth, which was also emphasized in the ICE report as a "beacon for teachings," or a transference of knowledge rooted in the land (2018, 47; also see Young in this section). Such knowledge transfer in itself is a form of healing for our people and in particularly for our youth (also see Dhillon 2020, 495).

What I am attempting to articulate here is that the politics of recognizing Indigenous knowledges in conservation practice take on an additional layer of gender issues that needs to be explored when espousing policies such as co-management or shared governance or perhaps even Indigenous-led governance. Centring the knowledge and experience of Indigenous women and 2SLGBTQQIA persons themselves, particularly in Indigenous governance, can serve as a way to further decolonize, reconcile, and transform conservation practice. Otherwise, conservation practice either directly or indirectly risks iterating gender violence and displacement. Further, IK in conservation must also undertake a healing process that restores knowledge and Indigenous knowledge systems to the descendants of ancestral knowledge holders, many of whom are women and 2SLGBTQQIA persons, and including generational transference by engaging youth. Conservation must not just serve as a patriarchal form of reconciliation for conservation's sake, it must also include a process for healing that includes Indigenous women, 2SLGBTQQIA persons, and youth, along with healing (restoring) the lands and waters from which Indigenous relational knowledge derives.

Concluding Considerations

I remember a year or so before my Grandmother had passed into the spirit world, she wanted to go to her ancestral homelands in Kejimkujik National Park, particularly to visit the ancestral burial ground and Jeremy's Bay. Jeremy's Bay is named after a long line of Jeremy's including my Grandmother's parents who were medicine and healing people, canoe builders, leaders, and crafts people. I caught a glimpse of my Grandmother that day standing on the shore of Jeremy's Bay with tears of joy flowing down her cheeks and maybe a bit of sadness. She was so relieved to be there, as though she thought she would never return. Many of her stories are from there. She was home.

The TRC Calls to Action (CTA) in 2015 (along with UNDRIP) gave way to exerted efforts for reconciliation with Indigenous Peoples in the Western sciences (and other disciplines), and in the formation of national and international governmental policies, in efforts to transform colonial approaches to conservation on one hand, while exploiting natural resources for economic development as another form of reconciliation on the other. These two extremes of reconciliation continue to impact Indigenous Peoples and especially Indigenous women and 2SLGBTQQIA persons in multiple ways that emanate patriarchal and colonial governance systems regarding nature and natural resources. As a way to disrupt these dichotomies, I propose that Indigenous/Mi'kmaw concepts of relationality with an ethical responsibility for healing between Indigenous–non-Indigenous–all-of-creation offer ways to mobilize reconciliation beyond current political economies and political ecologies in conservation practice.

The inseparability of the human, natural, and spiritual worlds was also emphasized throughout the ICE Report (2018) in response to Canada's 2020 Biodiversity Goals and Targets for Canada focusing on terrestrial and inland waters. Mi'kmaw Elder/Dr. Albert Marshall reminds us that, while as humans we rely on natural worlds, we must do so with an ethical responsibility by not compromising the integrity of those same natural worlds. Ethical and relational responsibilities form Indigenous ways of knowing with all of Creation, including our ancestors, in land- and water-based practices (an epistemological embodiment of the ontological). Just as important, healing is a crucial element in Indigenous/Mi'kmaw concepts of reconciliation and must include healing of current processes that enact violence against land, waters, and Indigenous Women and 2SLGBTQQIA persons. Therefore, because of how patriarchal colonial governance systems continue to be imposed and internalized in Indigenous communities, I further assert that conservation practices must also take into consideration impacts on gender in order to achieve truthful and genuine reconciliation.

In closing, it is important to note that Indigenous ways of knowing in human–all-of-creation relationality are also transferred through ceremonies, songs, dances, and stories, which is very similar to how healing in reconciliation is achieved. Therefore, as we learn to listen to these stories with an ethical and relational responsibility to both the human and non-human worlds, perhaps then, we can together, create more stories from these places in a good way that does not compromise the integrity of all of our relatives living there or work towards restoring the integrity to those struggling to stay alive. Either way, when recovering, restoring, conserving, or protecting, we are learning to re-story the land and waters in ways that will ensure they will continue to be storied by future generations.

NOTE

1 "Fortress conservation" refers to conservation that is exclusionary in practice and not participatory in planning and policy processes (see for example, Binnema and Niemi 2006; Moola and Roth 2018; Sandlos 2008; Youdelis 2016).

WORKS CITED

Artelle, Kyle A., Melanie Zurba, Jonaki Bhattacharyya, Diana E. Chan, Kelly Brown, Jess Housty, and Faisal Moola. 2019. "Supporting Resurgent Indigenous-Led Governance: A Nascent Mechanism for Just and Effective Conservation." *Biological Conservation* 240. https://doi.org/10.1016/j.biocon.2019.108284

Binnema, Theodore (Ted), and Melanie Niemi. 2006. "'Let the Line Be Drawn Now': Wilderness, Conservation, and the Exclusion of Aboriginal People from Banff National Park in Canada." *Environmental History* 11, no. 4: 724–50. https://doi.org/10.1093/envhis/11.4.724

Canada. 2019. *Advancing Reconciliation with Indigenous Peoples.* Canada Budget 19. Retrieved March 27, 2021. https://www.budget.gc.ca/2019/docs/nrc/indigenous-autochtones-en.html

CBC News. 2021. "Site C Dam Budget Nearly Doubles to $16B, but B.C. NDP Forging on with Megaproject." https://www.cbc.ca/news/canada/british-columbia/site-c-announcement-friday-1.5928719

Cormier, Paul, and Lana Ray. 2018. "A Tale of Two Drums: Kinoo'amaadawaad Megwaa Doodamawaad – 'They Are Learning with Each Other while They Are Doing.'" In *Indigenous Research: Theories, Practices, and Relationships*, edited by Deborah McGregor, Jean-Paul Restoule, and Rochelle Johnston, 112–25. Toronto: Canadian Scholars.

Corntassel, Jeff. 2012."Re-envisioning Resurgence: Indigenous Pathways to Decolonization and Sustainable Self-Determination." *Decolonization: Indigeneity, Education & Society* 1, no. 1. https://jps.library.utoronto.ca/index.php/des/article/view/18627

Coulthard, Glen Sean. 2014. *Red Skin, White Masks: Rejecting the Colonial Politics of Recognition*. Minneapolis: University of Minnesota Press.

Daigle, Michelle. 2019."The Spectacle of Reconciliation: On (the) Unsettling Responsibilities to Indigenous Peoples in the Academy." *Environment and Planning D: Society and Space* 37, no. 4: 703–21. https://doi.org/10.1177/0263775818824342

Désilets, C., G. Jiménez, and B. Lorimer. 2020. "Large-Scale Resource Extraction Exacerbates the Threat of COVID-19 across the American Hemisphere." *Rabble.ca.* https://rabble.ca/blogs/bloggers/kairos-witness/2020/05/large-scale-resource-extraction-exacerbates-threat-covid-19

Dhillon, Carla M. 2020. "Indigenous Feminisms: Disturbing Colonialism in Environmental Science Partnerships." *Sociology of Race and Ethnicity* 6, no. 4: 483–500. https://doi.org/10.1177/2332649220908608

Finegan, Chance. 2018. "Reflection, Acknowledgement, and Justice: A Framework for Indigenous-Protected Area Reconciliation." *International Indigenous Policy Journal* 9, no. 3. https://doi.org/10.18584/iipj.2018.9.3.3

Garnett, Stephen T., Neil D. Burgess, John E. Fa, Álvaro Fernández-Llamazares, Zsolt Molnár, Cathy J. Robinson, James E.M. Watson et al. 2018. "A Spatial

Overview of the Global Importance of Indigenous Lands for Conservation." *Nature Sustainability* 1, no. 7: 369–74. https://doi.org/10.1038/s41893-018-0100-6

Global News, The Canadian Press. 2020. "MMIWG Action Plan Delayed Due to Coronavirus Pandemic, Minister Says." https://globalnews.ca/news/6988871/mmiwg-coronavirus-action-plan-indigenous/

Hill, Rosemary, Çiğdem Adem, Wilfred V. Alangui, Zsolt Molnár, Yildiz Aumeeruddy-Thomas, Peter Bridgewater, Maria Tengö et al. 2020. "Working with Indigenous, Local and Scientific Knowledge in Assessments of Nature and Nature's Linkages with People." *Current Opinion in Environmental Sustainability* 43: 8–20. https://doi.org/10.1016/j.cosust.2019.12.006

Indigenous Circle of Experts (ICE). 2018. *We Rise Together: Achieving Pathway to Canada Target 1 through the Creation of Indigenous Protected and Conserved Areas in the Spirit and Practice of Reconciliation.* Canada. https://static1.squarespace.com/static/57e007452e69cf9a7af0a033/t/5ab94aca6d2a7338ecb1d05e/1522092766605/PA234-ICE_Report_2018_Mar_22_web.pdf

Intergovernmental Science-Policy Platform on Biodiversity and Ecosystem Services. 2019. "Indigenous and Local Knowledge in IPBES." IPBES. Retrieved March 26, 2021. https://www.ipbes.net/indigenous-local-knowledge#:~:text=IPBES%20recognizes%20that%20indigenous%20peoples,on%20biodiversity%20and%20ecosystem%20trends.&text=This%20commitment%20has%20now%20been,indigenous%20and%20local%20knowledge%20systems%E2%80%9D

IUCN World Conservation Congress. 2021. "World Summit of Indigenous Peoples and Nature." Fontainebleau, France: IUCN. Retrieved March 26, 2021. https://www.iucn.org/sites/dev/files/content/documents/ip_summit_note_jan_2021.pdf

Jung, Courtney. 2009. "Canada and the Legacy of the Indian Residential Schools: Transitional Justice for Indigenous People in a Nontransitional Society." *Aboriginal Policy Research Consortium International (APRCi)* 295. https://ir.lib.uwo.ca/aprci/295

Kejimkujik National Park and National Historic Site. (n.d.) "Kejimkujik National Park and National Historic Site Management Plan." Parks Canada. Retrieved March 26, 2021. https://www.pc.gc.ca/en/pn-np/ns/kejimkujik/info/plan-gestion-management

Kittinger, John N., Samantha H. Cheng, Jenna H. Neher, Amy Scoville-Weaver, Jorge A. Ahumada, Aradhna Tripati, and Gabrielle E. Lout. 2021. "Preparing Conservation Practitioners for the Anthropocene." *Frontiers in Ecology and the Environment* 19, no. 2: 88–90. https://doi.org/10.1002/fee.2308

Kruse, Mark, and Carrie Robinson. 2019. *Injunctions by First Nations: Results of a National Study.* Toronto: Yellowhead Institute. Retrieved March 27, 2021. https://yellowheadinstitute.org/2019/11/14/injunctions-by-first-nations-results-of-a-national-study/

Loucks, Laura. 2021. "Clayoquot Sound, Canada Community Engagement in a UNESCO Biosphere Reserve." In *Communities, Conservation and Livelihoods*, edited by A. Charles, 128–32. Gland, Switzerland: IUCN; Halifax: Community Conservation Research Network. https://doi.org/10.2305/IUCN.CH.2021.01.en

M'sit No'kmaq, Elder A. Marshall, K.F. Beazley, J. Hum, S. Joudry, A. Papadopoulos, S. Pictou, J. Rabesca, L. Young, M. Zurba. 2021. "Awakening the Sleeping Giant': Re-Indigenization Principles for Transforming Biodiversity Conservation in Canada and Beyond." *FACETS* 6: 839–69. https://doi.org/10.1139/facets-2020-0083

Marshall, M. (n.d.) "On Tribal Consciousness – The Trees That Hold Hands." http://www.integrativescience.ca/uploads/articles/2005November-Marshall-WIPCE-text-On-Tribal-Consciousness-Integrative-Science.pdf

McGregor, D. 2004. "Traditional Ecological Knowledge and Sustainable Development: Towards Coexistence." In *In the Way of Development: Indigenous Peoples, Life Projects and Globalization*, edited by M. Blaser, H.A. Feit, and G. McRae, 72–91. London and New York: Zed Books with International Development Research Centre. https://www.idrc.ca/en/book/way-development-indigenous-peoples-life-projects-and-globalization

McGregor, Deborah. 2018. "Toward an Anishinaabe Research Paradigm: Theory and Practice." In *Indigenous Research: Theories, Practices, and Relationships*, edited by Deborah McGregor, Jean-Paul Restoule, and Rochelle Johnston, 243–56. Toronto: Canadian Scholars Press.

McGregor, Deborah, Jean-Paul Restoule, and Rochelle Johnston, eds. 2018. *Indigenous Research: Theories, Practices, and Relationships*. Toronto: Canadian Scholars Press.

McMillan, L. Jane. 2016. "Living Legal Traditions: Mi'kmaw Justice in Nova Scotia." *University of New Brunswick Law Journal* 67: 187. https://journals.lib.unb.ca/index.php/unblj/article/view/29078

MMIWG National Inquiry. 2019. *Reclaiming Power and Place: The Final Report of the National Inquiry into Missing and Murdered Indigenous Women and Girls*. MMIWG National Inquiry Canada. https://www.mmiwg-ffada.ca/final-report/

Moola, Faisal, and Robin Roth. 2018. "Moving beyond Colonial Conservation Models: Indigenous Protected and Conserved Areas Offer Hope for Biodiversity and Advancing Reconciliation in the Canadian Boreal Forest." *Environmental Reviews* 27: 200–1. https://doi.org/10.1139/er-2018-0091

Nuna, R., T. Sable, D. Foxcroft, and M.d.G.Z Simbine. 2021. "Indigenous Perspectives on Community Conservation." In *Communities, Conservation and Livelihoods*, edited by A. Charles, 49–54. Gland, Switzerland: IUCN; Halifax, Canada: Community Conservation Research Network. https://doi.org/10.2305/IUCN.CH.2021.01.en

Office of the Auditor General of Canada. 2021. "Report 3 – Access to Safe Drinking Water in First Nations Communities – Indigenous Services Canada." Retrieved March 27, 2021. https://www.oag-bvg.gc.ca/internet/English/att__e_43754.html

Painemilla, K.W. 2021. "Foreword." In *Communities, Conservation and Livelihoods*, edited by A. Charles. IUCN and Community Conservation Research Network. https://doi.org/10.2305/IUCN.CH.2021.01.en

Parks Canada. 2019. "Mapping Change: Fostering a Culture of Reconciliation within Parks Canada." Retrieved March 26, 2021. https://www.pc.gc.ca/en/agence-agency/aa-ia/reconciliation

Penak, Nicole. 2018. "The Trickiness of Storytelling with Indigenous Social Workers: Implications for Research in the Era of Reconciliation." In *Research and Reconciliation: Unsettling Ways of Knowing Though Indigenous Relationships*, edited by S. Wilson, A.V. Breen, and L. Dupré, 139–51. Toronto: Canadian Scholars Press.

Pictou, Sherry. 2018. "Mi'kmaq and the Recognition and Implementation of Rights Framework." Policy Brief, Yellowhead Institute Policy Briefs. Retrieved March 26. 2021. https://yellowheadinstitute.org/yellowhead-briefs/

Pictou, Sherry. 2019. "What Is Decolonization? Mi'kmaw Ancestral Relational Understandings and Anthropological Perspectives on Treaty Relations." In *Transcontinental Dialogues. Activist Research and Alliances from and with Indigenous Peoples of Canada, Mexico, and Australia*, edited by R.A.H. Castillo, S. Hutchings, and B. Noble, 37–64. Tucson: University of Arizona Press.

Pictou, Sherry. 2020. "Decolonizing Decolonization: An Indigenous Feminist Perspective on the Recognition and Rights Framework." *South Atlantic Quarterly* 119, no. 2: 371–91. https://doi.org/10.1215/00382876-8177809

Potter, C.A. 2016. In "We Story the Land." Documentary Film, directed by M. Stiegman and S. Pictou. V. Tape: Rippling Current Media. http://westorytheland.ca/

Price, Karen, Audrey Roburn, and Andy Mackinnon. 2009. "Ecosystem-Based Management in the Great Bear Rainforest." *Forest Ecology and Management* 258: 495–503. 10.1016/j.foreco.2008.10.010.

Sable, Trudy, and Bernie Francis. 2012. *The Language of This Land, Mi'kma'ki*. Sydney, NS: Cape Breton University Press.

Sandlos, John. 2008. "Not Wanted in the Boundary: The Expulsion of the Keeseekoowenin Ojibway Band from Riding Mountain National Park." *Canadian Historical Review* 89, no. 2 (2008): 189–221. https://doi.org/10.3138/chr.89.2.189

Schuster, Richard, Ryan R. Germain, Joseph R. Bennett, Nicholas J. Reo, and Peter Arcese. 2019. "Vertebrate Biodiversity on Indigenous-Managed Lands in Australia, Brazil, and Canada Equals That in Protected Areas." *Environmental Science & Policy* 101 (2019): 1–6. https://doi.org/10.1016/j.envsci.2019.07.002

Simpson, Leanne. 2001. "Traditional Ecological Knowledge: Marginalization, Appropriation and Continued Disillusion." Indigenous Knowledge Conference, University of Saskatchewan, May 28, vol. 30.

Simpson, Leanne Betasamosake. 2017. *As We Have Always Done: Indigenous Freedom through Radical Resistance*. Minneapolis: University of Minnesota Press.

Sowman, M., W. Rice, A.M. Arce-Ibarra, and I. Peña-Azcona. 2021. "Meanings and Motivations: Communities and Conservation." In *Communities, Conservation and Livelihoods*, edited by A. Charles, 19–23. Gland, Switzerland: IUCN; Halifax, Canada: Community Conservation Research Network. https://doi.org/10.2305/IUCN.CH.2021.01.en

Starblanket, Gina, and Heidi Kiiwetinepinesiik Stark. 2019. "Towards a Relational Paradigm– Four Points for Consideration: Knowledge, Gender, Land, and

Modernity." In *Resurgence and Reconciliation*, 175–208. Toronto: University of Toronto Press.

Stiegman, Martha, and Sherry Pictou, 2016 [2012]. "Resource Privatization, Treaty Rights Recognition and Community Resistance in Maritime Canada." In *Aboriginal History: A Reader*, 2nd ed., edited by K. Burnett and G. Read, 226–42. Toronto: Oxford University Press, .

UN Human Rights Council Forty-Fifth Session. 2020. *Visit to Canada: Report of the Special Rapporteur on the Implications for Human Rights of the Environmentally Sound Management and Disposal of Hazardous Substances and Waste*. United Nations Digital Library. Retrieved March 27, 2021. https://digitallibrary.un.org/record/3879377?ln=en

Washington, Haydn, Guillaume Chapron, Helen Kopnina, Patrick Curry, Joe Gray, and John J. Piccolo. 2018. "Foregrounding Ecojustice in Conservation." *Biological Conservation* 228: 367–74. https://doi.org/10.1016/j.biocon.2018.09.011

Whitlow, Kawennakon Bonnie, and Vanessa Oliver. 2019. "Tentsitewatenronhste: We Will Become Friends Again." In *Research and Reconciliation: Unsettling Ways of Knowing through Indigenous Relationships*, edited by S. Wilson, A.V. Breen, and L. Dupré, 195–209. Toronto: Canadian Scholars Press.

Wilson, Shawn, and Margaret Hughes. 2019. "Why Research Is Reconciliation." In *Research and Reconciliation: Unsettling Ways of Knowing through Indigenous Relationships*, edited by S. Wilson, A.V. Breen, and L. Dupré, 5–20. Toronto: Canadian Scholars Press.

Wilson, Shawn, Andrea V. Breen, and Lindsay DuPré, eds. 2019. *Research and Reconciliation: Unsettling Ways of Knowing through Indigenous Relationships*. Toronto: Canadian Scholars Press.

Youdelis, Megan. 2016. "'They Could Take You out for Coffee and Call It Consultation!': The Colonial Antipolitics of Indigenous Consultation in Jasper National Park." *Environment and Planning A: Economy and Space* 48, no. 7: 1374–92. https://doi.org/10.1177/0308518X16640530

Young, Tuma. 2016. "L'nuwita'simk: A Foundational Worldview for a L'nuwey Justice System." *Indigenous Law Journal* 13: 75. https://jps.library.utoronto.ca/index.php/ilj/article/view/26700

Young, Tuma. 2020. "Reconciliation in Canada Is Hard Work." Op-ed, *Cape Breton Post*. https://www.capebretonpost.com/opinion/local-perspectives/op-ed-reconciliation-in-canada-is-hard-work-419140/

Zurba, Melanie, and John Sinclair. 2020. "Learning and Reconciliation for the Collaborative Governance of Forestland in Northwestern Ontario, Canada." In *Pathways of Reconciliation*, edited by Aimée Craft and Paulette Regan, 142–72. Winnipeg: University of Manitoba Press,.

Zurba, Melanie, Karen F. Beazley, Emilie English, and Johanna Buchmann-Duck. 2019. "Indigenous Protected and Conserved Areas (IPCAs), Aichi Target 11 and Canada's Pathway to Target 1: Focusing Conservation on Reconciliation." *Land* 8, no. 1. https://doi.org/10.3390/land8010010

7 "*Etuaptmumk*/Two-Eyed Seeing and Reconciliation with Earth"

DEBORAH McGREGOR, JESSE POPP, ANDREA REID, ELDER ALBERT MARSHALL, JACQUELYN MILLER, AND MAHISHA SRITHARAN

The discussion among the contributors to this chapter began in October 2020, when they participated in an online dialogue about *Etuaptmumk*/Two-Eyed Seeing and other ways of understanding across ways of knowing. This dialogue was organized as part of the Reconciling Ways of Knowing: Indigenous Knowledge and Science (RWoK) project, which began facilitating a series of online dialogues (https://www.waysofknowingforum.ca/online) when its May 2020 in-person gathering was postponed indefinitely because of COVID-19.

The RWoK project was created by a group of Indigenous and non-Indigenous people with backgrounds in governance, policy, research, stewardship, and environmental advocacy, with the objective of building understanding and relationships across Indigenous and Western scientific ways of knowing. In so doing, the RWoK project aims to bring together the best and most comprehensive knowledges and wisdom for living in balance with the Earth and to facilitate a just reconciliation and genuine nation-to-nation relationships between Indigenous Peoples and Canada. To achieve such nation-to-nation relationships requires building understanding and respect between Peoples, which – after more than 150 years of colonization – must involve building understanding of and respect for Indigenous Peoples' ways of being and ways of knowing by Canadians and their institutions.

RWoK is working to facilitate such understanding and relationships among a wide range of constituencies, including those practicing, teaching, researching, and making stewardship policy and decisions from within a Western science framework; Indigenous Elders / Knowledge Keepers, leaders, land and cultural stewards, and youth; representatives of civil society organizations, including industry and non-governmental organizations; and other interested members of the public. Through bringing together and building understanding among these groups, RWoK hopes to help change the way in which policies and decisions about the land and our relationships with it are made, to help ensure our common survival for generations to come.

The 28 October 2020 RWoK dialogue "Two-Eyed Seeing and Beyond," between Drs. Deborah McGregor (Anishinabek), Jesse Popp (Anishinabek), and Andrea Reid (Nisga'a), and Mi'kmaw Elder Albert Marshall, facilitated by Jacquelyn Miller (settler Canadian) on behalf of the RWoK project, engaged with the notion of *Etuaptmumk* / Two-Eyed Seeing[1] and other Indigenous ways of understanding across Peoples / knowledge systems, including the *Kaswentha*/Two Row Wampum and the Dish with One Spoon. Each of these frameworks have both an epistemological and an ontological/political aspect, dealing with ways of relating across ways of knowing and between Peoples. They may involve relationships between Indigenous and settler/newcomer Peoples and their respective ways of knowing, or they may involve relationships among Indigenous Peoples and their respective ways of knowing, as is the case of the Dish with One Spoon. Each framework necessarily involves not only a relationship among Peoples but with place, with the Earth, and includes guidelines for living together in balance.

Reconciliation with the Earth

While Canada has made many statements of commitment to reconciliation with Indigenous Peoples, questions remain about the real impact on the ground of such commitments on the lived experiences of Indigenous Peoples (McGregor 2019a). Kyle Whyte (2018) critiques settler-colonial approaches to reconciliation and is skeptical of their meaningfulness, given how mainstream approaches typically fail to include Indigenous perspectives and knowledges. A meaningful definition of reconciliation informed by the on-the-ground injustice experienced by Indigenous Peoples through ongoing colonialism is provided by Chance Finegan, who describes it as "a process of dismantling of oppressive structures and coming-to-terms with how settlers continue to benefit from, enable, and perpetuate settler colonialism" (2018, 4). Also, the Truth and Reconciliation Commission of Canada's (TRC) *Final Report* expressed that reconciliation with Indigenous Peoples also requires reconciliation with the land and all living things: "If human beings resolve problems between themselves but continue to destroy the natural world, then reconciliation remains incomplete" (2015a, 18).

Reconciliation with Indigenous Peoples and the Earth is a real challenge, as is clear from the well-known and well-documented environmental injustices against Indigenous Peoples, such as environmental contamination of drinking water sources, poor housing conditions, and exposure to environmental hazards (McGregor 2018; Waldron 2018). Reconciliation with the Earth encompasses the need to halt and redress environmental injustice against Indigenous Peoples (McGregor 2016). For many Indigenous Peoples, the land / environment / nature have immense cultural and spiritual significance, and from a holistic perspective it is inextricably linked to the health and well-being of Peoples (Tobias and Richmond 2014). Scholars working at the forefront of the relationships among Peoples have supported the holistic view of well-being contained in the TRC's conceptualization of "reconciliation," arguing for a call to action that recognizes the role of nature or creation in realizing reconciliation (Borrows 2018; McGregor 2018; Berkes 2017). As Anishinaabe legal scholar John Borrows states:

> Reconciliation with the earth is the kind of resurgence I value most. In my view, resurgent relations with the natural world are key to the revitalization of Indigenous peoples' relationships with the rocks, waters, insects, plants, birds, animals, and other forms of life around us. They are also key to our reconciliation with other peoples (Borrows 2018, 50).

In the "Two-Eyed Seeing and Beyond" RWoK dialogue, Elder Marshall states:

> I think it should be – especially in the current dilemma we're in at this point in time – obvious to all of us that there is a great need for some kind, some form of a transformative change in which we really reflect and look back, and see where we've come from and how we got here and at what expense, we have actually created imbalance with our natural world.
>
> And having acknowledged that, I think it should become incumbent on all of us to make an effort that from here on forward business cannot be as usual. We have to reflect into our past and really, clearly see and identify where we come from and how we got here and at the expense we have cost this wonderful Creation of ours. And that should propel us, that should motivate us, to make every concerted effort to ensure that this, this different perspective has to be a hundred degrees different … than what we had before. Because the Earth, our Earth Mother really needs us. We have allowed her to, for the environment to be completely compromised. Air, water, and soil. And unless we accept that responsibility and do everything in our power to, to improve our ways then I believe then we will then fail as humanity for the responsibility that we have been given because of something that we had that no other creature has and that's that cognitive mind. Yes, this cognitive mind has created a monster for us and these monsters that I would call this arm of destruction. But I believe this mind of ours could also transform that monster to be the arm of mitigation, of repairing and undoing some of the harms that we have done in the past. Unless we are committed to that, to that idea which I believe it's constantly encouraged and reinforced when we invoke that, when we invoke the Two-Eyed Seeing perspective. (RWoK 2020)

Through these words, Elder Marshall contends that transformative change is required between humanity and our relationship with the Earth. This form of reconciliation with the Earth is everyone's responsibility and, while our cognitive mind can be destructive, we can also use the gifts it has to offer to repair what has become a harmful relationship with the Earth.

From a Canadian state perspective, reconciliation is focused on recognition and alleviating conflict between Peoples, "presuming that forgiveness is the end goal of reconciliation" (Finegan 2018, 3). However, this view is deeply inadequate. Deborah McGregor (2018) emphasizes that the limitation in this approach to reconciliation is that from an Indigenous perspective reconciliation is needed not only between Peoples but also with the Earth. McGregor draws on *Mino-bimaatisiwin*, an Anishinabek concept of living in a good way, and notes how reconciliation with the Earth relates to "the connection between how we as peoples treat each other, and how we treat the natural world," underscoring that "[w]e cannot restore balance to one set of relationships without doing the same to the other" (McGregor 2018, 229).

Restoring balance to both sets of relationships – with each other and with the Earth – requires acknowledging and valuing Indigenous knowledges, as outlined in two of the principles outlined in the TRC's *What We Have Learned: Principles of Truth and Reconciliation* (2015b):

- The perspectives and understandings of Indigenous Elders and Traditional Knowledge-Keepers about the ethics, concepts, and practices of reconciliation are vital to long-term reconciliation.
- Supporting Indigenous Peoples' cultural revitalization and integrating Indigenous knowledge systems, oral histories, laws, protocols, and connections to the land into the reconciliation process are essential. (4).

Attaining reconciliation inclusive of Indigenous Peoples and nature requires greater understanding of and respect for Indigenous knowledges, which will support building relationships across ways of knowing, in balance with the Earth (Abu, Reed, and Jardine 2019; Finegan 2018; Martin 2012). In other words, reconciliation with Indigenous Peoples and the Earth requires respect for Elders and Traditional Knowledge Keepers and requires different ways of knowing and knowledge systems coming together respectfully, as called for by the TRC. The task of reconciling knowledge systems has been a decades-old challenge in Canada. Recognition of the need for linking knowledge systems is well established – it is the question of how this is to be done that remains challenging. Based on teachings from Elders and Knowledge Holders and Keepers, Indigenous and non-Indigenous scholars have advocated for approaches that respect Indigenous and Western systems of knowledge (Kimmerer 2012; Popp et al. 2020; Reid et al. 2020).

A Dialogue on Reconciling Ways of Knowing for Each Other and the Earth

This contribution is based on the October 28, 2020, RWoK-hosted dialogue "Two-Eyed Seeing and Beyond" between Drs. McGregor, Popp, and Reid with commentary from Elder Albert Marshall, facilitated by Jacquelyn Miller, RWoK project coordinator and a student in the joint common law-Indigenous legal orders degree program at the University of Victoria. The dialogue focused on *Etuaptmumk*/Two-Eyed Seeing and other Indigenous conceptions of understanding across ways of knowing. Through the discussion, the participants engaged in a practice of building understanding across ways of knowing and drawing on their experience doing so in service of reconciliation with the Earth. The discussion focused on different Indigenous ways of knowing and understanding the world and our relationships to it, and on how these concepts for understanding across ways of knowing can be applied, particularly in reconciliation with Indigenous Peoples and the Earth, addressing problems or challenges through a holistic lens (Bartlett, Marshall, and Marshall 2012; Moorman, Evanovitch, and Muliaina 2021; Reid et al. 2020). Excerpts of the transcription from the discussion are shared in this chapter to illustrate how these concepts for understanding across ways of knowing can help forge a path towards reconciliation with the Earth and Indigenous Peoples and how they can be applied in research and practice.

Conversation Method

We write this piece first and foremost as Indigenous scholars, an Indigenous Elder, and two non-Indigenous partners involved in and working with Indigenous and Western knowledges in our research and practice. We also express an Indigenous perspective as people who uphold storytelling as both cultural and academic practice (Archibald 2008; Todd 2018; McGregor 2019b). Thomas Peacock observes that engaging in stories is one of the oldest ways of teaching, which assists societies in making sense of and giving meaning to their experiences, and which provides "the experiential knowledge necessary for solving complex problems" (Peacock 2013, 103). From this perspective, we understand very deeply that stories are also pedagogical – they "illuminate our world" (Doerfler, Stark, and Sinclair 2013, 3). Likewise, Sweeney Windchief and Tim San Pedro focus on what they refer to as storied conversations that are shared in order to strengthen relationships (2019). Shawn Wilson, Andrea Breen, and Lindsay Dupré discuss storytelling as a way to understand how their authors hold "unique ways of seeing and speaking about the world" in their edited volume *Research and Reconciliation: Unsettling Ways of Knowing through Indigenous Relationships* (2019, xi). Thus, in understanding storytelling as knowledge sharing and pedagogy, and as essential to research, we too seek to nurture the integrity of stories in this work. Stylistically, this means that each contributor speaks from their own voice and in their own way.

The Influence of *Etuaptmumk*/Two-Eyed Seeing on Conservation

Jacquelyn initiated the dialogue by asking the panellists how the concept of *Etuaptmumk* or Two-Eyed Seeing has influenced their approach to their work.

DR. JESSE POPP: It wasn't so long ago that I really felt like I was standing alone in thinking that we could reconcile ways of knowing in science. Two-Eyed Seeing, or other frameworks for bringing together ways of knowing in science, wasn't something I learned about in school, even though I have several degrees in biology.

I am a member of Wiikwemkoong Unceded Territory. I did not grow up in the community. I grew up in northern Ontario. I did not experience as many Elder teachings as I would have liked, partly because my mom was part of the Sixties Scoop and because she experienced a rather negative upbringing in foster care, she shied away from culture. However, I do have somewhat of a foot in two worlds, or at least a toe. I always wondered how I could bring these worlds that I was part of into things that I am so passionate about – conservation biology and wildlife ecology. Because I did not have the opportunity to learn about ways that one could bring ways of knowing together in my academic training, I started a journey of learning on my own. I started talking to Elders and Knowledge Holders; I started doing what I knew best at the time with my Western academic training: reading literature. That is where I came across terms like "Traditional Ecological Knowledge" and "Two-Eyed Seeing" as presented in Elder Albert Marshall's paper and Robin Wall Kimmerer's book *Braiding Sweetgrass*. All of this information I was learning about really transformed my path from what I knew. I always wanted to contribute to conservation ecology, and through my journey of learning, I began to know that the way that I wanted to move forward was through a path that brought together ways of knowing in support of reconciliation in Canada and beyond.

Two-Eyed Seeing is a conceptual framework for how we can bring together ways of knowing to better understand the world. Two-Eyed Seeing is described by Mi'kmaq Elder Albert Marshall and states that you can better understand the world through seeing through two eyes, or two lenses: one through Indigenous ways of knowing and seeing the world and another through Western ways of knowing are seeing the world. Both of these ways of seeing the world can be complementary to one another and so we can better see or understand the world. In the research I do specifically, we can better understand ecology and ecological relationships. The work that I do today takes a Two-Eyed Seeing approach, much like many ecology researchers across Canada and the world. Some amazing research has been accomplished by taking a Two-Eyed Seeing or similar approach. From things like optimizing wildlife monitoring, to understanding causes of species declines, to delineating populations and so on, the list goes on and on. In my research particularly, we have used Two-Eyed Seeing to identify negative impacts to species at risk, impacts that Western science had not previously known about. By identifying these impacts, we can work towards mitigation to help improve conservation.

DR. ANDREA REID: I'm joining today from Algonquin Anishinaabe territory in Ottawa, Canada, where I just completed my PhD and which ... centered on interweaving knowledge to better understand the fate and the state of Pacific salmon, which are very dear to my nation, the Nisga'a Nation in northern British Columbia. Jesse and I share a great deal of parallels and, like Jesse, for very similar reasons due to the residential school system and the sixties scoop, I didn't have the privilege of growing up in Nisga'a community or ceremony or culture and I was actually raised in *Mi'kma'ki* on *Epekwitk* on Prince Edward Island surrounded by ocean and fish and fisheries and just grew up loving them, but still very disconnected from that part of my heritage, and so for me, I think that Two-Eyed Seeing – this idea to really bring together multiple ways of knowing – it really resonates with people in similar positions as Jesse and I that are straddling multiple worlds that have Western science training but also see the power and the expertise that comes from within our communities.

For me, I wasn't taught about Two-Eyed Seeing in any formal way. I never heard about it in school. It was something that I organically arrived at through my research on fish and fisheries and making myself useful to my community. I was able to reconnect with Nisga'a culture and community, and in doing that I wanted to find ways to interweave knowledge systems. I was seeking a framework – I was seeking that kind of validation. So like Jesse, through literature review and as well as through contacts, I was able to find out about Two-Eyed Seeing, and because the Indigenous scholarship world is small it turned out that Albert and I have many people in common, especially with my growing up in *Mi'kma'ki*, and I was able to connect with Albert.

We also looked to Australia and New Zealand where the Yolngu and the Māori have very equivalent kinds of ways of thinking about bringing together distinct knowledge systems so that they can interact and interface and innovate and create new solutions to problems, but they don't disrupt the integrity of the other. They remain separate and come together temporarily to work on a common goal, and it's very much like the concept of Two-Eyed Seeing and so the last thing I want to say on this subject while we get this going is that Albert is really adamant that he is a carrier of this knowledge. He did not dream up Two-Eyed Seeing; it as a tradition that has been carried through Mi'kmaq culture, and it really embraces this conservation ethic called *Netukulimk*, which is really about conserving our natural world. Looking ahead seven generations and back seven generations. It's really a teaching that we all have a responsibility to once we have the privilege of knowing more about it.

DR. DEBORAH McGREGOR: I came across this concept over 20 years ago and from a presentation that Elder Albert Marshall and some of other folks from his community were presenting as part of an initiative by the Department of Ocean and Fisheries (DFO) to develop a Traditional Knowledge framework to guide their work.... DFO was examining different models for how Aboriginal traditional knowledges would be considered in the work, in very science-based departments like DFO and they knew that the extractive model was not something that Indigenous Peoples supported or wanted. The Two-Eyed Seeing approach being offered was a different theoretical and conceptual framework for how to think about knowledge systems interacting. So, it wasn't just you know, some people talking about these ideas. It was actually theory; it was actually about how we understand knowledge and how we want to interact with knowledge and how different peoples can relate to each other in relation to knowledge ….

I find non-Indigenous research frameworks and science don't do that because it's all about the science and the data and collecting it, putting data in models. Two-Eyed Seeing is a different framework that could be about data, but also about a relationship between people, so Two-Eyed Seeing can inform us about reconciliation between Indigenous and non-Indigenous Peoples. While I was completing my PhD studies in forestry, I found that some students and faculty were threatened by the idea of traditional knowledge as saw it as a rejection of science. I believe in part because they weren't familiar with any kind of Indigenous conceptual theoretical frameworks, they thought it is primitive and is going to displace our knowledge. Two-Eyed Seeing, I believe, is to some extent comforting for them because it didn't require them to reject their training and everything that they knew, that Two-Eyed seeing actually seeks to embrace other knowledge into trying to solve whatever the common problem or challenge of the day was. I believe the concept means you are going to have to learn how to get along with Indigenous People because that's actually where the knowledge is: embedded within people and within the community.

Two-Eyed Seeing enabled for this interchange and interaction to occur in a respectful way, respecting different knowledge systems on their own terms. Two-Eyed seeing is a way to decolonize research-it disrupts the power that Western knowledge has over Indigenous knowledge and challenges the status quo. Indigenous knowledge is equally important, significant, and valid.

Another aspect of Two-Eyed Seeing that I learned over the last couple of decades is it doesn't always just apply to Western science and Indigenous knowledge. Different Indigenous Nations can also engage in the Two-Eyed Seeing approach. Indigenous Peoples are very diverse – their nations with their own knowledge systems languages, etc. We interacted with each other and developed our own ways of engaging in each other's knowledge systems. The Two-Eyed Seeing just wasn't invented by the Mi'kmaq upon encountering settlers and colonizers; they had this concept long before that. Indigenous people already had ways of how we wanted different knowledge to interact with each other and how different peoples were going to respectfully interact with each other based on the assumption that these knowledge systems have something to offer, and it's not appropriate for one to dominate the other.

Kaswentha/*Two-Row Wampum*

JACQUELYN MILLER: So, would you be able to tell us a little bit more about how you use the idea of the *Kaswentha* or Two Row Wampum or the Dish with One Spoon and other frameworks for thinking across ways of knowing and maybe just a quick recap on what those are for anyone who might not have the knowledge on that.

DR. DEBORAH McGREGOR: I think part of the underlying assumption that I come from with this is that as Indigenous Nations we had our own theories, conceptual frameworks for knowledge exchange. In our history, we have had to face destruction, and [it] is usually because we weren't behaving properly in relation to the natural and spirit world/all of creation. We had our own ideas and theories, philosophies, knowledge, and legal orders of which there is a great diversity. So, different nations develop different ways of how they were going to interact with other nations' knowledge systems in mutually beneficial ways.

I am not Haudenosaunee. I can only speak to my experience working with Haudenosaunee communities and peoples while engaged in the State of the Great Lakes work. State of the Great Lakes reports are science-based and lacked representation of Indigenous Peoples and their knowledge. Canada and the United States, as the part of the Great Lakes Water Quality Agreement, were trying to figure out how to work with Indigenous peoples and their knowledge as part of assessing the health of the Great Lakes and did not know how to go about this work.

James Ransom, who was Mohawk from Akwesasne, was the former director of environment for the Assembly of First Nations. [He] introduced me to the idea of the *Kaswentha* and it's actually a treaty originally between the Haudenosaunee and the Dutch for how they were going to function together as societies, that they weren't going to interfere with one another. The principles set out in the *Kaswentha* (a treaty) means that people were going to work together in peace and friendship and that they weren't going to interfere with each other's autonomy. It took, you know, some time for me to understand that the *Kaswentha* informs us how knowledge systems interact equitably, guided by a set of principles (see Ransom and Ettenger 2001).

One principle is that the integrity of the knowledge systems remain intact, there is not absorbing into another knowledge system. Unfortunately, [there has been] a lot of Indigenous knowledge appropriation from Indigenous peoples. The *Kaswentha* and Two Row Wampum influenced my PhD research because at the time there were not any Indigenous conceptual frameworks in the academy for how to deal with different knowledge systems appropriately and ethically. People were more comfortable with the idea of the *Kaswentha*, but they still struggled with the idea that traditional knowledge is part of a distinct knowledge system that you didn't have to tinker with in order for it to be valuable. I was influenced by the Haudenosaunee people that I was working with because I needed to be able to convey that Indigenous knowledges can stand on their own. They always did, and they can continue to do so and that we would bring the best that we have to offer to the situation at hand. We ask ourselves, "What's the best that we have to offer to try to resolve this common situation, problem, or challenge that we're facing?" The Dish with One Spoon treaty between the Haudenosaunee and the Anishinabek is another conceptual framework that also involves knowledge sharing. Again, as a Nation, we ask ourselves, "How are we going to sustain the resources or the land – the creation that we share – how are we going to support that? How are you going to ensure the sustainability for future generations? How are we going to honour that?" And that treaty informs that process. So, the Haudenosaunee and Anishinabek would bring again the best that they have to offer to ensure the sustainability of the land we shared in coexistence.

Indigenous knowledges have thousands of years on these territories. They can stand on their own, and they continue to stand on their own. But how are we going to relate to other knowledge systems that can also help us address some of the big challenges of the day?

Applying Concepts for Including Different Ways of Knowing

JACQUELYN MILLER: Firstly how do you use these frameworks for thinking and understanding across ways of knowing in your applied work? And ... tie the two together also – the ethical responsibility, relations, reciprocity, and partnership that is inherently involved in using these frameworks.

DR. ANDREA REID: Two-Eyed Seeing is really a reflexive practice that we can carry with us through the lifetime of a project and use it as a guiding principle at every research choice and action and every turn basically to guide how we move forward in the work in a good way. And so [to give] one example that actually comes from my nation, the Nisga'a Nation has been employing amazing co-management strategies for nearly three decades in which they have very successfully married traditional methodologies for understanding our fisheries and for monitoring them alongside modern statistical approaches. And so in my work in partnership with the nation I combined radio telemetry, where I put radio tags inside of salmon to see where they go, how quickly they get there, if they reach their spawning grounds, to see if there are things we can do – things in the environment that can be improved to make sure that more reach spawning grounds. So I use this really quantitative approach, but I pair that with methodologies that are employed by the Nisga'a Nation, such as big fish wheels that are on the river and weirs that give us this opportunity to recapture my tagged fish, and so we can do health assessments on these fish as they're migrating through time and space. And so this gives us a different kind of insight, and the Nisga'a Fisheries and Wildlife technicians are very actively assessing the health and well-being of these fish, based on their knowledge and understanding of what the fish ought to look like at that point in time and how they should be doing. And so, I get to bring together these qualitative and quantitative ways of knowing together to improve our understanding of the state of our fish.

Another example from within the context of my thesis is that I performed two kinds of expert evaluation assessments in my thesis that looked at leading threats to freshwater ecosystems and the fish that inhabit them. On one end of that work, I worked with freshwater scientists from around the world to evaluate key threats and identify what those main considerations are, and we used data in that work from the World Wildlife Fund on all monitored populations of vertebrates in freshwater, marine, and terrestrial systems to look at how they've done over time, between the 1970s and today. On the other end of this work, I interviewed Elders and Knowledge Keepers from across the province of British Columbia about key threats that are endangering our salmon and what we can do about them, asking them how their access to the fish has changed since that same time frame, since the 1970s to the present day. And what I find fascinating is that they both find this staggering decline that is of the same magnitude– both find an average of 83 per cent decline over this 50-year time frame, which is a really big cause for concern that we're seeing. These fish, these waterways, [declining] to a point of 1/6 of what they used to be and what we used to know them as. And I just love that you can do this big global monitoring of all the populations of freshwater vertebrates on the planet, or you can talk to people who live and know the fish and live in that way, and we arrive at the same value. And so, I think it just really goes to show that we can learn from both of these ways, and they're both accurate, precise, and valuable.

DR. JESSE POPP: I come from a wildlife ecology perspective and understand that we are faced with some pretty important environmental issues today. Biodiversity is collapsing, and there are many examples of how Two-Eyed Seeing and similar frameworks can help us better understand and address these issues related to collapse and population declines. In thinking about interweaving ways of knowing through frameworks like Two-Eyed Seeing, it is important for us to ensure that we are proceeding in a good way – for example, by being respectful to one another and being inclusive and diverse in science. By proceeding in a good way, we can start building really great partnerships, partnerships that follow practices like the Two-Row Wampum. In building these partnerships – that will hopefully consist of equal seats at a shared table – we can better engage in joint decision-making, for example in wildlife or environmental management. Although there is a way to go, every journey begins with a single step. Through these steps, we are reconciling ways of knowing and bettering nation-to-nation relationships. We have a long way to go, but we are on a path to getting there, and it's really exciting to be to be part of this.

DR. ANDREA REID: I think what we're seeing currently in *Mi'kma'ki* with the lobster fishery, that's a pretty prime example of how our failure to reconcile ways of knowing and being is manifesting today, and so we're getting to a point as Jesse alluded to where we're not going to have much of a choice in how we move forward. We need to do something now before it's too late and that's very much the reality through my salmon-centred view of the world, but I really think it requires a fundamental shift in how we grow up through the education system.

DR. JESSE POPP: In institutions and places where we work, there is a lot that we can do to contribute to decolonization by bringing together multiple ways of knowing. We need more learning opportunities for students, but also for the teachers, because we have had this system where inclusive approaches like Two-Eyed Seeing were not taught to those individuals now teaching. When I was in school, I felt a lot of barriers in trying to learn about or practice Two-Eyed Seeing. Although I didn't have a lot of support, I quickly realized that these barriers I was up against were only perceived barriers that I could overcome and that I did overcome. We all have a fire within us, this fire to make change. That fire is protected within each of us, and nobody can extinguish that fire. We need to keep feeding our fires and continue letting them burn bright, because our future generations depend upon it.

Elder Marshall in his remarks spoke to the need for right relations with the natural word through the Two-Eyed approach. Action, he maintained, is inherent in the concept of *Etuaptmumk*. He states:

"The Two-Eyed Seeing perspective I think has to be with some action. **Action** for the better. I don't believe we have the luxury anymore to be continuously comfortable in our denial, in our silences, in our inactions because the rate of destruction is so rapid that she cannot heal herself, regenerate herself fast enough. And she cannot cleanse herself fast enough with the rate of chemicals … being pumped into her. Now, how much longer are we going to remain silent, inactive, and in denial before maybe it might be too late. This is what we Aboriginal People have been saying for years: Unless we commit ourselves to ensuring that no action of ours will ever compromise the ecological integrity of the area or the cleansing then, we will then fail. We would have then failed to live up to our inherent responsibilities because again we have something that no other creature has, and that's the cognitive mind. So, let's put that energy to work, to be the helping hand and not stop her from being the arm of destruction. Thank you!'

Conclusion

The movement around the rights of nature – such as the recent granting of legal rights to the Magpie River in Quebec – indicates that steps are being taken towards reconciliation with nature (Lowrie 2021). Reconciliation with the Earth is increasingly gaining attention through such movements around the rights of nature and legal personhood (Ruru 2018). The discussions among Jacquelyn Miller, Deborah McGregor, Jesse Popp, Andrea Reid, and Elder Albert Marshall highlight how Indigenous concepts – particularly those of Two-Eyed Seeing, the Two Row Wampum, and the Dish with One Spoon – offer a pathway towards reconciliation with the Earth. These Indigenous models of knowledge sharing offer unique ways of knowing and relating centred on how we can and must balance humanity's relationships with place and the Earth. Indigenous knowledges are embodied within the lived experience of the People and thus are not separate from place/land/nature. These conceptual frameworks offer an ethical space to ensure a coming together of Peoples in the spirit of respect and collaboration, to enable reconciliation with each other and the Earth. This contribution offered insights into the application of the concepts of *Etuaptmumk/*Two-Eyed Seeing, *Kaswentha/*Two Row Wampum, and Dish with One Spoon to help us collectively better understand our inter-relationships and inter-responsibilities in support of reconciliation between societies, nations, and the Earth.

NOTE

1 The notion of *Etuaptmumk/*Two-Eyed Seeing was coined by Elder Marshall and his late wife Murdena Marshall.

WORKS CITED

Abu, Razak, Maureen G. Reed, and Timothy D. Jardine. 2020. "Using Two-Eyed Seeing to Bridge Western Science and Indigenous Knowledge Systems and Understand Long-Term Change in the Saskatchewan River Delta, Canada." *International Journal of Water Resources Development* 36 (5): 757–76. https://doi.org/10.1080/07900627.2018.1558050
Archibald, Jo-Ann. 2008. *Indigenous Storywork: Educating the Heart, Mind, Body, and Spirit.* Vancouver: University of British Columbia Press.
Bartlett, Cheryl, Murdena Marshall, and Albert Marshall. 2012. "Two-Eyed Seeing and Other Lessons Learned within a Co-learning Journey of Bringing Together

Indigenous and Mainstream Knowledges and Ways of Knowing." *Journal of Environmental Studies and Sciences* 2 (4): 331–40. https://doi.org/10.1007 /s13412-012-0086-8

Berkes, Fikret. 2017. *Sacred Ecology*, 4th ed. London: Routledge. http:// web.b.ebscohost.com.ezproxy.library.yorku.ca/ehost/ebookviewer/ebook /bmxlYmtfXzE1ODg1NzNfNfX0FO0?sid=3c2bf9fb-bc5e-4cdd-a987-b6415fdbacf7 @sessionmgr103&vid=0&format=EB&rid=1

Borrows, John. 2018. "Earth-Bound: Indigenous Resurgence and Environmental Reconciliation." In *Resurgence and Reconciliation: Indigenous-Settler Relations and Earth Teachings*, edited by Michael Asch, John Borrows, and James Tully, 49–81. Toronto, Canada: University of Toronto Press. http://ebookcentral.proquest.com/lib /york/detail.action?docID=5592950

Doerfler, Jill, Heidi Kiiwetinepinesiik Stark, and Niigaanwewidam James Sinclair, eds. 2013. *Centering Anishinaabeg Studies: Understanding the World through Stories*. Winnipeg, Manitoba: University of Manitoba Press.

Finegan, Chance. 2018. "Reflection, Acknowledgement, and Justice: A Framework for Indigenous-Protected Area Reconciliation." *International Indigenous Policy Journal* 9 (3). https://doi.org/10.18584/iipj.2018.9.3.3

Kimmerer, Robin Wall. 2012. "Searching for Synergy: Integrating Traditional and Scientific Ecological Knowledge in Environmental Science Education." *Journal of Environmental Studies and Sciences* 2 (4): 317–23. https://doi.org/10.1007 /s13412-012-0091-y

Lowrie, Morgan. 2021. "Quebec River Granted Legal Rights as Part of Global 'Personhood' Movement." *CBC News*, February 28, 2021. https://www.cbc .ca/news/canada/montreal/magpie-river-quebec-canada-personhood -1.5931067

Martin, Debbie H. 2012. "Two-Eyed Seeing: A Framework for Understanding Indigenous and Non-Indigenous Approaches to Indigenous Health Research." *Canadian Journal of Nursing Research Archive* 44 (2): 20–43.

McGregor, Deborah. 2016. "Living Well with the Earth: Indigenous Rights and the Environment." In *Handbook of Indigenous Rights*, edited by Damien Short and Corinne Lennox, 167–80. New York: Routledge.

– 2018. "Reconciliation and Environmental Justice." *Journal of Global Ethics* 14 (2): 222–31. https://doi.org/10.1080/17449626.2018.1507005

– 2019a. "Reconciliation, Colonialism and Climate Change." In *Policy Transformation in Canada: Is the Past Prologue?*, edited by Carolyn Tuohy, Sophie Borwien, Peter Loewen, and Andrew Potter, 139–47. Toronto: University of Toronto Press.

– 2019b. "Truth Be Told: Redefining Relationships through Indigenous Research." In *Renewing Relationships: Indigenous Peoples and Canada*, edited by Karen Drake and Brenda L Gunn, 9–36. Saskatoon, SK: Indigenous Law Centre. https:// digitalcommons.osgoode.yorku.ca/scholarly_works/2822

Moorman, Lynn, Julia Evanovitch, and Tolu Muliaina. 2021. "Envisioning Indigenized Geography: A Two-Eyed Seeing Approach." *Journal of Geography in Higher Education* 45 (2): 201–20. https://doi.org/10.1080/03098265.2021.1872060

Peacock, Thomas. 2013. "Teaching as Story." In *Centering Anishinaabeg Studies: Understanding the World through Stories,* edited by Jill Doerfler, Heidi Kiiwetinepinesiik Stark, and Niigaanwewidam James Sinclair. Winnipeg: University of Manitoba Press.

Popp, Jesse N., Pauline Priadka, Megan Young, Kevin Koch, and James Morgan. 2020. "Indigenous Guardianship and Moose Monitoring: Weaving Indigenous and Western Ways of Knowing." *Human-Wildlife Interactions* 14 (2): 296–308. https://doi.org/10.26077/67f5-d36b

Ransom R, Ettenger K. 2001. "'Polishing the Kaswentha': A Haudenosaunee View of Environmental Cooperation." *Environ Sci Policy* 4, no. 4–5: 219–28. https://doi.org/10.1016/S1462-9011(01)00027-2

Reid, Andrea J., Lauren E. Eckert, John-Francis Lane, Nathan Young, Scott G. Hinch, Chris T. Darimont, Steven J. Cooke, Natalie C. Ban, and Albert Marshall. 2020. "'Two-Eyed Seeing': An Indigenous Framework to Transform Fisheries Research and Management." *Fish and Fisheries* 22 (2): 243–61. https://doi.org/10.1111/faf.12516

Ruru, Jacinta. 2018. "Listening to Papatūānuku: A Call to Reform Water Law." *Journal of the Royal Society of New Zealand* 48 (2–3): 215–24. https://doi.org/10.1080/03036758.2018.1442358

RWoK. 2020. "Reconciling Ways of Knowing." Reconciling Ways of Knowing Stewardship Society. https://www.waysofknowingforum.ca.

Tobias, Joshua K., and Chantelle A.M. Richmond. 2014. "'That Land Means Everything to Us as Anishinaabe …': Environmental Dispossession and Resilience on the North Shore of Lake Superior" 29 (Complete): 26–33. https://doi.org/10.1016/j.healthplace.2014.05.008

Todd, Zoe. 2018. "Refracting the State through Human-Fish Relations." *Decolonization: Indigeneity, Education & Society* 7 (1): 60–75.

Truth and Reconciliation Commission of Canada. 2015a. "Honouring the Truth, Reconciling for the Future: Summary of the Final Report of the Truth and Reconciliation Commission of Canada." IR4–7/2015E-PDF – Government of Canada Publications – Canada.Ca. http://publications.gc.ca/site/eng/9.800288/publication.html

– 2015b. "What We Have Learned: Principles of Truth and Reconciliation. Report of the Truth and Reconciliation Commission." http://www.trc.ca/websites/trcinstitution/File/2015/Findings/Principles_2015_05_31_web_o.pdf

Waldron, Ingrid R.G. 2018. *There's Something in the Water: Environmental Racism in Indigenous and Black Communities.* Winnipeg: Fernwood Publishing.

Whyte, Kyle Powys. 2018. "On Resilient Parasitisms, or Why I'm Skeptical of Indigenous/Settler Reconciliation." *Journal of Global Ethics* 14 (2): 277–89. https://doi.org/10.1080/17449626.2018.1516693

Wilson, Shawn, Andrea V. Breen, and Lindsay Dupré, eds. 2019. *Research and Reconciliation: Unsettling Ways of Knowing through Indigenous Relationships.* Toronto: Canadian Scholars Press.

Windchief, Sweeney, and Timothy San Pedro, eds. 2019. *Applying Indigenous Research Methods: Storying with Peoples and Communities.* New York: Routledge.

8 Beacons of Teachings

LISA YOUNG

The Beginning

The healing will begin in the east, where it all began, the Elder said.

The East. *Wabanaki. Mi'kma'ki.* The place I call home. It is where we, the Mi'kmaq, or L'nu, had our first encounter with the newcomers. "Come on in." Being from the East, I've heard that a few times from natives out West, teasingly, in irony, with a smile; "Come on in," as they gesture with their arms wide in welcome. Being from the East, I have also had many occasions to think back, on the moment when I first heard the prophecy – *the healing will begin in the east, where it all began* – from the Elder. I wonder, did our ancestors truly have the power to see into the future, or was our future made self-evident through early destructive actions of the colonizers of this land? Whatever I choose to believe, there is an undeniable truth to their warning and their hope. The path we choose moving forward will decided how our story ends.

Learning to "Think Like Them"

Although I am Mi'kmaq, the first time I was ever exposed to elements of my Mi'kmaw culture was at Kluskap Mountain. It is located in what is now called Cape Breton Island, Nova Scotia, Canada. At the time it was not yet a designated wilderness area, not part of the provincial protected area network, but it was frequented by many who wanted to explore the cave found there. This first time, my father had taken me on a hike. We didn't speak of Kluskap, the Creator's first living being,[1] or his legends. We didn't discuss the medicines along the trail, although I learned later in life that my father knew of many edible plants. I learned even later that he learned of them out of necessity. It was by happenstance that we ran into a few of his friends on Kluskap Mountain; they were there to fast. It was a brief encounter. A cheerful greeting and a well-wishing from my father: "I will think of you when I am eating," he had said to them. I remember thinking to myself, why would he say that, knowing that they must be so hungry. When I questioned him, he simply said that it was our culture. And that was it, nothing else.

I never learned my language, though my father was fluent in Mi'kmaq. I heard him many times conversing in Mi'kmaq with friends on the telephone or when they came to the house to visit. I overheard him speak a few choice words in Mi'kmaq when he struck his thumb with the hammer. And, of course, I knew the words for "make tea." But that was all I knew of my language. I was better off not learning it, he told me once. He said that I needed to learn how to think like "them," the English; there will be time to learn Mi'kmaw later. I am still waiting for that later.

I did learn to think like them. I received my biology degree from York University. Biology seemed like the logical choice at the time because I had done well in that class in high school. But I know now that I was his top student because he was the only teacher that ever showed any interest in my future. Though I do have to give a little credit for my biology interests to Lorne Green and his nature documentary series.[2] Through my four years of schooling, I was never really convinced that I was where I was meant to be. But for some reason the idea of quitting, giving up and going home, was far less appealing. I stayed. When I finished, I was fortunate to be recruited right out of university by Charlie Dennis. Charlie was the executive director of the Eskasoni Fish and Wildlife Commission, a Mi'kmaw-led organization.

I will never forget my first day at my first real job. No real staff orientation. No real job description or direction was given. Charlie simply said, "Make yourself useful." This wasn't hard to do, since at the time the organization was quite small. So, you found yourself filling in for many roles. As it happens, I was asked to take minutes at the newly formed moose management initiative, a joint effort by Parks Canada, the provincial Department of Natural Resources, and the Mi'kmaq. For anyone new to an organization, I can tell you taking minutes at various meetings is probably the fastest way to learn the ins and outs. It wasn't long before I was tagging along to meetings with Charlie, all over Cape Breton. Not long after that I was what I like to describe as "being desked." The Unama'ki Institute of Natural Resources (UINR) had just been formed by the five Unama'ki Mi'kmaw communities and was in need of an administrator. No more boating on the Bras d'Or or flying over the Cape Breton Highlands for me. A hard pill to swallow at the time. But seeing how I didn't really care for statistical analysis I probably would have made a poor scientist anyway.

Over the years, UINR has grown to be a leading organization in natural resource management among our First Nation communities. When people ask us how we got to where we are, I always credit Charlie. Charlie treated his staff like family. He was our mentor and friend, and he is dearly missed. I never met someone that didn't like Charlie. He made fast friends with everyone he met.

It didn't matter if you worked for the government, local industry, or a sports fishing organization, people believed in him and in his vision, and they wanted to be a part of it. He kept things simple. Stick to the "bread and butter issues," he would say. Focus on what matters and leave your hat at the door.

Charlie's belief in the power of collaboration led to the formation of the Collaborative Environmental Planning Initiative and many other partnerships. UINR owes its success to the strong foundation that Charlie built through his efforts at developing partnerships and the feeling of family that he instilled in his staff. He once shared that his dream was to see young Mi'kmaq people working on the Bras d'Or Lakes doing research and helping to preserve and protect our resources. I can confidently say that his dream has become a reality.

As you can imagine, Charlie was a hard man to say no to. So, when he said an opportunity had come up to do an internship with the Department of Fisheries and Oceans Canada (DFO) in Halifax, I soon found myself looking for an apartment in the city. It was the fall of 2000, roughly one year after the Marshall decision affirming a two-century-old treaty right allowing Indigenous Peoples to earn a moderate livelihood through commercial fishing in Atlantic Canada (R. *v.* Marshall, [1999] 3 S.C.R. 456). It was I and a young man from Acadia First Nation who found ourselves getting a crash course in aquaculture, genetics, and oceanography, learning by doing on the job. And on the ocean. Those first four days at sea were the longest days of my life, in part as a consequence of watching too many *Jaws*[3] movies as a kid I suppose. Of all the lessons we learned during the six-month internship, the one that had the most impact on me was our experience in Saint John, New Brunswick. The task was simple enough: participate in the Coastal Zone 2000 conference as rapporteurs and support the Indigenous Elders who were invited to the conference. But that comes later.

Learning Our Stories

Working with Elders had become an important part of my work at UINR. It was there where I first had the pleasure of meeting Elder Albert Marshall. He was a frequent visitor to our little office, offering his wisdom and guidance on issues that were close to his heart. He would go on to help create UINR's Elder and Knowledge Holders engagement process to ensure we took a "Two-Eyed Seeing" approach (Marshall 2004; Bartlett, Marshall, and Marshall 2012). Two-Eyed Seeing is the guiding principle brought into Cape Breton University's Integrative Science program by Albert in the fall of 2004. *Etuaptmumk* is the Mi'kmaw word for "Two-Eyed Seeing." As Albert explains it, *Etuaptmumk* refers to learning to see from one eye with the strengths of Indigenous knowledges and ways of knowing, and from the other eye with the strengths of Western knowledges and ways of knowing, and learning to use both these eyes together, for the benefit of all. Developing an *Etuaptmumk* approach is done through a journey of co-learning. It is a requisite to enable integrative science work, as well as other integrative or transcultural or transdisciplinary or collaborative work (Marshall 2004). Seeing our work through this perspective resonated more with me than any course I had taken at university. I can't imagine working any other way.

It was because of my experience working with Albert that I learned to respect my elders and to value their knowledge. Attending the Coastal Zone 2000 conference in Saint John, New Brunswick, was a welcome break from counting spat and cleaning fish tanks. There I was given the opportunity to learn from elders and knowledge holders from all over the world: Hawaii, Peru, New Zealand, Canada, and the United States. Their lessons and teachings were in such stark contrast to the Western knowledge sessions that we attended. They spoke about the importance of the connection between the heart and the mind. Of how you can respectfully harvest salmon simply by throwing a pebble into a stream of spawning salmon: if the fish swam away, you would know they were done spawning and that they could be safely harvested. It was so empowering to see that Indigenous Peoples from all over the world shared so much knowledge. There was much that was shared among the Indigenous delegates outside the confines of the conference's agenda.

At the conference, alongside the sharing of song and dance, our people shared their dark stories of colonization. When the settlers first started to come to Hawaii, the Indigenous People knew their culture was in danger of being lost. So, they hid their knowledge and cultural practices in dance and song to preserve it for future generations. These are not the dances that you will see as a tourist. We, the Mi'kmaq, have a similar story: the "Seven Fires" prophecy. There are many online references to the prophecy[4] (e.g., Dostou 2000; see also Benton-Banai 1988; Christmas 2011), but I will share it with you as it was told to me.

> When the settlers first came to Mi'kma'ki, the Mi'kmaw knew their culture was in danger. They travelled west to the land of the Anishinaabe, to the sacred Midewiwin Lodge, where their knowledge could be held for safekeeping.
>
> When the time came, our people would be able to relearn our traditional ways. Our people were told that the settlers will come as both friend and foe, and we will not be able to tell the difference. Our people will lose our language, our land, and our children. There will be a time, however, that the children of those settlers will come to our Elders for guidance on how to heal the damages that were done to this land. How badly we will be affected by these damages will depend on their ability to change their ways. It was said that the healing will begin in the east, the place where it all began.

This is the part of the prophecy that stuck with me the most: *the healing will begin in the east, the place where it all began.* My home. The home of the Wabanaki,[5] people of the dawn, of which the Mi'kmaq are part.

Our people love to laugh. I think our humour is part of why we are so resilient. I don't remember the joke the Elder told but it felt good to laugh at that moment. What had started out as a week of stories and laughter was quickly dampened by underlying feelings of anger and frustration. Throughout the conference there was always the feeling that our Indigenous voices were being lost, swallowed in a sea of western science and government bureaucracy.

But even this seemed pretty inconsequential compared to what was to come next. We were joined halfway through the gathering by an Elder from New Brunswick. I remember that he was a very humble, kind, and generous man. This made what he shared somehow even more disheartening. He shared that his community was being harassed by the 'military,' as he called them. Whatever department they were actually from is irrelevant: they were sent there on behalf of the Canadian Government. Helicopters had been circling the community of Burnt Church in an effort to scare and intimidate their warriors from setting their lobster traps. Their community had chosen to exercise their rights to a livelihood fishery, newly upheld under the 1999 Marshall decision (R. v. Marshall, [1999] 3 S.C.R. 456). This was what is now sometimes referred to as the Burnt Church Crisis (First Nations Drum Newspaper 2000; Obomsawin 2002; CBC 2012). The next day the Elder led us through ceremony. It was my first sunrise ceremony. He explained afterwards that the powerful feeling you feel from the northern direction is medicine. It provides healing to those in need. I felt as though he was speaking directly to me.

To better understand how we got here we need to go back 30 years. Donald Marshall, Jr., was a Mi'kmaq from my home community of Membertou, Nova Scotia. He was son of the late Donald Marshall, Sr., Grand Chief of the Mi'kmaq Nation. Junior was no stranger to the justice system. He had been sentenced to life in prison at the young age of 17 years, after being wrongfully convicted in 1971 for the murder of Sandy Seale (Hickman, Poitras, and Evans 1989). It wasn't until 12 years later that he was acquitted by the Nova Scotia Court of Appeal after a witness came forward. His wrongful conviction resulted in changes to the Evidence in Canada Act and an investigation by the Royal Commission as to the causes of this miscarriage of justice (Hickman, Poitras, and Evans 1989).

Ten years after his acquittal, in 1993, when exercising his Treaty rights to fish, Marshall was convicted for fishing eels out of season and without a licence (Wicken 2002). It wasn't until six years later, in 1999, that the Supreme Court of Canada ruled on the case, affirming that Marshall, as Mi'kmaq, had a legal right to catch and sell fish, consistent with the Mi'kmaq Treaties of 1760–1 (R. v. Marshall, [1999] 3 S.C.R. 456). Much later, at the twentieth anniversary of the Marshall Decision conference in September 2019, lawyer Eric Zscheile (2019) reminisced about the days leading up to the trial, as a new, young lawyer supporting the legal team. He reflected that Donald Jr. had not intended to take on the Crown when he set out that fateful day in August 1971; he was just looking to provide for his family. The last thing he was looking for was more notoriety. He was just happy to be out living his life, doing what he loved, fishing for eels. But he understood the importance of the case and the impact it could have for the Mi'kmaq Nation.

When the Supreme Court of Canada came back with its ruling on the Marshall case on 17 September 1999, it was a momentous day for all of us. It affirmed our treaty right to hunt, fish, and gather in pursuit of a "moderate livelihood," arising out of the Peace and Friendship Treaties of 1760 and 1761. Finally, after 240 years, our Treaties – which affirm our inherent right to live on our ancestral lands as Mi'kmaq, to maintain relationship with our lands and provide for our families – were being upheld by the highest court in Canada. This historic moment, a time that should have been a time to celebrate, was instead marred by hatred, jealousy, and greed. Over 100 non-native fishing vessels had headed out to Miramichi Bay, NB, to protest. Tensions were high and violence ensued as hundreds of Mi'kmaw lobster traps were destroyed at the hands of non-native fishers. Online you can find a haunting video of a DFO vessel running over small Mi'kmaw fishing vessels, forcing our fishers to jump into the water to save their lives (Obomsawin 2002). Many Mi'kmaw communities, including those in Nova Scotia, chose to enter into negotiations with DFO; interim licences were issued with the promise of entering into negotiation for the establishment of a livelihood fishery.

Now, 21 years later, we are still waiting for our rights to be fully implemented. In a recent interview on CBC Radio's *Mainstreet Nova Scotia*, lawyer Bruce Wildsmith, legal counsel to the Assembly of Nova Scotia Mi'kmaq Chiefs, and lead council for Donald in the Marshall case, spoke about it. He described the legal context behind the ongoing disputes between Mi'kmaw and commercial fishermen, and what the Marshall decisions say about federal regulation (Douglass 2020). On the podcast recording, Mr. Wildsmith sounds frustrated, and with good reason. Since the Supreme Court ruling on the Marshall case – upholding our Treaty rights – and the Burnt Church incident in 1999, another 21 years of inaction by the federal government had culminated in another confrontation between Mi'kmaw fishers and non-native lobster fishers. This time it was in St Mary's Bay, in southwest Nova Scotia, and in response to the launch of the Sipekne'katik First Nation rights-based fishery. The Mi'kmaq once again had chosen to exercise their Treaty rights by fishing under their own terms, guided by the concepts of *Netukulimk* (Micmac Grand Council et al. 1987, as cited in Young 2016; Prosper et al. 2011; UINR n.d.).

Mr. Wildsmith participated in the media interview with the intention of setting the record straight after government officials and media made false claims that the *Netukulimk* lobster fishery is an "illegal fishery." In the interview, he explained that our Treaty right allows for the Mi'kmaq "to continue to obtain necessaries through hunting and fishing by trading the products of those traditional activities." It is only subject to "restrictions that can be justified under the Badger test." He goes on to explain that the Badger test (R. *v.* Badger, [1996] 1 S.C.R. 771) states that there first needs to be an "important public objective such as conservation" to justify infringement, and even then it must be "the minimal infringement that is possible to meet the object of conservation." The federal government has to "consult" with the Mi'kmaq when they are considering "actions that infringe on those rights." He stresses that the existing commercial regime under DFO does not apply to the Mi'kmaq: those regulations have to be "justified" under the Badger test; they need to be "proposed" to the Mi'kmaq through a "duty to consult" in a "meaningful" way. "[T]he constitutional right supersedes the statutory rights. So, the highest law in the land are those Treaties; and the Supreme Court's interpretations of them: they're embedded in the Constitution" (Wildsmith, in Douglass 2020, np). In 1999, through the Marshal decisions, "the Supreme Court told DFO what they had to do. And what they had to do was have a regime for a livelihood fishery that was different than the commercial fishery, and to consult with the Mi'kmaq, have criteria for the issuances of licences for that fishery" (ibid.). And yet, DFO had failed to do this. They instead engaged the Mi'kmaq in a drawn-out process that is "a made-in-Ottawa solution," culminating in a "non-negotiable offer." "This wasn't consultation. This was negotiation .... Negotiations were not advancing the implementation of the Treaty right because it was an 'Ottawa top-down approach'" (ibid.).

And so, despite the Supreme Court's reaffirmation of our Treaty and Rights, Canada's commitment to implementing the United Nations Declaration on the Rights of Indigenous People (UNDRIP) (UN 2007), and their promise to honour the recommendations of the Truth and Reconciliation Commission (TRC 2015a,b.c), the Government of Canada has failed to act honorably when it comes to Mi'kmaq Rights to earn a modest living from the commercial fishery.

Ethical Space

The first time I was introduced to the concept of "ethical space" was by Dr. Reg Crowshoe, a renowned Elder and Former Chief of the Piikuni Nation in Alberta, Canada. This was in 2017, during the Indigenous Circle of Experts (ICE) Regional Gatherings for the Pathway to Canada Target 1 (ICE 2018a). Ethical space is a "foundational concept in cross-cultural research ethics within Canada," first popularized by Cree philosopher and educator Willie Ermine" (ICE 2018a, 19), who cites a concept by Poole (1972; Ermine 2000; 2007). Elder Dr. Reg Crowshoe has been instrumental in adapting the concept of ethical space for the work of ICE (2018a).

In the Indigenous Circle of Experts (2018b) report – We Rise Together: Achieving Pathway to Canada Target 1 through the Creation of Indigenous

Protected and Conserved Areas in the Spirit and Practice of Reconciliation –
we refer to the countless rights violations in Canada's history where Indigenous
land stewards and defenders have been criminalized along with their traditional
and contemporary relationships with lands and waters. The incidents in Burnt
Church and St Mary's Bay are testaments to this (e.g., Obomsawin 2002). It is
understandable, then, that Indigenous Peoples are hesitant to establish relationships with non-Indigenous governments. Indigenous Peoples are often put in a
position of having to defend our Indigenous systems of knowledge, laws, cus-
toms, and practices and, as we saw in Nova Scotia and New Brunswick, fight for
our Treaty rights that have already been affirmed by the highest court of the land.

In stark contrast, the concept of ethical space puts us on an equal footing
(ICE 2018b). In this space the integrity of both knowledge systems – Western
and Indigenous – are respected and valued, and neither system has more weight
or legitimacy than the other. It's about starting with UNDRIP, the TRC recommendations, and our Peace and Friendship Treaties as jumping-off points, to elevate the rights and responsibilities of Indigenous Peoples for the betterment of
all. Ethical space is a safe space to share, learn, and build the respectful relationships that are needed to move forward on what can sometimes be considered
difficult issues. As in any relationship, you need commitment from both parties
to make an effort to communicate, to see things from the other's perspective
and be prepared to hear some hard truths of Canada's dark history.

There are 42 National Parks in Canada, over 1000 Provincial and Territorial
Parks (YourCanada n.d.). As of March 2020, there were 14 Oceans Act Marine
Protected Areas (MPAs), comprising over 350,000 km^2 or roughly six per cent
of Canada's marine and coastal areas (DFO website). All were created to protect
terrestrial and marine ecosystems, to preserve special landscapes and biodiversity, or simply to give people places to enjoy and escape the stress of their daily
lives. So, if there is such a value placed on nature, why are there 810 wildlife species in various risk categories listed by COSEWIC in their 2019–2020 annual
report, despite having protected areas and legislation in place that is supposed
to protect our wildlife? The answer is in how people view their relationship to
land and water. Traditional parks and protected areas were created to protect
nature from man. This comes from a mindset that man is somehow superior
to or outside of nature. The perception was, and in many cases continues to be,
that in order to preserve nature we must protect it from the exploits of man
(Binnema and Niemi 2006; Sandlos 2008; Youdelis 2016).

In the Indigenous Circle of Experts' report, we refer to the dark history of
protected areas in Canada (2018b). It speaks to the time when people, both
Indigenous and non-Indigenous, were forcefully removed from the land in the
misguided attempt to protect nature from man (Moola and Roth 2018; Zurba et
al. 2019; Artelle et al. 2019). It speaks to the time in our history that was fraught
with rights violations, forcible displacements, losses of access to traditional

territories and resource, and other substantial inter-generational cultural, social, economic, and spiritual impacts (Pictou 2018, 2019; National Inquiry into Missing and Murdered Indigenous Women and Girls 2019; Berger 1977).

This is the same mentality, the same set of values and belief systems that are at the core of nearly every legislation, policy, and program that was put in place to exert dominion and control not only over Canada's natural resources but its Indigenous populations. When our people speak of self-governance and self-determination, it is these constraints that we seek to free ourselves from. It is the freedom to govern our people and set our own paths guided by our own values and belief systems.

Indigenous people understand that man and nature are one and the same (M'sit No'kmaq et al. 2021; Battiste 1997; Henderson 2000; Young 2016). They are interdependent. All that we have comes from the land and waters. The earth provides not only for our well-being, but it holds our history, our teachings, and our languages. We did not have a written language, but these ways of knowing were written in the stars, the landscapes, the plants and animals, and this knowledge was passed down in our stories, songs, and dance. All that the Earth holds is sacred. These are the values and belief systems at the core of how we governed ourselves and how we conducted ourselves on these lands. *Netukulimk* is the word we use today to communicate this connection, the sense of responsibility we have to the land and future generations. Simply stated, *Netukulimk* is "the use of the natural bounty provided by the Creator for the self-support and well-being of the individual and the community at large" (Micmac Grand Council et al. 1987, as cited in Young 2016, 90). *Netukulimk* is achieving adequate standards of community nutrition and economic well-being without jeopardizing the integrity, diversity, or productivity of our environment. Sustainability – such a simple concept, yet as a country Canada is struggling to achieve this.

How does a country, in just a few hundred years, go from a virtual paradise to one struggling to address climate change and biodiversity loss at such an astounding rate? How did we get to this point in our history that many have deemed to be a crisis? It began the first time Canada decided to break treaty. It began with the creation of the first "Indian reserve." It began with the passing of the first law that claimed to make it illegal for our people to hunt and fish in our traditional territories. It began with the first child whose spirit was broken because they dared speak their own language. But change is on the horizon.

Beacons of Teachings

In Nova Scotia the Mi'kmaq have entered into dialogues with the provincial and federal governments to discuss our Treaties, under the Mi'kmaq-Nova Scotia-Canada Umbrella and Framework Agreements, signed in 2002 and 2007, respectively (Government of Canada 2010a,b). I say 'our' because we are all treaty people: there were two signatories on those Treaties and it is the responsibility of both parties to honour those promises. Through discussions we are working to rebuild the relationship that was entered into in peace and friendship, to determine how Mi'kmaq can exercise our inherent right in this modern age. One of the things we are exploring is the concept of IPCAs, or Indigenous Protected and Conserved Areas (ICE 2018b). IPCA is a term to describe Indigenous-led conservation initiatives such as tribal parks, Indigenous protected areas, Indigenous conserved areas, or Indigenous cultural landscapes. IPCAs are not only an opportunity to create new protected and conserved areas but also an opportunity to re-imagine the role of Indigenous peoples in existing protected areas. They are how, by making space for Indigenous conservation within existing protected areas, we can begin to address some of the injustices that resulted from Canada's dark history of protected areas.

The Mi'kmaq communities in Unama'ki, through the work of the Unama'ki Institute of Natural Resources, have developed a relationship with the staff at both the Cape Breton Highlands National Park and the Louisburg National Historic Site. In my opinion, these relationships exemplify the meaning of reconciliation. To me, reconciliation is not simply the acknowledgment of the inequalities that Indigenous people have faced throughout our shared history. That is the "truth" part of truth and reconciliation. Reconciliation is a sincere and on-going effort to build a meaningful relationship that seeks to rectify those inequalities while having the resolve to withstand the inevitable trials and tribulations that relationships can bring. The commitment is to create an ethical space where there is a conscious effort to understand each other's differences and limitations but also to see the strength and value that these differences can bring to the relationship. It has taken many years of working together to build this relationship. And although a departmental or agency directive to work with Indigenous people is an important first step, I can tell you that this goes nowhere if the people on the ground leading the work are not fully committed and open to the process.

In 2012 Parks Canada entered into a National Parks Interim Arrangement with the Mi'kmaq of Nova Scotia in which they identified areas where the two would like to work together (Government of Canada 2019). Included areas of mutual interest are cultural and natural resources, consultation, access and entry to the parks, gathering of plants and other natural objects, and the establishment of advisory committees. This arrangement also opened the door for the Mi'kmaq to assist in restoring balance to the Cape Breton Highlands National Park (CBHNP) ecosystem. The lack of natural predation within the park along with an abundance of food and low disease levels had allowed the moose population to grow to unsustainable numbers. This imbalance was impacting the ecosystem to the extent that large areas of the boreal forests were in danger of changing into grasslands, threatening the native plants and wildlife of the park (Smith et al. 2010; CBC 2015a). The removal of moose from a small section of the park was part of a larger Bring Back the Boreal project that also looked at other solutions to habitat conversion, including tree planting and the erection of moose exclusion zones (Parks Canada 2020). Annually, from 2015 to 2018, Parks Canada provided space for Mi'kmaq to conduct our traditional hunting practices, including space to perform ceremony, as a way to restore natural balance to the area (CBHNP 2016). As part of this act of reconciliation, 190,440 servings of moose meat from the harvest was shared not only with the Mi'kmaq communities but with surrounding non-native communities (Parks Canada 2020; CBC 2019). If any of you were tuned into the news during that time you would know that at times things got heated (e.g., CBC 2015b; 2016). But Parks Canada stood their ground and allowed the Mi'kmaq to continue to exercise what is not only our right but our responsibility.

Awakening the Sleeping Giant in the East

One of the other areas the Mi'kmaq are exploring, this time with the province of Nova Scotia, is designation of the Kluskap Wilderness Area as an IPCA. In 2015, Kluskap Mountain was designated as Kluskap Wilderness Area and added to the provincial parks system, at which time the province made a commitment to work towards a collaborative management arrangement with the Mi'kmaq. "Kluskap Wilderness Area protects much of the northern part of Kelly's Mountain, between St. Ann's Bay and the Great Bras d'Or" (Nova Scotia Environment [NSE] 2017, n.p.). The area is considered to be high in biodiversity, supporting stands of black spruce, balsam fir, white pine, hemlock, and hardwood forests, and a diverse ecosystem of "cobble beaches, coastal cliffs and caves, and barachois ponds …. Nesting bald eagles can be seen overhead, and pilot whales and dolphins swim in the adjacent waters of St. Ann's Bay" (NSE 2017, n.p.). From the province's perspective "the diversity of ecosystems there ensures a good representation of Kelly's Mountain's natural landscape in the provincial protected areas network" (NSE 2017, n.p.). For the Mi'kmaq, Kelly's Mountain is also a sacred Mi'kmaq site. It is said that Kluskap "once dwelled in the ocean-side cave near Cape Dauphin, at the northern tip of the wilderness area" (NSE 2017, n.p.).

Legend[6] has it that after the Mi'kmaq world was created and after the animals, birds, and plants were placed on the surface, Creator caused a bolt of lightning to hit the surface of the Earth. This bolt of lightning caused the formation of an image of a human body. It was Kluskap, first shaped out of the basic element of the Mi'kmaq world, sand. Creator unleashed another bolt of lightning which gave life to Kluskap. Kluskap watched the animals, the birds, and the plants grow and pass around him. He asked Kisu'lk, the Great Spirit, to give him freedom to move about the Mi'kmaq world. So it was that a third blast of lightning came, and that caused Kluskap to become free and to be able to stand on the surface of the Earth.

Kluskap then went out to explore the Earth, to see what he might learn about where he lived. He travelled in the direction of the setting sun, until he came to an ocean. He then went south until the land narrowed, and he could see two oceans on either side. He journeyed back to where he started from, and then continued towards the North, to the land of ice and snow. Finally, he came back to the East, where he decided to stay, because it was here where he came into existence. He again watched the animals, the birds, and the plants. He watched the water and the sky. Creator taught him to watch and learn about the world. Kluskap learned that mutual respect of his family and the world around him was a key ingredient for basic survival. Kluskap's task was to pass this knowledge to his fellow Mi'kmaq people, so that they too could survive in the Mi'kmaq world. This is why Kluskap became a central figure in Mi'kmaq storytelling. The Kluskap Wilderness Area is the home of Kluskap's cave, which is said to be his last home on Earth before he left to the sky world. Legend says that he will return once again to the Mi'kmaq people when they need him.

Designation of the Kluskap Wilderness Areas as an IPCA will provide the Mi'kmaq with the opportunity to take a primary role in the protection and conservation of a sacred Mi'kmaq site. This will aid in the revitalization of traditional Mi'kmaq government systems grounded in Indigenous laws and knowledge systems. It will be an opportunity to exercise our inherent rights and responsibilities as stewards of this land. It will play a vital role in the revitalization of Indigenous language and culture. It will provide space for the Mi'kmaq to reconnect with the land and heal from the centuries of trauma that our people have endured. And it will create opportunities to explore sustainable conservation economies and holistic approaches to governance and planning.

The Yellow Prayer Flag

The healing will begin in the East, where it all began, the Elder had said. This was strong in my mind as we gifted the yellow prayer flag to the Mi'kmaw Bear River First Nation, in the East. Regional Gatherings were a key part in the process of creating the recommendations for the Pathway to Target 1. They were hosted across Canada, according to the four directions: West (Tofino, BC), East (Digby, NS), North (Yellowknife, NWT) and Central/South (Winnipeg, MB). At each gathering a prayer flag was given to the host community to honour the "participants' commitment in that territory, and to offer protection, both to the work being done at that place and generally," to the territory itself (ICE 2018, 22). The flags were prayed over in ceremony at the start of the work of ICE. They are an important representation of those "sacred actions, which cannot be fully described in writing, represent how we live in relationship – to each other and to Mother Earth" (ICE 2018, 69). The Eastern gathering, although the second one held, was the first in which the region received a prayer flag.

"Come on in." At times it seems I am living in two realities, in which our lands and waters are in separate realms lorded over by a ruling body that wears two faces. And as the Seven Fires prophecy foretold, it is difficult for us to tell if Canada's ruling class is indeed friend or foe. When it comes to forestry and protected areas management the Mi'kmaq are making a lot of headway towards developing co-management arrangements that create space for Indigenous-led conservation in the true spirit of reconciliation. Concepts of Two-Eyed Seeing and *Netukulimk* are recognized as valid and essential. On the water, it is a different story. The Canadian government continues to ignore our Treaty rights and acknowledges Indigenous knowledge only when it is convenient and does not threaten their monopolization of a lucrative fishery.

They refuse to recognize that the Mi'kmaq have our own laws and governance systems. They are derived from this land and are older than the Constitution and Canada itself. The legends of Kluskap hold many of the values and teachings that are at the core of these systems and laws. They speak of the need for mutual respect for the land and all our relations – *m'sit no'kmaq*, to ensure our continued interdependence, existence, and survival. They form the founding principles from which Mi'kmaw IPCAs will be created. These teachings serve as beacons to light the path to reconciliation that will heal not only our relationship with Canada but with our lands and waters, ensuring a more sustainable future for all Canadians. It is my hope, and the hope of our communities, that the declaration of Kluskap Wilderness Area as an IPCA will aid in the revitalization of *Netukulimk* in *Mi'kma'ki* and awaken the sleeping giant, whose return was promised to occur when the Mi'kmaq, and Canada, need him most.

NOTES

1 A published version of the Mi'kmaw, or L'nuwey, Creation Story is presented in T. Young (2016, 84): "The following L'nu creation story was published by an L'nu woman [Battiste 1997] who received it from an L'nu man [S.J. Augustine] who in turn heard it from his grandmother, who had heard it from her great-grandparents." Stephen J. Augustine (Ekkian) is a curator of Ethnology at the Museum of Civilization, Ottawa, and "is also a Keptin of the Santé Mawiomi, the traditional government of the L'nu people" (Young 2016, 84). For online versions see Red Path (n.d.) and Mikmaw Spirit (n.d.), the latter of which cites the story as adapted from "Mi'kmaq Knowledge in the Mi'kmaq Creation Story: Lasting Words and Deeds," by Stephen Augustine, April 8, 1977.

2 Lorne Greene's *New Wilderness* was a Canadian television nature documentary series that debuted in 1982.

3 *Jaws* is an award-winning 1975 fictional thriller movie about a series of attacks by a great white shark near a Massachusetts beach resort and the heroic efforts to hunt it. It was based on Peter Benchley's 1974 book of the same name and followed by three sequels.

4 See for example, "Prophecy of the Seven Fires: Passamaquoddy at Sipayik," Pleasant Point Tribal Government. Available: http://www.wabanaki.com/wabanaki_new /Seven_Fires_Prophecy.html; retrieved March 19, 2021

5 *Wabanaki*, literally translated, means "people of the dawn" or "dawnland people," meaning easterners, and at times all five tribes of the Wabanaki Confederacy have referred to themselves this way. Also, the Mi'kmaq and Maliseet of New Brunswick collectively refer to themselves as Wabanaki, and some information about these two tribes has this name on it" (Native Languages of the Americas website, 1998–2020).

6 A published version of the L'nuwey Creation Story is presented in T. Young (2016, 84): "The following L'nu creation story was published by an L'nu woman [Battiste 1997] who received it from an L'nu man [S. J. Augustine] who in turn heard it from his grandmother, who had heard it from her great-grandparents." Stephen J Augustine (Ekkian) is a curator of Ethnology at the Museum of Civilization, Ottawa, and "is also a Keptin of the Santé Mawiomi, the traditional government of the L'nu people" (Young 2016, 84). For online versions see Red Path (n.d.) and Mikmaw Spirit (n.d.), the latter of which cites the story as adapted from "Mi'kmaq Knowledge in the Mi'kmaq Creation Story: Lasting Words and Deeds," by Stephen Augustine, 8 April 1977.

WORKS CITED

Artelle, Kyle A., Melanie Zurba, Jonaki Bhattacharyya, Diana E. Chan, Kelly Brown, Jess Housty, and Faisal Moola. 2019. "Supporting Resurgent Indigenous-Led Governance: A Nascent Mechanism for Just and Effective Conservation." *Biological Conservation* 240. https://doi.org/10.1016/j.biocon.2019.108284

Augustine, Stephen. 1977. ªMi'kmaq Knowledge in the Mi'kmaq Creation Story: Lasting Words and Deeds" (April 8, 1977). *Mi'kmaw Spirit*. http://www.muiniskw .org/pgCulture3a.htm

Bartlett, Cheryl, Murdena Marshall, and Albert Marshall. 2012. "Two-Eyed Seeing and Other Lessons Learned within a Co-learning Journey of Bringing Together Indigenous and Mainstream Knowledges and Ways of Knowing." *Journal of Environmental Studies and Sciences* 2, no. 4: 331–40. https://doi.org/10.1007 /s13412-012-0086-8

Battiste M. 1997. "Nikanikinutmaqn." In *The Míkmaw Concordat*, edited by J.S. Youngblood Henderson. Halifax: Fernwood.

Benton-Banai, E. 1988. *The Mishomis Book: The Voice of the Ojibway.* St. Paul, Minnesota: Indian Country Communications.

Berger, Thomas R. 1977. *Northern Frontier, Northern Homeland.* Vol. 1. Toronto: J. Lorimer & Company.

Binnema, Theodore Ted, and Melanie Niemi. 2006. "'Let the Line Be Drawn Now': Wilderness, Conservation, and the Exclusion of Aboriginal People from Banff National Park in Canada." *Environmental History* 11, no. 4: 724–50.

Canadian Parks Council (CPC). (n.d.) "Pathway to Canada Target 1." Available from https://www.conservation2020canada.ca/home

Cape Breton Highlands National Park. 2016. "Bring Back the Boreal Project." Parks Canada. http://parkscanadahistory.com/publications/cbreton/bring-back-the-boreal-newsletter-e-2.pdf

CBC. 2015. "Moose Cull Opponent Spots Just 5 Moose on North Mountain ahead of Cull." https://www.cbc.ca/news/canada/nova-scotia/moose-cull-anti-north-mountain-1.3304261

– 2015a. "A Tale of Two Moose." *Land & Sea.* CBC.ca. https://www.cbc.ca/player/play/2651378999

– 2016. "Moose Cull Protesters Block Cabot Trail into National Park." https://www.cbc.ca/news/canada/nova-scotia/moose-cull-protesters-return-1.3849032

– 2019. "Moose Cull." *Land and Sea.* https://gem.cbc.ca/media/land-and-sea-network/season-2015/episode-10/38e815a-00a0672d999

CBC Digital Archives. 2012. "The Battle for Aboriginal Treaty Rights – Aboriginal Rights: Overfishing, Out of Season." *CBC News.* Retrieved March 1, 2021. https://www.cbc.ca/archives/entry/aboriginal-rights-overfishing-out-of-season

Christmas, Kevin. 2011. "Aboriginal Consultation." *Mawqatmuti'kw.* (Winter/Spring): 16–25. Retrieved March 19, 2021. https://www.ikanawtiket.ca/pdf/Winter-Spring10-11.pdf.

Dostou, T. 2000. "Seven Fires Prophecy of the Anishnabe People and the Process of Reconciliation." Prayer Vigil for the Earth: Creating a Culture of Peace. Retrieved March 19, 2021. http://www.oneprayer.org/Seven_Fires_Prophecy.html.

Douglass, Jeffrey. 2020. "The Legal Context behind the Unfolding Dispute between Mi'kmaw and Commercial Fishermen." *Mainstreet Nova Scotia.* CBC Radio. Halifax. September 18, 2020. Retrieved February 25, 2021. https://podknife.com/podcasts/mainstreet-halifax-from-cbc-radio.

Ermine, Willie. 2000. "A Critical Examination of the Ethics in Research Involving Indigenous Peoples." Unpublished master's thesis, University of Saskatchewan, Saskatoon, Canada

Ermine, Willie. 2007. "The Ethical Space of Engagement." *Indigenous Law Journal,* 6 (1): 193–203.

First Nations Drum. 2000. "Matthew Coon Responds to the Burnt Church Crisis." December 26, *First Nations Drum.* Retrieved March 1, 2021. http://www.firstnationsdrum.com/2000/12/matthew-coon-responds-to-the-burnt-church-crisis/

Government of Canada 2010a. "Mi'kmaq – Nova Scotia – Canada Umbrella
    Agreement." https://www.rcaanc-cirnac.gc.ca/eng/1100100028635/1539610878232
– 2010b. "Mi'kmaq – Nova Scotia – Canada Framework Agreement." https://www
    .rcaanc-cirnac.gc.ca/eng/1100100031915/1529422708421
– 2019. "Negotiations in Atlantic Canada." Accessed March 2, 2021. https://www
    .rcaanc-cirnac.gc.ca/eng/1100100028583/1529409875394?wbdisable=true.
– 2021. "Species at risk public registry." Species search. Accessed March 2, 2021.
    https://species-registry.canada.ca/index-en.html#/species?sortBy=common
    NameSort&sortDirection=asc&pageSize=10.
Henderson, J.S. Youngblood. 2000. "Ayukpachi: Empowering Aboriginal Thought." In
    Reclaiming Indigenous Voices and Vision, edited by Marie Battiste. Vancouver: UBC
    Press. Royal Commission on the Donald Marshall, Jr., Prosecution (NS), and
    T.A. Hickman. *Royal Commission on the Donald Marshall, Jr. Prosecution*. The
    Commission, 1989.
Indigenous Circle of Experts (ICE). 2018a. "Pathway to Canada Target 1
    Indigenous Circle of Experts (ICE) Regional Gatherings Reports." https://static1
    .squarespace.com/static/57e007452e69cf9a7af0a033/t/5ab9504c0e2e7246a9551
    a5a/1522094157137/Regional+Gathering+Reports+EN.pdf
– 2018. *We Rise Together: Achieving Pathway to Canada Target 1 through the Creation
    of Indigenous Protected and Conserved Areas in the Spirit of Practice of Reconciliation.*
    https://static1.squarespace.com/static/57e007452e69cf9a7af0a033/t/5ab94aca6d2a73
    38ecb1d05e/1522092766605/PA234-ICE_Report_2018_Mar_22_web.pdf.
M'sit No'kmaq, Elder A. Marshall, K.F. Beazley, J. Hum, S. Joudry, A. Papadopoulos,
    S. Pictou, J. Rabesca, L. Young, and M. Zurba. 2021. "'Awakening the Sleeping
    Giant': 'Re-Indigenization' Principles for Transforming Biodiversity Conservation in
    Canada and Beyond." *FACETS*. https://doi.org/10.1139/facets-2020-0083
Marshall, A. 2004. "Two-Eyed Seeing." Institute for Integrative Science and Health.
    Accessed October 14 2019. http://www.integrativescience.ca/Principles/TwoEyedSeeing/.
Micmac Grand Council, L.L. Patterson, D.B. Clarke, Union of Nova Scotia Indians,
    and Native Council of Nova Scotia. 1987. *Mi'kmaq Treaty Handbook*. Native
    Communications Society of Nova Scotia.
Mikmaw Spirit (n.d.) *Mi'kmaw Creation Story*. http://www.muiniskw.org/pgCulture3a
    .htm#:~:text=The%20Creation%20of%20Kluskap%20After%20the%20Mi%27kmaq
    %20world,formation%20of%20an%20image%20of%20a%20human%20body
Moola, Faisal, and Robin Roth. 2018. "Moving beyond Colonial Conservation Models:
    Indigenous Protected and Conserved Areas Offer Hope for Biodiversity and
    Advancing Reconciliation in the Canadian Boreal Forest. *Environmental Reviews*
    27: 200–1. https://doi.org/10.1139/er-2018-0091.
National Inquiry into Missing and Murdered Indigenous Women and Girls. 2019.
    "Reclaiming Power and Place." Executive Summary of the Final Report. National
    Inquiry into Missing and Murdered Indigenous Women and Girls. https://www
    .mmiwg-ffada.ca/wp-content/uploads/2019/06/Executive_Summary.pdf

Native Languages of the Americas website. 1998–2020. Wabanaki Confederacy (Wabenaki, Wobanaki). Accessed February 26, 2021. http://www.native-languages .org/wabanaki.htm.

Nova Scotia Environment. 2017. "Kluscap Wilderness Area." Government of Nova Scotia. https://novascotia.ca/nse/protectedareas/wa_kluscap.asp

Obomsawin, Alanis. 2002. *Is the Crown at War with Us?* National Film Board of Canada. https://www.nfb.ca/film/is_the_crown_at_war_with_us/

Parks Canada. 2020. "Bring Back the Boreal: Restoring Forest Health in the Highlands." Summary report. https://www.pc.gc.ca/en/pn-np/ns/cbreton/decouvrir-discover /conservation/foret-forest

Pictou, Sherry. 2018. "The Origins and Politics, Campaigns and Demands by the International Fisher Peoples' Movement: An Indigenous Perspective." *Third World Quarterly* 39, no. 7: 1411–20.

Pictou, Sherry M. 2019. "What Is Decolonization? Mi'kmaw Ancestral Relational Understandings and Anthropological Perspectives on Treaty Relations." *Transcontinental Dialogues: Activist Research and Alliances from and with Indigenous Peoples of Canada, Mexico, and Australia*: 37–64. https://doi.org/10.2307/j.ctvdjrpm6.6

Poole, Roger. 1972. *Towards Deep Subjectivity.* New York: Harper & Row,

Prosper, Kerry, L. Jane McMillan, Anthony A. Davis, and Morgan Moffitt. 2011. "Returning to Netukulimk: Mi'kmaq Cultural and Spiritual Connections with Resource Stewardship and Self-Governance." *International Indigenous Policy Journal* 2, no. 4: 7. https://doi.org/10.18584/iipj.2011.2.4.7

R. v. Badger. 1996. 1 S.C.R. 771. Retrieved March 2, 2021. https://scc-csc.lexum.com /scc-csc/scc-csc/en/item/1366/index.do.

R. v. Marshall, 1999 CanLII 665 (SCC). 1999. 3 SCR 456. Retrieved March 1, 2021. https://canlii.ca/t/1fqkq,

Red Path. 1999. "A Micmac Creation Story. American Indian Legends." 1999. https:// www.firstpeople.us/FP-Html-Legends/MicmacCreationStory-Micmac.html

Sandlos, John. 2008. "Not Wanted in the Boundary: The Expulsion of the Keeseekoowenin Ojibway Band from Riding Mountain National Park." *Canadian Historical Review* 89, no. 2: 189–221. https://doi.org/10.3138/chr.89.2.189

Smith, Craig, Karen Faye Beazley, Peter Duinker, and Karen A. Harper. 2010. "The Impact of Moose (*Alces alces andersoni*) on Forest Regeneration Following a Severe Spruce Budworm Outbreak in the Cape Breton Highlands, Nova Scotia, Canada." *Alces: A Journal Devoted to the Biology and Management of Moose* 46: 135–50.

Truth and Reconciliation Commission. 2015a. "Honouring the Truth, Reconciling for the Future: Summary of the Final Report of the Truth and Reconciliation Commission of Canada." Truth and Reconciliation Commission of Canada, Winnipeg, MB.

– 2015b. "What We Have Learned: Principles of Truth and Reconciliation." Truth and Reconciliation Commission of Canada, Winnipeg, MB.

– 2015c. "Calls to Action." Truth and Reconciliation Commission of Canada, Winnipeg, MB. https://www.documentcloud.org/documents/2091412-trc-calls-to-action.html

Unama'ki Institute of Natural Resources (UINR). (n.d.) "Netukulimk." Accessed February 20, 2020. https://www.uinr.ca/programs/netukulimk/

United Nations. 2007. "Resolution 61/295." United Nations Declaration on the Rights of Indigenous Peoples. Published 2008. https://www.un.org/esa/socdev/unpfii/documents/DRIPS_en.pdf

Wicken, William C. 2002. *Mi'kmaq Treaties on Trial: History, Land, and Donald Marshall Junior.* Toronto: University of Toronto Press.

WWF Canada. 2020. "Living Planet Report Canada: Wildlife at Risk." World Wildlife Fund Canada, Toronto, ON.

Youdelis, Megan. 2016. "'They Could Take You Out for Coffee and Call It Consultation!': The Colonial Antipolitics of Indigenous Consultation in Jasper National Park." *Environment and Planning A: Economy and Space* 48, no. 7: 1374–92. https://doi.org/10.1177/0308518X16640530

Young, Tuma. 2016. "L'nuwita'simk: A Foundational Worldview for a L'nuwey Justice System." *Indigenous LJ 13*: 75.

YourCanada. (n.d.) "National Parks." Retrieved March 2, 2021. http://yourcanada.ca/parks/

Zscheile, E. 2019. "R. v. Marshall & September 17, 1999." 20th Anniversary of the Marshall Decision Conference. Kwilmu'kw Maw-klusuaqn Mi'kmaq Rights Initiative. Membertou, NS. September 17–18, 2019. Retrieved February 25, 2021. www.youtube.com/watch?v=cdZ9ggHjjUg;

Zurba, Melanie, Karen F. Beazley, Emilie English, and Johanna Buchmann-Duck. 2019. "Indigenous Protected and Conserved Areas (IPCAs), Aichi Target 11, and Canada's Pathway to Target 1: Focusing Conservation on Reconciliation." *Land* 8, no. 1: 10. https://doi.org/10.3390/land8010010

Disruptions, Part C

Indigenous Knowledge as a Disruption to State-Led Conservation

NATASHA MYHAL

Across North America, treaties established a legal relationship between the settler governments and Indigenous Nations. These treaties include, as retained rights, our ability to hunt, fish, and gather. I view Treaty rights as a framework for understanding tribal sovereignty with non-humans. Paul Nadasdy (2007) proposes that Indigenous accounts of hunting are necessary to understand human-animal relations. Viewing those relations simply as beliefs reinforces the state's control over Indigenous knowledge through discourses of natural resources. The refusal to consider human-animal reciprocity as a set of social practices and a figurative meaning prohibits the consideration of the ways animals interact with Indigenous societies (ibid., 32). Natural resource management as a field needs to take seriously Indigenous accounts of, first, fishing, hunting, and gathering and, second, how non-humans speak to humans. This will enable the field to re-frame the human-centred narrative of biodiversity conservation and climate change literature. Non-humans' narratives through time depict encountering and learning from Indigenous Peoples, in addition to interactions with settlers (Cruikshank 2007). These relations influence the local availability to fish, hunt, and gather. Furthermore, the role that non-humans play for Indigenous nations provides insights into their partnerships with the state through sovereignty.

Indigenous nations use sovereignty, their basis for authority, as a way to protect their land and water and negotiate its use with the state. In the United States, tribal natural-resource management utilization of sovereignty through social boundaries transforms community relations. Jessica Cattelino's work (2008) builds upon the concept of "social reproduction," or the process whereby Indigenous Peoples reproduce themselves as both contemporary *and* Indigenous and how their frameworks of value contribute to this, underscoring how Indigenous social life reproduces itself through land- and water-based practices rather than the capitalist need to control these lifeways (ibid., 61). Tribal natural-resource management examines the aforementioned everyday practices to show how Native peoples themselves exercise their own forms of sovereignty that value more-than-human relationships as necessary for their own understandings of sovereignty.

Clint Carroll (2015) provides a framework that theorizes the *resource-based* and *relationship-based* approach of tribal natural resource departments for the Cherokee Nation of Oklahoma. This framework illustrates how Indigenous knowledge complicates environmental governance, calling upon Indigenous governments to address concerns of traditional knowledge-keepers as central to their own initiatives. Thus, tribal natural resource management produces new forms of Native American governance and insights into non-humans. Tribal natural resource departments are crucial to the sovereignty that enables their land- and water-based practices.

Moreover, tribal natural resource management explores what it means for Indigenous Peoples themselves to address the role of non-humans in their lives. Through the interactions between humans and more-than-humans, land and water have become a site of analysis that informs Indigenous governance structures. John Borrows (2018) describes this through Indigenous law as originating from political, economic, spiritual, and social values via Anishinaabe teachings and behaviour (13). Indigenous law guides current tribal natural resource management strategies as a legitimate source for formulating responses to climate change and biodiversity declines. As such, I foresee changing climate conditions, for example, as producing new iterations of treaties that influence human and more-than-human relations – thus calling for ethnographic research that centres these issues and their complex social and political realms.

Conservation practitioners must understand and grapple with North American colonial histories in order to understand conservation's role in Indigenous land theft (Carroll 2014). Indigenous environmental studies offer approaches, grounded in Indigenous methodologies and ways of knowing, that address the impact of climate change and other colonialisms on Indigenous Peoples today (Whyte 2017). The land and water for Indigenous Peoples are grounded in responsibilities towards more-than-humans rather than management of them. To move forward, conservation must not only include Indigenous Peoples and their knowledges in their policies, but rather treat Indigenous environmental experiences and assertions as truth. Thus, Indigenous nations can help to renew and restore the ecosystems and cultural systems upon which they rely, supporting global biodiversity overall.

The Misipawistik Cree Nation *kanawenihcikew* Guardians Program

HEIDI COOK

It was the river that made this our home, and the same river that centred our nation here thousands of years ago is again central to the rebuilding of our nation. Our name, *Misipawistik*, references the mighty "Grand Rapids" of the Saskatchewan River on its final descent to the mouth at Lake Winnipeg. We are *Misipawistiko ininiwak* ("people from Grand Rapids"), officially named the Misipawistik Cree Nation (MCN), and we belong to this place.

Pre-contact, the river drew people from hundreds of kilometres in all directions to its abundant sturgeon and whitefish spawn. Some of us stayed in the area year round. During the fur trade and colonization, the river became the major route for western travel, declining in importance after the railway was built. In the 1960s, the magnificent rapids were silenced by colonizers who had long dreamed of harnessing the water's power to generate electricity.

The fortunes of our nation are tied to this river. The greatest devastation imaginable – the silencing of the rapids, alternately dried up and flooded beyond recognition on either side of a spillway gate – had a devastating effect on our people. It went to the core of who we are, destroying our nourishment, travel routes, and social connections, invalidating knowledge, creating poverty, trauma, loss of language, and social upheaval.

The rapids live on in the stories told by our Elders and in the hearts and imaginations of all the generations born after they were silenced. We are resilient, hanging on to traditional livelihoods and our identity as Cree people. We had to learn new landscapes and water bodies, but the river and rapids remained our home.

Recognition of this injustice grew in successive generations, who challenged the assault on our people (and its basis in the notion we were inferior). Compensation and relationship agreements with Manitoba Hydro in the 1990s and 2010s were intended to address injuries but fall short of meaningful redress.

A fish hatchery stocks the river with pickerel as part of the remediation effort. The fish sustain the commercial fishing livelihoods that are central to the local economy and draw many tourists to the area. Dozens of boats drift the two-kilometre stretch of river every day from the May long weekend until October. In the winter, fishers move to a bay at the mouth where ice can form unaffected by the swift current.

By 2018, Misipawistiko ininiwak had reached the limit of our tolerance at the heavy and largely unsupervised catch on the river. Having tried and failed at getting fishing restrictions put in place through provincial regulation, and with no provincial conservation enforcement presence, the situation was calling on us to restore the authorities we have as the original peoples to govern activity in our home. In November, the MCN *kanawenihcikew* ("one who looks after") Guardians were formed and immediately put in place a winter closure on the Saskatchewan River. The MCN lands department administers the MCN kanawenihcikew Guardians with proposal-based stewardship funding from non-government and government sources.

The MCN kanawenihcikew Guardians monitored the river and communicated with would-be fishers to relocate to the lake. First Nation members voluntarily restricted sustenance fishing on the river in recognition of the need for conservation. A safe trail was cleared and marked to fishing areas on Lake Winnipeg for tourists. The only access to the frozen bay is through the reserve, and the possible consequences for trespassing dissuaded visitors.

The following summer, in 2019, the kanawenihcikew Guardians were joined by newly appointed Youth Guardians, and teams of youth and senior kanawenihcikewak set up at the boat launch to conduct a creel survey. Voluntary restrictions on rights-based fishing on the river matched the limits for recreational fishers (six fish per person per day). Abuse of the fishery was curtailed, and MCN compiled data to back up assertions of heavy pressure on fish stocks. At the same time, commercial fishers noted increased abundance on Lake Winnipeg and filled their summer quotas in a shorter time, which was attributed to the winter closure.

The high level of community support for the measures taken to protect the river fishery was critical to its success, and the MCN kanawenihcikew Guardians quickly gained respect and authority in conservation matters. The MCN kanawenihcikew Guardians awakened a sense of pride in the community and renewed confidence in our knowledge and rights as Misipawistiko ininiwak. Our roles to look after the land and water, to protect our food and livelihood, are firmly based in Cree recognition of natural laws and respect for our relationship to the land, water, and other beings.

In January 2019, the kanawenihcikew Guardians began a monitoring program to collect data to address a declining moose population. Again, the issue was already prominent within the community and was not being addressed adequately by the provincial government. Licensed moose hunting closures in all areas to the south made the territory north of MCN the most readily

Figure C.1. MCN *kanawenihcikew* Guardians and Youth Guardians expedition in MCN territory on Lake Winnipeg, February 2020. Credit: MCN Lands Department.

accessible to sport hunters in the province. With no conservation officers in the area and no requirement for hunters to report kills, the impact of sport hunting on moose population and availability for rights-based harvest was left to differences of opinion.

MCN kanawenihcikew Guardians collected moose mortality data, with records including type of mortality (single/multiple, roadkill/predator/hunter and rights-based/licensed), location, age and sex. Public communication focused on the need to protect the cow moose and calving. The presence established by MCN kanawenihcikew Guardians in the territory led to a decrease in poaching. Highway patrols in winter months drove moose away from the roadway and identified high traffic areas for future signage and interventions.

With both fishery and moose monitoring programs, biological samples and select mortality data are shared with the province through data sharing agreements. MCN kanawenihcikew Guardians are recognized for our leadership and detailed knowledge of Misipawistik territory. The success of our monitoring programs stems from the focus and methods being shaped by the community members with the most knowledge of the territory or species being monitored. While there has of yet been no change in provincial regulation brought about, the need for it has decreased with the influence of MCN kanawenihcikew Guardians.

Our kanawenihcikew Guardians program continues to grow with more capacity, tools, and partners to work with. The articulation of the natural laws, which are the foundation of the program, ensure that these important elements of our cultural knowledge and identity are preserved. These Cree Laws are serving as the foundation for restoring jurisdiction and self-governance in other areas, such as education, health, child and family services, lands governance, and administration of the MCN.

The MCN kanawenihcikew Guardians and Youth Guardians are at the forefront of our national rebuilding. Young people are being mentored in teachings about our home and our place in it. Their monitoring and patrols connect and teach about our history and language. While the power of our river is transformed, it remains, and it has brought us to find new expressions of our own power as Misipawistiko ininiwak.

WORKS CITED

Borrows, John. 2018. "Earth-Bound: Indigenous Resurgence and Environmental Reconciliation." In *Resurgence and Reconciliation: IndigenousSettler Relations and Earth Teachings*, edited by Michael Asch, John Borrows, and James Tully. Toronto: University of Toronto Press.

Carroll, Clint. 2015. *Roots of Our Renewal: Ethnobotany and Cherokee Environmental Governance*. Minnesota: University of Minnesota Press.

– 2014. "Shaping New Homelands: Environmental Production, Natural Resource Management, and the Dynamics of Indigenous State Practice in the Cherokee Nation." *Ethnohistory* 61 (1): 123–47. https://doi.org/10.1215/00141801-2376105

Cattelino, Jessica. 2008. *High Stakes: Florida Seminole Gaming and Sovereignty*. Durham: Duke University Press.

Cruikshank, Julie. 2007. *Do Glaciers Listen?: Local Knowledge, Colonial Encounters, and Social Imagination*. Vancouver: University of British Columbia Press.

Nadasdy, Paul. 2007. "The Gift in the Animal: The Ontology of Hunting and Human–Animal Sociality." *American Ethnologist* 34, no. 1: 25–43. https://doi.org/10.1525/ae.2007.34.1.25

PART D

Transformation through Action

Metamorphoglia

9 Transforming University Curriculum and Student Experiences through Collaboration and Land-Based Learning

MELANIE ZURBA, JAMES DOUCETTE, AND BRIDGET GRAHAM

Introduction

Land-based learning experiences are integral to education that aims to impart knowledge and create an understanding with students regarding Indigenous perspectives and experiences (Wildcat et al. 2014). In addition to providing valuable and culturally appropriate educational experiences centred on Indigenous topics, land-based curriculum development can also act as an important vehicle for decolonizing education systems and building relationships between the academy and communities (Simpson 2014; Coulthard 2014). Acknowledging the wrongdoing of educational institutions and improving relationships between communities and universities that often have long histories and persisting characteristics steeped in colonialism can also be important first steps towards the process of reconciliation (Jansen 2009). This chapter describes the outcomes of a collaboration between a grass-roots Mi'kmaw organization and a university professor who developed a relationship to deliver land-based learning curriculum in the context of the "Indigenous perspective for resource and environmental management course" (referred to as "the course" from here on) at Dalhousie University, which is a blended graduate and undergraduate course that is taken by all students as an elective. Through working together the partners eventually built enough trust to engage in collaborative research focused on understanding the learning outcomes for the students engaged in the land-based learning experiences. This chapter also presents the approach and findings of this research and engages in critical reflection towards highlighting the aspects of collaboration that promoted relationship building and authentic student learning opportunities.

Background

Indigenous Land-Based Learning in Canadian Post-Secondary Education Contexts

Indigenous land-based learning is a relatively recent development in Canadian post-secondary education contexts, and most of the literature on this topic is from the past seven years. Most Indigenous land-based learning education programs that are run by post-secondary institutions are geared to Indigenous students who are interested in connecting with traditional practices and ways of life. An example is the Land-Based Learning Program that is part of Indigenous education at Red River College in Winnipeg, Manitoba. Students receive credits for this program, which offers experiential learning and skill development guided by Anishinaabe ancestral teachings (Red River College n.d.). Other non-credit courses of study also exist at post-secondary institutions, such as the free Land and Water: Land-Based Education program at the University of Manitoba. All students are welcome to apply to the program, which has 12–18 spaces, but Indigenous applicants are given priority (University of Manitoba n.d.). The Dechinta Centre for Research and Learning (also known as Dechinta Bush University; referred to as "Dechinta" from here on) is located on Chief Drygeese Territory in the North West Territories and offers the most extensive university accredited land-based learning courses to a diverse group of students led by community leaders, Elders, and professors from partnering universities (University of Alberta, University of British Columbia and the University of McGill) (Dechinta Centre for Research and Learning n.d.; UArctic n.d.).

In Ballantyne's (2014) paper entitled "Dechinta Bush University: Mobilizing a Knowledge Economy of Reciprocity, Resurgence, and Decolonization," Dechinta was used as a case study of land-based education and knowledge "within a comprehensive strategy of resistance to settler capital" (67). The article chronicled five years of the Yellowknife-based program, from its conception to its implementation. Ballantyne (2014) recounted how Dechinta encountered challenges associated with its inception and was logistically difficult but received a large amount of support, which made it possible. Ballantyne (2014) explained how the establishment of Dechinta made it possible for community Elders and other educators to learn together and for students to experience "the Dechinta Transformation" through the learning of skills that will last them throughout their lives and shifting "from guilt to gift" (79). Ballantyne (2014) described how the program measures learning outcomes (as they are called, to engage the language of the university) "by how students are transformed and transforming colonial and capitalist realities in themselves and around them" (84). Students can often feel transformed after an experience such as this, and in telling others they continue to expand the impact and reach of the program.

Wildcat and colleagues (2014) explain that we must move "from talk about the land within conventional classroom settings, to studying instances where we engage in conversations with the land and on the land in a physical, social, and spiritual sense" (2). By bringing students onto the land, along with educators and Elders, this exchange of knowledge can transpire. Wildcat and colleagues (2014) also state that "land-based education, in resurging and sustaining Indigenous life and knowledge, acts in direct contestation to settler colonialism and its drive to eliminate Indigenous life and Indigenous claims to land" (3). Leanne Betasamosake Simpson (2014), in her paper "Land as Pedagogy: Nishnaabeg Intelligence and Rebellious Transformation," explains the importance of fostering intergenerational relationships and storytelling and how it has been possible to "advocate for a reclamation of land as pedagogy, both as process and context for Nishnaabeg intelligence" (1). Bang and colleagues (2014), in their delivery of land-based learning for Indigenous youth and families in urban contexts, explored how the potential for dismantling settler-colonial constructs in environmental education and found that land-based pedagogy created opportunities for transforming education through "land re-becoming itself" and guiding the learning process (37).

Community-University Partnered Curriculum Development

Aikenhead and Elliott (2010) describe the tensions that exist between Indigenous knowledge and Western education and how Indigenous students in mainstream post-secondary context have "to cross a cultural border between their own everyday culture and the culture of academic school science" (5). They state that it is important to promote cross-cultural curriculum that promotes decolonization in such settings. Aikenhead and Elliott (2010) also explain how there is increasing collaboration between educators and Indigenous knowledge keepers and that it is essential that such collaborations do not perpetuate tokenism and neo-colonialism. When discussing the goal of integrating Indigenous content into the curriculum, Benton (2017) wrote, "To be successful, both Indigenous teachers and non-Indigenous teachers will need to be supported through their learning processes and they will need to be provided with materials that are locally relevant to their communities" (28).

There are several different approaches and guiding principles that can be used to support community-university partnered curriculum development. One such concept is called "ethical space." Ermine (2007) states that "'ethical space' should be formed when two societies, with disparate worldviews, are poised to engage each other" (193) and must include a respect for different knowledge systems and action towards ethical transformation beyond that which is only found in discourse. Two-Eyed Seeing is a concept rooted in Mi'kmaw traditional knowledge that was brought forward by Elder Albert

Marshall, which has been used in several contexts, including in the teaching of Integrative Sciences (Marshall and Bartlett 2010; Hatcher et al. 2009). Two-Eyed Seeing "refers to learning to see from one eye with the strengths of Indigenous ways of knowing and from the other eye with the strengths of Western ways of knowing and to using both of these eyes together" (Hatcher et al. 2009, 146). When Two-Eyed Seeing was applied to Integrative Science it was found to be powerful approach for bringing together Indigenous and non-Indigenous worldviews; however, challenges arose, including in the sensitive treatment of spirituality in a conventional classroom, the development and translation of living knowledge held by Elders and other knowledge keepers, the availability of classroom resources to support Indigenous pedagogy, and the connection that many students lack with their natural environment (Hatcher et al. 2009).

In 2017, Melanie Zurba (postdoctoral fellow at The University of Winnipeg at this time), Elder George Land (Elder and Medicine Man from Wabaseemoong Independent Nations) and Ryan Bullock (professor at The University of Winnipeg) initiated a pilot project to explore collaborative land-based learning as a way of decolonizing and Indigenizing university curriculum (Zurba et al., under review). The pilot project was grounded in a long-term friendship between Melanie and Elder George Land and was guided by "boundary work"[1] principles that were transformed to apply to collaboration in the context of curriculum development. Like other forms of boundary work, their "collaborative boundary education" approach aimed to "diminish structural injustices, build equity, and enhance relationships" (Zurba et al. under review, 4). Collaborative boundary education involved centring Indigenous knowledge and shifting leadership in curriculum design and delivery. This enabled Elder Land to determine precisely what knowledge was shared and how, and meant that the university partners were in a more supportive role where they managed university bureaucracy and protocols (e.g., safety briefings, research ethics board applications, etc.). Key outcomes of the pilot project included insights about logistical challenges (i.e., weather related), deepened understanding of the importance of trust and relationships, an enthusiastic and supportive response from students who participated in the land-based learning excursion, student reflections that cited unique and important learning that could not be easily obtained in the classroom setting, and a structural shift in power dynamics related to curriculum that supported greater decision-making by Elder George Land as a community partner.

Building Collaboration

Chenise Hache and James Doucette founded the Mi'kmaw-led organization Reclaiming Our Roots in 2018. The organization "aims to reconnect Indigenous youth with meaningful land-based knowledge rooted in Mi'kmaw values" and has the vision that "through mentorship and workshops, youth embark on a journey of decolonization by reclaiming their confidence in traditional skills" (Reclaiming Our Roots n.d.). Using a youth-centred approach, our guiding values include *Netukulimk* and *M'sit No'kmaq*, which can be broadly translated to "a commitment to stewardship and sustainability and respectful relationships among all living and non-living things." Reclaiming Our Roots facilitates land-based learning sessions through workshops and mentoring opportunities year round, which include activities such as harvesting, fishing, plant medicines, material collection, and more. Chenise and James both direct administration, strategic vision, and planning, and James draws on knowledge passed down to him by his family to deliver the land-based programming.

In the fall of 2018, Melanie Zurba, a newly appointed assistant professor at the School for Resource and Environmental Studies and the College of Sustainability at Dalhousie University, reached out to Chenise and James to explore the potential for collaboration and land-based learning for the course that she was to teach the following winter. She had come across an article in a local newspaper about Reclaiming Our Roots and, having engaged in partnered land-based learning in northwestern Ontario, was interested in the potential to develop a new partnership to connect to her new teaching roles at Dalhousie. Melanie, Chenise, and James had their first meeting over coffee and started by describing what was important to them and what working together could look like. Through several subsequent meetings it was determined that there was value on both sides to start a working relationship and provide students in the course with a land-based learning curriculum. Following the development and first delivery of land-based learning within the course, Melanie approached Chenise and James with an opportunity to research student learning outcomes that would be funded through a Dalhousie Scholarship of Teaching and Learning Grant. Chenise and James felt that the delivery of programming to university students would enable them to develop their workshop delivery skills and that the evidence-based research could be of value to their future program development. They were also interested in the students' experiences and learning outcomes.

The grant was awarded in the summer of 2019, and Bridget Graham, a research assistant working with Melanie, was assigned data handling and analysis aspects of the project. Bridget has experience with land-based learning, and during her undergraduate degree she participated in the University of Manitoba Pangnirtung Bush School program, where she spent five weeks living on the Arctic tundra, studying the history and ecology of Cumberland Sound, as well as learning the Inuktitut language. Chenise and Melanie had a discussion around this time about how Reclaiming Our Roots would have preferred to see an Indigenous person in this role, especially because it could afford an opportunity for training. However, they agreed that Bridget could remain in the role, and Melanie committed to collaboratively recruiting Indigenous students for future research employment and training opportunities. This was an important part of the relationship-building journey since partnerships for research have the potential to become more trusting and meaningful if collaborators listen, critically reflect, and adapt their practices based on such experiences. All decisions about the project from this point forward, including research logistics and analysis, were made together by Chenise, James, and Melanie. In our next section we explain how research themes were determined in collaboration and applied to student reflections so that we could develop knowledge around learning outcomes that would have relevance to Reclaiming Our Roots as an organization.

Approach

Collaborative Development of Curriculum and Educational Research

When engaging community partners in the development of curriculum it is particularly important to consider roles: How can the process be used to improve university–community relationships and provide meaningful outcomes for community partners (Austin and Rust 2015; Preece 2016)? Melanie, Chenise, and James had different roles in the development of land-based learning curriculum and the research on student learning outcomes. Chenise and James were given full autonomy to determine the type of land-based learning excursion activities and the knowledge that they would share. This was communicated with Melanie ahead of the excursion so that Melanie could handle logistical components of the excursion (e.g., transportation). Chenise and James also expressed that they thought it would be best if a Mi'kmaw youth could also co-facilitate the excursion as a way of continuing to support the intergenerational knowledge transmission that is central to their work. This was possible during the first cohort, which took place in the winter and involved learning that was centred around eel spearing (figure 9.1). Students met at a site next to a frozen estuary and were given an orientation on eel spearing and safety before following Chenise and James onto the frozen lake to learn more about the process. This involved first cutting holes into the ice and then plunging the spear down the hole into the substrate where eels would be resting. Each student attempted to catch an eel, but unfortunately none were successful. Nevertheless, they learned about the harvest and what would be expected if they caught an eel, including offering the first catch back to the land. The second cohort entered in the fall, and this time learning was centred around the identification and harvesting of plants (figure 9.2). Students learned about the traditional uses of plants such as wintergreen and cranberries and had an opportunity to learn about important Mi'kmaw principles for engaging with

Figure 9.1. James Doucette demonstrating an eel spearing technique on a frozen lake (winter 2019).

the land, such as *Netukulimk*, which is a complex cultural concept guiding individual and collective beliefs around resource protection and sustainability for future generations. Students were encouraged to make offerings; they were only shown plants that were abundant, and asked to take only plants that they thought they would use.

Most students enrolled in the course were in graduate programs at the Dalhousie School for Resource and Environmental Studies (SRES) or had a major in Environment, Society, and Sustainability, taken through the College of Sustainability; however, some students did come from other educational fields, such as engineering and planning. Students were asked to submit two assignments relating to the excursions towards grades in their course. The first was a preparatory reflection based on readings. Chenise and James selected one reading (a master's thesis on land-based learning), and Melanie provided the

Figure 9.2. James Doucette starting a fire to prepare Apuistekie'ji'jit (Labrador tea) (fall 2019).

students with an additional two readings (i.e., Bang et al. 2014; Wildcat et al. 2014). Following the excursion, the students completed a learning reflection assignment. The students were given a set of guiding questions (e.g., Has your understanding of Mi'kmaw traditional livelihoods practices, culture, and resurgence expanded as a result of your engagement in land-based learning?) to assist them with their reflections but were also directed to express their learning in ways that are most authentic to them.

The development of the research followed boundary work principles, beginning with the scoping of objectives and following through to knowledge mobilization (co-authoring of this chapter). Principles followed those outlined in Zurba et al. (under review) and included (1) identifying the boundary to be overcome by the educational experience/the knowledge to be shared; (2) initiating the boundary education work/curriculum partnership; (3) establishing ethical protocols, such as those relating to how knowledge is shared; (4) deciding on curriculum design; (5) establishing ownership and custodianship of the curriculum; and (6) interpreting student outcomes. The first five principles were established before the research component of the partnership. Chenise and James had full autonomy to decide what knowledge was shared and how it was shared, and maintained full ownership of the land-based curriculum that they delivered. The application of the sixth principle, concerning the analysis of the students' reflections, is described further in the following section.

Identifying and Applying Learning Themes

Mi'kmaw Ethics Watch[2] was contacted, and they stated that a full review was not required because the project was not focused within a community and did not focus on recording Indigenous knowledge. After receiving ethics approval from the Dalhousie University Research Ethics Board, it was possible to contact the first cohort of students who had participated in the land-based excursion with Reclaiming our Roots in winter 2019. These students were contacted by the Bridget, the research assistant in the summer of 2019. Students were asked by Bridget to enter their reflection assignments anonymously (identifiers removed) into a pool of data following the completion and grading of the course. Within the first cohort, five of the 13 undergraduate students chose to participate in the study, and five of the 11 graduate students also agreed to participate. Participants were enthusiastic, and many expressed their gratitude to participate in this sort of study. The research assistant was able to speak to the second cohort of students during the fall 2019 semester. After this initial introduction, the students were contacted once all their course work had been submitted and they had received their final grades. In the second cohort, three of the 14 undergraduate students participated, while seven of the 13 graduate students submitted their work to the study. Participation is this research project was completely voluntary, and 20 of the 51 students in the two cohorts participated, which was approximately 39 per cent of students.

Students were given the option of submitting both their preparatory reflection as well as their final reflection, or just one of the two. Students were asked to situate themselves in their learning and to base their reflections on the readings for the course and the lived experience of the land-based excursions. These submissions were organized by Bridget, who used NVivo 12 to code the documents, which were organized by student and by reflection type. Bridget conducted two rounds of coding for all reflections. The first round involved Bridget identifying emergent themes. Once this was complete, Bridget and Melanie met with Chenise and James of Reclaiming our Roots, who identified five themes that were important to them upon reflecting on the emergent themes. These five became the final coding structure:

1. Willingness to engage
2. Group dynamic and relationality (as it connects to msit no'kmaq/acknowledging connection to "all my relations")
3. Knowledge transferral

4. Types of knowledge and what was learned
5. Value of the experience and emotional reactions

Results

The students' learning reflections were coded according to the five themes identified above, and the interpretations of these reflections involve input from all parties (Zurba, Hache, Doucette and Graham).

Willingness to Engage

All the students' reflections indicated that they were willing to engage and learn through the land-based learning excursions. Some approached the excursion with trepidation, given their inexperience with land-based learning, and others embraced and felt excited about the unknown. Students often wrote they saw this as an opportunity to not only connect with the land, but also with each other, and with their guides. In Chenise and James, they saw leaders, two Indigenous people who embraced traditional land-based practices and had a desire to transmit the knowledge to the next generation through their organization, Reclaiming Our Roots. Many students wrote about their personal learning outcomes in their preparatory and reflective assignments. Given the short timeframe for the excursions, the students had to be realistic and diligent when setting goals for themselves. This exercise in goal setting allowed them to take an active role in their learning. They often reflected on how the learning experience engaged them in a different way from other forms of education they had been involved in. One student wrote:

> A majority of my formal education has always felt like I am working to satisfy requirements or to please someone else ... land-based education challenged that idea for me. Suddenly my education was no longer about pleasing someone else, it was now about understanding myself and the natural world around me and how to live in relation to that world. (Student Q)

Students like the one quoted here are seeking a different way to learn and are eager to engage in models of learning that extend beyond the confines of the traditional classroom. Another student wrote a similar statement in their preparatory assignment:

> Although I have taken courses that involved field work, the driving force behind this work was to collect scientific data to gain an understanding of the ecosystems, not to create a connection with them. (Student J)

This point is quite poignant because the student started to see their relationship to the land in a different way. Finally, in addition to engaging with their guides and the land and the environment that surrounded them, students were also given the opportunity to engage with others in their cohorts. One student wrote:

> The excursion allowed me to connect with the land and my peers in a way that I would not have otherwise had a chance. (Student H)

Students were able to connect and foster relationships with those present, and some relationships continued to develop after the excursions ended, especially as students interacted with Reclaiming Our Roots through social media or by email (personal correspondence, Chenise and James). Although the willingness to engage was a decision made at an individual level, a collective impact was felt by many. As one student wrote,

> These kinds of experiences allow for the "[b]uilding [of] student capacity for intercultural understanding, empathy, and mutual respect" which is just part of one of the [Trust and Reconciliation Commission of Canada] 94 Calls to Action. (Student T)

This sort of willingness to engage enabled students to connect with themselves, their colleagues and guides, the environment, as well as external factors as demonstrated here with the mention of the Truth and Reconciliation Commission's 94 Calls to Action.

Group Dynamic and Relationality

Students often reflected on the group dynamics and different types of knowledge. As previously mentioned, students reported being able to connect with their class peers in a meaningful way. Students from the first cohort also felt that the group dynamic and learning was enhanced by the youth facilitators (Mi'kmaw youth) who helped to facilitate alongside James and Chenise. One student wrote:

> [The youth facilitator] talked about the impact of land-based learning on his life; it was quite clear how land can really teach skills and bolster a person's confidence. (Student S)

Students realized that they were not just learning from their peers, their guides, and their instructor, but that someone younger than them with a very different lived experience could also teach them many lessons. Several students reflected upon privilege in their reflections, both the privilege associated with identity, as well as the privilege of the experience itself. This manifested itself differently for each student because of their different personal identities. One student wrote:

> I am honoured, as a non-Indigenous person and a beneficiary of settler colonialism, for the privilege of being invited to experience a land-based learning exercise by Reclaiming Our Roots. (Student P)

This student chose to reflect on their own personal privilege based on their identity, while another student wrote about the existence of both forms of privilege by stating,

> I feel that the opportunity to experience knowledge-sharing on Indigenous land with Indigenous people is a great privilege. Though Indigenous peoples owe us settlers nothing – it is very much the opposite – their invitation of us to their land and teachings demonstrates profound kindness on their part, which I feel honoured to experience. (Student I)

This student saw this whole opportunity as a privilege, not only to learn from Mi'kmaw people of Indigenous, but also from the land. Learning to see the land as more than a resource, and in fact as a being in which they were able to interact with and form a relationship with created a profound impression on several students.

When discussing privilege, some students were eager to understand their role in large and historically oppressive systems, such as resource and environmental management in Canada. A number of students wrote about a specific conversation that they had with Chenise during their excursion. Chenise was discussing roles in decolonization, reconciliation, and the job market, and she encouraged students against taking jobs from Indigenous people and students. One student reflected on this conversation by saying,

> Settlers, like many of us that took part in the excursion, have many opportunities for work and career – those which are not as plentiful for Indigenous peoples. For this reason, when roles, jobs and careers arise that fit Indigenous cultures, traditions, or ways of life, these should belong to the Indigenous people interested in the work; settlers should not take this opportunity from Indigenous peoples like we have taken other things over time. (Student M)

The student went on to say that what Chenise said really resonated with them and that they will consider this statement in the future. While Reclaiming our Roots is focused in land-based learning with Indigenous youth, they also believe it is important to facilitate conversations about challenging issues relating to Mi'kmaw livelihoods, culture, and land. The students involved in the excursion benefitted from these conversations, and many of them stated that they would remain mindful of the space that they occupy, the conversations that they participate in and the knowledge that they acquire.

Knowledge Transferral

The students from both cohorts began acquiring knowledge about land-based learning through readings before their excursion took place. Some knowledge that they brought to their learning experiences also came from their lived experience. Students wrote about this candidly and openly in both the preparatory and land-based excursion reflections. One student wrote:

> My overall objective for the excursion is to be open-minded about the teachings and to try and immerse myself in the land-based learning. I feel that this objective, though obvious, will be important because coming from a European background and being part of the academy has shaped the way I learn and create knowledge. Thus, my first objective is to be open to different ontologies of knowledge. (Student F)

During the excursion itself, the students respected Chenise and James as knowledgeable guides in their learning. The students had a collective understanding that Chenise and James possessed traditional and Indigenous knowledge and an understanding of the land that they were sharing and exploring together. The transfer of knowledge from Chenise and James to the students happened in many ways during these land-based learning excursions. One example from the first cohort year that students wrote about was when Chenise and James discussed the eel harvest with the group. The students understood that the current eel harvests are less plentiful than they have been in the past. One student wrote:

> We learned from Chenise and James and experienced harsh winter conditions with them; however, after this experience, many of us returned to our comfortable dwellings and likely consumed food from a grocery store ... there are no cultural ties to store-bought food, no reciprocity with Mother Earth, no ability to share the harvest with the community, and no ability to transfer this knowledge to future generations. (Student D)

This student realized that food systems are connected to privilege and that they have a relationship and play a role in the environment in which they live.

Another student wrote:

> James spoke about some Mi'kmaw values and the importance of eels in sustaining their culture and food source all year long. One idea and word that James talked about was Netukulimk. (Student S)

Another student also wrote about Netukulimk, saying:

> In Mi'kmaq culture, Netukulimk is expressed through their right to exercise traditional rituals and practices. For instance, one ritual involves thanking Mother Nature after having harvested an animal, such as an eel, by offering that eel to another animal, such as a hawk. The practice of giving thanks is intended to maintain respectful co-existence and co-dependence between their people and nature. (Student O)

While one student focused on the practice of eel spearing, another wrote about their keen interest in dance. The student wrote:

> I have a background in dance, so I am interested in learning about the dances of different cultures. (Student P)

Given their interest, the student discussed the topic of dances with Chenise and James during their land-based excursion. Chenise and James spoke about some Mi'kmaw dances, and how they are still commonly practised at modern gatherings like Mawio'mis. The student went on to write:

> It was interesting to learn from James that there were two traditional Mi'kmaq dances regrettably whose choreography had either been lost or there were only a couple of people who knew the dance's steps still.

This quote speaks to the importance of knowledge transfer and the sharing of knowledge. The examples of eel spearing and dance, while quite different from one another, demonstrate how connected things and beings are, and they demonstrate the importance of knowledge transfer to sustain a tradition and community.

Types of Knowledge and What Was Learned

In preparing for their land-based learning excursions, the students were asked to choose and establish some learning objectives for themselves. The students were asked to write about these objectives in their preparatory assignments, and a number of students wrote about wanting to be open to the experience to deepen their knowledge about Mi'kmaw culture. One student wrote:

> One of my objectives for our excursion is [to] open myself up to experiencing learning not just through definitive ideas and words, but through conscious sensation and abstract feeling as well. (Student A)

Being on the land helped students experience sensations and feelings and allowed them to immerse themselves in learning. These excursions were quite short, but opportunities for learning were still plentiful. Students commented on the fact that learning on the land was different from conventional classroom learning and a welcomed change. Chenise and James could look around to draw inspiration for the knowledge being shared. One student wrote in their preparatory assignment,

> sharing such knowledge within the constraints of conventional Western academia, such as that employed at Dalhousie, is no small feat. (Student C)

Many students believed that in order to learn in a more holistic sense, that they needed to learn about both Western and Indigenous knowledge, through time spent in a classroom and on the land. They believed it is necessary for the two knowledge systems to exist, not in competition, but in a complementary manner. One student wrote in their land-based learning reflection:

> I now am more aware that [Indigenous] concepts can't be separated from education on the land. I needed this experience with Reclaiming Our Roots to understand this. Talking about Indigenous knowledge and culture in a classroom has been an important part of my education; however, to understand the concepts we discuss I needed to get out on the land with Reclaiming Our Roots to put the discussion into feelings. (Student L)

By being outside and on the land, the students from both cohorts were able to think differently about their learning. They were able to think about how knowledge had been acquired traditionally, and what is missing from the current Western way of learning. Language was another way in which knowledge was being exchanged throughout the land-based learning excursions. One student wrote in their preparatory assignment:

> I hope to learn more about how traditional knowledge is imbedded in the Mi'kmaq language during our excursion, and I will remember to reflect deeply on any translations our Mi'kmaq leaders share with us. (Student A)

This student linked traditional and Indigenous knowledge with language, understanding that when both are being discussed together, learning can be deepened. Chenise and James were able to demonstrate this first-hand by identifying place names and giving the Mi'kmaw and traditional names of plants and being. This experience also allowed students to think about their learning on a personal level, outside of a traditional classroom and beyond the expectations in a syllabus or reading list. The knowledge that was being shared by Chenise and James with the students who participated in the excursion would not only inform their experience in the course, but potentially could also affect and inform a great deal of their future learning.

Value of the Experience and Emotional Reactions

While it is not possible to put a definite value on a student's experience, it is possible to note their emotional response and thoughts associated to the experience. Students prepared for the land-based excursions in different ways, and they also approached the excursions with different stories and lived experiences. One student wrote in their preparatory assignment,

> Everyone and everything in this world is connected to the land. Our food and water come from the land and because of that, the land has defined our communities and culture ... The most recent ancestral connection I have with the land is through my grandmother. My grandmother grew up on a farm in the Netherlands and as the eldest of eight children, helped raise all of her siblings to be a part of the running of the farm. Their house was directly connected to the barn so they slept close to the animals at night and gave each other heat and protection during the difficult times of the winter and war. Though my relatives lived a very Westernized agrarian life, with a mindset of ruling over animals, their lives were solely dependent on their daily work with the animals and the land. Due to a variety of factors such as health, money, and war, my grandmother's knowledge of agrarian life was not passed down to her children or grandchildren. (Student R)

This student approached this land-based learning excursion with questions about their own connection to the land. While this work can be challenging and quite personal, the same student wrote the following in their reflective assignment:

> At first, land-based learning felt a bit uncomfortable because I was unfamiliar to this type of learning. Once we were encouraged to ask questions, share knowledge, and explore the area on our own, this experienced started to feel more natural and less stressful. Often in a classroom setting I feel an underlying stress and pressure to ask the right questions or say nothing at all. With land-based learning, I was able

to learn without stress and found I was able to express my thought and questions freely. I found that as I grew in my understanding and relationship with the land, I become increasingly relaxed and thoroughly enjoyed being in that setting. Unlike an indoor classroom where the longer I am there, the more tired I become, with this excursion, the longer I was on the land the more curious and aware of my surrounding I became. I believe that this is because I was not just learning head knowledge, which is often the focus in the classroom, but I was learning practical hands-on knowledge. (Student R)

This quote clearly demonstrates an emotional reaction to the land-based learning excursion, and while it is but one example, countless others exists within the students' preparatory and reflective assignments. This knowledge and experience will shape the students' experiences moving forward and allowed them to experience the value of land-based learning within the context of a university class without the context of a traditional classroom.

Discussion and Conclusion

The collaboration for land-based learning curriculum design in the context of a university course produced different types of outcomes for the partnership itself, the research and for students. Through the collaborative curriculum design, Chenise, James, and Melanie built a relationship and an understanding of the different roles and qualities of the curriculum that were important to each other. The partnership put Reclaiming Our Roots in a leadership position for the delivery of all aspects of the land-based learning (preparatory materials, excursion, and reflections). This was essential for respecting Indigenous knowledge and avoiding the perpetuation of tokenism and neo-colonialism within the partnership (Aikenhead and Elliott 2010). Partners supported one another in their respective roles (delivering materials, guiding land-based excursion, grading assignments) and maintained a high level of coordination to ensure that supports for one another were appropriately placed, thereby reducing miscommunications and process errors and maintaining boundaries related to each other's roles. Clear and frequent communication and the understanding of roles and responsibilities was essential for supporting the learning and relationship-building process that eventually resulted in the trust and confidence to move forward to collaborative research on land-based learning curriculum design and student learning outcomes (Benton 2017; Zurba et al. 2019). Relationship building took time, and it was important to communicate what was possible on both sides of the partnerships so that expectations could be collectively managed. In terms of challenges, the main one encountered was the processing time for remunerations for facilitating the workshop in the first year. Melanie worked with the university administration in the second year to make sure that the issue would not recur.

The research design was guided by boundary work principles that had been modified for the context of collaborative curriculum development (Zurba et al. under review). Principles relating to the development of the curriculum (the boundary object) were applied at the beginning of the partnership, even prior to deciding to engage in partnered research, and continued into the knowledge translation (data analysis) and mobilization (co-authorship) phase of the overall work. Ethics translation, in particular what knowledge should be shared and what should not be, was important for both the curriculum design and research phases and involved continuous consultation and iterative cycles of feedback on curriculum design and research processes and products (e.g., preliminary results of findings). Communication also contributed to relationship building, which was integral to the collaboration. Chenise reflected on this and emphasized that she felt that academics, such as Melanie, who work at universities in Indigenous Peoples' territories, should collaborate with the peoples in those territories even if they have relationship elsewhere (e.g., Melanie's relationship with Elder George Land from Wabaseemoong traditional territory).

The student reflections provided valuable insights for understanding learning related to the themes that were of interest to Chenise and James, as the Indigenous knowledge-holders and facilitators of land-based learning: willingness to engage; group dynamic and relationality (as it connects to M'sit No'kmaq/ acknowledging connection to "all my relations"); knowledge transferral; types of knowledge and what was learned; and value of the experiences and emotional reactions. Student learning reflections demonstrated that engaging with the land itself, the facilitators and each other were all meaningful learning experience that could not be easily accessed in a conventional classroom setting. Students also had opportunities to critically reflect on their position and the spaces that they occupy in relation to the land and Indigenous Peoples. This type of reckoning and critical reflection is essential for learning that leads to the transformation of attitudes and practices (Mezirow 1991), such as in how students might engage in their current and future/post-education work. The student reflections also demonstrated a desire to continue to deepen understanding of Indigenous knowledge and worldviews and foster relationships with the Indigenous Peoples and the land. Therefore, many of the outcomes of collaborative land-based curriculum development, such as relationship building and an appreciation for Indigenous knowledge and respect for one another, were similar for the collaborating partners and for students.

NOTES

1 MacMynowski (2007, 3) describes "boundary work" as "those acts and structures that create, maintain, and break down boundaries."

2 Mik'maw Ethics Watch is a Mi'kmaw ethics committee "appointed by the Sante'
   Mawio'mi (Grand Council) to establish a set of principles and protocols that will
   protect the integrity and cultural knowledge of the Mi'kmaw people" (Founding
   Committee of Mi'kmaw Ethics Watch n.d.).

WORKS CITED

Aikenhead, Glen S. 2006. "Towards Decolonizing the Pan-Canadian Science Framework."
   Canadian Journal of Science, Mathematics and Technology Education 6, no. 4: 387–99.
   https://doi.org/10.1080/14926150609556712
Aikenhead, Glen S., and Dean Elliott. 2009. "An Emerging Decolonizing Science
   Education in Canada." *Canadian Journal of Science, Mathematics and Technology
   Education* 10 (October): 321–38. https://doi.org/10.1080/14926156.2010.524967
Austin, M. Jill, and Dianna Zeh Rust. 2015. "Developing an Experiential Learning
   Program: Milestones and Challenges." *International Journal of Teaching and Learning
   in Higher Education* 27, no. 1: 143–53. https://files.eric.ed.gov/fulltext/EJ1069800.pdf
Ballantyne, Erin Freeland. 2014. "Dechinta Bush University: Mobilizing a Knowledge
   Economy of Reciprocity, Resurgence and Decolonization." *Decolonization: Indigeneity,
   Education & Society* 3, no. 3: 67–85.
Bang, Megan, Lawrence Curley, Adam Kessel, Ananda Marin, Eli S. Suzukovich III, and
   George Strack. 2014. "Muskrat Theories, Tobacco in the Streets, and Living Chicago
   as Indigenous Land." *Environmental Education Research* 20, no. 1 (February): 37–55.
   https://doi.org/10.1080/13504622.2013.865113
Benton, D. 2017. "Land-Based Pedagogies: A Path to Decolonizing Environmental
   Education in British Columbia." Master's thesis. Lakehead University.
Coulthard, Glen S. 2014. *Red Skin, White Masks: Rejecting the Colonial Politics of
   Recognition*. Minneapolis: University of Minessota Press.
Dechinta Centre for Reseach and Learning. (n.d.) "About." Accessed February 25, 2021.
   https://www.dechinta.ca/about
Ermine, Willie. 2007. "The Ethical Space of Engagement." *Indigenous Law Journal* 6,
   no. 193.
Founding Committee of Mi'kmaw Ethics Watch. (n.d.) "Mi'kmaw Ethics Watch."
   https://www.cbu.ca/wp-content/uploads/2019/08/MEW-Principles-and-Protocols.pdf
Hatcher, Annamarie, Cheryl Bartlett, Albert Marshall, and Murdena Marshall. 2009.
   "Two-Eyed Seeing in the Classroom Environment: Concepts, Approaches, and
   Challenges." *Canadian Journal of Science, Mathematics and Technology Education* 9,
   no. 3 (September): 141–53. https://doi.org/10.1080/14926150903118342
Jansen, Jonathan D. 2009. *Knowledge in the Blood: Confronting Race and the Apartheid
   Past*. Redwood City, CA: Stanford University Press.
MacMynowski, Dena P. 2007. "Pausing at the Brink of Interdisciplinarity: Power and
   Knowledge at the Meeting of Social and Biophysical Science." *Ecology and Society*
   12, no. 1 (June): Art 20. https://doi.org/10.5751/ES-02009-120120

Marshall, Albert, and Cheryl Bartlett. 2010. "Two-Eyed Seeing for Environmental Sustainability." Environment, Sustainability and Society Lecture Series. Dalhousie University (September 23). http://integrativescience.ca/uploads/articles/2010September -Marshall-Bartlett-Integrative-Science-Two-Eyed-Seeing-environment-sustainability -Aboriginal.pdf

Mezirow, Jack. 1991. *Fostering Critical Reflection in Adulthood: A Guide to Transformative and Emancipatory Learning.* San Francisco: Jossey-Bass.

Preece, Julia. 2016. "Negotiating Service Learning through Community Engagement: Adaptive Leadership, Knowledge, Dialogue and Power." *Education as Change* 20, no. 1 (April): 1–22. https://doi.org/10.17159/1947-9417/2016/562

Reclaiming Our Roots. (n.d.) "Reclaiming Our Roots: Land-Based Learning and Community Stewardship." Accessed February 25, 2021. https://www.facebook.com /ReclaimingOurRootsNS

Red River College. (n.d.) "Indigenous Education: Land-Based Learning." Accessed February 25, 2021. https://www.rrc.ca/indigenous/land-based-learning/

Simpson, Leanne Betasamosake. 2014. "Land as Pedagogy: Nishnaabeg Intelligence and Rebellious Transformation." *Decolonization: Indigeneity, Education & Society* 3, no. 3 (November): 1–25.

UArctic. (n.d.) "Dechinta Bush University Centre for Research and Learning." Accessed February 25, 2021. https://www.uarctic.org/member-profiles/canada/32803/dechinta -bush-university-centre-for-research-and-learning

University of Manitoba. (n.d.) "Land and Water: Land-Based Education." Accessed February 25, 2021. https://umanitoba.ca/community-engaged-learning /land-and-water-land-based-education

Wildcat, Matthew, Mandee McDonald, Stephanie Irlbacher-Fox, and Glen Coulthard. 2014. "Learning from the Land: Indigenous Land-Based Pedagogy and Decolonization." *Decolonization: Indigeneity, Education and Society* 3, no. 3 (December): I–XV.

Zurba, Melanie, Kirsten Maclean, Emma Woodward, and Durdana Islam. 2019. "Amplifying Indigenous Community Participation in Place-Based Research through Boundary Work." *Progress in Human Geography* 43, no. 6: 1020–43. https://doi.org /10.1177/0309132518807758

Zurba, Melanie, George Land, Ryan Bullock, and Bridget Graham. (under review). "Boundary Education: Collaborative Land-Based Learning as a Way of Decolonizing and Indigenizing University Curriculum." *Journal of Cultural Geography.*

10 Ecological Networks and Corridors in the Context of Global Initiatives

JODI A. HILTY AND STEPHEN WOODLEY

Transformation through policy and governance at all levels is critical for advancing conservation. Enabling policies, guidance, and practices set at the global level, such as international instruments and bodies, can support nations, regions, and local efforts. As ecologists, we understand that conservation of biodiversity requires shifting from protecting individual parcels to protecting ecological networks across larger regions. The aim is to conserve large landscapes and seascapes, which requires building connectivity between protected areas such that the whole network functions to conserve nature in ways that the parts cannot achieve alone. This is similar to the way many Indigenous Peoples have explained to us that they see the world as interconnected and functioning across many scales (e.g., L. Little Bear).

To support this paradigm shift, we engaged with a global community to advance a key policy tool, standards for conserving ecological corridors. Ecological corridors are one key component in addition to protected areas that could help move us from just protected areas to ecological networks at landscape and seascape scales. We worked within the IUCN Connectivity Specialist Group (described further below) and sought the engagement of more than 900 members from at least 119 countries around the world to provide input at in-person and online meetings to help 59 contributing authors from around the world to ultimately provide globally agreed-upon guidelines for ecological networks and corridors. We also extensively drew on other existing globally agreed-upon standards. For example, we utilized global governance standards that specify a range of governance types such as by a government to shared forms of governance (e.g., transboundary shared between governments, collaborative, private, and Indigenous Peoples or local communities). Finally we provided illustrative case studies for a range of connectivity initiatives to illustrate a range of approaches, principles, and governance types. This chapter offers a much-condensed summary of the need and the new guidance.

Background

We are in a time of crisis, where a diversity of life on Earth is rapidly disappearing and the very survival of humanity also may be imperilled as a consequence. The combined impact of unprecedented change of the surface of Earth by humans together with a human-caused rapidly changing climate means that up to one million species are at imminent risk of extinction (IPBES 2019).

More than 7.6 billion people inhabit Earth, a number projected to continue to grow. Accordingly, human impacts across the world are enormous and expanding. Already evidence of human impacts in the marine environment include overfishing, nutrient run-off, and climate change that occur in more than 85 per cent of the marine biomes (Jones et al. 2018).

Similarly, more than three-quarters of the terrestrial world is affected by anthropogenic activities (Venter et al. 2016). The impacts vary from place to place. Across the terrestrial surface, about 17 per cent of lands have been fundamentally changed by cities and agriculture. Lower intensity developments and ranching impact more than 50 per cent of shared lands, defined as places where more than half the landscape is still largely untransformed. That leaves about a quarter of terrestrial Earth as mostly intact areas (Locke et al., 2019). To avert global species extinctions will require a suite of different strategies depending on the condition of the place.

It is clear, though, that while protected and conserved areas – defined by the Convention on Biological Diversity as "other effective area-based conservation measures" or OECMs (IUCN-WCPA 2019) – are important in conserving biodiversity, the current protected and conserve area system is not adequate for stemming biodiversity loss. We need to address conservation at larger spatial scales, where well-designed protected and conserved areas are ecologically connected to ultimately create functional ecological networks. The creation of ecological networks is an essential requirement for conserving biodiversity given the nature of the threats to biodiversity. These threats include habitat loss, fragmentation, and climate change.

What is ecological connectivity? The United Nations Convention for Migratory Species (CMS) defines ecological connectivity as "the unimpeded movement of species and the flow of natural processes that sustain life on Earth" (CMS 2020). This definition importantly recognizes that ecological connectivity is not just about the movement of individual organisms but about supporting the function of entire ecosystems. Loss of function due to human-induced habitat loss and fragmentation, or the breaking up of once continuous habitat into smaller pieces, ultimately leads to the slow unravelling of the ecosystem. This can imperil many organisms dependent on those processes and intact habitats (Ceballos 2017).

The Need for Ecological Connectivity

In the twentieth century, the focus for area-based conservation was on new and expanded protected areas. Now in the twenty-first century we still need a focus on dramatically upscaling protected and conserved areas, but also to understand and implement conservation at the large scales, beyond and specific parcel, the scale that nature needs to be resilient in the long term. There is clear scientific and public support for a significant increase in protected areas around the world. As we discuss in more depth later, the preponderance of evidence suggests that a minimum of 30 per cent and likely somewhere around 50 per cent of various ecosystems require protection to function in the long term (Woodley et al. 2019a). The public actually agrees with these large numbers. Various public surveys of how much humans think should be set aside show people around the world believing that approximately 50 per cent of land and sea should be set aside for nature (e.g., Wright et al. 2019). Current conservation movements, including the 2020 Global Biodiversity Framework of the Convention on Biological Diversity, reflect this and continue to press for new and expanded protected areas. Target 3 of the Global Biodiversity is now international law, with countries agreeing to protect, by 2030, at least 30 per cent of terrestrial and inland water, and of coastal and marine areas (CBD/COP/DEC/15/4). It is critical to understand that conservation is not only about percent coverage figures. Protected and conserved areas must be located in areas that are important for conserving biodiversity, properly designed, well governed, and effectively managed. Only where these conditions are met will protected and conserved areas deliver effective conservation outcomes (Hockings et al. 2019).

Proper ecological design is a challenge for most of the world's protected and conserved areas simply because most of them are not big enough to sustain large-scale ecological processes or provide everything all organisms need (Newmark 1995), and thus need functional ecological connectivity between these areas. Ecological connectivity increases the effective size of protected and conserved areas because it builds smaller units into ecological networks. Ecological connectivity is particularly critical with global climate change because many species ranges are already shifting to adapt to new conditions. Those species that cannot move through human-modified landscapes especially need conserved ecological corridors (Hilty et al. 2019). Ultimately, ecological networks of protected and conserved areas and ecological corridors offer an ecological design solution to best manage climate change and habitat fragmentation. We will dive deeper into this later, but generally such networks have emergent properties that enable the network to better conserve biodiversity and ecological processes than the protected and conserved areas in isolation.

Table 10.1. Examples of international instruments and bodies that arguably depend on ecological connectivity to achieve their purpose

---

- Convention on Biological Diversity (CBD)
- Ramsar Convention
- Convention on the Conservation of Migratory Species (CMS)
- World Heritage Convention
- UN Convention for the Law of the Sea (UNCLOS)
- UN Framework Convention on Climate Change (UNFCC)
- UNESCO's Man and the Biosphere Programme
- Revised African Convention on the Conservation of Nature and Natural Resources (Maputo Convention)
- Convention on the Conservation of European Wildlife and Natural Habitats (Bern Convention)
- United Nations Convention to Combat Desertification
- UN Convention on Non-Navigational Uses of International Watercourses
- Convention on the Protection and Use of Transboundary Watercourses
- Migratory Bird Treaty Act of 1918
- International Fur Seal Treaty of 1961

The Global Conservation Agenda

Despite the fact that IUCN guidelines for connectivity were only published in 2020 (Hilty et al. 2020), the concept of ecological connectivity is not new and has become increasingly visible in the global policy arena over the last decades. We need only to look at the United Nations Convention for Biological Diversity (CBD), a global instrument that all but two countries (the United States and the Vatican have ratified. In the CBD targets set forth for all countries to achieve by 2030, connectivity is mentioned in one goal and four targets. As examples, Goal A and Target 2 read:

- Goal A: The integrity, connectivity [bold emphasis added] and resilience of all ecosystems are maintained, enhanced, or restored, substantially increasing the area of natural ecosystems by 2050;
- TARGET 2: Ensure that by 2030 at least 30 per cent of areas of degraded terrestrial, inland water, and coastal and marine ecosystems are under effective restoration, in order to enhance biodiversity and ecosystem functions and services, ecological integrity and connectivity [bold emphasis added].

Likewise, the Convention on Migratory Species, formed in 1979, concerns itself exclusively with providing a global platform to address the needs of migratory species between states, laying the legal foundation for coordinated international conservation measures (http://CMS.int). Many other global international instruments also arguably depend on ecological connectivity at least in part to achieve their purpose (table 10.1).

Global Guidance: IUCN and Conservation

Much of the global effort to avert the biodiversity crises is led by civil society, also called non-government organizations, working in collaboration with governments, citizens, communities, and the business community. Unique among these organizations is the International Union for the Conservation of Nature (IUCN). It is one of the world's oldest conservation organizations, created in 1948 as the world was reorganizing after the Second World War. At its core, the IUCN is a membership union composed of 1,300 members – including states, government agencies, civil society (non-government organizations or NGOs), and Indigenous Peoples' Organizations. In addition to the members, there are seven IUCN commissions, composed of over ten thousand experts, that are the scientific and knowledge engine of the union. The members and commissions are supported by the IUCN Secretariat, with staff located in offices in 11 operational regions around the world.

The seven IUCN commissions and their mandates are as follows:

- Commission on Education and Communication (CEC), driving change through leading communication, learning, and knowledge
- Commission on Ecosystem Management (CEM), promoting ecosystem-based approaches for the management of landscapes and seascapes
- Commission on Environmental, Economic and Social Policy CEESP, harmonizing nature conservation and the critical social, cultural, environmental, and economic justice concerns of human societies
- Species Survival Commission (SSC), influencing, encouraging, and assisting societies to conserve biodiversity by building knowledge on the status and threats to species
- World Commission on Environmental Law, advancing environmental law to strengthen the legal foundations of conservation of nature and sustainable development
- World Commission on Protected Areas, developing knowledge-based policy, advice and guidance on the full suite of issues surrounding protected areas
- IUCN Climate Crises Commission – a new commission in development that will provide science and policy advice on the climate crises.

All of the commissions create standards, guidance, data, and science that helps the global conservation agenda. For example, the Species Survival Commission is a global collection of experts that develops the authoritative global inventory of the global conservation status of biological species, known as the Red List of Threatened Species. Major species assessors include BirdLife International, the Institute of Zoology (the research division of the Zoological Society of London), the World Conservation Monitoring Centre, and many Specialist Groups within the IUCN Species Survival Commission (SSC). Collectively, assessments by these organizations and groups account for nearly half the species on the Red List. It is worth reflecting that the global status of threatened species is done largely by a volunteer commission of experts. Can you imagine if the world's financial status were tracked by a volunteer commission of experts? It is indicative of the global priority, or lack thereof, on nature conservation.

The global leadership on standards and guidance for protected and conserved areas comes from the World Commission on Protected Areas (https://www.iucn.org/commissions/world-commission-protected-areas). As with all IUCN Commissions, much of the detailed work comes from working units termed Specialist Groups or Task Forces. The work on ecological connectivity and ecological networks is carried out by the Connectivity Conservation Specialist Group (CCSG). The CCSG developed the set of guidelines on connectivity leading to ecological networks that is discussed in this chapter.

What Are the Needs for Large-Scale Conservation? A Review of the Evidence

The need for large-scale area-based conservation is rooted in the fact that we face a global biodiversity crisis. Extinction rates are estimated to be 1,000 times the background rate and future rates could be 10,000 times higher (De Vos et al. 2015). The Intergovernmental Science-Policy Platform on Biodiversity and Ecosystem Services reports that 75 per cent of the Earth's land surface is significantly altered, 66 per cent of the ocean area is experiencing increasing cumulative impacts, and over 85 per cent of wetlands (by area) have been lost (Díaz et al. 2019). On average, population sizes of wild vertebrate species have declined precipitously over the last 50 years on land, in freshwater and in the sea, and around 25 per cent of species in assessed animal and plant groups are threatened (Díaz et al. 2019).

The most significant direct drivers of biodiversity loss are habitat loss and fragmentation (changes in land and sea use) and direct exploitation, with over-exploitation being more significant in marine systems. Factors of climate change, invasive alien species, disease, and pollution are also important (Díaz et al. 2019). Many of these drivers of biodiversity loss can be managed through area-based conservation, with connected systems of protected areas and conserved areas being the backbone of area-based conservation. Because biodiversity loss is being driven primarily by habitat loss and fragmentation and over-harvest, protected and conserved areas are key policy and practical solutions to biodiversity loss. Area-based conservation may be less effective for addressing some drivers, including widespread pollution, widespread disease, and invasive species.

The key conclusions from a scientific review of evidence for large-scale conservation apply equally to terrestrial, marine and freshwater ecosystems (Woodley et al. 2019a), as follows:

1. Under the previous Strategic Plan for Biodiversity of the Convention on Biological Diversity, Aichi Biodiversity Target 11 called for the protection of 17 per cent terrestrial area and 10 per cent marine area by 2020. No published research considered that Aichi Biodiversity Target 11 was adequate for the area-based conservation of biodiversity, either on sea (O'Leary et al. 2016) or on land (Butchart et al. 2015; Rodriguez and Gaston 2001; Noss et al. 2012; Svancara et al. 2005). Even with the best locations for protected areas, there is simply too much species diversity and too high levels of endangerment to cover these elements in relatively small percentages of the global surface. Almost universally, when conservation targets are based on the research and expert opinion of scientists, they far exceed targets set to meet political or policy goals (Svancara et al. 2005; Noss et al. 2012). This is supported by a global survey of conservation scientists conducted in 2017, who massively supported very large percent area targets to conserve biodiversity (Woodley et al. 2019b).

2. Percentage area targets cannot be considered in isolation from the quality considerations presented in Aichi Biodiversity Target 11. There is some concern that a focus on percent area targets might draw away from a focus on quality (Visconti et al. 2019). Protected and conserved areas are policy tools to achieve nature conservation and need to be selectively located, properly designed, equitably governed, and effectively managed in order to achieve biodiversity outcomes. Questions of ecological design, equitable governance, and management effectiveness that lead to conservation outcomes are included in the IUCN Green List of Protected and Conserved Areas Standard (IUCN and World Commission on Protected Areas (WCPA) 2017). The question of where to locate protected and conserved areas is complex, but there is good agreement in the literature that they should focus on areas of importance for biodiversity, including Key Biodiversity Areas (IUCN 2016), Ecologically or Biologically Significant Marine Areas (EBSAs; https://www.cbd.int/ebsa/), and equivalent national and open ocean priorities.

3. There are different approaches to considering percent areas targets, but they all agree that the large percentages of the globe need to be kept in a natural condition in order to conserve biodiversity. There is no one unequivocal

answer to the question of what per cent of the earth, or a region, should be protected in order to maintain biodiversity. The answers are complicated by spatial scale, patterns of biodiversity, and weaknesses in selection approaches. The answers are further complicated by the selected conservation values used in systematic conservation planning approaches. Each selected conservation element raises the percentage targets. For example, selecting only for endangered or rare biodiversity elements will result in a lower percent area than if ecological connectivity or ecosystem services are also considered. Studies that include a more complete set of values are universally very high, well over 50 per cent and up to 80 per cent. Studies that include a narrower subset of biodiversity values result in lower percent area targets but are never under 30 per cent and always include caveats that they are likely inadequate and represent minimum estimates. As such, protected area conservation targets should be established based on the desired outcomes (e.g., halting biodiversity loss by 2030). It is clear in this respect that decisions already taken by the global conservation community on, for example, at least 30 per cent protection of the ocean, can only be but way points on to what is really needed to address current crises in biodiversity and climate.

Large area-based targets should never be considered as percentages for percentages' sake. They should always be determined and implemented, whether at the global, regional or local scale through systematic conservation planning or other science-based approaches. However, there is strong evidence that percentage targets materially increase national conservation efforts. Target 11 is being seen as one of the most successful targets reached including in mega-diverse countries (Bacon et al. 2019; Green et al. 2019).

Area targets alone are insufficient to halt biodiversity loss, and must be accompanied by a focus on quality, notably the equitable governance and effective management of systems of protected and conserved areas. For example, most new protected areas in Canada are advancing as Indigenous Protected and Conserved Areas (Indigenous Circle of Experts 2018; also discussed further in chapter 6). Protected and conserved areas must also be carefully located in areas where they make a conservation impact for nature conservation and they should be ecologically connected to function as conservation networks. It is clear we need a dramatic increase in both the quality and quantity of protected and conserved areas as an essential means to halt and reverse the catastrophic loss of biodiversity that is undermining all life on earth. They must also be set in truly sustainable actions across the whole ocean and land space to realize the true benefits.

4. The key conclusion from a review of the evidence is that calls for the global protection of a minimum of 30 per cent and up to 70 per cent or even more of the land and sea on earth are supported in the literature whether through studies based on species-area curves, systematic conservation planning, or minimum system size approaches. Importantly these suggested higher conservation targets are not discounted in any of the biodiversity literature. The call for conserving 50 per cent of the earth is a mid-point of these values and is supported by a range of studies. More importantly there are no studies that argue that we can maintain biodiversity with low percent coverage targets. There is consistent scientific agreement that very large-scale conservation is required to deal with the known drivers of biodiversity loss. Suggested conservation targets of 30 per cent or 50 per cent or even 70 per cent, while not based on precision, are consistent with scientific literature on what is required to conserve biodiversity.

Coming to a Globally Agreed-Upon Definition of Ecological Connectivity

The IUCN connectivity specialist group was formally established in 2016 under the IUCN World Commission on Protected Areas. Despite the recent establishment of the group, much discussion and work focused on the need for ecological connectivity had advanced from the IUCN mountains specialist group prior until formalization of the connectivity specialist group. Although being a relatively new group, membership is greater than 920 individuals representing more than 450 institutions, ranging from government agencies, academic and other scientific entities, non-profit, and the business sector enterprises. Members are from at least 119 countries around the world. The purpose of the connectivity group is to "advance science, policy, and practice to protect ecological connectivity that is key to maintaining the integrity of protected areas, saving biodiversity, and increasing resilience to climate change" (IUCN no date). It operates as a large umbrella, but also has subgroups such as marine and transportation work groups.

Advancing the idea of ecological connectivity and corridors has been several decades in the making. Some of the early efforts by IUCN to promote ecological connectivity arose through the Mountain Specialist Group a few decades ago (table 10.2). The specialist group builds on this considerable body of work on connectivity, led by the late Dr. Graeme Worboys among others. It has taken a while for more general agreement on concepts and ways forward. From academics to policy-makers to practitioners, everyone had their own ideas of what ecological connectivity was and how to advance policy and on-the-ground

Table 10.2. Nearly two decades of work led up to the IUCN global guidelines for connectivity. Below are some of the key milestones representing the advancement of the concept by IUCN

Date	Milestones
2003	• Didima Camp, uKhahlamba-Drakensberg Park, South Africa: International gathering of mountain protected area managers, organized by Larry Hamilton prior to Durban World Parks Congress.
	• Harmon, D., and G.L. Worboys, eds. 2004. "Chapter 4, Corridors for Conservation." In *Managing Mountain Protected Areas: Challenges and Responses for the 21st Century*. Colledara, IT: Andromeda Editrice.
	• Bennett, A.F. 2003. *Linkages in the Landscape: The Role of Corridors and Connectivity in Wildlife Conservation*. IUCN
2004	• Banff, Canada: An International Workshop Protecting the Worlds Mountain Corridors and Peace Parks
2006	• Papallacta, Ecuador: *The Papallacta Declaration*
	• Lockwood, M., and T. Sandwith. 2006. "Chapter 22, Linking the Landscape." In *Managing Protected Areas, A Global Guide,* edited by M. Lockwood, G.L. Worboys, and A. Kothari. Oxfordshire: Routledge.
2008	• Dhulikhel, Nepal: *A Connectivity Conservation Workshop of International Corridor Managers* (IUCN WCPA Workshop facilitated by Graeme L. Worboys and Nakul Chettri of ICIMOD)
2010	• Worboys, G.L., Francis, W.L., and Lockwood, M. *Connectivity Conservation Management, A Global Guide*
2013	• Fitzsimons, J., I. Pulsford, and G. Wescott. *Linking Australia's Landscapes: Lessons and Opportunities from Large-Scale Conservation Networks,* CSIRO Publishing.
	• Lausche et al. *The Legal Aspects of Connectivity Conservation: A Concept Paper,* IUCN
2015	• Pulsford et al. "Chapter 29: Connectivity Conservation Management." In *Protected Area Governance and Management*, edited by G.L Worboys, M. Lockwood, A. Kothari, S. Feary, and I. Pulsford. IUCN WCPA
2016	• Worboys et al. *Connectivity Conservation Area Guidelines* (Advanced Draft)
	• IUCN Resolution *WCC-2016-Res-087,* "Awareness of connectivity conservation definition and guidelines"
2017–2020	• Global consultations (Colombia, Brazil, Romania, Kenya, Tanzania, Australia, online, India)
2020	• Hilty, J..* G.L. Worboys, A. Keeley,* S. Woodley,* B. Lausche, H. Locke, M. Carr, I. Pulsford, J. Pittock, J.W. White, D.M. Theobald, J. Levine, M. Reuling, J.E.M. Watson, R. Ament, and G.M. Tabor.* 2020. *Guidelines for Conserving Connectivity through Ecological Networks and Corridors. Best Practice Protected Area Guidelines* Series No. 30. Gland, Switzerland: IUCN. xiii + 122pp.
Post 2020	• Work to develop a database with the Protected Planet to track conserved ecological corridors at a global level using the guidelines

Table 10.3. Differences in the role of protected areas, OECMs, and ecological corridors. Note that all three terms refer to areas with conservation outcomes

	Protected Areas	OECMS	Ecological corridors
MUST conserve in situ biodiversity	•	•	
MAY conserve in situ biodiversity			•
MUST conserve connectivity			•
MAY conserve connectivity	•	•	

conservation of it. While general agreement on the importance of movement existed, the particulars took years of in-person meetings and publications. Even now that there is a globally agreed-upon set of guidelines, some dialogue will undoubtedly continue and new challenges will continue to be hashed out in the global arena.

Of fundamental importance was to agree that an area-based conservation approach was important for conserving ecological connectivity. In early discussions, some individuals expressed concern about yet another area-based tool for conservation because IUCN had worked hard to move from solely protected areas to conserved areas or OECMS. Some wondered whether protected and conserved areas on their own might be adequate area-based approaches that could be applied to conserve connectivity. Others wanted to define areas of connectivity to include protected and conserved areas, while still others didn't want overlapping designations such that connectivity areas needed to be distinct and separate. Some worried that proposing ecological corridors as an area-based tool could distract governments and practitioners from the essential business of continuing to expand protected and conserved areas. In many places, first steps towards the conservation of connectivity may need to be voluntary, so that the larger matrix of lands between protected and conserved areas should be the focus of more general voluntary actions, not limiting connectivity solely to defined geographical areas of ecological corridors.

These are all legitimate concerns. Ultimately, the guidelines moved forward to recognize ecological corridors as distinct and separate from protected and conserved areas (table 10.3). We also recognized that while ecological corridors may conserve biodiversity in their own right, they only have to conserve ecological connectivity. Many corridors will not be habitat for focal species and only permit movement of that species. Other corridors may provide for continuous habitat for a variety of species between protected and conserved areas. Ecological corridors may also be important for conserving cultural or spiritual values, one example being Indigenous or Local Peoples travel routes (Hilty et al. 2020). The guidelines provide for a range of different types of ecological corridors suitable to a range of connectivity goals including incorporating socio-political considerations.

It is understood that different regions of the world have variable ability to implement the guidelines now. The guidelines establish what might be aspirational connectivity futures in some places. They clarify what would be required to conserve an ecological corridor-based on a defined set of connectivity objectives. We hope that as new governments consider laws and policies pertaining to connectivity that they utilize this guidance. If human impacts were not so pervasive and increasing, we might be able to address all lands between protected and conserved areas and manage for connectivity. Unfortunately, only about 9–11 per cent of all current protected areas have any structural connectivity, and likely little of that is conserved at this time (Ward et al. 2020). We have limited time for nature to get on with the implementation of effective connectivity conservation.

Given this, the new global guidelines for connectivity were advanced with significant global input over the last three years. Ultimately, the purpose of reaching global agreement on ecological connectivity guidelines was multifold:

- to consolidate a wealth of knowledge and best available practices;
- to agree upon global definitions that function across terrestrial, freshwater, and marine environments much the way that the protected area definition is agnostic of ecosystem type;
- to outline the fundamentals of what needs to be in place to refer to an ecological corridor as conserved;
- to highlight an approach to start tracking conserved corridors at a global level because up until now we can only assess whether structural connectivity exists but not whether it is conserved.

The guidelines were subject to global peer review and vetted through the IUCN publications process and are now available in the four languages of the IUCN including English, French, Mandarin, and Spanish (Hilty et al. 2020).

The Need for Ecological Corridors and Ecological Networks

The need and scientific basis for ecological corridors is well articulated elsewhere including in chapters 1 through 3 in the guidelines (Hilty et al. 2020). For those interested in taking a deeper dive into the cumulative science on connectivity, we refer you to the book *Corridor Ecology* (Hilty et al. 2019). In addition, the science is rapidly becoming more sophisticated, so some new manuscripts have already come out since that synthesis.

In brief, we need ecological corridors because the preponderance of science tells us that this tool, if used together with expanding protected and conserved areas, will help to conserve biological diversity in all its forms (e.g., Heller et al. 2009). The challenge we face is that human impacts on the earth continue to expand and at the expense of species. Even well-managed, existing protected areas are increasingly becoming isolated from other protected areas and being surrounded by a sea of human influence, and with that comes the loss, sometimes delayed by decades, of species and functionality of such parks (Hansen and DeFries 2007). At the same time, climate change is altering once predictable connectivity pathways, such as those that migratory ungulates traditionally followed. In order to survive the twin threats of ecosystem fragmentation and climate change, ungulates and other animals need more room to roam in order to survive. At this time, we see the opposite trend with movement being truncated. Global migration routes are being shortened and or being lost (e.g., Williams et al. 2020) at a time when we need to be maintaining and restoring connectivity.

In order to significantly improve our efforts to conserve biological diversity, we need to move from a focus only on protected and conserved areas to a broader focus on ecological networks – systems of protected and conserved areas with ecological connectivity in the context of large landscapes and seascapes. Ecological networks ensure ecological connectivity but also help meet a number of other ecological values, such as representativeness, redundancy, and other variables beyond the scope of this chapter.

Ecological networks are made up of two basic elements including (1) protected and conserved areas and (2) ecological corridors (figure 10.1). It is the emergent properties of both of these elements functioning together that can enable increased conservation effectiveness and are considered, when well designed, to be important to facilitate adaptation during this time of climate change.

Key considerations for the different elements are whether the protected and conserved areas are in the right places and appropriately sized. Likewise, ecological corridors need to be well designed and managed. If not, the compromised elements will affect the overall integrity of the entire ecological network. Assuming that the elements are decently designed, together the ecological network will function to better conserve biological diversity over time and through space than any individual element on its own. (Bennett and Mulongoy 2006; Hilty et al. 2020).

Figure 10.1. This shows an example of an ecological network and all its elements, including protected and conserved areas (OECMS) and both continuous and discontinuous ecological corridors.

Planning and Implementing Ecological Corridors

It is important to restate that ecological corridors are only effective if protected and conserved areas already exist, as they can increase the effectiveness of them in nature conservation. Simply put, you need something to connect. This is true whether in terrestrial, marine, or freshwater environments. Some preliminary work on connectivity has begun for airspaces, but this was considered too preliminary to be formally included in the guidelines. No matter the environment, various research and modelling approaches can identify where conserving ecological connectivity may be important (Hilty et al. 2019). Once the specific area is identified, moving to conserving connectivity requires a number of steps, ranging from documenting basic information, selecting objectives, choosing a governance model, delineating boundaries, implementing management, and designing monitoring plans that reach the objectives. Following are the basic requirements to achieve a conserved ecological corridor (Hilty et al. 2020):

- Objectives – what biodiversity elements are to be connected?
- Contribution to ecological network – what role does this corridor plan in the larger network?

- Social and economic values – what are the interactions between keeping the areas a corridor and other social and economic values?
- Delineation – what are the boundaries of the corridor?
- Governance – who owns and managed the corridor area?
- Tenure – who owns the corridor?
- Legal mechanisms – what legal protection is in place for the corridor?
- Longevity – what arrangements are in place for the corridor to be in place for the long term?
- Management – what management is required within the corridor so it can meet its conservation objectives?
- Monitoring, evaluation, reporting – how will the corridor be monitored, evaluated and reported?

While we will not go through each of these, we will highlight a few matters. Every corridor should have specific ecological objectives and be governed and managed to achieve connectivity outcomes. Ecological corridors may consist partly or entirely of natural areas managed primarily for connectivity. So long as their conservation objectives are supported, they also may include compatible human activities that practise sustainable resource use. However, ecological corridors should be differentiated from non-designated areas by specific uses that are allowed or prohibited. Likewise, they should have the governance and/or legal mechanisms in place that ensure that these are managed for the connectivity objective in perpetuity, for without the permanence, they become subject to human pressures like any other land and thus cannot guarantee their connectivity goals.

Case Study: Yellowstone to Yukon

Articulated in 1993, the Yellowstone to Yukon vision in western North America is an interconnected system of wild lands and waters harmonizing the needs of people with those of nature. Significant progress has been achieved through using best available science and knowledge and building shared collaborative efforts to advance on-the-ground conservation.

As a result of collaborative efforts with governments, Indigenous Peoples, non-profits, businesses, and local communities, and others, protected areas increased by more than 80 per cent in the first 25 years (figure 10.2), and increased conservation of connectivity occurred through voluntary private land conservation and the building of at least 117 wildlife over- and underpasses to help keep wildlife connected across highways. Some of these were and are being advanced through Indigenous leadership. Today, as part of Canada's Truth and Reconciliation Commission objectives, conservation is advancing with Indigenous leadership. Currently, one-quarter of the protected areas are managed or co-managed by Indigenous Peoples. Since 2018, more than 12,000,000 additional acres have been formally agreed upon to be Indigenous Conserved and

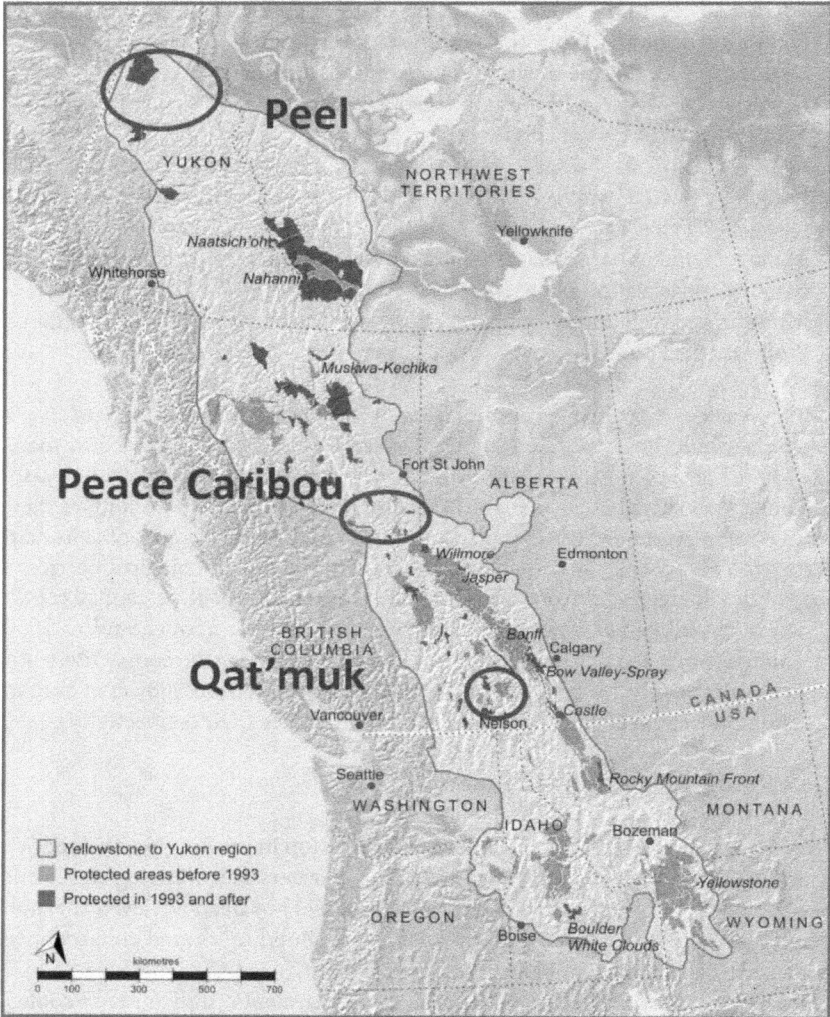

Figure 10.2. Increasing human activities threaten to fragment the more than 3,000-km-long Yellowstone to Yukon (Y2Y) mountain region in western North America and more than 75 Indigenous Territories. Protected areas increased by more than 80 per cent in from 1993–2018. Three Indigenous Protected and Conserved Areas that are moving forward through formal agreements will soon be designated in the Peel Watershed Regional Land-Use Plan in the Peace region (Caribou Agreement) and in the Upper Columbia (Qat'muk Agreement) contributing further growth to protected areas in the region.

Protected Areas (figure 10.2). In addition, Nahanni and Náátsʼihch,oh National Park Reserves were already designated and are co-managed by Parks Canada and First Nations. Collectively, these demonstrate a paradigm shift from provincial, territorial, and national government governance to shared governance approaches that recognize Indigenous governments as having a primary role in conservation, and such new protected areas help increase connectivity across the Y2Y landscape. Other case studies of Indigenous and local people advancing corridors can be found in the IUCN connectivity guidelines.

Closing Remarks

As of the writing of this document, the IUCN Connectivity Specialist Group is working with the Protected Planet Database (https://www.protectedplanet.net/en) to build a database that will track conserved ecological corridors similar to how we track protected areas today. We can only truly begin to understand how effective ecological networks are now and are likely to be into the future if we are able to assess where ecological networks exist, including all the elements – protected and conserved areas and ecological corridors.

How do we define a new area-based conservation tool? The leading entity that maintains the definitions of areas-based conservation tools, such as protected and conserved areas, is the IUCN. With recent science clearly showing the need for large land and seascape conservation approaches that would anchor protected and conserved areas into larger ecological networks, the need to define conserved ecological corridors has never been greater. With the new IUCN connectivity guidelines now available, the focus shifts from what is area-based connectivity to how we advance policy and practice from local to regional and to national and global. Fortunately, there are many governments at different levels that are already advancing connectivity conservation as well as practitioners. With the United Nations Convention for Biological Diversity having set ambitious global targets, including emphasizing the need for connectivity, globally we have an opportunity – even a mandate – to move the biodiversity conservation focus from solely protected and conserved areas to also consider ecological connectivity and shift the paradigm to ecological networks for conservation.

ACKNOWLEDGMENTS

The summary of this work is a built off the work of the co-authors of the IUCN Guidelines including Jodi Hilty, Graeme L. Worboys, Annika Keeley, Stephen Woodley, Barbara Lausche, Harvey Locke, Mark Carr, Ian Pulsford, James Pittock, J. Wilson White, David M. Theobald, Jessica Levine, Melly Reuling, James E.M. Watson, Rob Ament, and Gary M. Tabor, as well as the myriad reviewers and case study authors. Thank you to all for such a collection of work.

WORKS CITED

Bacon, Elizabeth, Patrick Gannon, Sarah Stephen, Edjigayehu Seyoum-Edjigu, Megan Schmidt, Barbara Lang, Trevor Sandwith, et al. 2019. "Aichi Biodiversity Target 11 in the Like-Minded Megadiverse Countries." *Journal for Nature Conservation* 51. https://doi.org/10.1016/j.jnc.2019.125723

Bennett, Graham, and Kalemani Jo Mulongoy. 2006. "Review of Experience with Ecological Networks, Corridors and Buffer Zones." In *Secretariat of the Convention on Biological Diversity, Montreal, Technical Series* 23.

Butchart, Stuart H.M., Martin Clarke, Robert J. Smith, Rachel E. Sykes, Jörn P.W. Scharlemann, Mike Harfoot, Graeme M. Buchanan, et al. 2015. "Shortfalls and Solutions for Meeting National and Global Conservation Area Targets." *Conservation Letters* 8, no. 5: 329–37. https://doi.org/10.1111/conl.12158

Ceballos, Gerardo, Paul R. Ehrlich, and Rodolfo Dirzo. 2017. "Biological Annihilation via the Ongoing Sixth Mass Extinction Signaled by Vertebrate Population Losses and Declines." *Proceedings of the National Academy of Sciences* 114, no. 30: E6089–E6096. https://doi.org/10.1073/pnas.1704949114

CMS. 2020. "Improving Ways of Addressing Connectivity in the Conservation of Migratory Species, Resolution 12.26 (REV.COP13)," Gandhinagar, India, February 17–22, 2020. UNEP/CMS/COP13/CRP 26.4.4. https://www.cms.int/sites/default /files/document/ cms_cop13_crp26.4.4_addressing-connectivity-in-conservation -of- migratory-species_e_0.docx.

De Vos, Jurriaan M., Lucas N. Joppa, John L. Gittleman, Patrick R. Stephens, and Stuart L. Pimm. 2015. "Estimating the Normal Background Rate of Species Extinction." *Conservation Biology* 29, no. 2: 452–62. https://doi.org/10.1111/cobi.12380

Díaz, Sandra, Josef Settele, Eduardo S. Brondízio, Hien T. Ngo, John Agard, Almut Arneth, Patricia Balvanera, et al. 2019. "Pervasive Human-Driven Decline of Life on Earth Points to the Need for Transformative Change." *Science* 366 (6471). https:// doi.org/10.1126/science.aax3100

Gardner, Toby A., Amrei Von Hase, Susie Brownlie, Jonathan M.M. Ekstrom, John D. Pilgrim, Conrad E. Savy, R.T. Theo Stephens, et al. 2013. "Biodiversity Offsets and the Challenge of Achieving No Net Loss." *Conservation Biology* 27, no. 6: 1254–64. https://doi.org/10.1111/cobi.12118

Hansen, Andrew J., and Ruth DeFries. 2007. "Ecological Mechanisms Linking Protected Areas to Surrounding Lands." *Ecological Applications* 17, no. 4: 974–88. https://doi.org/10.1890/05-1098

Heller, Nicole E., and Erika Zavaleta. 2019. "Biodiversity Management in the Face of Climate Change: A Review of 22 Years of Recommendations." *Biological Conservation* 142: 14–32. https://doi.org/10.1016/j.biocon.2008.10.006

Hilty, Jodi A., Annika T.H. Keeley, Adina M. Merenlender, and William Z. Lidicker Jr. 2019. *Corridor Ecology: Linking Landscapes for Biodiversity Conservation and Climate Adaptation.*Washington DC: Island Press.

Hilty, Jodi, Graeme L. Worboys, Annika Keeley, Stephen Woodley, Barbara Lausche, Harvey Locke, Mark Carr et al. 2020. "Guidelines for Conserving Connectivity through Ecological Networks and Corridors." *IUCN, International Union for Conservation of Nature.* https://doi.org/10.2305/IUCN.CH.2020.PAG.30.en

Hockings, Marc, James Hardcastle, Stephen Woodley, Trevor Sandwith, J. Wildson, Marnie Bammert, Sandra Valenzuela, Béatrice Chataigner, Thierry Lefebvre, and Fiona Leverington. 2019. "The IUCN Green List of Protected and Conserved Areas: Setting the Standard for Effective Area-Based Conservation." *Parks* 25, no. 25.2: 57–66. https://doi.org/10.2305/IUCN.CH.2019.PARKS-25-2MH.en

Indigenous Circle of Experts. 2018. *We Rise Together – Achieving Pathway to Canada Target 1 through the Creation of Indigenous Protected and Conserved Areas in the Spirit and Practice of Reconciliation.* Report and Recommendations of the Indigenous Circle of Experts. March 2018.

IPBES (Intergovernmental Science-Policy Platform on Biodiversity and Ecosystem Services). 2019. "Summary for Policymakers of the Global Assessment Report on Biodiversity and Ecosystem Services of the Intergovernmental Science-Policy Platform on Biodiversity and Ecosystem Services," edited by S. Díaz, J. Settele, E. S. Brondizio, H.T. Ngo, M. Guèze, J. Agard, A. Arneth, P. Balvanera, K.A. Brauman, S.H.M. Butchart, K.M.A. Chan, L.A. Garibaldi, K. Ichii, J. Liu, S.M. Subramanian, G.F. Midgley, P. Miloslavich, Z. Molnár, D. Obura, A. Pfaff, S. Polasky, A. Purvis, J. Razzaque, B. Reyers, R. Roy Chowdhury, Y.J. Shin, I.J. Visseren-Hamakers, K.J. Willis, and C.N. Zayas. Bonn: IPBES Secretariat.

IUCN. 2016. *A Global Standard for the Identification of Key Biodiversity Areas, Version 1.0.* 1st edition. Gland, Switzerland: IUCN.

IUCN and World Commission on Protected Areas (WCPA). 2017. *IUCN Green List of Protected and Conserved Areas: Standard, Version 1.1.* Gland, Switzerland: IUCN.

IUCN-WCPA Task Force on OECMs. 2019. *Recognising and Reporting Other Effective Area-Based Conservation Measures.* Gland, Switzerland: IUCN.

Jones, Kendall R., Oscar Venter, Richard A. Fuller, James R. Allan, Sean L. Maxwell, Pablo Jose Negret, and James EM Watson. 2018. "One-Third of Global Protected Land Is under Intense Human Pressure." *Science* 360, no. 6390: 788–91. https://doi.org/10.1126/science.aap9565

Klein, Carissa J., Christopher J. Brown, Benjamin S. Halpern, Daniel B. Segan, Jennifer McGowan, Maria Beger, and James EM Watson. 2015. "Shortfalls in the Global Protected Area Network at Representing Marine Biodiversity." *Scientific Reports* 5, no. 1: 1–7. https://doi.org/10.1038/srep17539

McCullough, Dale Richard. 1996. *Metapopulations and Wildlife Conservation.* Washington DC: Island Press.

Newmark, William D. 1995. "Extinction of Mammal Populations in Western North American National Parks." *Conservation Biology* 9, no. 3: 512–26. https://doi.org/10.1046/j.1523-1739.1995.09030512.x

Noss, Reed F., Andrew P. Dobson, Robert Baldwin, Paul Beier, Cory R. Davis, Dominick A. Dellasala, John Francis et al. 2012. "Bolder Thinking for Conservation." *Conservation Biology.* 26 (1) 1–4. https://doi.org/10.1111/j.1523-1739.2011.01738.x

O'Leary, Bethan C., Marit Winther-Janson, John M. Bainbridge, Jemma Aitken, Julie P. Hawkins, and Callum M. Roberts. 2016. "Effective Coverage Targets for Ocean Protection." *Conservation Letters* 9, no. 6: 398–404. https://doi.org/10.1111/conl.12247

Rodrigues, Ana S.L., and Kevin J. Gaston. 2001. "How Large Do Reserve Networks Need to Be?." *Ecology Letters* 4, no. 6: 602–9. https://doi.org/10.1046 /j.1461-0248.2001.00275.x

Svancara, L.K., J.R. Brannon, M. Scott, C..R. Groves, R.F. Noss, and R.L. Pressey. 2005. "Policy-Driven versus Evidence-Based Conservation: A Review of Political Targets and Biological Needs." *BioScience* 55: 989–95. https://doi.org /10.1641/0006-3568(2005)055[0989:PVECAR]2.0.CO;2

Svancara, Leona K, J. Ree Brannon, Michael Scott, Craig R. Groves, Reed F. Noss, and Robert L Pressey. 2005. "Policy-Driven versus Evidence-Based Conservation: A Review of Political Targets and Biological Needs." *BioScience* 55 (11): 989–95. https://doi.org/10.1641/0006-3568(2005)055[0989:PVECAR]2.0.CO;2

Venter, Oscar, Eric W. Sanderson, Ainhoa Magrach, James R. Allan, Jutta Beher, Kendall R. Jones, Hugh P. Possingham et al. 2016. "Sixteen Years of Change in the Global Terrestrial Human Footprint and Implications for Biodiversity Conservation." *Nature Communications* 7, no. 1: 1–11. https://doi.org/10.1038/ncomms12558

Visconti, Piero, Stuart H.M. Butchart, Thomas M. Brooks, Penny F. Langhammer, Daniel Marnewick, Sheila Vergara, Alberto Yanosky, and James E.M. Watson. 2019. "Protected Area Targets Post-2020." *Science* 364, no. 6437: 239–41. https://doi .org/10.1126/science.aav6886

Ward, Michelle, Santiago Saura, Brooke Williams, Juan Pablo Ramírez-Delgado, Nur Arafeh-Dalmau, James R. Allan, Oscar Venter, Grégoire Dubois, and James E.M. Watson. 2020. "Just Ten Percent of the Global Terrestrial Protected Area Network Is Structurally Connected via Intact Land." *Nature Communications* 11, no. 1: 1–10. https://doi.org/10.1038/s41467-020-18457-x

Williams, Sara H., Robin Steenweg, Troy Hegel, Mike Russell, Dave Hervieux, and Mark Hebblewhite. 2021. "Habitat Loss on Seasonal Migratory Range Imperils an Endangered Ungulate." *Ecological Solutions and Evidence* 2, no. 1. https://doi .org/10.1002/2688-8319.12039

Wright, Pamela A., Farhad Moghimehfar, and Alison Woodley. 2019. "Canadians' Perspectives on How Much Space Nature Needs." *FACETS* 4, no. 1: 91–104. https:// doi.org/10.1139/facets-2018-0030

Woodley, Stephen, Harvey Locke, Dan Laffoley, Kathy MacKinnon, Trevor Sandwith, and Jane Smart. 2019. "A Review of Evidence for Area-Based Conservation Targets for the Post-2020 Global Biodiversity Framework." *Parks* 25, no. 2: 31–46. https:// doi.org/10.2305/IUCN.CH.2019.PARKS-25-2SW2.en

Woodley, Stephen, Nina Bhola, and Harvey Locke. 2019. "A Global Survey of Conservation Scientists on Global Conservation Targets." *Parks* 25: 19–30. https:// doi.org/10.2305/IUCN.CH.2019.PARKS-25-2SW1.en

11 The Imperative for Transformative Change to Address Biodiversity Loss in Canada

JUSTINA C. RAY

While biodiversity – or the variety of life on earth – is "overwhelmingly perceived as positive, something to conserve, to enhance and to admire" (Brunet et al. 2020), the deteriorating status of ecosystems and species in Canada is not usually a hot topic in public discourse. Rather than a crisis, this is a drama unfolding behind the scenes at an imperceptible rate that occasionally attracts attention in the news or sparks conversations in the playground. One day, it might occur to someone in passing – while having a drink on the porch on an early evening when the spring weather finally turns warm – that she hasn't seen nearly as many bats swooping in the gathering dusk as she used to. Someone else might ask herself what happened to the barn swallows that nested nearby at this time of year, or why, come to think of it, he has seen fewer turtles or snakes crossing the roads this spring than in some others he remembers. Although continued expansion of the human enterprise is more evident than species loss, with nature being paved over and converted to housing and parking lots, even this happens incrementally. The result of numerous independent decisions and actors, the process of change is not perceptible in the day to day. Overall, most individuals will confess a lack of direct connection to this slowly unfolding and largely invisible drama. This ultimately leads to a societal acceptance of such changes to the natural environment due to a collective loss of memory and understanding over just a few generations.

It is an altogether different situation for those who are monitoring, measuring, or tracking such developments or are otherwise intimately connected to species, ecosystems, and the services provided by nature. To us, there is a mounting compilation of evidence for biodiversity loss that is impossible to ignore. What is also evident is the lack of progress on addressing the problem. Those who are involved in the documentation of the problem are the ones most likely to call for transformative change as key to attaining sustainability. (UNEP 2021; McNeely 2021; Grumbine & Xu 2021). The simplest explanation for the recurring use of the term "transformation" in this context is an acknowledgment that business as usual is failing to ameliorate ecological degradation. The crescendo of voices is rising not only because of consolidating consensus that the problems are acute but that they have actually accelerated since the alarm bell first rang. Any measures that have been put in place to ameliorate and manage impacts have had little discernible effect. Quite simply, transformation is a wholesale change to how humans manage and safeguard our natural systems. Díaz et al. (2019) refer to transformation as "a fundamental, system-wide reorganization across technological, economic, and social factors, making sustainability the norm rather than the altruistic exception," while the World Business Council for Sustainable Development (WBCSD 2021) referred to it as "change at a root cause level to deliver fundamentally new outcomes … will require radical ambition, intent and effort across business and governments, throughout economies and societies." In short, "transformative change means doing things differently – not just a little more or less of something we're already doing" (Chan 2019).

Such statements about the condition of the world and the need for structural and systemic change are similar to other calls for transformational change that have arisen from social justice, anti-racism, and the COVID-19 pandemic itself, which collectively make a case for a re-boot in the name of a "green and just" recovery. As explained by McNeely (2021), for example, "COVID-19 provides a powerful incentive and opportunity to address the interconnected issues of human health, climate change, and biodiversity loss in a coordinated and effective manner: to develop a biodefense system for Planet Earth." What is therefore needed is a fundamental re-design that would require wholesale changes in mindset – a reboot as an alternative to incremental change that has maintained the status quo for so many years. And transformative change to achieve sustainability outcomes cannot be considered a success without social justice (Bennett et al. 2020).

What does such a transformation look like for Canada? This chapter addresses this question from the perspective of a conservation scientist who works at the science-policy interface as both a leader within a global non-government organization and an academic. I argue that transformative change should come through mainstreaming biodiversity considerations in decision-making, which itself can only come about through a fundamental shift in values away from an unsustainable and exploitive growth ideology. Transformation should be buoyed by an embrace of Indigenous-led conservation and strong federal leadership with committed actions designed to truly implement the goals and targets in the Kunming-Montreal Global Biodiversity Framework (hereafter, KMGBF; CBD 2022) adopted by Parties to the Convention on Biological Diversity, including law reform across all jurisdictions. I end by reflecting on the vital roles and responsibilities of scientists in particular in providing key support to so many aspects of this endeavour.

The Moment for Canada

Preceded by the United Nations Decade of Biodiversity, 2020 was intended to be the "Year of Biodiversity," and culminate in a Conference of the Parties of the Convention on Biological Diversity (CBD) in October in Kunming, China, where a new strategic plan for achieving the three objectives of the CBD through 2030 was to be decided. Interrupted by the global COVID-19 pandemic, the parties to the CBD slowly built this successor to the Aichi Biodiversity Targets set for 2020 through discussions and documentation on virtual platforms, with the expectation for this framework to serve as the nature counterpart to the 2015 Paris Agreement for climate change. Although none of the Aichi Biodiversity Targets for 2020 was met following 10 years of (attempted) implementation (Secretariat of the CBD, 2020), generally high levels of global motivation have remained nevertheless evident. This is likely explained by a combination of factors, such as the development of the UN Sustainable Development Goals in 2015, the coalescence of distinct but interlocking environmental and justice crises in 2020, and the urgent calls in reports of successive global-scale scientific analyses that are increasing understanding of the consequences of continued degradation of the life support systems of the planet (IPBES 2019; Bradshaw et al. 2021). Following several postponements of the 15th Conference of the Parties (COP15) to the CBD, the summit was held in Montreal in December 2022, with Canada as host and China as president. The framework (CBD 2022) that was ultimately agreed to by the 188 parties who were present is indicative of considerable new ambition. While the protected area targets in land and sea of 30 per cent has received the most attention, many other necessary elements comprise the 23 targets: These range from restoring and halting the loss of areas important to biodiversity and of high ecological integrity and addressing key drivers of biodiversity loss, to many aspects of implementation that include finance and resource mobilization, full integration of biodiversity into policies and regulations, addressing destructive financial subsidies, and the need for business disclosure of "risks, dependencies and impacts" on biodiversity. And it all comes with a monitoring framework with measurable indicators to track progress of goals and targets through 2030. In some ways it can be said that Canada is a leading voice in this global conversation. Canada enjoys a global reputation as an active player in the implementation of Multi-Lateral Environmental Agreements (MEA), such as CBD and the Convention on the International Trade in Endangered Species (CBD). Canada was among the first 50 countries to sign on to the High Ambition Coalition, as per its domestic 30x30 protected area commitment (ECCC 2020), well before the adoption of the KMGBF. In 2021, representatives of the Canadian federal government served as co-chairs of several committees and working groups central to the implementation of both the CBD and CITES, and held leadership positions in multi-lateral funding agencies, such as the Global Environmental

Facility and the Global Climate Fund. Canada stands out in contrast to the US, Australia, and most countries in Europe, Asia, and southern South America, as among those countries at the highest tier of human development (in relation to life expectancy, education, and per capita income) but without pervasive environmental degradation (Blicharska et al. 2019). Indeed, a significant portion of Canada still has intact ecosystems in the north that have not yet been crisscrossed by road networks and large-scale land-clearing activities, and a relatively small human population, with most inhabitants settled within a few hundred kilometres of the border with the US.

That a relatively large proportion of Canada's ecosystems has high levels of ecological integrity is not, however, an indicator of strong protection policies or special consideration of protection of nature as a high political priority. Much has been written about the documentation by the early European "explorers" and colonial settlers of the tremendous abundance of nature and natural resources in Canada, leaving impressions of unlimited wealth to be exploited (Lakanen 2018). Such exploration and discovery came with the subjugation by settlers of Indigenous Peoples and served as the basis for the natural resource-driven economy that defines Canada today, with the third largest per-capita natural resource endowment in the world, contributing to 17 per cent of the country's GDP in 2021 (NRCan 2022). The Canadian approach over the centuries since then has been variously described as favouring resource exportation over domestic processes, heavy subsidization of infrastructure and exploration in order to open areas to development interest, charging of relatively low rents or royalties, and actively welcoming foreign direct investment to develop and remove the products of natural resources from the country. Canada is among 10 economies responsible for more than 68 per cent of global extraction in 2017, with the second highest material extraction per capita (behind Australia; IRP 2019). Aspirations for developing northern areas that remain in ecologically intact condition have been thwarted more by access and economic considerations than by any policy barriers. It seems that the vast size of Canada provides cover for what is in fact expansive industrial development, as the relative proportion of intact ecosystems will remain for some time, even if the development proceeds in an unsustainable fashion (Blicharska et al. 2019).

Other metrics provide more indication of Canada's contribution to environmental degradation. For example, Canada is still the only G7 country to have rising greenhouse gas emissions since the signing of the Paris Agreement in 2015. Canada's resource extraction footprint extends a good deal further than that of settlement, carrying out operations for forestry, oil and gas, hydroelectricity and, increasingly, mineral products. Meanwhile, the status and condition of species and ecosystems in the country exhibit numerous worrying trends (Federal Provincial and Territorial Governments of Canada, 2010), as summarized throughout this book and Ray et al. (2021).

In collaboration with Jaime Grimm and Andrea Olive, I undertook a recent analysis (Ray et al. 2021) of relevant federal and sub-national laws, strategies, plans, and policies to measure how well Canada has implemented the CBD as well as overarching national commitments related to biodiversity and sustainable development. Declining biodiversity trends in many areas of the country indicate that Canada is not displaying particular effectiveness at confronting or addressing the biodiversity crisis within its borders in spite of the many statutes that include provisions to do so. Our analysis of the existing regulatory regime – a patchwork of laws and policies across the 14 jurisdictions – revealed an overall system that has been unable to keep pace with rapidly changing environmental conditions. As of late 2020, there were 201 federal, provincial, and territorial laws that collectively provide fragmented and inadequate protection to biodiversity. Most jurisdictions have laws providing various degrees of land protection, directed attention at species at risk, or limiting overexploitation of biodiversity by managing fisheries or hunting. However, 30 per cent of the 201 statutes are composed of a subset of natural resource extraction laws that explicitly contain provisions for biodiversity but rely on mitigation of impacts with respect to individual activities carried out by various resource sectors. This compilation did not include the numerous statutes in jurisdictions throughout the country, mostly related to oil and gas, coal, mining, and a subset of forestry and so on, that contain no mention of environment or sustainability, with the primary purpose of maximizing yield.

Through powers derived from section 92 of the Constitution, authority over lands and resources gives the provinces the right to regulate their natural-resource industries – an enormously important driver of economic development decisions and concomitant land use change (Kwasniak 2016). This has meant that laws governing natural resource development were originally designed to facilitate development activities under the assumptions that any impacts would be successfully mitigated under largely separate processes and that public land can simultaneously meet the needs of multiple users (Hughes 2016). We now know that this is largely wishful thinking. Yet we remain largely stuck in a mindset that impacts can always be somehow ameliorated – rather than avoided – and that development rather than conservation is the primary purpose of land use and resource planning. Environment ministries that are usually given responsibility for regulating for biodiversity protection are often left directly at odds with natural resource development ministries that, thanks to revenue generation power and status quo decision-making processes, exert far more influence in government.

The Role of Policy and Law in Achieving Transformative Change

Authors of the 2019 landmark report by the International Panel for Biodiversity and Ecosystem Services (IPBES 2019) saw laws and policies as critical levers for achieving change, from setting rules to enforcement. Indeed, this is the premise by which a number of environmental statutes were created following increasing recognition of environmental impacts in both the US and Canada. Canada awakened to environmental problems like pollution and acid rain around the same time as the United States; it wasn't until the early 1970s that a federal ministry of the environment was constituted, although it remained a junior ministry until 1988. This period was defined by positive disposition towards environmental issues and social movements, but nevertheless the federal government at the time conducted largely performative actions, focusing on reporting voluntary measures, with little investment apart from increased bureaucratic capacity (Toner and Meadowcroft 2009; Lakanen et al. 2018). Environmental policy was never effectively operationalized in this period. The focused attention that began only 30 years ago resulted in environmental laws that were layered on top of a chaotic system of natural resource extraction, wildlife and fisheries management laws, and statutes conferring land protection of various strengths (Ray et al. 2021).

There is the sobering realization, as far as biodiversity is concerned, that many laws that exist in Canada have passed their expiration date and are collectively ineffective in addressing impacts from direct threats, especially habitat loss and degradation. These pressures come about primarily through clearing of forests, wetlands, grasslands, and other natural areas for human dwellings, infrastructure, and development activities, with varying success at replacing this habitat. By and large, the pace and scale of the change is not being matched, even remotely, by mitigation and restoration efforts. And while the original definition of "sustainable development" by the Brundtland Commission (WCED 1987) was very careful to emphasize the well-being of future generations, the use of this term has since devolved mostly into a balancing act between the competing interests of economy, environment, and society (Locke et al. 2021).

The counterview to this depiction of weak biodiversity protection is that Canada is already over-regulated (a negative sign of strong governance; Worldwide Governance Indicators), and is therefore falling behind in economic opportunities. Such a perception tends to consider threats from biodiversity loss and climate change to be exaggerated – or certainly not sufficient to stand in the way of economic progress or the achievement of self-sufficiency. Even without oil and gas resources, mineral riches should be contributing to the transition to a low-carbon economy (Critical Minerals; NRCan 2022), but there is a chorus of concern regarding the lack of progress in developing these precious resources. Joining this view is the notion that all harm to biodiversity can and is already being routinely and successfully mitigated through measures that render activities less harmful than they otherwise would be were they to have no such attention, with progress fueled by technological advances. That approval processes that proponents are subjected to take years and foster reams of paperwork and preparation only accentuate concerns of over-regulation. Accompanying this have been multiple efforts to streamline processes and reduce the regulatory burden by various governments, both federal and provincial/territorial, across the political spectrum, with progress tracked each year by the *Provincial Red Tape Report Card* (CFIA 2021). This was, to a certain extent, accentuated by the pandemic, whereby the federal government and most provinces relaxed environmental rules to make way for much needed economic growth following lockdowns (Goodday 2021).

Calls to Action

Amid such tensions, the IPBES (2019) assessment and the COVID-19 pandemic have nevertheless placed biodiversity, and human connections to wildlife, on the public agenda worldwide. The pandemic not only exposed once again the links between zoonotic disease risk and environmental degradation, but the enormous economic consequences of failing to invest in preventative actions (Dobson et al. 2020; Bernstein et al. 2022) and the essential role of natural areas and green spaces for human well-being (WHO 2020). Habitat loss and degradation as the primary cause of terrestrial biodiversity loss points to the need to make area-based conservation a major anchor of action, and Canada has made significant progress in the past few years on its promise to meet its Aichi Biodiversity Target 11 for land and marine protection and proactive commitment to the 30x30 agenda. However, such efforts must be complemented by effective sustainable development measures outside protected areas. Indeed, Article 8 of the CBD makes clear that there are many additional needs relevant to in situ protection of biodiversity, including (but not limited to) sustainable development outside protected areas. Looking ahead, and particularly in view of domestic implementation of the new KMGBF, it is clear that more ambition will be necessary, and that we need to quickly step up our game.

Mainstreaming Biodiversity

Traditionally speaking, conservation actions are primarily executed by altogether different actors from those directly responsible for the damage. In a collective sense, such actions lag behind impacts, as they tend to be undertaken in a piecemeal and reactive fashion, consistently compromising the need to address indirect and cumulative effects at meaningful scales (Millner-Guiland et al. 2021). Government organizational structures universally reflect this kind of siloed approach, with those departments or offices focused on biodiversity goals being entirely separated from those focused on development and economic growth, and comparatively underfunded. With economic prosperity being the prime overarching goal of most governments, this sets up a situation whereby biodiversity conservation will not receive political, social, and financial support that is so necessary for success (Redford et al. 2015). This challenge and the need to "integrate, as far as possible and as appropriate, the conservation and sustainable use of biological diversity into relevant sectoral or cross-sectoral plans, programs, and policies" was already recognized in the text of the Convention itself back in 1992. And amid growing appreciation for the direct links between biodiversity and human well-being, the concept of "mainstreaming" has received increasing attention.

Defined as "embedding biodiversity considerations into policies, strategies, and practices of key public and private actors that impact or rely on biodiversity, so that it is conserved, and sustainably used, both locally and globally" (Huntley and Redford, 2014), mainstreaming calls for a whole-of-government approach. In practice, this would mean bringing biodiversity into the core agenda and objectives of decision-making and being deliberately considered at the outset by all policy sectors. This would have to replace the current system, which places the safeguarding of species and ecosystems as an afterthought to core government business – actions that environmental agencies are left largely on their own to execute or coordinate, once many options are precluded.

In Canada, discussion of mainstreaming of biodiversity and ecosystem services has been virtually absent from any government documentation. In the CBD *2010–2020 Strategic Plan for Biodiversity*, containing the Aichi Goals and Targets and signed by Canada, mainstreaming was articulated as an explicit goal (Aichi Strategic Goal A). This was not, however, even mentioned in the *2020 Biodiversity Goals and Targets for Canada*, formulated in 2015 as a belated expression of adoption of the global goals and targets. Mainstreaming likewise received no mention in the latest reports by Canada to the CBD (ECCC 2019), other than in reference to integrating biodiversity into the elementary and secondary school curricula. The notion of applying a "green lens" to some policies and programs has had some recognition in the context of federal sustainable development as early as the 90s, in the form of a cabinet directive. This places a requirement on federal government agencies to incorporate environmental considerations in their reviews of national-level proposals, plans, and programs – including positive and negative effects – and report these to the public. Implementation of this directive has, however, had a weak history (ENVI 2016; Noble et al. 2019). The reality in Canada is that the primacy of revenue generation in the context of profit maximization in competitive markets has traditionally driven government actions, leaving biodiversity considerations out of the mainstream of planning and decision-making, (M'Gonigle and Takeda 2013; Bond et al. 2020).

When it comes to combatting climate change, the federal government is somewhat further ahead in applying a "climate lens" to decision-making, for example as a requirement for proposed large infrastructure projects seeking federal funding. Fighting climate change, or at least a "clean environment," appears at the top of many mandate letters to federal ministers, and a federal climate plan released in late 2020 (ECCC 2020b) contained a pledge to "apply a climate lens to integrate climate considerations throughout government decision-making". While no implementation details were included in this aspirational document, it did characterize this move as a "transformation." But still, it may be telling that the plan was issued by Environment and Climate Change Canada and not the Office of the Prime Minister. Nevertheless, domestic implementation of the KMGBF will certainly spark conversations about broadening this lens beyond climate to biodiversity.

True implementation of mainstreaming of environmental issues would of course require significant institutional reform and shifts in the prevailing mindset. For biodiversity mainstreaming, there appears to be greater impetus for implementation in those countries that can readily perceive the short-term economic advantages of doing so, where they have intimate connections with biodiversity and ecosystem services, including a tight reliance on primary production sectors, and where there has been less accumulation of laws and regulations over time (Whitehorn et al. 2019). While addressing the impacts of climate change is being increasingly recognized as imperative for economic prosperity in Canada, similar recognition of such linkages between biodiversity and humanity lags further behind (ENVI 2016).

Valuing Biodiversity

Opening a pathway to achieving this necessary transformation could be enabled by increased levels of understanding by decision-makers and society at large of how biodiversity loss is indeed connected to the well-being of humanity (Bradshaw et al. 2021). To this end, the voices of other disciplines are starting to add to the chorus of ecologists and conservation biologists raising alarm bells. In its most recent annual Global Risks Report (WEF 2023) issued in January 2022 in the middle of a global pandemic by the World Economic Forum, environmental risks once again dominate the highest global risks in a 5–10-year time frame. To put this into perspective, environmental issues were not even mentioned among the top global risks in WEF's 2007 report. By contrast, in 2023 "biodiversity loss and ecosystem collapse is viewed as one of the fastest deteriorating global risks over the next decade." An independent report commissioned by the UK Treasury (Dasgupta 2021), stated among several headline messages that "our unsustainable engagement with Nature is endangering the prosperity of current and future generations" with demands outstripping capacity. Put in economic terms, "we have failed to manage our global portfolio of assets sustainably … endangering the prosperity of current and future generations." The author, a leading economist at Cambridge University, went on to stress that because the prevailing measure of economic activity, GDP, does not account for the depreciation of natural capital assets, its use encourages the pursuit of unsustainable economic growth and development. Liquidating biological systems in order to finance economic growth and ignoring this element in decision-making must end (Rees 2020). This would require not only a drive to increase the global supply of natural assets and a halt to subsidies and other financial flows that harm them but also a move to measure wealth in a more inclusive fashion by including natural capital into national accounting. Again, accomplishing this would require a transformation of our institutions and systems (Dasgupta 2021).

The pandemic itself has put this imbalance into even sharper focus, which may help heighten the imperative for change. As remarked by McNeely (2021), "COVID-19 has exposed some of the major environmental problems caused by the dominant economic model that has been pushing global growth in resource consumption for the past 75 years." Similarly, the World Health Organization issued a manifesto several months into the pandemic, placing biodiversity, and the mainstreaming thereof, as a central pillar of a healthy and green recovery. Their number one "prescription" was to "protect and preserve the source of human health: Nature," in recognition that lessening humanity's impact on the environment will be necessary to "reduce the risk at source" (WHO 2020). At the same time, however, the pandemic has exposed profound disparities and societal weaknesses, like the widening and persistent inequality and resulting disproportionate costs (measured in illness and death) borne by racialized communities in particular. And with the Black Lives Matter movement having reached new heights during this same period, all this carries with it a common thread that continuing much longer with business as usual is just not an option. It also reminds us that tackling the biodiversity crisis cannot be resolved without addressing a number of entwined, but still separate, fundamental social justice issues. As such, transformation will require an intersectional approach to addressing the systemic issues at the root of all these problems (Bennet et al. 2020; Massarrella 2021).

Making Way for Indigenous-Led Conservation

One key feature of any strategy moving forward will be the resurgent role of Indigenous-led conservation. Already in Canada, this is at the leading edge of potential transformative change. In their landmark report, the Indigenous Circle of Experts (ICE 2018) put forward a case for how Indigenous Protected and Conserved Areas (IPCAs) represent a long-term commitment to conservation while elevating Indigenous rights and responsibilities. A pivot away from the negative legacy of protected area creation in Canada that resulted in the displacement of Indigenous Peoples and their practices to make way for recreational experiences – the principal impetus for park creation in the early days – marks an opportunity to "rebuild our natural heritage for future generations."

Additional imperatives relate to the increasing recognition of inherent Indigenous rights, as confirmed by numerous high court decisions, and the need for Indigenous consent in land-use decisions, thereby supporting meaningful reconciliation and enacting the principles of the United Nations Declaration on the Rights of Indigenous Peoples.

The fact is that there is room for substantial growth for this model of governance. This is particularly (although not exclusively) the case in as-yet ecologically intact northern regions where there are opportunities at appropriate scales for complete ecosystem conservation and where Indigenous communities are already demonstrating leadership, supported in part by federal government expenditures (Zurba et al. 2019; Artelle et al. 2019). Similar to ecosystem protection, there is a good case to be made that species conservation would benefit from the implementation of management approaches that are grounded in traditional Indigenous systems. For one thing, their multi-generational scope could be a welcome alternative to prevailing models of contemporary resource management that emphasize extraction for short-term profits (Atlas et al. 2020).

The Need for Federal Leadership and a New Biodiversity Strategy and Action Plan

The ICE report and the process underlying its development was made possible by targeted investment by the federal government, both financially and through its public embrace of IPCAs as a cornerstone to achieving the so-called Pathway to Canada Target 1, or "at least 17% of terrestrial areas and inland water ... conserved through networks of protected areas and other effective area-based conservation measures." Launched in 2017, the Pathway process stimulated new excitement in the country about the potential for enhanced (in both quality and quantity) protection of nature, through use of a fiscal lever whereby a relatively small federal expenditure of less than $200 million incentivized cooperation and action. This represented a marked departure from the usual deferential treatment of provinces in matters of biodiversity protection (e.g., species-at-risk recovery), in contrast to traditionally high policy priorities such as health, education, and infrastructure. While constitutional realities place real limits on the use of federal authority to address biodiversity conservation that cannot deny the right of provinces and territories to regulate their natural-resource industries, there is an important place for skilful use of federal government authority to play an effective leadership role without abandoning cooperative federalism. In his multi-decadal examination of policy failures related to climate change, Macdonald (2020) made a strong case not only for the necessity of federal leadership to effectively implement a collaborative national policy in this arena, but that this must be led by first ministers, and not only environmental ministers. A National Advisory Panel struck at the same time as the ICE as part of the Pathway to Canada Target 1 process, placed similar emphasis in its recommendations on the need for federal leadership and financial investment, but also called for structural change. A new nature conservation architecture, consisting of a new federal Nature Conservation Department and associated federal law, "would facilitate the alignment of provincial and territorial governments' conservation institutions and responsibilities with Canada's international commitments" (NAP 2018).

Recent federal government budgets have included a similar scale of investment to nature protection in keeping with campaign and platform pledges and membership in the international High Ambition Coalition. For example, hidden as an annexe in the 724-page 2021 federal budget document was a "quality of life framework," intended to "bring a long-term perspective to its decision-making and ensure today's prosperity and quality of life is not achieved at the expense of future generations, whether through environmental degradation, unsustainable debt levels, or under-investment in the productive capacity of the economy" (Government of Canada 2021).

Less encouraging indicators of federal leadership are illustrated by Canada's implementation history of its "National Biodiversity Action Plan and Strategy" – the principal implementation instrument of the CBD and its reporting obligations as a party to the Convention (Ray et al. 2021). While the federal government clearly has the power to negotiate and ratify an international treaty, its implementation of such commitments relies a great deal on provincial and territorial actions. Yet, the CBD envisions NBSAPs to be strong instruments of implementation, intended to be whole-of-government policies that facilitate "biodiversity mainstreaming at all relevant levels within political, economic, and social sectors" (see CBD Subsidiary Body on Implementation 2018, 1). The current Biodiversity Strategy for Canada is more than 25 years old (Government of Canada 1995). And while the Canadian translation of the 2010–20 *Aichi Biodiversity Targets* (CBD 2010) is much more recent (2015; biodivcanada n.d.), it represents a cherry-picked version of the global goals and targets, which was focused primarily on sustainable use, and paid far less attention to reducing pressures on biodiversity.

As National Focal Point for the CBD, the federal government's role in Canada has been primarily devoted to coordinating and reporting on the progress on implementation of the biodiversity strategy, similar to sustainable development (ENVI 2016). Reporting represents a "roll up" of provincial inputs and is generally conducted without any accompanying analysis of the degree to which the country as a whole is meeting its international obligations under the treaty, and without comment on potential course adjustments that could or should be made.

A comprehensive NBSAP for domestic implementation of the post-2020 Global Biodiversity Framework will now be needed to replace the aged and incomplete Canadian Biodiversity Strategy. The process to develop the new strategy and associated action plan could play a key role in defining how transformative change to address biodiversity loss could be achieved. It could include actions discussed here, such as mainstreaming biodiversity considerations into policymaking across jurisdictions, proper valuation of nature as an asset, and defining the nature of cooperative implementation across Canada, including Indigenous-led conservation. This would provide an opportunity to identify the regulatory, legislative, enforcement, financing, and accountability measures required to deliver the strategy and address the ongoing loss of biodiversity and ecosystem services.

Biodiversity Law Reform

There will be some imperative to consider the compendium of relevant laws that are currently layered on top of one another in any given jurisdiction. Until very recently, there were no statutes in Canada devoted to biodiversity conservation per se, that is, with conservation of species and ecosystems as the overriding objectives. Yet, over 200 laws (as of 2020) across all 14 jurisdictions are currently in place that address certain elements of biodiversity, usually as secondary to other objectives (Ray et al. 2021). Law reform in Canada designed to address biodiversity loss would be best to proceed in two directions: (1) reform of natural resource sector laws to rebalance laws that have economic considerations as overriding factors built in; and (2) new comprehensive biodiversity statutes that integrate issues other than protected areas, species at risk, and management of hunting and fishing into regulatory frameworks that include accountability mechanisms.

Statutory reforms will, however, not succeed without fundamental structural and cultural shifts. For example, at present the structure in which environmental law is embedded is impossible to divorce from the imperative of production, forcing environmental regulation to take a back seat. As such, jurisdictions have an inherent conflict of interest between protecting and developing the resources that they rely on for revenue and economic growth (M'Gonigle & Takeda 2013; Ray et al. 2021). Viewed in this light, the bureaucratic scale of the modern "administrative state is geared almost entirely to the legalization of natural resource damage … [with] the majority of agencies spend[ing] nearly all of their resources to permit, rather than prohibit, environmental destruction" (Wood 2012). The broader goal of expanding and intensifying production goes effectively unchallenged, on the increasingly weak premise that negative impacts can be mitigated. It remains "economic heresy and political suicide" to speak of limits to growth (M'Gonigle & Takeda 2013), even as evidence piles up that the cumulative impacts of human activities in many respects have already exceeded even planetary boundaries (Steffen et al. 2015).

Accordingly, effective biodiversity governance will require a regulatory environment that builds much greater awareness of natural limits into planning and decision-making processes and reverses the current approach of land-use conversion being a foregone conclusion (possibly with mitigation). Instead, such governance would result in a system where all such conversion must be considered within the context of clear evidence-based limits – similar to the notion of a carbon budget for climate. Shifting to such a regime will have to be accompanied by investment in biodiversity monitoring and cumulative effects assessment at appropriate planning scales and tightly linked to transparent decision-making. This, after all, is in keeping with the conceptual vision of sustainable development, that is "to create 'strong, healthy, and just societies,' and yet remain within the ecological limits of a finite planet (Daly 1991; Steffen et al. 2015).

In March 2021, a Biodiversity Act: An Act to Provide for the Conservation and Sustainable Use of Biodiversity in Nova Scotia was introduced and then enacted the following month. While its debate and passage went largely unnoticed outside the province, the passage of this statute represents an important lesson for us in at least two ways. First, the words of the law itself are unique in including a complete definition of biodiversity with all its elements that must be managed for future generations, as well as an explicit acknowledgment that conservation and sustainable use of biodiversity is a "complex, cross-cutting imperative" that is not being addressed at present in the patchwork of existing laws. However promising this may seem, the more sobering lesson became apparent during the controversy of its passage, when enormous pushback generated by an organized industry-sponsored campaign eventually led to the removal of numerous whole sections of the bill. While the pure existence of the bill, and by a provincial government, provides some not insignificant promise of a step in the right direction, it remains a purely enabling statute that merely grants the responsible ministry the power to take certain actions. The Act will not come into force until regulations are developed, and this in turn will rely on the forward thinking of future politicians and bureaucrats who have the courage to be indeed enabled by the possibilities for transformation inherent in this statute. However, anyone who doesn't want to take such action, will not, for the time being at least, be punished due to their recalcitrance. Biodiversity remains a bread-and-butter issue only until it is perceived to interfere with economic priorities or personal freedom.

The Role of Scientists

In closing, I am compelled to reflect on the particular role of conservation scientists during what may be an inflection point for the biodiversity crisis in Canada. For one thing, affecting the needed societal transformation discussed in this paper will require enhanced public understanding of the extent and urgency of the problem. As explained by Eden and Geoghegan (2017, 2):

> Many environmental issues originate in scientific work, which often identifies and measures the issue, for example, stratospheric ozone pollution or climate change. This is one reason why opinion polls often report that the public trust scientists more than any other profession in society, including business and government, to tell the truth about environmental issues. Because of their specialized training and expertise, scientists are often regarded as being knowledgeable about environmental issues and as having solutions or answers to environmental problems as well as pursuing facts, data, and truth for its own sake without being affected by the need to make a profit as a business might do. Scientists and scientific writings, such as journal articles or reports, can be particularly important in influencing public understanding of environmental issues because many environmental problems cannot be perceived by ordinary people.

The numerous articles and high-profile reports that have been issued in recent years by scientists testifying to the deteriorating state of global biodiversity have been often accompanied by major investments in plain language summaries, infographics, and blogs to support the clarity of key messages. This has represented a kind of a shift for scientists, who have engaged in much debate over the years about the appropriate roles and responsibilities of scientists in policy-making, and the extent to which evidence-based science drives, or even influences, environmental policy-making. But there have been more recent calls for the scientific community in particular to be more vocal about their warnings to humanity. For example, under the grim title "Underestimating the Challenges of Avoiding a Ghastly Future," Bradshaw et al. (2021) make a convincing argument that it is "incumbent on experts in any discipline that deals with the future of the biosphere and human well-being to eschew reticence, avoid sugar-coating the overwhelming challenges ahead and 'tell it like it is.'" Scientists are indeed bringing themselves from background voices to the frontlines, yielding impressive reports and media hits, with more individuals comfortable in the spotlight, to explain in clear terms what is happening and what is at stake with global biodiversity. Science communications has emerged as a special skill that is being taught in university and training programs. Some notable biodiversity-related examples include the release of the flagship inaugural IPBES report in 2019, the flurry of peer-reviewed papers by scientists bringing insight and evidence to bear on the development of the Global Biodiversity Framework (e.g., Grumbine et al. 2021; Williams et al. 2021), and the rising interest of individual scientists in speaking directly to policy makers and others via social media, especially Twitter (Côté and Darling 2018).

In Canada, biodiversity research, ranging from basic inventory and monitoring to analysis of impacts across knowledge systems, to identification of Key Biodiversity Areas (kbacanada.org), should play an ever-increasing role, supported by sustained funding. There are, of course, so many biodiversity topics that are ripe for innovation, but we should first and foremost be humbled by our overall ignorance of the natural world. For example, we know there are about 80,000 species at present, but also that there are potentially many more. Around a third of those species that have been assessed lack any information to evaluate their status (CESCC 2023). We simply do not know enough about the creatures with which we share our planet to provide them with proper safeguards. As E.O. Wilson pointed out recently (Wilson 2017), "the discovery and description of Earth's biodiversity is the oldest biological science, yet it is the least developed," and he wasn't even addressing the detailed knowledge on biodiversity and ecosystem trends possessed by Indigenous Peoples that must be deliberately included in applied ecosystems research and ecological assessments. The irony is that the prevailing approach to managing our impacts assumes that actions to mitigate our damage are universally successful. This calls for increased investment to achieve much better understanding of our natural world and responses of species and ecosystems to environmental change, combined with the development of accurate and efficient monitoring systems.

With most attention to biodiversity decline focused on tropical regions of the world, the global assessments that dominate the literature do not always have obvious relevance to Canada from a policy-maker's vantage point. Therefore, scientific energy in Canada could be harnessed in the near term towards the conduct of Canada-focused collection data and information across this vast country to help ensure that any transformation is underpinned by the best available evidence. A Dasgupta-style report focused on Canada would be likewise beneficial, so as to make the process of proper valuation of biodiversity as a quantifiable asset that feels real to Canadians. And Canadian natural and social scientists alike are needed to help translate the results of the global reports to Canadian audiences and explain their relevance to Canada, and why and how actions in Canada can make a difference.

Conclusion

The time for transformative change to address biodiversity loss and degradation in Canada is now. The COVID-19 pandemic and the ensuing economic upheaval have shown the dangers of ecosystem degradation, as well as the need for international cooperation and greater social and economic resilience. Although the sustainable future of biodiversity receives less attention than climate change (e.g., Legagneux et al. 2018) in Canada, the condition of lands and oceans as functional carbon sinks will be critical for combatting the climate crisis (Carroll and Ray 2021). Accordingly, biodiversity can no longer be regarded as a boutique issue, important only to those who have time to consider it, but instead as a critical asset that has tangible value for human well-being. It is simply not possible to ignore the welfare of species and ecosystems with which we share the planet, because similar to the climate emergency, ecosystem collapse will impact us all.

Clearly, the biodiversity crisis won't be resolved by small solutions, which is all that has been attempted so far in Canada. Rather, actions that will be required to resolve problems must be conceived of and executed at the scale of the problems themselves. This chapter has argued that transformative change in Canada will necessitate a whole-of-government approach to everything from budgeting to policy-making, a shift in mindset to how we value nature, an embrace of Indigenous-led conservation, strong federal leadership, and accompanying law reform.

Naturally, transformative change will continue to be opposed by those with economic interests vested in the status quo; this will persist as long as biodiversity remains relegated to the margins as an ignored externality and while biodiversity is disregarded as an asset (Dasgupta 2021). We can take heart both that societal transformation has occurred multiple times before in history and that an increasingly diverse set of voices (including business) is calling for a shift in mindset for transformative change, given the convergent global challenges of the loss of nature with the climate emergency and growing inequality (WBSCD 2021).

WORKS CITED

Artelle Kyle A., M. Zurba, J. Bhattacharyya, D.E. Chan, K. Brown, J. Housty, and F. Moola. 2019. "Supporting Resurgent Indigenous-Led Governance: A Nascent Mechanism for Just and Effective Conservation." *Biological Conservation* 240. https://doi.org /10.1016/j.biocon.2019.108284

Atlas W.I., N.C. Ban, J.W. Moore, A.M. Tuohy, S. Greening, A.J. Reid, et al. 2020. "Indigenous Systems of Management for Culturally and Ecologically Resilient

Pacific Salmon (*Oncorhynchus spp.*) Fisheries." *BioScience* 71, no. 2: 186–204. https://doi.org/10.1093/biosci/biaa144

Bennett, Nathan J., Jessica Blythe, Andrés M. Cisneros-Montemayor, Gerald G. Singh, and U. Rashid Sumail. 2020. "Just Transformations to Sustainability." *Sustainability* 11 (14): 3881; https://doi.org/10.3390/su11143881

Bernstein, Aaron S. et al. 2022. "The Costs and Benefits of Primary Prevention of Zoonotic Pandemics." *Scientific Advances* 8, no. 5. https://doi.org/10.1126/sciadv .abl4183

Blicharska, Malgorzata, Richard J. Smithers, Grzegorz Mikusiński, Patrik Rönnbäck, Paula A. Harrison, Måns Nilsson, and William J. Sutherland. 2019. "Biodiversity's Contributions to Sustainable Development." *Nature Sustainability* 2: 1083–93. https://doi.org/10.1038/s41893-019-0417-9

Bond, Alan, J. Pope, M. Fundingsland, A. Morrison-Saunders, F. Retief, and M. Hauptfleisch. 2020. "Explaining the Political Nature of Environmental Impact Assessment (EIA): A Neo-Gramscian Perspective." *Journal of Cleaner Production* 244. https://doi.org/10.1016 /j.jclepro.2019.118694

Bradshaw, Corey J.A., Paul R. Ehrlich, Andrew Beattie, Gerardo Ceballos, Eileen Crist, Joan Diamond, Rodolfo Dirzo, Anne H. Ehrlich, John Harte, Mary Ellen Harte, Graham Pyke, Peter H. Raven, William J. Ripple, Frédérik Saltré, Christine Turnbull, Mathis Wackernagel, and Daniel T. Blumstein. 2021. "Underestimating the Challenges of Avoiding a Ghastly Future." *Frontiers in Conservation Science* 1. https://doi.org/10.3389/fcosc.2020.615419

Brunet, Nicolas D., Danielle Dagenais, Sandra Breux, and Tanya Handa. 2020. "A Characterization of Media Representation of Biodiversity and Implications for Public Perceptions and Environmental Policy: The Case of Québec, Canada." *Environment, Development and Sustainability* 22: 1655–69. https://doi.org/10.1007 /s10668-018-0244-6

Carroll C., and J.C. Ray. 2021. "Maximizing the Effectiveness of National Commitments to Protected Area Expansion for Conserving Biodiversity and Ecosystem Carbon under Climate Change." *Global Change Biology*. https://doi.org /10.1111/gcb.15645. PMID: 33852186.

CBD (Convention on Biological Diversity). 2010. "The Strategic Plan for Biodiversity 2011– 2020 and the Aichi Biodiversity Targets." 10th Conference of the Parties, Nagoya, Japan. https://www.cbd.int/sp/.

CBD. 2022. "COP15: Final Text of Kunming-Montreal Global Biodiversity Framework. Decision 15/4." 15th Conference of the Parties, Montreal, Quebec, Canada. https:// www.cbd.int/doc/c/e6d3/cd1d/daf663719a03902a9b116c34/cop-15-l-25-en.pdf

CESCC (Canadian Endangered Species Conservation Council). 2022. "Wild Species 2020: The General Status of Species in Canada." National General Status Working Group. https://www.registrelep-sararegistry.gc.ca/virtual_sara/files/reports /Wild%20Species%202015.pdf.

Chan, Kai. 2019. "What Is Transformative Change, and How Do We Achieve It?: Think Globally: Act Locally," Intergovernmental Science-Policy Platform on Biodiversity and Ecosystem Services Guest Blog, November 2019. https://ipbes.net/news/what -transformative-change-how-do-we-achieve-it

Côté, Isabelle M., and Emily S. Darling. 2018. "Scientists on Twitter: Preaching to the Choir or Singing from the Rooftops?" *FACETS.* https://doi.org/10.1139/facets -2018-0002

Daly, Herman E. 1991. *Steady-State Economics: With New Essays.* Washington, DC: Island Press.

Dasgupta, Partha 2021. *The Economics of Biodiversity: The Dasgupta Review.* London: HM Treasury.

Díaz, Sandra, Josef Settele, Eduardo S. Brondizio et al. 2019. "Pervasive Human-Driven Decline of Life on Earth Points to the Need for Transformative Change." *Science* 366 (6471). https://doi.org/10.1126/science.aax3100

Dobson, Andrew P., Stuart L. Pimm, Lee Hannah, et al. 2020. "Ecology and Economics for Pandemic Prevention." *Science* 369 (6502): 379–81. https://doi.org/10.1126 /science.abc3189

ECCC (Environment and Climate Change Canada). 2019. "Summary of Canada's 6th National Report to the Convention on Biological Diversity." Gatineau, QC, Government of Canada. https://biodivcanada.chm-cbd.net/sites/biodivcanada /files/inline-files/EN_Summary%20of%20Canada%27s%206th%20National %20Report_Final_2.pdf.

– 2020a. "Canada Joins the High Ambition Coalition for Nature and People." https:// www.newswire.ca/news-releases/canada-joins-the-high-ambition-coalition-for -nature-and-people-847311784.html.

– 2020b. "A Healthy Environment and a Healthy Economy: Canada's Strengthened Climate Plan to Create Jobs and Support People, Communities and the Planet." Ottawa. https://www.canada.ca/content/dam/eccc/documents/pdf/climate-change /climate-plan/healthy_environment_healthy_economy_plan.pdf

Eden, Sally, and Hilary Geoghegan. 2017. "Environmental Issues and Public Understanding." In *International Encyclopedia of Geography: People, the Earth, Environment and Technology,* edited by D. Richardson, N. Castree, M.F. Goodchild, A. Kobayashi, W. Liu, and R.A. Marston. Wiley Online Library. https://doi.org /10.1002/9781118786352.wbieg1065

ENVI (Standing Committee on Environment and Sustainable Development). 2016. "Federal Sustainability for Future Generations: A Report Following an Assessment of the Federal Sustainable Development Act." ENVI Committee Report. June 2016, 42nd Parliament, 1st Session. https://www.ourcommons.ca/DocumentViewer/en /42-1/ENVI/report-2/page-5.

Federal, Provincial and Territorial Governments of Canada. 2010. "Canadian Biodiversity: Ecosystem Status and Trends." Canadian Councils of Resource Ministers.

Ottawa, ON. https://biodivcanada.chm-cbd.net/ecosystem-status-trends-2010
/canadian-biodiversity-ecosystem-status-and-trends-2010-full-report

Goodday, Victoria. 2021. "Environmental Regulation and the COVID-19 Pandemic: A
Review of Regulator Response in Canada." The School of Public Policy Publications
Briefing Paper 14, no. 1. Calgary: University of Calgary. http://dx.doi.org/10.11575
/sppp.v14i.71913.

Government of Canada. 1995. "Canadian Biodiversity Strategy Canada's Response to
the Convention on Biological Diversity 1995." https://biodivcanada.chm-cbd.net/sites
/biodivcanada/files/2017-12/CBS_e.pdf

– 2021. "Measuring What Matters: Toward a Quality of Life Strategy for Canada."
https://www.canada.ca/en/department-finance/services/publications/measuring
-what-matters-toward-quality-life-strategy-canada.html#Toc61968295

Grumbine, R. Edward, and Jianchu Xu. 2021. "Five Steps to Inject Transformative
Change into the Post-2020 Global Biodiversity Framework." *BioScience* vol. 71, no. 6:
637–46. https://doi.org/10.1093/biosci/biab013

Hughes Elaine L. 2016. "The Future of Public Lands and Natural Resources Law." In
Public Lands and Resources Law in Canada, edited by E.L. Hughes, A.J. Kwasniak,
and A.R. Lucas. Toronto, Ontario: Irwin Law Inc.

Huntley, Brian J., and Kent H. Redford. 2014. "Mainstreaming Biodiversity in Practice:
A STAP Advisory Document." Global Environment Facility, Washington, DC.
http://www.thegef.org/sites/default/files/publications/Mainstreaming-Biodiversity
-LowRes_1.pdf

Indigenous Circle of Experts. 2018. *We Rise Together: Achieving Pathway to Target 1 through
the Creation of Indigenous Protected and Conserved Areas in the Spirit and Practice of
Reconciliation*. https://static1.squarespace.com/static/57e007452e69cf9a7af0a033
/t/5ab94aca6d2a7338ecb1d05e/1522092766605/PA234-ICE_Report_2018_Mar_22
_web.pdf

International Resource Panel. 2019. "Global Resources Outlook 2019: Natural
Resources for the Future We Want." UN Environment Programme. https://www
.resourcepanel. org/reports/global-resources-outlook

IPBES. 2019. "Global Assessment Report of the Intergovernmental Science-Policy
Platform on Biodiversity and Ecosystem Services," edited by S. Díaz, J. Settele,
E. Brondízio, and H.T. Ngo. Bonn, Germany: IPBES Secretariat. https://doi.org
/10.5281/zenodo.3553579.

Kwasniak, Arlene J. 2016. "Source of Jurisdiction and Control." In *Public Lands and
Resources Law in Canada*, edited by E.L. Hughes, A.J. Kwasniak, and A.R. Lucas.
Toronto, Ontario: Irwin Law Inc.

Lakanen, Raili. 2018. "Dissent and Descent: Tracing Canada's Environmental
Governance from Regulatory Beginnings to Dismissal and Reversals by the Harper
Government." *Local Environment* 23 (5): 549–64. https://doi.org/10.1080/13549839
.2018.1444589

Legagneux, Pierre, et al. 2018. "Our House Is Burning: Discrepancy in Climate Change vs. Biodiversity Coverage in the Media as Compared to Scientific Literature." *Frontiers in Ecology and Evolution*, 5. https://doi.org/10.3389/fevo.2017.00175.

M'Gonigle Michael, and Louise Takeda. 2013. "The Liberal Limits of Environmental Law: A Green Legal Critique." *Pace Environmental Law Review*, 30 (3). http://digitalcommons.pace.edu/pelr/vol30/iss3/4

Massarella, Kate et al. 2021. "Transformation beyond Conservation: How Critical Social Science Can Contribute to a Radical New Agenda in Biodiversity Conservation." *Current Opinion in Environmental Sustainability* 49 (April 2021): 79–87. https://doi.org/10.1016/j.cosust.2021.03.005

McNeely, Jeffrey A. 2021. "How to Conserve Biological Diversity: Perspectives from *Ambio*." *Ambio* 50, 957–61. https://doi.org/10.1007/s13280-020-01479-6

NAP (National Advisory Panel). 2018. "Canada's Conservation Vision: A Report of the National Advisory Panel." https://static1.squarespace.com/static/57e007452e69cf9a7af0a033/t/5b23dce1562fa7bac7ea095a/1529076973600/NAP_REPORT_EN_June+5_ACC.pdf.

Natural Resources Canada (NRCan) 2022. "10 Key Facts on Canada's Natural Resources." https://www.nrcan.gc.ca/sites/nrcan/files/emmc/pdf/NRCan_Key_Facts_Figures_Update_EN-2022.pdf

NRCan 2021. "Canada Announces Critical Minerals List," news release, Ottawa, March 11, 2021. https://www.canada.ca/en/natural-resources-canada/news/2021/03/canada-announces-critical-minerals-list.html.

Noble, Bram et al. 2019. "Effectiveness of Strategic Environmental Assessment in Canada under Directive-Based and Informal Practice." *Impact Assessment and Project Appraisal* 37 (3–4): 344–55. https://doi.org/10.1080/14615517.2019.1565708

Ray, Justina, Jaime Grimm, and Andrea Olive. 2021. "The Biodiversity Crisis in Canada: Failures and Challenges of Federal and Sub-National Legal Frameworks." *FACETS* 6 (January): 1044–68. https://doi.org/10.1139/facets-2020-0075

Redford, Kent H., et al. 2015. "Mainstreaming Biodiversity: Conservation for the Twenty-First Century." *Frontiers in Ecology and Evolution*. https://doi.org/10.3389/fevo.2015.00137

Resources of the Future Table. 2018. "The Innovation and Competitiveness Imperative: Seizing Opportunities for Growth." https://www.ic.gc.ca/eic/site/098.nsf/vwapj/ISEDC_ResourcesFuture.pdf/$file/ISEDC_ResourcesFuture.pdf

Steffen Will, et al. 2015. "Planetary Boundaries: Guiding Human Development on a Changing Planet." *Science* 347 (6223). https://doi.org/10.1126/science.1259855

Toner, Glen, and James Meadowcroft. 2009. *Innovation, Science, Environment, 1987–2007*. Montreal/Kingston: McGill-Queen University Press.

Watson, James E.M., et al. 2018. "The Exceptional Value of Intact Forest Ecosystems." *Nature Ecology & Evolution* 2: 599–610. https://doi.org/10.1038/s41559-018-0490-x

Williams, Brooke A., James E.M. Watson, Stuart H.M. Buchart et al. 2020. "A Robust Goal Is Needed for Species in the Post-2020 Global Biodiversity Framework." *Conservation Letters* 14 (3). https://doi.org/10.1111/conl.12778

Wilson, Edward O. 2017. "Biodiversity Research Requires More Boots on the Ground." *Nature Ecology & Evolution*, 1: 1590–1. https://doi.org/10.1038/s41559-017-0360-y

World Economic Forum (WEF). 2023. "The Global Risks Report 2023." 18th edition.

World Health Organization (WHO) 2020. https://www.who.int/news-room/feature -stories/detail/world-environment-day-2020

Whitehorn Penelope R. et al. 2019. "Mainstreaming Biodiversity: A Review of National Strategies." *Biological Conservation* 235: 157–63. https://doi.org/10.1016/j .biocon.2019.04.016

World Business Council for Sustainable Development (WBCSD). 2021. *Time to Transform: How Business Can Lead the Transformation It Needs.* https://www.wbcsd .org/contentwbc/download/11765/177145/1

– 1987. *Our Common Future.* Oxford: Oxford University Press.

Zurba M., K. Beazley, E. English, and J. Buchmann-Duck. 2019. "Indigenous Protected and Conserved Areas (IPCAs), Aichi Target 11 and Canada's Pathway to Target 1: Focusing Conservation on Reconciliation." *Land* 8 (1). https://doi.org/10.3390/land8010010

Disruptions, Part D

Conservation Bright Spots: Focusing on Solutions Instead of Reacting to Problems

BARBARA FREI

Humans and nature have had a long-standing, tumultuous relationship in the history of conservation biology. The very field was a reactive creation for the need to protect nature from the threat of human destruction and degradation (Kareiva and Marvier 2012). The framing of conservation biology has shifted over the decades from a species-centric view in which humans were painted dually as both nature's antagonist and saviour, to a more recent multi-layered, multi-faceted relationships of human's dependence on, and role within, nature (Mace 2014). As a research community we recognize that for conservation to be successful in the long term, we must recognize human well-being as part of the equation to success (Marvier 2014), and likewise how human well-being is dependent on conserving and managing a healthy, resilient ecosystem that provides services such as clean water, food production, carbon storage, and nature recreation (Bennett 2017).

Yet in practice, conservation policy and action remains reactive in nature with a focus on the most dire of circumstances. The strength of habitat and species protection measures are all too often at their strongest at the brink of population extinction or extensive loss, rather than a focus on prevention (Gerber 2016, Martin et al. 2018). Public outreach and education highlights conservation disasters or warns of dystopian futures. The general public have grown jaded by the overwhelming and predictable message of crisis, and scare scenarios often fail to drive positive societal or policy change (Fischer et al. 2012).

What if, instead of searching for problems and highlighting conservation crises, we search for existing solutions and aim to emulate those? So-called bright spots (Cinner et al. 2016, Frei et al. 2018) or seeds (Bennett et al. 2016) may be quantitatively or qualitatively identified outliers (locations or initiatives) where conditions exceed expectations. The premise of this approach is that the solutions to difficult problems are often known or practised by uncommon members of the group or community (Marsh et al. 2004); in other words, someone, somewhere, is already doing it right. Optimism is a rare resource in conservation biology and as such a powerful tool in inspiring change (Cvitanovic and Hobday 2018, McAfee et al. 2019). While bright spots may in fact be common and widespread, they are rarely documented (Cvitanovic and Hobday 2018), and thus the opportunities to learn from them are lost.

With over 75 per cent of the land surfaces in the world being anthropogenically modified (Ellis and Ramankutty 2008), it is imperative to include the human dimension in future conservation efforts. Using the bright spot approach allows researchers to employ a social-ecological lens in research, by blending rigorous quantitative model building using ecological variables followed by further exploration of social dynamics where data may be more qualitative in nature. In conservation research this provides insights to identify and understand possible levers of change and feasible management recommendations in complex social-ecological systems (Cinner et al. 2016, Frei et al. 2018, Heinicke et al. 2019). It further allows space to move towards a transdisciplinary approach and avoid disciplinary-siloed thinking when approaching conservation conflicts and exploration of solutions (Harrison and Loring 2020). Failure to include social aspects and create conservation policy or natural resource management solely focused in ecological theory may have fatal flaws unforeseen by researchers, making incomplete solutions unsuitable for the real world (Bennett et al. 2017).

While there is a strong need for solution-focused conservation research, such work is often time-consuming and challenging, and demands a multidisciplinary skill set that many researchers are unprepared for in traditional academic training (Williams et al. 2020). Additional challenges, such as the difficulty of receiving funding for and publishing multi-disciplinary research (Bromham et al. 2016) and lower recognition for applied work in academic settings (Roy et al. 2013), present serious deterrents particularly for early career researchers. This means that as a community conservationists must be more supportive of transdisciplinary and location/system-specific research (Williams et al. 2020), co-designed with multiple stakeholders, to build solution-driven policy and management. Only then will conservation science reach its ultimate goal in conserving nature with people, for people, and for itself.

Disrupting Current Approaches to Biodiversity Conservation through Innovative Knowledge Mobilization

VIVIAN NGUYEN

Knowledge generators have traditionally operated independently from knowledge users, with the assumption that knowledge would eventually be used by conservation practitioners. This has led to the knowledge-action gap (reviewed in Nguyen et al. 2017). To be relevant and applicable for informing decisions and implementing conservation strategies, effective conservation requires the best and up-to-date evidence (Rose et al. 2019; Sutherland et al. 2004). Thus, *knowledge mobilization* (KM) or *knowledge exchange* (KE), may achieve impact and increase return on investments in conservation (Cvitanovic et al. 2015; Nguyen, Young, and Cooke 2017; Young et al. 2013). Principles of KM/KE include iterative exchanges between knowledge producers, holders, and users, developing and maintaining interpersonal relationships and trust, as well as leveraging networks and influencers (Cvitanovic, McDonald, and Hobday 2016; Fazey et al. 2014; Nguyen et al. 2019). The implementation of these KM/KE principles have spurred transformative approaches and new perspectives for conservation action including knowledge co-production and co-evolution frameworks, citizen or community science projects, and the Living Labs research model, to name a few.

The co-evolution of knowledge promotes inclusive research and equal partnerships with knowledge users; this entails conducting research collaboratively, inclusively, and in a respectful manner (Cooke et al. 2021 Nel et al. 2016; Westwood et al. 2020). Knowledge coevolution is a disruptive innovative framework, bringing together different knowledge systems in an inclusive, iterative manner to promote self-determination of communities and cultural resilience (Chapman and Schott 2020; Schott et al. 2020). Through this approach, traditional colonial research and decision-making processes are disrupted as different ways of knowing, and worldviews are unified to achieve a common goal. The co-existence of multiple knowledge systems is also captured in the two-eyed seeing concept developed by Mi'kmaq Elder Albert Marshall (Marshall et al. 2015, Reid et al. 2021). Together, these concepts are transformative.

By integrating knowledge users and communities into the knowledge generation phase, citizen and community science can promote engagement with and uptake of research. Citizen and community science can have different meanings to different people but, generally, it is the practice of engaging the public in a scientific project; it has grown exponentially in recent years (McKinley et al. 2017). Information gathered from citizen and community science projects can be critical to meet information needs as well as address shortages in conservation tools. By involving people around the globe, it can help projects to increase in spatial-temporal scales through long-term and geographically vast monitoring of ecological and environmental baselines, the gathering of opportunistic and observational data, and the garnering of support and financial backing for conservation activities. If leveraged and done properly, citizen and community science can be transformative by positively involving humans in conservation (Ellwood, Crimmins, and Miller-Rushing 2017). Ballard et al. (2017) demonstrated the measurable impact of citizen science programs on conservation at three museums through research programs, education programs, policy, and livelihoods. For example, ongoing monitoring programs for the Reptiles and Amphibians of Southern California (RASCals) project, the Southern California Squirrel Survey, and the L.A. Spider Survey resulted in multiple recordings of new locations of species (reviewed in Ballard et al. 2017). Citizen and community science offers a promising option for addressing complex conservation challenges (McKinley et al. 2017).

Living Laboratories (LLs) is a novel concept that has not yet been explored in conservation. The concept of Living Labs refers to the involvement of a variety of stakeholders – including users, citizens, partners – in the exploration, co-creation, testing, and evaluation of innovations or tools within real-world environments (Ballon, Van Hoed, and Schuurman 2018; Hossain, Leminen, and Westerlund 2019). In LLs, users can shape innovation in their daily real-life environments based on practices and preferences, whereas in traditional innovation networks or labs, users are observed, and their insights are captured and interpreted by experts (Almirall and Wareham 2009). This innovative model is popular in the field of information, communication, and technology. It has only recently been explored in environmental sustainability (Schuurman and Leminen 2021, Hossain et al. 2019, Bronson et al. 2021, Beaudoin et al. 2022). LLs can help elucidate for their participants the connection between environmental and human systems; significant potential exists for academic, public, private, and not-for-profit sectors to apply LLs to conservation issues. Increased LL uptake might accelerate adoption of best practices and tools as well as promotion of behavioural change for supporting transition to a sustainable future, but LLs remain relatively underexplored (Hossain et al. 2019, Bronson et al. 2021). This research model and concept is highly disruptive to a technocratic model, where decisions and interpretations of research are highly directed by experts. With the rapid changes in environment, innovative research is required, Living Labs presents an approach for researchers and practitioners to adapt and keep up with this rate of change.

WORKS CITED

Almirall, E., and J. Wareham. 2009. "Innovation: A Question of Fit – The Living Labs Approach." *Mobile Living Labs* 9: 87–102.

Ballard, Heidi L. et al. 2017. "Contributions to Conservation Outcomes by Natural History Museum-Led Citizen Science: Examining Evidence and Next Steps." 208: 87–97. https://doi.org/10.1016/j.biocon.2016.08.040

Ballon, Pieter, Miriam Van Hoed, and Dimitri Schuurman. 2018. "The Effectiveness of Involving Users in Digital Innovation: Measuring the Impact of Living Labs." *Telematics and Informatics* 35 (5): 1201–14. https://doi.org/10.1016/j.tele.2018.02.003

Beaudoin, C., S. Joncoux, J.F. Jasmin, A. Berberi, C. McPhee, R.S. Schillo, and V.M. Nguyen. 2022. "A Research Agenda for Evaluating Living Labs as an Open Innovation Model for Environmental and Agricultural Sustainability." *Environmental Challenges* 7: 100505.

Bennett, E.M. 2017. Changing the Agriculture and Environment Conversation. *Nature Ecology and Evolution* 1: 1–2. https://doi.org/10.1038/s41559-016-0018

Bennett, Elena M., Martin Solan, Reinette Biggs, Timon McPhearson, Albert V. Norström, Per Olsson, Laura Pereira et al. 2016. "Bright Spots: Seeds of a Good Anthropocene." *Frontiers in Ecology and the Environment* 14, no. 8: 441–8. https://doi.org/10.1002/fee.1309

Bennett, Nathan J., Robin Roth, Sarah C. Klain, Kai Chan, Patrick Christie, Douglas A. Clark, Georgina Cullman et al. "Conservation Social Science: Understanding and Integrating Human Dimensions to Improve Conservation." 2017. *Biological Conservation* 205: 93–108. https://doi.org/10.1016/j.biocon.2016.10.006

Bromham, Lindell, Russell Dinnage, and Xia Hua. 2016. "Interdisciplinary Research Has Consistently Lower Funding Success." *Nature* 534, no. 7609: 684–87. https://doi.org/10.1038/nature18315

Bronson, K., R. Devkota, and V. Nguyen. 2021. "Moving toward Generalizability? A Scoping Review on Measuring the Impact of Living Labs." *Sustainability* 13 no. 2: 502.

Chapman, J.M., and Stephan Schott. 2020. "Knowledge Coevolution: Generating New Understanding through Bridging and Strengthening Distinct Knowledge Systems and Empowering Local Knowledge Holders." *Sustainability Science* 15, no. 3: 931–43. https://doi.org/10.1007/s11625-020-00781-2

Cinner, Joshua E., Cindy Huchery, M. Aaron MacNeil, Nicholas A.J. Graham, Tim R. McClanahan, Joseph Maina, Eva Maire et al. 2016. "Bright Spots among the World's Coral Reefs." *Nature* 535, no. 7612: 416–19. https://doi.org/10.1038/nature18607

Cvitanovic, Christopher, and Alistair J. Hobday. 2018. "Building Optimism at the Environmental Science-Policy-Practice Interface through the Study of Bright Spots." *Nature Communications* 9, no. 1: 1–5. https://doi.org/10.1038/s41467-018-05977-w

Cvitanovic, Christopher, Alistair J. Hobday, Lorrae van Kerkhoff, Shaun K. Wilson, Kirstin Dobbs, and N. A. Marshall. 2015. "Improving Knowledge Exchange among Scientists and Decision-Makers to Facilitate the Adaptive Governance of

Marine Resources: A Review of Knowledge and Research Needs." *Ocean & Coastal Management* 112: 25–35. https://doi.org/10.1016/j.ocecoaman.2015.05.002

Cvitanovic, Christopher, Jan McDonald, and A. J. Hobday. 2016. "From Science to Action: Principles for Undertaking Environmental Research that Enables Knowledge Exchange and Evidence-Based Decision-Making." *Journal of Environmental Management* 183: 864–74. https://doi.org/10.1016/j.jenvman.2016.09.038

Ellis, Erle C., and Navin Ramankutty. 2008. "Putting People in the Map: Anthropogenic Biomes of the World." *Frontiers in Ecology and the Environment* 6, no. 8: 439–47. https://doi.org/10.1890/070062

Ellwood, Elizabeth R., Theresa M. Crimmins, and Abraham J. Miller-Rushing. 2017. "Citizen Science and Conservation: Recommendations for a Rapidly Moving Field." *Biological Conservation* 208: 1–4. https://doi.org/10.1016/j.biocon.2016.10.014

Fazey, Ioan, Lukas Bunse, Joshua Msika, Maria Pinke, Katherine Preedy, Anna C. Evely, Emily Lambert, Emily Hastings, Sue Morris, and Mark S. Reed. 2014. "Evaluating Knowledge Exchange in Interdisciplinary and Multi-Stakeholder Research." *Global Environmental Change* 25: 204–20. https://doi.org/10.1016/j.gloenvcha.2013.12.012

Fischer, Joern, Robert Dyball, Ioan Fazey, Catherine Gross, Stephen Dovers, Paul R. Ehrlich, Robert J. Brulle, Carleton Christensen, and Richard J. Borden. "Human Behavior and Sustainability." 2012. *Frontiers in Ecology and the Environment* 10, no. 3: 153–60. https://doi.org/10.1890/110079

Frei, Barbara, Delphine Renard, Matthew G.E. Mitchell, Verena Seufert, Rebecca Chaplin-Kramer, Jeanine M. Rhemtulla, and Elena M. Bennett. 2018. "Bright Spots in Agricultural Landscapes: Identifying Areas Exceeding Expectations for Multifunctionality and Biodiversity." *Journal of Applied Ecology* 55, no. 6: 2731–43. https://doi.org/10.1111/1365-2664.13191

Gerber, Leah R. 2016. "Conservation Triage or Injurious Neglect in Endangered Species Recovery." *Proceedings of the National Academy of Sciences* 113, no. 13: 3563–66. https://doi.org/10.1073/pnas.1525085113

Harrison, Hannah L., and Philip A. Loring. 2020. "Seeing beneath Disputes: A Transdisciplinary Framework for Diagnosing Complex Conservation Conflicts." *Biological Conservation* 248. https://doi.org/10.1016/j.biocon.2020.108670

Heinicke, Stefanie, Roger Mundry, Christophe Boesch, Bala Amarasekaran, Abdulai Barrie, Terry Brncic, David Brugière et al. 2019. "Characteristics of Positive Deviants in Western Chimpanzee Populations." *Frontiers in Ecology and Evolution* 7. https://doi.org/10.3389/fevo.2019.00016

Hossain, Mokter, Seppo Leminen, and Mika Westerlund. 2019. "A Systematic Review of Living Lab Literature." *Journal of Cleaner Production* 213 (March): 976–88. https://doi.org/10.1016/j.jclepro.2018.12.257

Kareiva, Peter, and Michelle Marvier. 2012. "What Is Conservation Science?" *BioScience* 62, no. 11: 962–9. https://doi.org/10.1525/bio.2012.62.11.5

Mace, Georgina M. 2014. "Whose Conservation?." *Science* 345, no. 6204: 1558–60. https://doi.org/10.1126/science.1254704

Marsh, David R., Dirk G. Schroeder, Kirk A. Dearden, Jerry Sternin, and Monique Sternin. 2004. "The Power of Positive Deviance." *The BMJ* 329, no. 7475: 1177–9. https://doi.org/10.1136/bmj.329.7475.1177

Marshall, M., A. Marshall, and C. Bartlett. 2015. "Two-Eyed Seeing in Medicine." In *Determinants of Indigenous Peoples' Health in Canada: Beyond the Social*, 2nd ed., edited by M. Greenwood, S. de Leeuw, and N.M. Lindsay, 16–24. Toronto: Canadian Scholars' Press.

Martin, Tara G., Laura Kehoe, Chrystal Mantyka-Pringle, Iadine Chades, Scott Wilson, Robin G. Bloom, Stephen K. Davis et al. 2018. "Prioritizing Recovery Funding to Maximize Conservation of Endangered Species." *Conservation Letters* 11, no. 6. https://doi.org/10.1111/conl.12604

Marvier, Michelle. 2014. "New Conservation Is True Conservation." *Conservation Biology* 28, no. 1: 1–3. https://doi.org/10.1111/cobi.12206

McAfee, Dominic, Zoë A. Doubleday, Nathaniel Geiger, and Sean D. Connell. 2019. "Everyone Loves a Success Story: Optimism Inspires Conservation Engagement." *BioScience* 69, no. 4: 274–81. https://doi.org/10.1093/biosci/biz019

McKinley, Duncan C., Abe J. Miller-Rushing, Heidi L. Ballard, Rick Bonney, Hutch Brown, Susan C. Cook-Patton, Daniel M. Evans et al. 2017. "Citizen Science Can Improve Conservation Science, Natural Resource Management, and Environmental Protection." *Biological Conservation* 208: 15–28. https://doi.org/10.1016/j.biocon .2016.05.015

Nguyen, Vivian M., Nathan Young, Jacob W. Brownscombe, and Steven J. Cooke. 2019. "Collaboration and Engagement Produce More Actionable Science: Quantitatively Analyzing Uptake of Fish Tracking Studies." *Ecological Applications* 29, no. 6. https://doi.org/10.1002/eap.1943

Nguyen, Vivian M., Nathan Young, and Steven J. Cooke. 2017. "A Roadmap for Knowledge Exchange and Mobilization Research in Conservation and Natural Resource Management." *Conservation Biology* 31, no. 4: 789–98. https://doi .org/10.1111/cobi.12857

Reid, Andrea J., Lauren E. Eckert, John-Francis Lane, Nathan Young, Scott G. Hinch, Chris T. Darimont, Steven J. Cooke, Natalie C. Ban, and Albert Marshall. 2021. "'Two-Eyed Seeing': An Indigenous Framework to Transform Fisheries Research and Management." *Fish and Fisheries* 22, no. 2: 243–61. https://doi.org/10.1111 /faf.12516

Roy, Eric D., Anita T. Morzillo, Francisco Seijo, Sheila M.W. Reddy, Jeanine M. Rhemtulla, Jeffrey C. Milder, Tobias Kuemmerle, and Sherry L. Martin. 2013. "The Elusive Pursuit of Interdisciplinarity at the Human–Environment Interface." *BioScience* 63, no. 9: 745–53. https://doi.org/10.1093/bioscience/63.9.745

Schott, Stephan, James Qitsualik, Peter Van Coeverden de Groot, Simon Okpakok, Jacqueline M. Chapman, Stephen Lougheed, and Virginia K. Walker. 2020. "Operationalizing Knowledge Coevolution: Towards a Sustainable Fishery for Nunavummiut." *Arctic Science* 6, no. 3: 208–28. https://doi.org/10.1139/as-2019-0011

Schuurman, D., and S. Leminen. 2021. "Living Labs Past Achievements, Current Developments, and Future Trajectories." *Sustainability*, 13, no. 19.

Sutherland, William J., Andrew S. Pullin, Paul M. Dolman, and Teri M. Knight. 2004. "The Need for Evidence-Based Conservation." 19 (6): 4–7. https://doi.org/10.1016/j.tree.2004.03.018

Westwood, Alana, Nicole Barker, Sam Grant, Amy Amos, Alaine Camfield, Kaytlin Cooper, Francisco Dénes et al. 2020. "Toward Actionable, Coproduced Research on Boreal Birds Focused on Building Respectful Partnerships." *Avian Conservation and Ecology* 15, no. 1. https://doi.org/10.5751/ACE-01589-150126

Williams, David R., Andrew Balmford, and David S. Wilcove. 2020. "The Past and Future Role of Conservation Science in Saving Biodiversity." *Conservation Letters* 13, no. 4. https://doi.org/10.1111/conl.12720

Young, Nathan, Isabelle Gingras, Vivian M. Nguyen, Steven J. Cooke, and Scott G. Hinch. 2013. "Mobilizing New Science into Management Practice: The Challenge of Biotelemetry for Fisheries Management, a Case Study of Canada's Fraser River." *Journal of International Wildlife Law & Policy* 16, no. 4: 331–51. https://doi.org/10.1080/13880292.2013.805074

PART E

Conclusion

12 Achieving Transformative Change: Conservation in Canada, 2023 and Beyond

ANDREA OLIVE AND KAREN F. BEAZLEY

To transform itself into a monarch butterfly, a "caterpillar must first digest itself" (Jabr 2012). This collection is an attempt at such a process for scholars and practitioners of Canadian biodiversity policy. Collectively, the authors present two fundamental propositions. First, there are significant obstacles to effective conservation practices in Canada (see part B). Second, and more importantly, transformative change is possible, and possible right now (see parts C and D).

Alongside other international partners, Canada has been working towards the Paris Agreement targets for climate change (UN 2015a), Sustainable Development Goals across 17 different targets (UN 2015b), and post-2020 targets for biodiversity (UN CBD 2020). As we were writing, a G7 Climate and Environment Ministers' Meeting Communiqué on May 21, 2021, strongly reported,

> We acknowledge with grave concern that the unprecedented and interdependent crises of climate change and biodiversity loss pose an existential threat to nature, people, prosperity and security ... [S]ome of the key drivers of global biodiversity loss and climate change are the same as those that increase the risk of zoonoses, which can lead to pandemics. We highlight that urgent and concrete action is needed to ... maximise the opportunities to solve these crises in parallel. (G7 2021, 1)

These developments signal that we may have reached a tipping point in the global nature crisis. This is a critical moment in which we believe immense socially and ecologically just changes are crucial as well as politically and economically feasible. As a promising signal, on the eve of the production of this collection, the 15th Conference of Parties to the UN CBD adopted the landmark "Kunming-Montreal Global Biodiversity Framework" on December 19, 2022, with four goals and 23 targets for achievement by 2030 (UN CBD 2022).

The science on biodiversity loss in Canada is clear and bleak. Indeed, scientists have been ringing the alarm bells for decades (e.g., Union of Concerned Scientists 1992; Willison et al. 1992). Yet, things are only getting worse. So, where is the policy? Why are the policies that do exist not effective in stemming the declines? We know what biodiversity is, what biodiversity loss means, and what – from a scientific perspective – needs to occur to reverse declining trends and restore ecosystem function. Why do policy-makers fail to respond effectively? While we do see a similar pattern in climate change and other "wicked problems" that are "incomprehensible and resistant to solution" (Churchman 1967; Rittel and Webber 1973; Head and Alford 2015), a lack of progress appears even more pronounced with biodiversity loss. Most Canadians now know what climate change is, can define it, understand the causes (although perhaps disagree about it), and name a handful of individual and societal actions that could address it. The same cannot be said of biodiversity loss.

The authors in this volume suggest that the barriers to more effective biodiversity conservation, as well as transformative pathways towards overcoming those barriers, hinge on societal values and specific political and governance actions. In this concluding chapter, we reflect on the political barriers identified in part B as well as society's potential for transformative change in values (parts C) and actions (part D). Overall, we editors hope this digestive process enables readers to reflect carefully on how Canada can make lasting change in complex human relations to reshape/restore the natural environment in socially just ways, and, like the caterpillar, thereby transform ourselves.

As editors, by way of situating ourselves, we declare that we write this chapter and reflect on this curated collection as non-Indigenous academics. Olive was born on Treaty 4 lands in Saskatchewan, and Beazley was born on the ancestral and unceded territory of the Mi'kmaq nation in Nova Scotia. Although we editors are white, with the privilege it entails, many authors in this volume identify as Indigenous or Person of Colour. One goal of this collection is to bring a diversity of voices into the discussion about conservation in Canada. We are especially attentive to the voices of Indigenous scholars and activists because Canadian settler-colonialism remains a significant barrier to healing humanity's relationship with the earth and each other. To move forward in transformational ways will require that we all work together, with open hearts, ears, eyes, minds, and spirits, to think and act in new ways to heal people and nature – all our relations.

Transformative Change

How does transformation come about – through values or through actions? Do we have to change our values first or change our actions first? Can we change both at the same time? This is a large and ongoing debate in conservation biology and many other fields. As noted in this volume's introduction, Donella Meadows's (1999) seminal work on leverage points highlights the potential to change entire social systems through a mix of strategies that range from small,

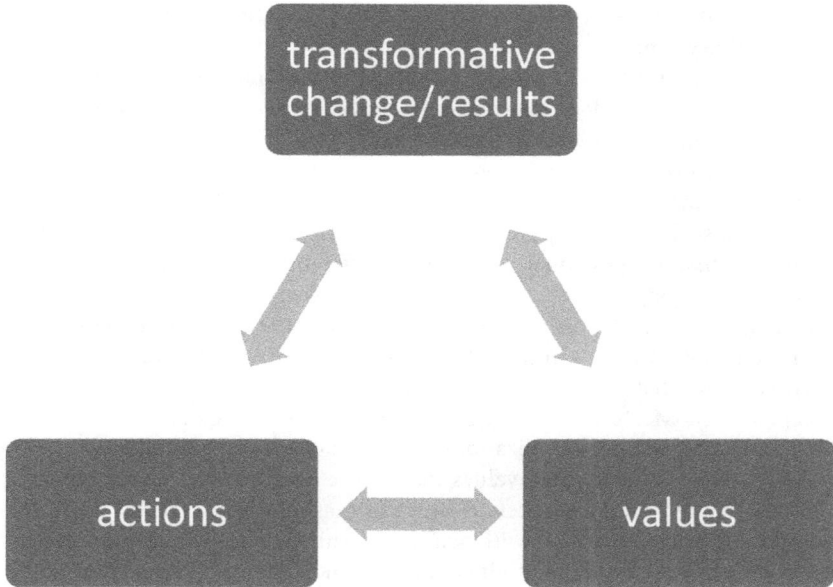

Figure 12.1. Looping relationship between values, actions, and transformative changes.

discrete actions to paradigm shifts. She focuses on the importance of concrete actions, like changes to the tax system, as well as more fundamental or pervasive levers, like changes to values, mindsets, and worldviews. However, not all scientists are convinced about the feasibility of the latter. Manfredo et al. (2016) recently reignited a long-standing debate in the journal *Conservation Biology* with the argument that values cannot be changed; and thus, scientists (and perhaps politicians) should work within prevailing value systems (such as capitalism). In direct response, Ives and Fischer (2017) argued that such an approach would be "self-sabotaging conservation" and that value change is both necessary and possible. Ultimately, they advocated for more research into what values are and how values can change, thereby bolstering support for the crucial role of social sciences in conservation science.

While not wanting to side-step this important conversation, we suggest that values and actions are connected, and both impact each other in a continual loop while at the same time bringing about transformative changes (figure 12.1). Consistent with Meadows, we acknowledge that "a small shift in one thing can produce big changes in everything" (1999, 1). We also accept that values can and do change – sometimes quickly. These value changes are a result of complex processes, and we are not suggesting that changes to the status quo would be easy. And yet, there are strong arguments, including within this collection, that support the necessity of changes in predominant worldviews and values if we are to address crucial fundamental causes and underlying issues, such as humanity's relationship with nature.

Consequently, the inter-relationships between values and actions are important in our conceptualization of transformation. We know from a diverse range of sources, such as social psychology or Indigenous teachings and Guardian Programs, that an individual needs to act differently to think and feel differently. And as thoughts and feelings change, it is easier for behaviours to change. We suggest that actions to address biodiversity declines will reshape societal values on conservation. On the other hand, we also know that value shifts are occurring and that these will reshape what actions are considered possible or acceptable. As McDermott and Roth observe, there is "a global awakening of how damaging" Western civilization's economically driven paradigm is.

Many people already hold values that centre equity, social justice, and the rights of nature, and their voices are being increasingly heard. To our point, the question of where we start – with actions or with values – is not important. It is not an either-or situation; both are needed and can occur concurrently. The two are connected and nourish each other. We have cognitive minds that can think differently and physical bodies that can take action in mutually reinforcing ways, to the benefit of people and the planet.

Barriers to Effective Conservation

Key barriers to effective conservation were highlighted by authors in this collection (table 12.1). Actions and values are linked through a continuous loop; it is impossible to completely separate them. Despite this, we have attempted to organize the barriers according to those we consider to be primarily action based, followed by barriers comprising both action and value, and then those that are value based.

The barriers that are about actions (or inactions) are mainly aimed at the federal and provincial governments and are highlighted in the first few chapters in this volume. As Lemieux et al. argue, "Canada is deeply affected by pathological management and chronic organizational dysfunction." Some of these barriers exist because of the way the Canadian Constitution divides powers between the federal and provincial governments. Other barriers exist because government agencies at either or both levels have failed to take action for, or acted in ways counter to, the conservation of biodiversity. At the same time as committing unprecedented levels of funding for biodiversity conservation, climate change mitigation and adaptation, and Indigenous leadership and guardian programs (Government of Canada 2021), governments are also approving mega-projects,

Table 12.1. List of barriers to effective conservation in Canada and the chapters in this volume that discuss each barrier

Political/Governance Barriers	Value or Action	Chapter
Failure to learn	Action	Lemieux et al.; McDermott and Roth; Finegan; Frei
Procrastination	Action	Lemieux et al.; Boan and Plotkin
Risk averse decision-making	Action	Lemieux et al.
Lack of accountability and transparency	Action	Lemieux et al.
Economy and political elites dominated/captured by natural resource extraction; conflict of interest	Action	Colla; Pictou; Ray
Failure in leadership	Value and Action	Lemieux et al.; Hilty and Woodley; Ray
Unfulfilled treaties	Value and Action	McDermott and Roth; Pictou; Young; Myhal
Acceptance of status quo	Value	Williamson et al.; Boan and Plotkin
Lack of engagement; Lack of local support	Value	Lemieux et al.; Nguyen; Boan and Plotkin
Ideology (including growth without limits, human-nature binary, anthropocentrism, colonialism)	Value	Boan and Plotkin; McDermott and Roth; Pictou; Young; Ray
Failure to understand reconciliation as about human/Creation relationships	Value	McDermott and Roth; Pictou; Young; Popp; Myhal

such transcontinental pipelines and large-scale dams (Gilchrist 2018; Datta and Hurlbert 2020; Elkaim 2020), which cause severe social and ecological impacts to these same systems and communities. Biodiversity and the climate suffer as a consequence, with disproportionate distribution of the burdens across peoples, species, and places, and posing threats to us all.

While federalism and the Constitution allow wildlife management to be defined and organized in ways that serve the state, the fact that so many Canadians accept this system is troubling. As Williamson et al. argue, "Most Canadians, across all regions, think the government is doing an adequate job of managing wildlife. There is a general acceptance and preference for federal and provincial involvement in wildlife issues, with little appetite for other actors, including Indigenous governments." These authors, and others in the volume, take issue with status-quo governance as there is ample scientific and policy data to suggest that Canadian governments are not doing a very good job. While there have been recent initiatives that are promising and may signal a shift in governance and policy priorities towards biodiversity conservation, climate adaptation and recognition of Indigenous rights (e.g., NAP 2018; ICE 2018; ECCC 2020; G7 2021), the aims, actions, and outcomes to date have been ineffective, and much remains to be done to move from recommendations to change on the ground.

It should be noted that many of the Indigenous scholars and writers have focused on barriers related to values, and many of these are rooted in unfulfilled treaties, which is both an action and a value. McDermott and Roth draw the reader's attention to the need to honour treaties signed between the Crown and Indigenous Peoples as the cornerstone of Canadian conservation practice. Without recognizing and respecting all nations and honouring our relationship and responsibilities to the whole web of life, they argue, conservation may fail.

Many authors point to barriers associated with settler-colonialism and capitalist ideology as well as Western frameworks and practices that preclude reconciliation with land. Indeed, in their chapter on caribou, Boan and Plotkin call for more sustainable practices in which "social and cultural dimensions, Indigenous practices and ethics, creative framing of new approaches, and a commitment to transparency should each play a primary role." Beyond this, many of the Indigenous contributors highlight that reconciliation extends beyond human–human to human–Creation relationships. Limiting reconciliation to a primarily state-sponsored process aimed at increasing the legitimacy of Canadian sovereignty hinders conservation, as we discuss below. This insistence on a human–Creation binary (or, rather, the presumption of the validity of the dominant approach to human–Creation relationships) is but one example of the persistent, harmful ideologies that underpin setter society in Canada and threaten biodiversity conservation.

Recent conservation research suggests using our values for just and fair economies: "we need to consider what levels of consumption are sustainable and how a more equitable distribution of resources can be achieved" (Turnhout et al. 2021). These sorts of justice and equity considerations require the active involvement of not only conservation professionals, but political elites and society generally. Yet, as Lemieux et al., Nguyen, and Boan and Plotkin highlight, many Canadians simply are not engaged – or at least, not to the extent necessary – in thinking around biodiversity conservation. Instead, most of society is content with the status quo (in which provinces have the greatest ability to support conservation while they are also charged with developing natural resources to extract maximum, ever-growing economic returns). Many academics, on the other hand, critique the status quo and offer alternatives, but are often invested in knowledge-production foci and dissemination methods that may not align with what policy elites need to inform their decision-making.

Transformation Pathways

What will it take to overcome the barriers and transform nature conservation policy in Canada? The authors in this collection suggest over a dozen actions government and society could immediately take as well as half a dozen shifts in values that are required in the short, medium, and long term (Table 12.2). Many of the actions necessary for transformation are of a practical nature and focus not on conservation theory, but on conservation practice. For example, Ray as well as Hilty and Woodley are direct in their calls for protected areas and ecological networks. They both leave open the role of Indigenous-led efforts in these protected and connected spaces. Both see ecological networks as fitting into a larger framework for transformative changes. Ray is bold, yet justified, in her calls for federal leadership, law reforms, and reshaped policy approaches around the idea of mainstreaming for biodiversity. She is mindful – and frank – about the necessity of Indigenous-led and co-led endeavours. Such approaches confront a "lack of effective and meaningful engagement," positioned by Lemieux et al. as a pathology that yields "… narrow management objectives rather than a whole-systems approach." Hilty and Woodley directly challenge contemporary conservation practitioners to take such a whole-system approach, writing that both protected areas and corridors can, together, "enable increased conservation effectiveness … [and] facilitate adaptation during this time of climate change." While none of these actions are easy to enact, especially given general acceptance of the status quo in Canada, they are feasible and practical policy changes that any government could implement in the next five to ten years.

The most fundamental action discussed throughout parts C and D of this volume is reconciliation with land. As Pictou importantly points out "a key underlying message identified in the ICE report is that reconciling tensions between conservation practice and Indigenous knowledges relies on a process of "healing" by restoring a sustainable human relationship to the land/waters (ICE 2018, 36, 48, 103; also see Zurba et al. 2019, 14; Nuna et al. 2021)." Pictou grounds conservation in Mi'kmaw (Indigenous) ideas about human/nonhuman relationships and reciprocity. This, Pictou argues, can lead to improved conservation outcomes within and outside of protected areas and more successful attempts at reconciliation. McGregor et al. also point out that the 2015 TRC reports build around a holistic understanding of well-being through conceptualizing "reconciliation as a process that must also include the Earth." In their chapter, Elder Marshall "contends that transformative change is required between humanity and our relationship with the Earth."

Table 12.2. List of transformative potential actions and values and the chapters that discuss each

Society's Transformative Potential	Value-Led or Action-Orientation	Chapter
Indigenous-led conservation; IPCAs; Indigenous Guardian programs	Action	Young; Cook; Ray
Ecological corridors and connectivity; protected areas	Action	Hilty and Woodley; Ray
Federal leadership; law reforms; mainstreaming	Action	Ray
Educational reform; land-based learning	Action	Zurba et al.; Finegan
Sustainable development/ Netukulimk outside protected areas	Action	Boan and Plotkin; Pictou; Young; Ray
Indigenous relationality; relationship-based management	Action and value	McDermott and Roth; Pictou; Young; Popp; Finegan; Myhal
Reconciliation with land	Action and value	Pictou; McGregor et al.; Young
Decolonizing conservation	Value	Pictou; Young; Ray; Myhal
Ethical space (including gender and sexuality)	Value	Pictou; Young
Two-Eyed Seeing	Value	McGregor et al; Young; Myhal
Ideology (worldview/paradigm centring all my relations; Natural Law; rights of nature; ecocentrism/ecojustice; Indigenous feminism)	Value	McDermott and Roth; Pictou; McGregor et al.; Young

As with Pictou and others, Young emphasizes the deep connections between humans and Creation, and the role of reconciliation in restoring these relationships. Young reminds the reader that successful conservation in Canada is dependent on respect for Indigenous laws and governance systems, in both terrestrial and water-based places. Young skilfully uses personal narrative and her experiences as a Mi'kmaw conservation practitioner to show readers how non-Indigenous conservation actors (e.g., Parks Canada; Nova Scotia Protected Areas and Ecosystems) can support Indigenous-led conservation, and how the Mi'kmaq are shaping conservation in Mi'maki through IPCA creation with both federal and provincial government agencies.

The main transformation pathways that are value driven hinge on decolonization, ethical space, Two-Eyed Seeing and ideology or worldview.

Essentially, Canada must continue with the work started through ICE (2018) and Canada Pathway to Target 1 (NAP 2018) to meaningfully respect and engage both Indigenous knowledge and Western science in conservation practices. Indigenous insights offer ways to see the world as reciprocal relationships and responsibilities among all peoples and all ecologies. They remind us that healing requires human reconnection with the land, counter to Western systems that perpetuate a false dichotomy between humans and nature. As noted in the introduction and discussed by many authors (Lemiex et al., Ray, Boan and Plotkin, and Pictou especially), "status-quo continues in resource extraction sectors, including oil and gas, renewal energy, mining and forestry, and through the ongoing tendency to privilege private property and corporate rights over more equitable and reciprocal relations among people, lands and waters" (Beazley et al. this volume, citing MMIWG 2019; Kruse and Robinson 2020; MERE 2021). Thus, transformation work has only just begun.

At heart, scholars and practitioners must interrogate their ontological and epistemological assumptions about conservation. Canadians who purport to care about wildlife must be open to reconceptualizing "wildlife" as a term and as a category of being. McDermott and Roth confront this in their discussion of "All of Our Relations" as something different than "wildlife." Pictou also discusses, in the context of decolonizing conservation practices, how Indigenous knowledge is grounded in land- and water-based lifeways and as such is an "embodiment of the wild or wild species as our relatives: an Indigenous relationality that encompasses the human and non-human or more-than-human world including our ancestors and 'all of Creation.'"

The discussion of Indigenous knowledges foregrounds the concept of ethical space. Many authors in this volume draw on Ermine (2007), who states "'ethical space' should be formed when two societies, with disparate worldviews, are poised to engage each other" (193) and must include a respect for different knowledge systems and action towards ethical transformation beyond that which is only found in discourse. In her essay, Young highlights the importance of ethical space, saying that it puts Indigenous and non-Indigenous society on an equal footing where "the integrity of both knowledge systems – Western and Indigenous – are respected and valued, and neither system has more weight or legitimacy than the other." She, like other authors in the collection, concludes that ethical space is a "safe space to share, learn, and build the respectful relationships that are needed to move forward on what can sometimes be considered difficult issues."

The disruption essays that close part D of the volume focus on the implications of knowledge production and draw attention to the need to implement emerging knowledge creation and mobilization strategies (such as "Living Labs") to enhance conservation practice. In many respects, the disruptions throughout the collection suggest that one can disrupt conservation by thinking about thinking. Deliberate attention to knowledge and knowledge systems, in all their complexities, disrupts and enhances biodiversity conservation. Such attention should come in the form of questioning dominant narratives, actively supporting Indigenous knowledge systems and relationships with Creation, and considering new and more inclusive ways of knowledge production, or re-thinking from whom, how, and where we learn.

From Values and Actions to Transformation

If the actions and values (table 12.2.) discussed in this collection were realized, would it be enough to reverse declines in biodiversity and address the main threats, like habitat loss? We think yes. But one important aspect not yet discussed – but raised by a few authors – is our ability to set goals and measure progress. We must be able to hold ourselves accountable. To date, the federal government has largely failed to produce metrics for measuring progress on sustainability and biodiversity goals. Turnhout et al. (2021) argue that "changing metrics is a well-recognized strategy for effecting structural change in values and paradigms: by better measuring what we value, changes in values can be reflected in and catalyzed by changes in metrics" (see also Stiglitz et al. 2009). This echoes Ray's call for a strategic biodiversity assessment, Boan and Plotkin's critiques about cumulative effectors, and Lemieux et al.'s observations about inadequate monitoring programs, lack of clear measurable goals, lack of timelines, and poor reporting. It also confronts the standard practice of valuing and measuring almost everything in terms of economic indicators such as GDP/GNP. Thus, we suggest that metrics and assessments that reflect biodiversity, healing, and other values that centre nature and people in socially and ecologically just ways must be part of the overall transformative process (figure 12.2).

The transformative loop we envision is illustrated by figure 12.2. We do not include a specific reference to science or scientific data because we believe that Western science and Indigenous knowledge have already provided us with more than enough information to shift values and actions. Moreover, we agree with Boan and Plotkin (this volume) that "wildlife management must be based on science, but science alone cannot shape management decisions. Social and cultural dimensions, Indigenous practices and ethics, creative framing of new approaches, and a commitment to transparency should each play a primary role." Essentially, socially and ecologically just transformation for all of Creation is possible through measured and assessed changes in our values and actions. As transformation happens, new values and actions will emerge, disrupt the status quo, and become entrenched.

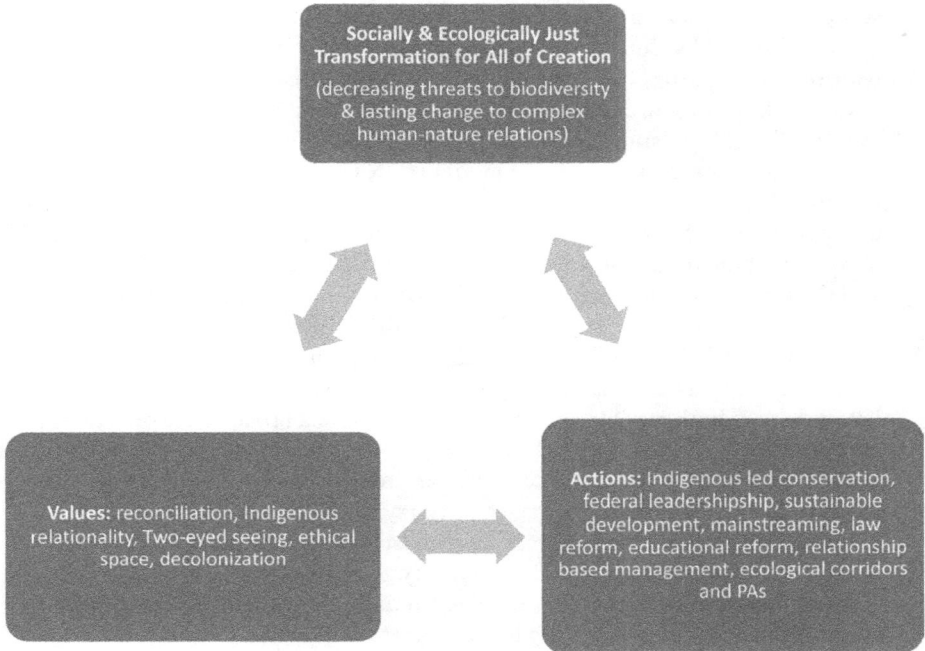

Figure 12.2. Relationship of values, actions, and ecologically and socially just transformation for conservation in Canada.

Looking Ahead

In the realm of conservation, Canada has lofty goals. While the post-Aichi biodiversity framework (UN CBD 2020) was delayed by COVID-19 disruptions, Prime Minister Trudeau committed to conserve 25 per cent of Canada's land and 25 per cent of Canada's oceans by 2025, working towards 30 per cent of each by 2030, and joined other countries in the High Ambition Coalition working towards 30 per cent by 2030 (Trudeau, 2019; Canada (Governor General) 2020; ECCC 2020; Government of Canada 2021). Two sequential federal budgets allocated unprecedented levels of funding to direct protection of additional lands and waters in Canada, through initiatives such as Indigenous Protected and Conserved Areas, Indigenous Guardians programs, provincial and territorial protected areas, and protecting species at risk (Government of Canada 2021). Additional funds were earmarked for marine protected areas, natural infrastructure, and nature-based disaster and climate adaptation and mitigation. Commitments in the 2021 budget totalled nearly 4.9 billion CAD over the subsequent five years. In December 2022, Canada hosted the 15th Conference of Parties to the UN Convention on Biological Diversity in Montreal and, along with the other parties, adopted the "Kunming-Montreal Global Biodiversity Framework" (GBF), including a protected area target of at least 30 per cent of the world's lands, inland waters, coastal areas and oceans, along with 22 other conservation targets to be achieved by 2030 (UN CBD 2022).

Canada's biodiversity conservation commitments also augment pledges to address climate change and efforts to reach sustainable development goals. They contribute to global targets, such as the Paris Agreement (UN 2015a), and the G7 Climate and Environment Ministers' Meeting Communiqué (G7 2021). They additionally align with the Truth and Reconciliation Commission of Canada's Calls to Action (2015) and support further action on the recommendations from ICE (2018) and NAP (2018). Further, they represent levers that are both feasible and effective and engage a broad range of actions and values.

Change is underway. Significant barriers remain, and many seem insurmountable. For example, Lemiuex et al. worry that "the pathologies we detail have become so entrenched, there is little reason to believe that they will change in the short- to medium-term." However, they go on to note that learning, especially from past failures, will be key. Indeed, if there is one main take-away from this collection, it is a call for deep learning as the foundation to transformative changes in society and governance. Canada must reflect on what constitutes a relational ethic of care between all people and the lands, waters, and wildlife. As a society, we need to work together to co-develop ways to acknowledge and value diverse knowledge systems and weave them together using Two-Eyed Seeing to reconnect people with the land, both as a form of learning about land and wildlife and as a means of healing. These conditions will require ethical space and may involve innovations like living laboratories and land-based curriculums. Genuine learning requires an openness to learn not just from each other but also from the land and entails a deepening of relationship. As Young says, humans and nature "are interdependent. All that we have comes from the land and waters. The earth provides not only for our well-being, but it holds our history, our teachings, and our languages."

Learning will require reflection on our past so we can honour the truth and learn from our mistakes and our successes. The disruption essays, for example, reflect on knowledge and suggest opportunities for learning that exist in places where conservation is successful, rather than solely where biodiversity is threatened. In some ways, this reinforces the lessons from part C of the collection. Since we know that Indigenous Guardians are successful, we should re-double our efforts to support and learn from them. By doing so, we can see, hear and feel that land needs people and people need land, and at the same time deepen the relationship and heal both.

The monarch butterfly is nature's most grand statement about the possibility for profound transformative change. Science tells us that moths can learn and remember. The butterflies "remember what they learned in later stages of their lives as caterpillars" (Jabr 2012; see also Blackiston et al. 2008). Our hope is this collection has provided interested readers with knowledge to digest and the inspiration to continue learning. Transformative change is possible, and the butterfly shows us that the result can be beautiful.

WORKS CITED

Blackiston D.J., E. Silva Casey, and M.R. Weiss. 2008. "Retention of Memory through Metamorphosis: Can a Moth Remember What It Learned as a Caterpillar?" *PLoS ONE* 3 (3). https://doi.org/10.1371/journal.pone.0001736

Canada (Governor General). 2020. A Stronger and More Resilient Canada: Speech from the Throne to Open the Second Session of the Forty-Third Parliament of Canada, September 23, 2020. Ottawa. Accessed April 22, 2021. Available www.canada.ca/throne -speech. Accessed April 22, 2021.

Churchman, C. 1967. "Wicked Problems." Guest editorial. *Management Science* 14, no. 2: B141–B142.

Datta, R., and M.A. Hurlbert. 2020. "Pipeline Spills and Indigenous Energy Justice." *Sustainability* 12, no.1: 47. https://doi.org/10.3390/su12010047

Elkaim, A.V. 2020. "State of Erosion: The Legacy of Manitoba Hydro." *The Narwhal.* November 7, 2020. https://thenarwhal.ca/state-of-erosion-the-legacy-of-manitoba -hydro/

Environment and Climate Change Canada (ECCC). 2020. "Canada Joins the High Ambition Coalition for Nature and People." News release, September 28, 2020. Ottawa, Ontario. https://www.canada.ca/en/environment-climate-change/news /2020/09/canada-joins-the-high-ambition-coalition-for-nature-and-people.html

G7. 2021. "G7 Climate and Environment Ministers' Meeting Communiqué." London, United Kingdom, May 20–21, 2021. https://assets.publishing.service.gov.uk /government/uploads/system/uploads/attachment_data/file/988551/g7-climate -environment-communique.pdf

Gilchrist, E. 2018. "The Real Reason Canada Is in Crisis over the Kinder Morgan Pipeline." *The Narwhal.* April 25, 2018. https://thenarwhal.ca/real-reason-canada -crisis-over-kinder-morgan-pipeline/

Government of Canada. 2021. "Budget 2021: A Recovery Plan for Jobs, Growth and Resilience." Department of Finance. Service Canada. https://www.canada.ca/en /department-finance.html. Accessed April 22, 2021.

Head, B.W., and J. Alford. 2015. "Wicked Problems: Implications for Public Policy and Management." *Administration & Society.* 47 (6): 711–39. https://doi.org/10.1177 /0095399713481601

Indigenous Circles of Experts (ICE). 2018. *We Rise Together: Achieving Pathway to Canada Target 1 through the Creation of Indigenous Protected and Conserved Areas in the Spirit of Practice of Reconciliation.* https://static1.squarespace.com/static /57e007452e69cf9a7af0a033/t/5ab94aca6d2a7338ecb1d05e/1522092766605/PA234 -ICE_Report_2018_Mar_22_web.pdf

Ives, C.D., and J. Fischer. 2017. "The Self-Sabotage of Conservation: Reply to Manfredo et al." *Conservation Biology* 31: 1483–5. https://doi.org/10.1111/cobi.13025

Jabr, Ferris. 2012. "How Does a Caterpillar Become a Butterfly?" *Scientific American* https://www.scientificamerican.com/article/caterpillar-butterfly-metamorphosis -explainer/

Manfredo, M.J., J.T. Bruskotter, T.L. Teel, D. Fulton, S.H. Schwartz, R. Arlinghaus, S. Oishi, A.K. Uskul, K. Redford, S. Kitayama, and L. Sullivan. 2016. "Why Social Values Cannot Be Changed for the Sake of Conservation." *Conservation Biology* 31: 772–80. https://doi.org/10.1111/cobi.12855

Meadows, D. 1999. "Leverage Points: Places to Intervene in a System." The Sustainability Institute, Hartland, Vermont. https://donellameadows.org/wp-content /userfiles/Leverage_Points.pdf

National Advisory Panel (NAP). 2018. "One with Nature: A Renewed Approach to Land and Freshwater Conservation in Canada. A Report of Canada's Federal, Provincial and Territorial Departments Responsible for Parks, Protected Areas, Conservation, Wildlife and Biodiversity." Ottawa. https://static1.squarespace.com /static/57e007452e69cf9a7af0a033/t/5c9cd18671c10bc304619547/1553781159734 /Pathway-Report-Final-EN.pdf

Rittel, H.W.J., and M.M. Webber. 1973. "Dilemmas in a General Theory of Planning." *Policy Sciences* 4: 155–69. https://doi.org/10.1007/BF01405730

Stiglitz, J., A.K. Sen, and J.P. Fitoussi. 2009. "Report of the Commission on the Measurement of Economic Performance and Social Progress." https://www .economie.gouv.fr/files/finances/presse/dossiers_de_presse/090914mesure_perf_eco _progres_social/synthese_ang.pdf

Trudeau, J. 2019. "Minister of Environment and Climate Change Mandate Letter." Retrieved from https://pm.gc.ca/en/mandate-letters/2019/12/13/minister -environment-and-climate-change-mandate-letter

Truth and Reconciliation Commission of Canada (TRCC). 2015c. "Calls to Action." Winnipeg, Manitoba: Truth and Reconciliation Commission of Canada. http://trc .ca/assets/pdf/Calls_to_Action_English2.pdf

Turnhout, Esther, Pamela McElwee, Mireille Chiroleu-Assouline, Jennifer Clapp, Cindy Isenhour, Eszter Kelemen, Tim Jackson, Daniel C. Miller, Graciela M. Rusch, Joachim H. Spangenberg, and Anthony Waldron. 2021. "Enabling Transformative Economic Change in the Post-2020 Biodiversity Agenda." *Conservation Letters.* https://doi.org/10.1111/conl.12805

Union of Concerned Scientists. 1992. "World Scientists' Warning to Humanity." Union of Concerned Scientists. Cambridge, MA. https://www.ucsusa.org/resources /1992-world-scientists-warning-humanity

United Nations Convention on Biological Diversity (UN CBD). 2020. "Update of the Zero Draft of the Post-2020 Global Biodiversity Framework." CBD/POST2020 /PREP/2/1. August 17, 2020. https://www.cbd.int/doc/c/3064/749a/0f65ac7f9def867 07f4eaefa/post2020-prep-02-01-en.pdf

United Nations Convention on Biological Diversity (UN CBD). 2022. "Nations Adopt Four Goals, 23 Targets for 2030 in Landmark UN Biodiversity Agreement," official CBD press release, December 19, 2022. Montreal. https://www.cbd.int/article/cop15 -cbd-press-release-final-19dec2022

United Nations (UN). 2015a. "Paris Agreement." UN Framework Convention on Climate Change. https://unfccc.int/sites/default/files/english_paris_agreement.pdf

United Nations (UN). 2015b. "Transforming Our World" 2030 Agenda for Sustainable Development. A/RES/70/1. https://sustainabledevelopment.un.org/content /documents/21252030%20Agenda%20for%20Sustainable%20Development%20web.pdf

Willison, J.H.M., S. Bondrup-Nielsen, C. Drysdale, T.B. Herman, N.W.R. Munro, and T.L. Pollock. 1992. Science and the Management of Protected Areas: Proceedings of an International Conference. Acadia University, Nova Scotia, Canada, May 14–19, 1991. Amsterdam; New York: Elsevier

Closing Ceremony

ONWARD

let these stories find a place to rest
not only in my mind
but the deepest and farthest reaches of self
i listened
i felt and heard
the pains and worries
of messengers
with maps spread out through the haze of unknown
i let them in
so that i would see further
into our country's cold night
let these barriers and crevices
be examined like art
let our hardship of heart and mind
be spoken
to waft around us in plain sight
and then let them land
while we stand here together
broke open
let the earth take our words
like the mixing of hard mineral
and acidity of tree needles
be the nourishment
of new growth
let embers of the hopeful
navigate this terrain
let my mind quiet again
be guided to waters, sky, and fire
where our ancestors still sing to us
for i am among the living
with a mind, heart, and hands
that can do tomorrow's work
but first, i must dream of it

shalan joudry

Author Biographies

Karen F. Beazley is a professor emeritus at Dalhousie University's School for Resource and Environmental Studies. Her applied, interdisciplinary scholarship focuses on biodiversity conservation, conservation through reconciliation, and justice from an eco-centric, kinship, "all-my-relations" lens. Her research interests include wildlife conservation in a climate-change context, re-Indigenization for people and nature, ecological (land and water) corridor design, and protected area network planning. She is a member of the Conservation through Reconciliation Partnership, IUCN World Commission on Protected Areas Connectivity Conservation Specialist Group, and Canada Pathway Connectivity Working Group.

Julee Boan is the boreal partnership manager for Natural Resources Defense Council, based in Thunder Bay, Ontario. She completed a PhD in forest sciences with research focused on mitigating the impact of industrial logging on boreal caribou. She has worked in the non-profit sector advocating for the protection of wildlife habitat for over 20 years.

Sheila R. Colla is a conservation scientist and associate professor at York University's Faculty of Environmental and Urban Change. She has studied the ecology and conservation management of native pollinators for over a decade and has co-authored *The Bumblebees of North America: An Identification Guide* (Princeton University Press, 2014).

Heidi Cook is from the Misipawistik Cree Nation (Grand Rapids, Manitoba). She grew up in a fishing family and returned home after leaving for university education. She worked in the Misipawistik Cree Nation lands department before being elected as a councillor and then Chief.

James Doucette (he/him) is a Mi'kmaw youth worker and land-based practitioner from Potlotek First Nation, located in the heart of the Mi'kmaw Nation,

Una'kmaki: Land of Fog, sometimes known as Cape Breton Island. Chenise Hache and James are the co-founders and directors of Reclaiming Our Roots: Land-Based Learning and Community Stewardship.

Chance Finegan was a postdoctoral research fellow in the Department of Political Science at the University of Toronto Mississauga. His academic work focuses on the role of parks and protected areas in reconciliation. Before coming to Canada, he worked as a seasonal park ranger/interpreter for the US National Park Service. He resides on Treaty 6 territory, in Edmonton, Alberta.

Adam T. Ford holds the Canada Research Chair in Wildlife Restoration Ecology at the University of British Columbia, where he and his students take a community ecology approach to support the recovery of nature's critical ecological processes. He works with a diversity of rights and stakeholders on issues related to wildlife harvest, connectivity, human-wildlife conflict, and road ecology.

Barbara Frei is a Research Scientist in the Science and Technology Branch of Environment and Climate Change Canada. She works at the intersection of people and nature within urban ecology, nature-based solutions for biodiversity conservation and climate change mitigation, and ecosystem services. Her work includes both complex analytical modelling as well as place-based conservation efforts that are co-developed with local NGOs and communities. She lives in Montreal, Quebec, with her two young children and husband, and loves spending time in nature and exploring the world through the optimistic and honest lens of her children's eyes.

Bridget Graham (she/her/elle) is a research assistant with Melanie Zurba at Dalhousie University. Bridget has a master of arts in history and is the current operations manager at the Marine Environmental Observation, Prediction and Response Network (MEOPAR). She is also a full spectrum doula (labour and birth, postpartum and abortion) based in Halifax.

Mark W. Groulx is an associate professor in the University of Northern British Columbia's School of Planning and Sustainability and supervises graduate students in the Natural Resources and Environmental Studies graduate program. Mark's research focuses broadly on sustainable and resilient communities, and specifically on the importance of community engagement and placemaking in effective collaborative planning. Inspired by the creativity and careful craft of place makers of all types, Mark explores how communities are tapping into local knowledge and values to ensure that resilient planning and design is people focused. Mark is currently working on projects examining community-based approaches to low-carbon resilience, and the influence of nature-based citizen science on transformative environmental learning.

Shannon Hagerman is an associate professor in the Department of Forest Resources Management and principal investigator of the Social-Ecological Systems Research Group at the University of British Columbia. Her research examines the diverse ways that individuals know, value, and interact with the non-human environment, the social and political processes by which these perspectives and experiences are (or aren't) incorporated into policy, and the impacts of policy as it shapes management and practice in specific locales. Her research on novel interventions (including assisted migration) over the past decade illustrates how values-based and institutional commitments shape preferences for new management options for forests and biodiversity in an era of rapid climate change.

Jodi A. Hilty is president and chief scientist of the Yellowstone to Yukon Conservation Initiative, a joint US-Canada non-profit organization. Y2Y's vision is an interconnected system of wild lands and waters stretching from Yellowstone to Yukon, harmonizing the needs of people with those of nature. She is a conservation biologist specializing in ecological corridor and large landscape research and has over 20 years of experience managing large landscape conservation efforts.

shalan joudry is a Mi'kmaw mother and narrative artist from L'sətkuk (Bear River First Nation). She is a poet, playwright, oral storyteller, as well as a "two-eyed seeing" conservation ecologist. shalan is the author of two books of poetry, *Generations Re-merging* and *Waking Ground,* and the play *Elapultiek*, inspired by real-life species-at-risk work.

Christopher J. Lemieux is a social scientist working at the science-policy interface on a number of issues related to parks and protected areas and conservation more broadly. His current research focuses on conservation standards, evidence-based decision-making, climate change adaptation, and the human health and well-being benefits associated with nature contact. He is a member of the IUCN World Commission on Protected Areas and director of the Canadian Council on Ecological Areas.

Stacy Lischka is a conservation social scientist and principal researcher at Social Ecological Solutions. Her research supports communities in understanding how human behaviour affects conservation outcomes and in designing and evaluating programs designed to change human behaviours. Her current work focuses on building systems to support food production and conservation on community-owned land in Northern Colorado.

Elder Albert Marshall is an Elder from the Mi'kmaw community of Eskasoni on Cape Breton Island, Nova Scotia. He is a fluent speaker of the Mi'kmaw language and a passionate advocate of Mi'kmaq culture, healing, and reconciliation.

Albert is a proponent of cross-cultural understanding and *Etuaptmumk*: Two-Eyed Seeing – the idea that combining multiple cultural perspectives will result in clearer focus and better comprehension.

Larry McDermott is an Algonquin Elder from Shabot Obaadjiwan First Nation and is the executive director of Plenty Canada. He is currently a member of numerous organizations, including the International Indigenous Forum for Biodiversity, Ontario Human Rights Commission, UNESCO, and the Elder's Circle for the Law Society of Ontario. He also co-authored the "Ontario Recovery Strategy for the American Eel." He holds an Honorary Doctor of Laws from the University of Guelph and is a founding member of the Elders Lodge of the Conservation through Reconciliation Partnership. He was a humble student for many years of the late Algonquin Elder, Grandfather William Commanda, who created the Circle of All Nations organization.

Deborah McGregor, Anishinaabe, associate professor and Canada Research Chair: Indigenous Environmental Justice. Osgoode Hall Law School and Faculty of Environmental and Urban Studies, York University. Her community-engaged research has focused on Indigenous knowledge systems and their various applications in diverse contexts including environmental and water governance, environmental justice, health and environment, climate change, and Indigenous legal traditions.

Jacquelyn Miller (settler) is a graduate of the first cohort of the University of Victoria's (UVic) Juris Doctor/Juris Indigenarum Doctor program in Canadian common law and Indigenous legal orders. She received her master of arts degree in political science and cultural, social, and political thought from UVic. She was a lead organizer for the Reconciling Ways of Knowing: Indigenous Knowledge and Science project, helping effect the vision of its conveners to build understanding across ways of knowing for better relationships among Peoples and with our planetary home. She is now articling to become a lawyer in the territory of the ləkʷəŋən People in Victoria, British Columbia.

Natasha Myhal is Sault Ste. Marie Anishinaabe and Ukrainian. She is a PhD candidate in the Department of Ethnic Studies at the University of Colorado Boulder, with an emphasis on Native American and Indigenous Studies. Her dissertation research explores the intersection of Indigenous ethnobotanical perspectives, environmental change, and ongoing colonial practices in the Great Lakes.

Vivian Nguyen is an assistant professor in the Institute of Environmental and Interdisciplinary Science and the Department of Biology at Carleton University in Ottawa, Canada. Her research is interdisciplinary and focuses on the interface of science, people, and policy within the themes of conservation, environmental change, and natural resource management. Dr. Nguyen's research program focuses on application and mobilizing various forms of knowledge into decisions, policy, and practice. She is interested in social-ecological systems, human dimensions of environmental issues, science policy, and community knowledge.

Andrea Olive is a professor in the Department of Political Science and Geography, Geomatics, and Environment at the University of Toronto Mississauga. Her area of research is environmental policy in Canada and the United States, especially species-at-risk policy. She is on the board of directors with CPAWS-SK. In 2019 she was awarded a SSHRC Connection Grant with Karen Beazley, entitled "Transformative Politics of the Wild."

Sherry Pictou is a Mi'kmaw woman from L'sɨtkuk (water cuts through high rocks) known as Bear River First Nation, Nova Scotia. She is an assistant professor in the Faculties of Law and Management at Dalhousie University focusing on gender and Indigenous governance. Dr. Pictou is also a former Chief for her community and the former co-chair of the World Forum of Fisher Peoples. Currently she is a member of the The Intergovernmental Science-Policy Platform on Biodiversity and Ecosystem Services (IPBES) Task Force on Indigenous and Local Knowledge.

Jeremy Pittman is an associate professor in the University of Waterloo's School of Planning. His research focuses on environmental governance and policy, and he works with a diverse range of communities and sectors in Canada and internationally on sustainability-oriented projects.

Rachel Plotkin is the boreal project manager at the David Suzuki Foundation, where she has worked for 15 years. Prior to that she worked for six years at the Sierra Club of Canada. Her highly collaborative work has focused on maintaining and restoring habitat for wildlife and supporting Indigenous land governance.

Jesse Popp is a Canada Research Chair in Indigenous Environmental Science at the University of Guelph, an emerging scholar, and member of Wiikwemkoong Unceded Territory. Dr. Popp partners with Indigenous communities in ecology research projects that strive to promote inclusive science that embrace multiple ways of knowing.

Justina C. Ray is president and senior scientist of Wildlife Conservation Society Canada. She is involved in research and policy activities associated with land use planning, impact assessment, and species conservation in northern landscapes. She has been appointed to numerous government advisory panels related to science and policy development for species at risk and land use planning in Ontario and Canada. She was the co-chair of the Terrestrial Mammals Subcommittee of COSEWIC (2009–2017) and is currently adjunct professor at University of Toronto and Trent University.

Andrea Reid is a citizen of the Nisga'a Nation, a descendant of the Gisk'aast (Killerwhale) clan, with her paternal family coming from Gingolx. She was raised, however, on Epekwitk (Prince Edward Island) by her mother and brothers, and now lives in the Nass River Valley, home of her Nation, in Gitlaxt'aamiks. As an Indigenous fisheries scientist, Dr. Reid joined the Institute for the Oceans and Fisheries at the University of British Columbia in 2021. She has launched and now leads the Centre for Indigenous Fisheries, committed to research and teaching approaches that are intergenerational, land-based, and profoundly relational.

Robin Roth is a professor in the Department of Geography, Environment, and Geomatics at the University of Guelph. She and her students have worked collaboratively with Indigenous Peoples and organizations to explore the social and ecological impacts of state-led conservation in Southeast Asia and the enabling and constraining factors that give rise to effective collaborative, Indigenous-led models of conservation in North America. She is one of the six-person Leadership Circle and the principal investigator for the Conservation through Reconciliation Partnership.

Mahisha Sritharan is a Tamil-Canadian settler and a research associate at York University. Her research focuses on environmental justice, climate change, social and environmental determinants of health, and Indigenous knowledge. She holds a masters in environmental studies from York University, and her graduate project focused on understanding the impacts of climate change on the Whitefish River First Nation community in Ontario, Canada.

Trevor Swerdfager recently left the Public Service of Canada after a thirty-year career, which included time in Environment Canada where he led the Canadian Wildlife Service; in Fisheries and Oceans Canada where he served as senior assistant deputy minister, Science and Ocean Protection Plan; and in Parks Canada where he served as senior vice-president, operations. He recently joined the University of Waterloo's Faculty of Environment where he teaches courses in oceans science and policy, federal environmental decision-making, and fish, forests, and wildlife conservation.

Matthew A. Williamson is an assistant professor in Human Environment Systems at Boise State University. His work focuses on understanding how the interactions between people, their environment, and the institutions that govern them inspire (or inhibit) conservation action and ultimately determine the effectiveness of those actions.

Stephen Woodley is an ecologist who has worked in the field of environmental conservation a consultant, field biologist, university researcher, and the first chief scientist for Parks Canada. He currently works as vice chair for Science and Biodiversity of IUCN's World Commission on Protected Areas. The focus of the work is to understand the role of protected areas as solutions to the current global conservation challenges.

Lisa Young is the executive director of Unama'ki Institute of Natural Resources (UINR), a leading Mi'kmaw natural resources and environmental management organization. Lisa joined UINR shortly after graduating with a BSc in biology from York University. Originally from Membertou First Nation, she currently resides in Eskasoni with her husband and two children.

Melanie Zurba (she/her) is an associate professor with the School for Resource and Environmental Studies (SRES) and the College of Sustainability at Dalhousie University, which is located in Kjipuktik (Halifax). Her work focuses on environmental governance, equity, and collaboration. She is originally from Treaty 1 territory (Winnipeg).

Index

Page numbers in *italics* denote tables and figures. Endnotes are indicated by "n" followed by the endnote number.

www.ingramcontent.com/pod-product-compliance
Lightning Source LLC
Chambersburg PA
CBHW020532030426
42337CB00013B/827